Managing Modernity

Managing Modernity

Beyond Bureaucracy?

Edited by

Stewart Clegg, Martin Harris,

and Harro Höpfl

OXFORD
UNIVERSITY PRESS

OXFORD

UNIVERSITY PRESS

Great Clarendon Street, Oxford OX2 6DP

Oxford University Press is a department of the University of Oxford.
It furthers the University's objective of excellence in research, scholarship,
and education by publishing worldwide in

Oxford New York

Auckland Cape Town Dar es Salaam Hong Kong Karachi
Kuala Lumpur Madrid Melbourne Mexico City Nairobi
New Delhi Shanghai Taipei Toronto

With offices in

Argentina Austria Brazil Chile Czech Republic France Greece
Guatemala Hungary Italy Japan Poland Portugal Singapore
South Korea Switzerland Thailand Turkey Ukraine Vietnam

Oxford is a registered trade mark of Oxford University Press
in the UK and in certain other countries

Published in the United States
by Oxford University Press Inc., New York

© Oxford University Press 2011

The moral rights of the authors have been asserted
Database right Oxford University Press (maker)

First published 2011

British Library Cataloguing in Publication Data

Data available

Library of Congress Cataloging in Publication Data

Data available

Typeset by SPI Publisher Services, Pondicherry, India
Printed in Great Britain
by
MPG Books Group, Bodmin and King's Lynn

ISBN 978–0–19–956364–7 (Hbk.)
ISBN 978–0–19–956365–4 (Pbk.)

1 3 5 7 9 10 8 6 4 2

⬚ FOREWORD

The last three decades have seen a profuse flowering of new organizational forms in both private and public sectors. This collection grapples with the problem of how to understand this profusion and the phrase 'beyond bureaucracy' marks the core of its preoccupation. To what extent, and in what ways, has bureaucracy been transcended, displaced, or transformed as the definitive organizational signifier of modernity? The following chapters explore different theoretical and empirical routes to resolving this question. Here, I want to pause briefly and puzzle about the implications of the word 'beyond' in the title.

For most of the book, the chapters engage with 'beyond' as involving a temporal dimension. This leads us to the world of the post—the possibility of post-bureaucratic organizations suggests a landscape of 'epochal' shifts: post-modern, post-national, post-feminist, post-rational, and many others. I will return to the problem of going 'beyond bureaucracy' in temporal terms later. But 'beyond' also works in a second dimension: spatial rather than temporal. To be beyond may refer to being outside of somewhere, beyond the reach or control of something, or simply being elsewhere. For me, this is a reminder that organizations—and the forms of power and authority they embody— occupy particular spaces in mundane and profound ways. Organizations are constructed in *places* (buildings, cities, regions, and nations); they link *multiple places*; they *locate* people in positions, places, and relationships. So 'beyond bureaucracy' also points to the ways in which the organization of power and authority may have moved beyond the organizational shapes of established bureaucratic forms.

Ideas of disaggregation, decentralization, and dispersal speak to the idea of moving beyond: they capture a sense of fragmentation in established organizational structures—whether in the classic integrated and integrative structures of industrial production or the machine and professional bureaucracies of European welfare states. In all sectors, we have been treated to a ferment of organizational innovation as new ways of coordinating commerce, capital, and governing are developed. Such new organizational forms *take place differently*—they occupy and order space in different ways and deploy new techniques and technologies to manage the problems of managing at a distance. The dynamics of disintegration create new types of relationship— principal–agent contracts, partnerships, clubs, cooperatives, networks, for example—for organizing the 'co-production' of economically and politically desired outcomes. In these turbulent processes of reinvention, many previously fixed boundaries become blurred: between previously separate organizations, between public and private sectors (and interests), between producers and consumers, and more. For someone like me whose research is centred on welfare states, uncertainty about where the state ends and other types of organization begin is an increasingly troubling—and increasingly important—question.

The spatial aspect of 'beyond bureaucracy' also makes me think about the other places in which organizational innovation has been taking place. Although most of the chapters gathered together in this volume are focused on the Euro-Atlantic zone, important developments have been taking place elsewhere—or at least in the lines of flow and connection that link the old Northern metropolitan societies and the emerging/developing regions. From micro-finance to the flourishing and contradictory world of Non-Governmental Organizations; from the authority of International Organizations to the Sovereign Wealth Funds of nation states; and from the capacity of the Chinese state to mobilize (and demobilize) labour on unimaginable scales to the enthusiasm for participatory forms of social action (e.g. the popular budget-setting movement that originated in Porto Alegre): organizational innovation is global in many senses.

The idea of venturing 'beyond bureaucracy' invites us to think in both spatial and temporal terms. Many of the contributors here take up the temporal challenge whilst avoiding the temptation to divide the world according to what Janet Fink and I have called 'sociological time': the simplifying binary division of Past and Present in which the Past is simple, all too well-known, and really rather boring, while the Present is mobile, complex, richly coloured, and fundamentally exciting. Bureaucracy—in both popular and academic discourse—lends itself to this process (bureaucracy being seen as old-fashioned, staid, unchanging, and so on). The current vicissitudes of academic publishing tend to fuel this phenomenon of sociological time: far better to announce an 'End', a Post-, or a New, than to struggle with formulations about the partial, incomplete, or unfinished processes of organizational innovation. In this collection, though, we discover that a thoughtful engagement with processes of emergence, hybridization, and reconstruction in which forms of bureaucracy persist, are reconfigured and assume a new importance or value. This is a more profound sense of being beyond—in which the existing archetypes of organizational sociology and popular politics no longer provide a way of mapping the emerging organizational landscape and its patterned flows and blockages, knots and lines, insides and outsides. The challenge of dealing with these emergent forms is as much that of tracing heterogeneous potentials, trajectories, and tendencies as it is to map a new set of systems and structures.

Forty years ago, I was as a student of Behaviour Sciences at the University of Aston (then famous for its Industrial Administration Research Unit). There I failed to learn to become a manager of any kind, much less one that would rise to the challenges of 'managing modernity'. But the experience did persuade me that organizations were of considerable academic and practical interest in their intimate entanglements with power. This book reminds me of the basic import of that observation, while adding to my understanding of the ways in which power and authority are being—and have been—recomposed. Organizations serve as sites for the contested recomposition of power: they are critical settings where such struggles take place. But they also constitute the modes and mechanisms through which power is enacted and put into practice. This is one reason why the politics of organizational design has been such a central feature of the last few decades—'bashing bureaucracy' served a variety of purposes in creating the discursive and political space for new organizational forms and new assemblages of power.

John Clarke

⬚ CONTENTS

☐ LIST OF FIGURES

☐ LIST OF TABLES

⬚ NOTES ON CONTRIBUTORS

Stephen Ackroyd is Emeritus Professor of Organizational Analysis at Lancaster University Management School. His research interests include public sector organizations and professions, expert labour and the 'hollowing out' of Britain's manufacturing base in the years since 1945. His recent books include: *The Organization of Business* (2002), *Critical Realist Applications in Management and Organization Studies* (with Steve Fleetwood, 2004), *The New Managerialism and the Public Service Professions* (with Ian Kirkpatrick and Richard Waller, 2005), *The Oxford Handbook of Work and Organisations* (with Rosemary Batt, Paul Thompson, and Pamela Tolbert, 2005), and *Redirections in the Study of Expert Labour* (with Daniel Muzio and Jean-francois Chanlat, 2005).

Mats Alvesson is Professor of Business Administration at the University of Lund and at the University of Queensland Business School. He is Honorary Professor at the University of St Andrews and Visiting Professor at Exeter University. His recent books include *The Oxford Handbook of Critical Management Studies* (with Todd Bridgman and Hugh Willmott, 2009), *Understanding Gender and Organizations* (with Yvonne Billing, 2009), *Reflexive Methodology* (with Kaj Skoldberg, 2005), and *Understanding Leadership in the Real World* (with Andre Spicer, 2010).

David A. Buchanan is Professor of Organizational Behaviour at Cranfield University School of Management. He has authored numerous articles and books including *The Sustainability and Spread of Organizational Change* (with Louise Fitzgerald and Diane Ketley, 2007), *Organizational Behaviour* (with Andrzej Huczynski, 2007), *Power, Politics, and Organizational Change* (with Richard Badham, 2008) and *The Sage Handbook of Organizational Research Methods* (with Alan Bryman, 2009). Current research projects include a study of the changing role of middle management in health care, and managing change in extreme contexts.

John Clarke is Professor of Social Policy at the Open University, where he has worked for more than twenty-five years on the political and cultural struggles involved in remaking welfare states. John has a particular interest in the ways in which managerialism and consumerism have reshaped the relations between welfare states and nations. He is currently working with an international group on a project called *Disputing Citizenship*. His books include *Changing Welfare, Changing States* (2004), *Creating Citizen-Consumers* (with Janet Newman and others, 2007), and *Publics, Politics and Power: Remaking the Public in Public Services* (with Janet Newman, 2009).

Stewart Clegg is Research Professor and Director of the Centre for Management and Organization Studies at the University of Technology, Sydney and is also a Visiting Professor at Copenhagen Business School and EM-Lyon. A prolific publisher in leading academic journals in social science, management, and organization theory, he is also the author and editor of many books, including *The Sage Handbook of*

Organization Studies (with Cynthia Hardy, Walter Nord, and Tom Lawrence, 2006) *The Sage Handbook of Power* (with Mark Haugaard, 2009), and *The Sage Handbook of Macro-Organization Behaviour* (with Cary Cooper 2009).

Paul du Gay is currently a Professor in the Department of Organization at Copenhagen Business School, and an associate Fellow of Warwick Business School. His work is located at the intersection of sociology, organizations, and cultural studies. Publications include *Consumption and Identity at Work* (1996), *In Praise of Bureaucracy* (2000), *Cultural Economy* (with Michael Pryke, 2002), and *Conduct* (with Anthony Elliot, 2009). Current research includes work on sovereign wealth funds and the revitalization of public services.

Louise Fitzgerald is Visiting Professor at Manchester Business School. Her previous career includes managerial work in the private sector and academic posts at Salford, Warwick, City, and De Montfort Universities. Her research is focused on the implementation of change in complex organizations. Previous projects include research on the management of networks in health care and the roles of clinical managers in leading service changes. Recent book publications include *From Knowledge to Action? Evidence Based Health Care in Context* (with Sue Dopson, 2005) and *The Spread and Sustainability of Organizational Change: Modernizing Health Care* (with David Buchanan and Diane Ketley 2007).

Martin Harris is a Senior Lecturer at the Essex University Business School. Martin has edited *Innovation, Organization Change and Technology* (with Ian McLoughlin, 1997) and published in journals such as the *Journal of Management Studies*, and the *Human Relations*. Martin's current research interests are centred on digital technology, 'post-bureaucracy', marketization and 'the politics of forgetting' in UK public institutions such as the BBC, the British Library, and the NHS. His most recent work is concerned with digitisation and the preservation of cultural memory.

Harro Höpfl is Research Professor at the Essex University Business School, and a former Senior Lecturer in Politics at Lancaster University; he is also a Visiting Professor at the Pedagogical University, Krakow. He has written *Jesuit Political Thought: the Society of Jesus and the State* (2004) and published extensively on the history of political thought, especially reason of state, and Machiavellism. His recent work is concerned with relating concepts of authority and political accountability to theories of post bureaucracy.

Jannis Kallinikos is Professor in the Department of Management at the London School of Economics. His research is focused on the ways in which new digital formats (text, voice, image) are reshaping contemporary organizations and institutions. His most recent work is concerned with the ways in which these technologies may be undermining the boundaries that once separated work from everyday life and production from consumption. Some of these issues are dealt with in *The Consequences of Information: Institutional Implications of Technological Change* (2006).

Dan Kärreman is Professor in Management and Organization Studies at Copenhagen Business School. Dan is also affiliated with the KLIO group at the School of Economics and Management, Lund University. His research interests include critical management studies, knowledge work, identity in organizations, leadership, organizational control, innovation, and research methodology. He has published in the *Academy of Management Review, Human Relations*, the *Journal of Management Studies, Organization, Organization Science, and Organization Studies*.

Michael Reed is Professor of Organisational Analysis at Cardiff Business School. Michael has published widely in major international journals, such as the *Journal of Management Studies* and *Organization Studies*, as well as book-length monographs in the areas of organization theory and analysis, expert work, knowledge organizations, public services organization and management, and organizational futures. He is a member of several leading international academic associations, including the European Group for Organisation Studies, and the British Academy of Management. He is one of the founding editors of the international journal, *Organization*.

Ewen Speed is a Lecturer at the University of Essex School of Health and Human Sciences. His current research is focused on the policy discourses that surround patient choice, patient involvement, and public engagement in the UK healthcare system. Ewen holds a PhD in Sociology from the University of Dublin (Trinity College), and he has published extensively in journals, such as *Sociology, Social Science and Medicine*, and the *Journal of Mental Health*.

Hugh Willmott, currently research Professor in Organization Studies, Cardiff Business School, has held professorial positions at the Universities of Cambridge, Manchester, Copenhagen, Lund, and Cranfield. Hugh currently serves on the boards of the *Academy of Management Review, Organization Studies*, the *Journal of Management Studies*, and *Organization*. Recent books include *Critical Management Studies: A Reader* (with Christopher Grey, 2005), *Introducing Organizational Behaviour and Management* (with David Knights, 2007), and *The Oxford Handbook of Critical Management Studies* (with Mats Alvesson and Todd Bridgman, 2009).

Introduction: Managing Modernity: Beyond Bureaucracy?

MARTIN HARRIS, STEWART CLEGG, AND HARRO HÖPFL

Bureaucracy has long been seen as a cornerstone of the advanced industrial societies, and even as constitutive of modernity itself. Yet, one of the most striking features of contemporary debate is that this hitherto dominant form has been dismissed as outmoded by commentators of virtually all persuasions. Whilst 'post-bureaucratic' has become one of the most widely used terms to describe a new and emergent organizational type, other coinages employed in the same sense include 'the boundaryless corporation', 'the virtual organization', and the 'network enterprise'. A recurrent theme is the belief that we are seeing an historical 'end' to the era of large complex organizations (Davidow and Malone 1992; Dent 1995; Miles et al. 1997; Heckscher 1991, 1994; Heckscher and Applegate 1994; Kofman and Senge 1993; Child and McGrath 2001). Thus, as Reed has argued:

> ...a neo-liberal management theorist such as Bennis, a neo-liberalist economist such as Schumpeter, a social democrat such as Schumacher, a neo-corporatist such as Elias, a technological determinist such as Bell or Castells and a theorist of radical participatory democracy such as Illich can all agree that the underlying currents of history will, eventually, make bureaucracy an obsolete form of administrative power and organization. (Reed 2005: 115–16)

The critiques noted by Reed are as old as modern bureaucracy itself. They also resonate strongly with a *Zeitgeist* whose acute sense of historical discontinuity came to define the closing decades of the twentieth century. During these years, the social sciences were permeated by a 'discourse of endings', premised in large part on the belief that the age of high modernity had given way to 'late' or 'post'-modernity. This *fin de siècle* mood manifested itself in a variety of different ways. The sense that the advanced industrial societies had reached an historic 'ending' was germane to Claus Offe's thesis of 'disorganized capitalism' (Offe 1985), and the master theme of discontinuity was reflected in the work of those who rejected the rationalist 'control' model of organization (Cooper and Burrell 1988; Clegg 1990). An even more momentous 'ending' derived from the perceived decline of the welfare state, disenchantment with heavily bureaucratized public sector organizations, and the rise of 'the new public management' (Hood 1998; Greenwood et al. 2002). The increasing power and ubiquity of information technology added to the growing sense that bureaucracy was being undermined in the emergent 'network society' (Castells 2000). Recent debate on the post-bureaucratic organization suggests, however, that this tale of 'endings' has not gone unchallenged. Research in this field points to a rather more nuanced view of bureaucracy and its contemporary relevance. Whilst large complex organizations have become increasingly heterodox, what has emerged is not the 'end' of bureaucracy, but a more complex and differentiated set of post-bureaucratic (or neo-bureaucratic) possibilities that have had the effect of undermining some distinctions previously deemed incontestable (e.g. market versus hierarchy; centralization versus decentralization; public versus private sectors). Whilst there can be little doubt that real and significant change is underway, changes in the bureaucratic form cannot be characterized as a straightforward trajectory of historical decline, still less a necessary one. On the contrary, the market reforms of the 1980s and 1990s were quickly followed by a proliferation of regulatory controls, and recent years have seen the return of the state as a central actor in the economic management of the advanced industrial societies. The social and cultural purposes of many public sector bodies have, meanwhile, been expanded rather than contracted, precisely because these societies have become more complex and diverse.

This volume gathers together scholarly contributions from academics working across a range of disciplines including political science, sociology, management studies, and organizational theory. Some chapters are centred on the issues of power, legitimacy, and historical embeddedness in contemporary bureaucracies. Others focus on organizational hybridity, professional identity, and new forms of 'soft domination'. The overall picture is one of paradox and contradiction: new hybrid forms promise new forms of social action and new conceptualizations of control (Ackoff 1994), but these new forms may also create new forms of 'centralized decentralisation' (Hill et al. 2000; Alvesson and Thompson 2005). Whilst the current preoccupation with 'networked' organizational forms seems to suggest a much more diverse and open future for the bureaucratic form, some of the research presented here suggests a much more perplexing view of those organizations (in both public and private sectors) whose core operations have been 'hollowed out' and fragmented by outsourcing and quasi-privatization.

As noted above, the last two decades have been dominated by an intellectual climate that has emphasized indeterminacy, market values, and the rolling back of the state. The neoliberal orthodoxies of the 1980s and 1990s suffered a setback of world-historical proportions (Gray 2009) as this volume was being prepared for publication in early 2009—yet the precipitous decline in the credibility of 'the market' has done little or nothing to dispel the prevailing climate of uncertainty that hangs over contemporary organizations. The chapters presented here paint a picture of complexity and variability across a diverse range of bureaucratic contexts. They are presented in four groupings. The first two contributions (by du Gay and Höpfl) address some fundamental issues raised by 'the post-bureaucratic turn' in government settings. Chapters 3, 4, and 5 (by Buchanan and Fitzgerald, Speed, and Harris, respectively) examine the changes now underway in the UK National Health Service, an institution that can be understood as a model 'traditional' bureaucracy and as a test bed for some ostensibly 'post-bureaucratic' reforms. The three succeeding chapters (respectively by Kallinikos, Alvesson and Karreman, and Ackroyd) show the diverse ways in which interactivity, power, and structures of control are conditioned in fundamental ways by a variety of 'bureaucratic' organizational forms. Finally, the chapters by Clegg, Reed, and Willmott draw more explicitly on social theory, reframing the bureaucratic archetype in the light of the preceding chapters.

Bureaucracy Old and New

Bureaucracy has a long and distinguished history, not least because of its central place in Max Weber's understanding of modernity (Weber 1978). For Weber, bureaucracy was neither a novel nor even a distinctively European phenomenon, but Germany's rapid development after 1871 owed much to its modern rational-legal form. This volume examines the idea that the management of late modern societies is now increasingly reliant on organizational forms that go 'beyond bureaucracy'. We begin with a chapter by Paul du Gay, one of the foremost contemporary interpreters of Max Weber and the bureaucratic archetype. Du Gay takes issue with the tendency of contemporary organizational theory to see Weber as a theorist of overarching rationalization. Weber was at pains to emphasize the social embeddedness of different value systems, and his account of bureaucracy centred not just on formal rules, but also on the idea that the ethics of office implied a form of practical wisdom. The chapter questions the tendency to dismiss Weber as either a celebrant of narrow instrumentalism or as a prophet of metaphysical pathos. Both tendencies underestimate the complexity of Weber's historical account. Du Gay links contemporary debates on governance to the Weberian corpus, arguing that there has been an 'unbedding' of public institutions and a tendency for political elites to abandon the existing norms and machinery of government. A closely related tendency is that due process is being usurped by an emphasis on 'delivery' and transformational leadership. One significant casualty of this 'unbedding' of public institutions has been the 'disinterested' public servant *sine ira et studio*, whose vocation was the impartial, impersonal, and efficient execution of official duties, independent of any political or moral 'enthusiasms'. For many contemporary critics of bureaucracy, it is precisely this ethical separation of person, office, and authority that has been seen as problematic. The search for greater control over state bureaucracies has undermined the important role played by the bureaucratic ethos—with its spirit of formalistic impersonality—in the responsible operation of a state and in the effective running of a constitution. Du Gay puts the case for bureaucratic reform based on a revived ethics of responsibility. Contemporary demands for an increased emphasis on 'responsiveness' and 'enthusiasm' on the part of political appointees and special advisors should be treated with considerable scepticism.

The chapter by Harro Höpfl examines the New Public Management (NPM) in specific relation to the question of bureaucratic accountability. NPM draws on elements of 'public choice' theory, the managerialist cult of 'excellence', and a belief that markets or quasi-markets should supplant 'bureaucracy' in public administration (Osborne and Gaebler 1992). The chapter points up the equivocal nature of the improvements promised by NPM. NPM may have created new modes of accountability, but it has done little or nothing to resolve the long-standing question of who is accountable to whom for what. The accountability of senior civil servants was traditionally framed by notions of 'ministerial responsibility' to Parliament and public, whilst the 'fourth estate' could be construed as a proxy for the public good. The internal work of departments and ministries was held to account internally, through the hierarchy of office. Today's senior civil servants are subordinate to the responsible minister, but responsibility for the implementation of policy has become much more diffuse as relations between ministers and civil servants have increasingly been mediated by the actions of *ad hoc* committees, task forces, and special advisors. Höpfl argues that these developments have produced an executive that is becoming progressively more detached from the *status quo ante* of the Westminster model. Both the old public administration and the new public management are rooted in the liberal/utilitarian tradition of institutional engineering and design. These cannot reconcile the 'operational autonomy' and expertise of bureaucratic agents with ministerial or Parliamentary control.

The Largest Civilian Bureaucracy in the World?

The British National Health Service (NHS) marked its 60th year in 2007, and we have devoted three chapters to this largest of European bureaucracies.[1] The chapter by Buchanan and Fitzgerald examines some of the organizational consequences of outsourcing, 'agentification', and continued experimentation with quasi-markets. The chapter shows that the old archetype of professional bureaucracy and clinician governance has not been displaced by these changes. The NHS is dominated by powerful clinical disciplines that have maintained their professional autonomy in the face of the managerial controls, and recent managerial reforms have added yet another layer to what is revealed as a deeply sedimented institutional form. This has created what Buchanan and Fitzgerald call an *accessorized bureaucracy*—an organizational form that retains many of the characteristics of professional bureaucracy whilst 'accessorizing' it with the trappings (structures, processes, discourses) of modern commercial enterprise. Accessorized bureaucracy mediates between a traditional, stable, and predictable system and one that is simultaneously characterized by innovation and radical change. Legitimacy is a perennial issue for those who seek to manage this elaborate *pas de deux*.

The chapter by Ewen Speed examines the ways in which market mechanisms are conditioned by the 'soft rhetorics' of bureaucratic power advocated by Courpasson (2000). Speed shows that currently influential notions of patient choice owe little or nothing to the consumer sovereignty favoured by neoliberal economics. Patient choice is discursively constituted, and practically constrained, by the preferences of NHS clinicians. The 1983 Griffiths Report established the idea that economic management could be seen as synonymous with better clinical management, and this in turn signalled a cultural shift away from professional judgement towards measureable targets. Subsequent waves of reform further entrenched managerialist doctrines of efficiency, internal markets, and competition. New Labour policy after 1997 replaced fiscal metrics with what Speed calls a 'quality metric' whose ostensible purpose of empowering patients is underpinned by a variety of centralized controls. Speed argues that the emphasis on quality operates not only as a formal measure, but also as a mode of governance exercised on the basis of 'soft domination'. The quality and differential pricing of health-care services remains tied to the expert judgements of clinicians whose control of diagnosis and treatment remains largely unhampered by managerial controls. UK healthcare professionals are, however, also being managed according to bureaucratic controls that are all the more constraining for being softer and more 'liquid'.

The following chapter, by Martin Harris, relates case study findings on the implementation of new information technologies to questions of organizational resistance and the restructuring of the NHS. Many commentators have noted the centralizing imperatives of the *National Programme for Information Technology* (NPfIT) and the recurrent tendency to subject the 'local' shaping of these technologies to the dictates of business process reengineering. This chapter shows that the specific form taken by this huge initiative has also been influenced by broader shifts in the political economy of health care, and by the 'networked' forms of governance now being enacted by *Connecting for Health*, the agency responsible for implementing the initiative. Moves towards networked forms of governance have resulted in a 'hollowing out' of NHS organizations—a theme that resonates strongly with post-bureaucracy and the 'politics of forgetting' (Harris and Wegg-Prosser 2007; Pollitt 2009). The chapter argues that the vision of a seamless digital future is fundamentally at odds with some long-standing questions of power and legitimacy that have dominated successive attempts to reform the NHS (Klein 2001; Webster 2002; Harrison and McDonald 2008). The broader picture is one of continued political dissension and resistance, as the values of NHS clinicians have conflicted with a new institutional logic of outsourcing and marketization.[2]

A New Hybrid Institutional Landscape?

The chapter by Jannis Kallinikos, examines new Internet-based modes of social production that blur the line between working and living, producing and consuming. Kallinikos sets great store by these developments, but questions the 'epochalist' tendency to view new production concepts in binary opposition to existing institutional and organizational forms. The chapter uncovers 'a deeper layer of relations' that transcends the stereotypical depiction of formal organizations as concentrated, monolithic, and inflexible. Seen in a wider context, the current 'informatization' of work organizations can be understood as part of a long-run cultural tendency to put the manipulation of symbols at the heart of social development.[3] The collaborative arrangements that underpin new forms of social production can also be understood as part of an institutional landscape that is fundamentally Janus-faced. The 'grand fusion' of text, sound, and vision creates a symbolically rich environment that creates new forms of communication and social experience. However it would also appear that this environment offers a medium of transactional exchange that is well suited to the creation of online value chains, interactive marketing techniques, and new forms of social codification. Kallinikos concludes that the precise character of the emerging information habitat will be determined in large part by battles over digital copyright and other impediments to the free exchange of information.

The next chapter, by Alvesson and Kärreman examines human resource management (HRM) practices in two detailed case study examples. The chapter shows that 'knowledge intensive' firms may be grounded in very different assumptions about how employee identities and structures of motivation are managed. Whereas the literature on psychological contracts has tended to focus exclusively on individual perceptions of mutual obligations, this chapter puts the case for a more robustly sociological view of identity formation and 'aspirational control' in 'high commitment' work environments. The authors develop the idea of a 'personnel concept', arguing that key elements of HRM strategy are reproduced as employees become 'normalized' and standardized in line with particular HRM practices. The chapter presents two contrasting manifestations of this concept. Management in one consultancy firm (described as a 'meritocratic technocracy') emphasized standards, rules, and procedures. In a second consultancy (described by the authors as a 'sociocracy'), technical qualifications were downplayed in favour of interpersonal skills and sociability. Here, the emphasis was on cooperation, close contact with clients, and the negotiation of shared understandings. Whilst the practices described have a strong bearing on the recruitment, motivation, and mobilization of key personnel, they are subject to a significant degree of variation. The personnel concept also appears to function as a politically 'hybrid' organizational form. HRM policies may, on one hand, facilitate cooperation and the creation of bonds that tie skilled personnel to the firm. But these policies may equally be played out in ways that contribute to conformist behaviours, thus delimiting the criteria set for recruitment, promotion, and reward. Alvesson and Kärreman put the case for further research in this field in the hope that this will encourage more ambitious and innovative employment practices.

The chapter by Stephen Ackroyd highlights the cultural embeddedness of the bureaucratic form. The chapter takes a broader historical view of the post-bureaucratic turn. Fragmentation and disaggregation, far from representing an emergent new paradigm, are revealed as long-standing and endemic features of British industrial organization. Whilst a number of large UK manufacturers emerged in the twenty-five years that followed the Second World War, the chapter shows that these firms lacked the centralized direction and unitary structures suggested by classic models of bureaucracy. UK firms may appear large when considered in aggregate, but they are frequently comprised of relatively small subsidiary companies that are governed in accordance with 'loose tight' models of management. Whilst this mode of governance confers a very substantial degree of operating autonomy on local management, culturally based constraints on the availability of capital have long inhibited the technological capabilities of UK industry. The institutional landscape of this British exceptionalism—based on radically 'disaggregated' firm structures—derives not from the exigencies of markets or functional requirements, but from the values, policies, and strategic objectives of UK managerial elites. The years since 1995 have seen the emergence of a new type of UK-based 'capital extensive' firm. These firms have ceased to operate in their original industrial sectors and now occupy strategic positions in a number of selected global supply chains. They are run by an increasingly internationalized cadre of shareholding managers who have little or no commitment to particular countries, locations, or industrial sectors.

The chapter by Stewart Clegg views the bureaucratic form through a dialectical lens, one that sees modern organizations as simultaneously decomposing and recomposing. The theme of decomposition is redolent of extended supply chains, outsourcing, the virtual organization, and call centres. The theme of recomposition takes us into the world of new, but as yet ill-defined organizational forms. Clegg notes that the shift to outsourcing and organizational disaggregation may coexist with some very familiar politics of surveillance and control. Recomposed (or 'refurbished') bureaucracies feature a range of more innovative developments in which the central figure of the bureaucrat has been superseded by that of the project leader. Clegg suggests that the 'politics of the project' has become the arena in which the strategic interests of aspirant elites are played out, and the chapter concludes that the theoretical object of 'bureaucracy' may now be of far more limited utility than was the case in the immediate post-War period.

Manuel Castells is one of the world's foremost commentators on the social, economic, and cultural consequences of the information revolution. Castells' work on 'the network society' and the 'network enterprise' (Castells 1996, 2000) continues to provoke intense debate on the nature of the transformations now under way in the organizations of the advanced capitalist societies. In the penultimate chapter, Mike Reed takes issue with Castells' dismissal of bureaucracy as an outmoded form, arguing that the 'network enterprise' thesis has emphasized collaboration, partnership, and high-trust working relationships whilst neglecting the key issue of power. The chapter offers a critique of the changing logics of control that inhere in 'bureaucratic', 'post-bureaucratic', and 'neo-bureaucratic' modes of organization. For Reed, the political reality of corporate life is one in which a diverse range of hybridized control regimes allow power elites to devolve operational autonomy whilst retaining a streamlined and effective centralized strategic control over productive organizations. The chapter concludes that separate, but related market, hierarchy, and networked modes of control are determined not by the abstract logic of a new informational paradigm, but by the 'dynamics of domination' that inhere in the process of network formation.

The final chapter, by Hugh Willmott, offers a comprehensive rethinking of the bureaucratic archetype and its significance for late modernity. Willmott questions the technicist bias of the ongoing debate on post-bureaucracy, arguing that the most pressing dilemmas confronting late modern societies are ethical and political, rather than technical in nature. An excessive preoccupation with the 'variable geometry' ascribed to new organizational forms has obscured the ways in which the constraints of formal rationality have been tightened at precisely the historical moment when the moral and technical capacities of many public sector bureaucracies have been 'hollowed out' and disaggregated. Willmott strikingly illustrates the ways in which an erosion of the bureaucratic ethos has led to the fragmentation of community and child-care services in a UK local authority, and he also notes the alacrity with which central government sought to re-assert bureaucratic principles when the dire consequences of this fragmentation were widely reported. Whilst we may yet see the emergence of institutions that break free of formal rationality, the chapter concludes that the exigencies of contemporary 'risk societies' demand a revitalization of the bureaucratic ethos. Willmott notes that the alternative prospect may be one of further 'descent into social division and disarray'.

NOTES

1. One media critic of President Obama's healthcare reforms noted that the huge scale of the NHS bureaucracy was matched only by that of the Chinese People's Liberation Army (Hannan 2009). Some commentators have argued that the Indian railway system should be regarded as the world's largest non-military bureaucracy (Lister 2004).
2. The *National Programme for Information Technology* (NPfIT), widely reported as the largest civil IT project in history, may yet be seen as a telling example of 'network failure'. Whilst the huge scale of the programme reflects a commitment to capacity-building and infrastructural development across the NHS, the NPfIT has been adversely affected by a succession of politically contentious project overruns, 'IT failures', and data security problems. Some senior managers within the NHS were predicting the collapse of the initiative as the final version of this volume was being prepared in December 2009. Pre-budget statements issued by the Chancellor of the Exchequer indicate that large parts of the initiative deemed to be 'not essential to the front line' will be scaled back in 2010 (BBC 2009).
3. Strathern (2002) offers an authoritative account of virtuality as a reflection of 'audit culture' and formalisation. This is cognate with Robert Cooper's 'bureaucratic' conception of information technology as 'abbreviation' and 'control at a distance' (Cooper, 1992).

BIBLIOGRAPHY

Ackoff, R. (1994) *The Democratic Corporation*, New York: Oxford University Press.

Alvesson, M. and Thompson, P. (2005) Bureaucracy at Work: Misunderstandings and Mixed Blessings, in P. du Gay (ed.), *The Values of Bureaucracy*, Oxford: Oxford University Press 89–114.

BBC News (2009) Troubled £12bn NHS IT system to be scaled back, http://news.bbc.co.uk/1/hi/uk_politics/8397854.stm (accessed 12 December 2009).

Child, J. and McGrath, R.G. (2001) Organizations Unfettered: Organizational Form in an Information-Intensive Economy, *Academy of Management Journal*, 44(6m): 1135–49.

Castells, M. (1996) *The Rise of the Network Society*, London: Blackwell.

—— (2000) Materials for an Exploratory Theory of the Network Society, *British Journal of Sociology*, 51(1): 5–24.

Clegg, S.R. (1990) Modern Organizations. *Organization Studies in the Post Modern World*, London: Sage.

—— Courpasson, D. and Phillips, N. (2006) *Power and Organizations*, London: Sage.

Cooper, R. (1992) Formal Organization as Representation: Remote Control, Displacement and Abbreviation, in M. Reed, and M. Hughes (eds), *Rethinking Organization: New Directions in Organizational Analysis*, London: Sage.

—— and Burrell, G, (1988) Modernism, Postmodernism and Organizational Analysis: An Introduction, *Organizational Studies*, 9(1): 1–12.

Courpasson, D. (2000) Managerial Strategies of Domination: Power in Soft Bureaucracies, *Organization Studies*, 21(1): 141–61.

Davidow, W.H. and Malone, M.S. (1992) *The Virtual Corporation*, New York: Edward Burlingame Books/Harper Business.

Dent, M. (1995) The New National Health Service: A Case of Postmodernism?, *Organizational Studies*, 16(5): 875–900.

Gray, J. (2009) *False Dawn: The Delusions of Global Capitalism*, 2nd edn, London: Granta Books.

Greenwood, J. et al. (2002) *New Public Administration in Britain*, London: Routledge.

Hannan, D. (2009) Glenn Beck: Daniel Hannan (MEP) Warns America about ObamaCare [FOX News], http://www.youtube.com/watch?v=1wcWlHTRcTE&eurl=http%3A%2F%2Fwww.dailymail.co.uk%2Fnews%2Farticle-1206264%2FBrowns-Tweet-nothings-NHS.html&feature=player_embedded (accessed on 9 October 2009).

Harris, M. and Wegg-Prosser, V. (2007) Post Bureaucracy and the Politics of Forgetting: The Management of Change at the BBC 1991–2002, *Journal of Organizational Change Management*, 20(3): 290–303.

Harrison, S. and McDonald, R. (2008) *The Politics of Healthcare in Britain*, London Sage Publications.

Heckscher, C. (1991) Can Business Beat Bureaucracy, *The American Prospect*, 2(5): 114–28.

—— (1994) Defining the Post-Bureaucratic Type, in Heckscher, C. and A. Donnelon (eds), *The Post Bureaucratic Organizational: New Perspectives on Organizational Change*, Thousand Oaks, CA: Sage.

Heckscher, C. and Applegate, L.M. (1994) Introduction, in C. Heckscher, and A. Donnelon (eds), *The Post Bureaucratic Organizational: New Perspectives on Organizational Change*, Thousand Oaks CA: Sage.

Hill, S., Martin, R. and Harris, M. (2000) Decentralisation, Integration and the Post Bureaucratic Organization: The Case of R&D, *Journal of Management Studies*, 37(4): 563–85.

Hood, C. (1998) *The Art of the State: Culture, Rhetoric and Public Management*, Oxford: Clarendon Press.

Klein, R. (2001) *The New Politics of the NHS*, 4th edn, Harlow: Pearson/Prentice Hall.

Kofman, F. and Senge, P.M. (1993) Communities of Commitment: The Heart of Learning Organizations, *Organizational Dynamics*, 22: 5–23.

Lister, S. (2004) NHS is World's Biggest Employer After Indian Rail and Chinese Army, Timesonline, 20 March 2004, http://www.timesonline.co.uk/tol/news/uk/health/article1050197.ece, (accessed 9 October 2009).

Miles, R.E., Snow, C.C., Matthews, J.A. and Coleman, H.J. (1997) Anticipating the Cellular Form, *Academy of Management Executive*, 11(4): 7–19.

Offe, C. (1985) *Disorganized Capitalism*, Oxford: Blackwell.

Osborne, D. and T. Gaebler (1992) *Reinventing Government*, Reading, MA: Addison Wesley.

Pollitt, C. (2009) Bureaucracies Remember, Post Bureaucratic Organizations Forget? *Public Administration*, 87(2): 198–218.

Reed, M. (2005) Beyond the Iron Cage? Bureaucracy and Democracy in the Knowledge Economy and Society, in du Gay (ed.), *The Values of Bureaucracy*, Oxford: Oxford University Press.

Rhodes, R.A.W. (1994) The Hollowing Out of the State, *Political Quarterly*, 65: 138–51.

Strathern, M. (2002) Abstraction and Decontextualisation: An Anthropological Comment, in S. Woolgar (ed.), *Virtual Society: Technology, Cyberole, Reality*, Oxford: Oxford University Press.

Weber, M. (1978) *Economy and Society. An Outline of Interpretive Sociology*. R. Guenther and C. Wittich (ed) Berkeley: University of California Press.

Webster, C. (2002) *The National Health Service: A Political History*, Oxford: Oxford University Press.

1 'Without Regard to Persons': Problems of Involvement and Attachment in 'Post-Bureaucratic' Public Management

PAUL DU GAY

It used to be reasonably easy to outline the contours of the administrative state, to distinguish public administration from other forms of organized activity, and to identify the professional role of state bureaucrats, public administrators, or career civil servants in the conduct of government. No longer. Over the last two to three decades, public administration, particularly but not exclusively its Anglo-Saxon variant, has been subject to extraordinary degrees of turbulence. As the American scholar of public management Gerald Caiden (2006: 515) has argued, there have been periods in the past when the public administration as an institution of government 'has undergone considerable upheavals . . . but rarely . . . at so fast and furious a pace, rarely so radical and revolutionary'. For another American scholar, Michael Lind (2005: 37), this continuous reform of the public administration is best seen as a vast political and managerial experiment 'as audacious in its own way, as that of Soviet Collectivism'. Among its most significant consequences has been what the French legal theorist Alan Supiot (2006: 2) terms the '*délite-ment*' or 'unbedding' of public institutions. He points in particular to the role of political elites themselves in this process of de-institutionalization, not least in their enthusiastic desire to be unencumbered by existing norms and machineries of government that might in some way abrogate their freedom to experiment (see also Quinlan 2004). He argues that one significant casualty of this process of *délitement* has been a prized achievement of Western political and juridical practice—the distinction between a public office and the person who occupies it. 'Initially intended to characterise the office of sovereign, this distinction signifies that the office does not die, that it has a dignity transcending the human being who provisionally occupies it and who must respect it. When that respect is erased, public office from the highest to the most modest is perceived as the private property of the present holder who can use it as he sees fit' (Supiot 2006: 3).

The chapter explores some of the reforms of the public administration as a bureaucratic institution of government that have contributed to this process of *délitement*, and examines their consequences for the relationship between 'person' and 'office' in the practice of governmental administration. I begin by highlighting certain key criticisms of the bureaucratic form that have circulated within sociology, social theory, and organization studies over the last three decades, and indicate briefly how each trades upon a particular representation of the work of the foremost theorist of bureaucracy, Max Weber. I then proceed to indicate how these criticisms feed into, and indeed help to frame, the changing ethical template that programmes of so-called 'post-bureaucratic' and 'responsive' managerial reform are held to require of civil servants. In so doing, I have cause to highlight certain political and administrative dangers that a subtle and insidious emphasis upon particular forms of loyalty and commitment to the current governing party ('the all on one team' approach), or of policy enthusiasm ('owning' the policy and championing its 'delivery') poses to the maintenance of what we might term the 'conservation standards' for responsible and effective government.

The main argument of the chapter is that many of the political and administrative virtues associated with the development and reproduction of an ethic of bureaucratic office in public administration—in particular the capacity to act with what Weber (1994*a*) famously termed a 'spirit of formalistic impersonality', and hence 'without affection or enthusiasm, and without anger or prejudice'—are either unappreciated or simply ignored in contemporary programmes designed to inculcate the requisite 'responsiveness'. This carries with it certain dangers of which earlier analysts of bureaucracy were more than aware. In particular, the work of Max Weber, and especially his theorization of bureaucracy as *officium*, and politics as a vocation, provides a continual source of inspiration for those who seek to hold onto an 'ethics of bureaucratic office' in an increasingly alien environment.

Max Weber and the Bureaucratic Form: Critic, Celebrant, or Historical Anthropologist?

Much of what passes for criticism of the bureaucratic form within sociology, social theory, and organization studies does so with reference to the work of Max Weber. For each, Weber is seen as the paradigmatic theorist of bureaucracy. However, interpretations of Weber's views of, and intellectual approach to, bureaucracy differ significantly. In certain forms of sociology, for example, Weber is represented as one of the chief critics of bureaucracy, and his work is referenced with respect to what is considered to be his perceptive, even prophetic, analysis of this organizational form's inherent 'dark side'. Here is a critic of modernity, so Bauman (1989) for instance argues, who highlights the instrumentalizing, rationalizing logic of bureaucratic action, and points to its role in undermining substantive forms of morality (see also Ritzer 2004). Within certain sections of management and organization studies, on the other hand, a rather different picture of Weber emerges. Here we find Weber positioned as a celebrant of bureaucracy as the most efficient form of organization known to humanity. This Weber is something akin to a para-digmatic adherent of the—largely discredited—'closed system–rational actor' school of organizational analysis. As two of his more histrionic critics make clear, Weber got it all wrong because 'he pooh-poohed charismatic leadership and doted on bureaucracy; its rule driven, impersonal form, he said, was the only way to ensure long term survival' (Peters and Waterman 1982: 5). In this reading, Weber is represented as a well-intentioned but ultimately misguided celebrant of bureaucracy; misguided because he pays too much attention to formal rationality and not enough to its inherent dysfunctions. The latter are seen ultimately to matter more than the former precisely because they eventually begin to paralyse the organization, making it unable to fulfil its instituted purposes except at tremendous cost—socially and emotionally, for instance—particularly to those working within its hyper-rational 'frame'.

What both images of Weber assume is the centrality of 'rationalization' to his work. The former locates Weber as a key critic of Western rationalism and its 'instrumental' logics, who views with horror the ethical and emotional disfigurements that the primary institutional carrier of this forms of rational-ization—bureaucracy—is producing. The latter locates Weber as a leading advocate of rational management and, hence, as an unconscious promoter of bureaucracy's inherent tendency to displace 'morality', 'emotion', etc. and all forms of substantive human value from organizational existence. What both approaches share, however, is first, the assumption that rationalization is Weber's key theme, and second, the belief that when we come to analyse the consequences of bureaucratic action, most especially the advances in efficien-cy and economy it registers, we can see that increasing instrumental rational-ization comes at too high a price for those immediately subject to its dictates, and also for the societies it helps to bring into being. In this way, both the image of Weber as a critic of bureaucracy, and that of Weber as its celebrant, point towards a similar conclusion: the importance of constructing a post-bureaucratic future where the human and social ends of organizing and managing are once again invested with more value than are their means, and the negative human consequences of hierarchy, instrumental rationality, and impersonality can be addressed and remedied (Heckscher and Donnellon 1994).

As two of the most impressive scholars of his work, Mommsen (1987) and Hennis (1988), have argued, it does not take much familiarity with Weber's *oeuvre* to see that Max Weber is innocent of the so-called Weberianism that adopts a uniform, monolithic conception of the historical phenomena of rationalization. As Weber argued, on a number of occasions, rationalism can mean many different things. In *The Protestant Ethic and the Spirit of Capitalism*, for instance, he warns that:

The history of rationalism shows a development which by no means follows parallel lines in the various departments of life ... In fact, one may—this simple proposition should be placed at the beginning of every study which essays to deal with rationalism—rationalise life from fundamentally different basic points of view and in very different directions. Rationalism is a historical concept which covers a whole world of different things. (Weber 1930: 77–8)

Many economic sociologists and scholars of organization studies who comment on his work often appear to imagine that the distinctions suggested by Weber are, so far as Weber's own studies are concerned, flattened out by the modern advance of that dead hand of instrumental rationality—bureaucracy (Bauman 1989; Ritzer 2004). However, it is relatively easy to point to the vital importance that Weber attaches to the lasting and intrinsic differences between, for instance, the style of rationality appropriate to the bureaucrat, and those of the entrepreneur and the politician, for example (Gordon 1987; du Gay 2000).

This still leaves open the question as to whether, and in what ways, the question of rationalization determines the overall themes and purposes of Weber's *oeuvre*. One response to this question has been provided by Wolfgang Schluchter (1981), who sees the varieties of rationalization that Weber's studies deal with as ultimately staging posts on the road to a complete theory of rationalization. However, one of perhaps the most problematic aspects of this proposal is Weber's own stated doubts concerning the extent to which the different historical 'problem-spaces within which questions about rationalisation come to be posed can usefully be merged together under the auspices of a single overarching theory' (Gordon 1987: 294).

If, as Weber argued, we need 'to remind ourselves that rationalism may mean very different things', then to represent him as involved in a project of tracing 'a universal–historical process of rationalization' is somewhat misleading, if not misplaced. The problematic of rationalization is more diverse and context-specific than such a grand narrative allows for or appreciates. Rather, Weber's work points to the ways in which different 'orders of life' (*Lebensordungen*) exhibit their own distinctive and non-reducible forms of 'organized rationality'. These have to be described and understood in their terms, rather than being 'coordinated' into a meta-theory of rationalization (Mommsen 1987: 42–3). As Wilhelm Hennis (1988: 94) puts it, the process of rationalization for Weber has 'to be related to each life order if we are to perceive the significance it has in his work'. Not only this, but the tensions between these forms of organized rationality need to be outlined and appreciated. They do not necessarily follow the same path, towards the same end. Rather, they often have non-uniform trajectories, not entirely unrelated to their rather differing purposes and the ethos framing them. Here, then, there is in principle a plurality of competing rationalizations, each of which 'is dependent upon a different value position, and these value positions are, in their turn, in constant conflict with one another' (Mommsen 1987: 44). As Weber (1994*b*: 357) famously asked, 'is it in fact true that any ethic in the world could establish substantively identical commandments applicable to all relationships, whether erotic, business, family or official, to one's relations with one's wife, greengrocer, son, competitor, with a friend or an accused man?'

In contrast to commentators seeking to find in Weber's work, or more likely, to imprint upon that work, the tracing of a uniform, unilinear, and monolithic process of rationalization, other interpretations of the Weberian *oeuvre* have stressed the importance of a more contextually specific focus on the organized forms of rationality that must be confronted by all those who become involved in particular 'life-orders'. Here the central focus is upon *Lebensführungen*: the conducts of life, and the various forms of their rationalization in specific life-orders (Hennis 1988, 2000; Turner 1992; Minson 1993, 1998; Saunders 1997).

The claim, most notably advanced by Wilhelm Hennis, that a focus on *Lebensführung* constitutes a, if not the, key object of Weber's work, involves three interlinked propositions. First, Hennis argues that most of Weber's work is centrally concerned with the conduct of life as its first and most pressing topic. Among the texts that Hennis refers to in order to back up this claim is, unsurprisingly, Weber's most famous essay *The Protestant Ethic and the Spirit of Capitalism*, with its focus upon the methodical conduct of life instilled by the Calvinist sects. Second, Hennis argues that the concern with *Lebensführung* inspires and illuminates the methodology of Weber's major works, pointing in particular to *Economy & Society*, where the 'arena of normative and *de facto* powers' is imagined and assessed in terms of the influence of collective forces upon individual life-conduct (1988: 84).

The point of departure is that of external given conditions. The life-orders, however, do possess an inner regularity,... each of these orders makes a demand, forms, characterises, a variety of 'impositions' or perhaps opens up possibilities for future conduct, involves a formative tendency for the 'personality'... What fate do these orders dictate, open up to or withhold from the persons placed in their power by conditions of time and place? Is this Weber's theme? (Hennis 1988: 65)

That this is indeed Weber's main theme is, as far as Hennis is concerned, evidenced by his third claim: for Weber, no ultimate moral or philosophical justification for a given form of life is possible in modern societies, 'because the different value systems of the world stand in conflict with one another' (1989: 22). Between these different life-orders there is frequently a battle of different gods of different religions: 'Destiny not science prevails over these gods and their struggles. One can only understand what the divine is for one system or another, or in one system or another' (Weber 1989: 22). In *Science as a Vocation*, Weber encourages his audience to be 'polytheistic', and to take on the persona specific to the life-order within which they are engaged. In the absence of a universal moral norm, or a conclusive victory for one form of organized rationality over all others, Weber asks, how are individuals to develop 'character' or 'personality' (*Persönlichkeit*)? In considering the future of modern societies, and the individuals existing within them, Weber's deepest concern, Hennis argues, is the cultivation of individuals with 'personality': those willing and able to live up to the ethical demands placed upon them by their location within particular life-orders, whose life-conduct within those distinctive orders and powers—the public bureau, the firm, the parliament—can combine practical rationality with ethical seriousness.

In *Science as a Vocation*, Weber's answer to this problem is clear and direct: 'Ladies and gentlemen: Personality is possessed in science by the man (*sic*) who serves only the needs of his subject, and this is true not only in science' (1989: 11). The individual with 'personality' is one who is capable of personal dedication to a cause (*Sache*), or the instituted purposes of a given life-order, in a manner that 'transcends individuality' (Hennis 1988: 88). It is in this sense that it is possible, for example, for bureaucrats to be 'personally' committed to the ethos and purposes of their distinctive office, even though that ethos lies outside their own personal (i.e. individual) moral predilections or principles. The possibility of different categories and practices of personhood requiring and expressing distinctive ethical comportments, irreducible to common underlying principles, appears quite foreign to those for whom a common or universal form of moral judgement is held to reside in the figure and capacities of the self-reflective person or individual agent (e.g. Habermas). This context-specific, and thus 'limited', conception of 'personality' cautions against the siren-calls of those political romantics—socialists, anarchists, the *littérateurs*—seeking to hold onto, or re-establish, the idea of the 'complete' human being: an ultimate, supra-regional persona that could function as the normative benchmark for all others.

Hennis argues passionately, and with a wealth of documentary evidence, that at the heart of Weber's work there is a moral anthropology profoundly at variance with both the positivistic tendencies and Kantian philosophical assumptions of the human sciences in the present and previous century. He argues that for both a positivistic and high theoretical social science, which in

Weber's own words sought to 'shift its location and change its conceptual apparatus so that it might regard the stream of events from the heights of reflective thought' (Weber, quoted in Hennis 1988: 104), questions of *Lebens-führung*, of 'personality' and life-orders, would have little interest. However, if we managed to descend from such heights, they might once again become very important indeed. For Hennis (1988: 104), Max Weber's work finds a place in the prehistory of this sort of social science only once his central problems, questions, and concerns are neglected. In Hennis's view, Weber's work belongs, rather, to the late history of a rather different practical science of mankind (*Menschentum*) and, we might add, to a distinctive ethical tradition: the ethics of office. Seen in this way, Max Weber's work provides a classic account of the ways in which a distinctive and important role for an ethics of office can be maintained in an increasingly alien environment, through, for example, his theorization of bureaucracy as *officium* and politics as a vocation (Hennis 1988: 104, 2000: 156; Condren 2006: 347).

Office as a Vocation: Weber and the Moral Economy of Bureaucracy

If, as I have suggested, Weber is approached first and foremost as a historical anthropologist of *Lebensführung*, then it becomes clear that his work on bureaucracy is neither celebratory nor overtly critical. Indeed, Weber was not simply or exclusively interested in offering a formal organizational theory of 'bureaucracy' at all, for good or ill, but rather, as Hennis (1988, 2000) has suggested, with describing the ethical–cultural attributes of bureaucratic conduct. In order to approach Weber's work in this way—as a historical anthropologist of *Lebensführung* or 'conduct of life'—it is first necessary to dispense with the detritus of the Parsonian inheritance in Weberian scholarship, and to focus instead upon Weber as a somewhat eccentric and isolated moral theorist in a tradition of the ethics of office (Condren 2006: 24). To put it in its most general propositional form: a presupposition of office was the expectation that people are educated (in the widest sense of that term) to live up to the demands and requirements of their respective offices. An office (*Lebensordnung*) was an

'identifiable and discriminate constellation of responsibilities and subordinate rights and liberties asserted to be necessary for their fulfilment' and manifested not in an individual, represented as a distinctive, reflective and autonomous 'self' but rather in a persona. In other words, individual identity was specific to office, referring only to bodies considered as personae, as instituted statuses or conditions. (Condren 2006: 29)

For Weber, bureaucracy was a historically contingent and variable 'life-order' (*Lebensführung*) constituting a distinctive ethical milieu in its own right, one whose practices of formalistic impersonality gave rise to certain substantive ethical goals. Thus, in his classic account of the 'persona' of the bureaucrat, for instance, Weber (1978, II: 978ff) treats the impersonal, expert, procedural, and hierarchical character of bureaucratic conduct as elements of a distinctive ethos. Here office itself constitutes a 'vocation', a focus of ethical commitment and duty, autonomous of and superior to the bureaucrat's extra-official ties to kith, kin, class, or conscience. The ethical attributes of the 'good' bureaucrat—strict adherence to procedure, commitment to the purposes of the office, abnegation of personal moral enthusiasms, and so on—represent a remarkable achievement (Hunter 1994: 157). In particular, Weber (1978, II: 983ff) stresses the ways in which the ethos of bureaucratic office-holding constitutes an important political resource, because it serves to divorce the administration of public life from private moral absolutisms. Without the historical emergence of the ethos and persona of bureaucratic office-holding, Weber argues, the construction of a buffer between civic comportment and personal principles—a crucial feature of liberal government—would never have been possible. Indeed, without the 'art of separation' (Walzer 1984) that the state bureau effected and continues to effect, many of the qualitative features of government that are regularly taken for granted—for instance, formal equality, reliability, and procedural fairness in the treatment of cases—would not exist.

As Weber makes clear, the crucial point of honour for bureaucrats is not to allow extra-official commitments to determine the manner in which they perform the duties associated with their office. 'On the contrary', the bureaucrat 'takes pride in preserving his impartiality, overcoming his own inclinations and opinions, so as to execute in a conscientious and meaningful way what is required of him by the general definition of his duties or by some particular instruction, even—and particularly—when they do not coincide with his own political views' (Weber 1994a: 160). 'The official has to sacrifice his own convictions to his duty of obedience' (Weber 1994a: 204). This does not mean that officials only do the boring, routine work of public or state administration:

Independent decision-making and imaginative organizational capabilities are usually also demanded of the bureaucrat, and very often expected even in large matters. The idea that the bureaucrat is absorbed in subaltern routine and that only the 'director' performs the interesting, intellectually demanding tasks is a preconceived notion of the literati and only possible in a country that has no insight into the manner in which its affairs are conducted. (Weber 1994a: 160)

The key to understanding the ethos of bureaucratic office, Weber argues, resides in 'the kind of responsibility' associated with it. It is this, and not simple divisions between task complexity and simplicity, or between policy making and routine administration, that distinguishes the 'demands addressed' to this 'position'. As Weber (1994*b*: 330) puts it:

An official who receives a directive which he considers wrong can and is supposed to object to it. If his superior insists on its execution, it is his duty, even his honour to carry it out as if it corresponded to his innermost conviction, and to demonstrate in this fashion that his sense of duty stands above his personal preference...This is the ethos of office.

Without this 'supremely ethical discipline and self-denial', Weber (1994*b*: 331) continued, 'the whole apparatus of the state would disintegrate, and with it all the political benefits deriving from it'.

Similarly, Weber (1978, I: 225–6) argued that it was odd for the *literati* to criticize bureaucratic conduct as antithetical to the realization of substantive ends; that is, as simply the organizational vehicle by which instrumental values supersede and/or eliminate all substantive values. Rather, as he made clear on a number of occasions, the 'formalism' of bureaucratic conduct, its instituted blindness to inherited differences of standing and prestige, produces the very substantive effects—enhancing democracy and equality, for example—that the *literati* claimed bureaucratic conduct would destroy (Weber 1978, I & II, 1994*b*):

The dominance of a spirit of formalistic impersonality: 'Sine ira et studio', without hatred or passion, and hence without affection or enthusiasm. The dominant norms are concepts of straightforward duty without regard to personal considerations. Everyone is subject to formal equality of treatment; that is, everyone in the same empirical situation. This is the spirit in which the ideal official conducts his office. The development of bureaucracy greatly favours the levelling of status, and this can be shown historically to be the normal tendency. Conversely, every social levelling creates a favourable situation for the development of bureaucracy by eliminating the office-holder who rules by virtue of status privileges and the appropriation of the means and powers of administration; in the interests of 'equality', it also eliminates those who can hold office on an honorary basis or as an avocation by virtue of their wealth. Everywhere, bureaucracy foreshadows mass democracy...(Weber 1978, I: 225–6)

In other words, the exclusion of extra-official considerations from the conduct of official business, and the strictly formalistic impersonality with which that business was conducted, was not only a prerequisite of impartial and efficient administration but also crucial to the production of mass democracy and increased social equality. This idea that the 'formal' rationality of bureaucratic conduct itself gives rise to substantive ethical goals and effects, and is rooted in its own *Lebensordnung* or ethical life-order—that of the bureau—has been largely ignored by critics keen to 'rehumanize' official life through 'post-bureaucratic' means. Like the *literati* chided by Weber in his own day, contemporary anti-bureaucrats in the arena of public or governmental administration focus much of their attention upon the presumed negative consequences of the bureaucrat's formalistically impersonal obligations of office, and demand a shift in the relationship between these obligations and what they conceive of as the official's principal duties—to deliver the policies that their political governors demand of them with maximum enthusiasm and conviction. It is to the work of these critics that I now turn.

Enthusiasm, Responsiveness, and 'Post-Bureaucracy'

It would be difficult to overestimate the importance allocated to qualities of enthusiasm and enterprise in recent discourses of organizational reform in both private and public sector management. From the hyperbolic commandments of Tom Peters (1989) to 'develop a public and passionate hatred of bureaucracy' through to Gary Hamel's demands for 'revolutionary management' (2000), the emphasis has been on breaking with bureaucratic norms and forms of conduct in the name of innovation, risk-taking, and organizational and personal liberation (Armbrüster 2005; du Gay 2005). While, in the aftermath of the corporate scandals at Enron, WorldCom et al., and indeed the recent and ongoing 'financial crisis', the shine has been somewhat taken off the tropes of revolutionary rule-breaking, nonetheless the equation of entrepreneurial enthusiasm with getting things done or delivering results, as the current wisdom has it, has far from disappeared from programmes of organizational reform.

In discussions of public sector performance, for instance, governments of many different political hues have come to the conclusion that Weberian bureaucracy is not a solution but rather a barrier to 'delivery'. In their search for responsive forms of public management, party-political governments rail against the obstruction and inertia of conservative bureaucrats, and seek instead to surround themselves with enthusiastic, committed champions of their policies. The testimony of the former head of (former) Prime Minister Blair's Public Service Delivery Unit offers a taster of precisely such an attitude. 'Most of all there is the danger of underestimating the extraordinary deadweight of institutional inertia. Senior civil servants generally recognised the need for change, but found it hard to bring about—the deadweight of the culture held them back...Bold sustained leadership is a pre-requisite for transformation, professions left to themselves rarely advocate more than incremental change ...' (Barber 2007: 72, 124–5, and 144). Here, the demand is for a break with bureaucracy in the name of transformation, performance, passion, and much else besides. There is, from this perspective, no recognition of, and thus no respect for, the possible positivities of attention to precedent, for institutionalized caution, and for consultation and cross-checking.

As the former Senior Civil Servant Sir Michael Quinlan (2004: 128) notes, such a focus on 'delivery' and 'performance' as part and parcel of a sustained focus on the achievement of practical results can

[s]lide into a sense that outcome is the only true reality and that process is flummery. But the two are not antithetical, still less inimical to one another. Process is care and thoroughness; it is consultation, involvement and co-ownership; it is (as we were reminded by the failure of international process in the run-up to the Iraq war) legitimacy and acceptance; it is also record, auditability and clear accountability. It is accordingly a significant component of outcome itself; and the more awkward and demanding the issue—especially amid the special gravity of peace and war—the more it may come to matter.

For Quinlan (2004), such bureaucratic practices are less the epitome of inefficiency and anachronism than crucial material means through which responsible democratic governance is practically achieved. As John Uhr (1993: xvii) puts it, 'the bureaucratic vocation therefore helps furnish many of the "conservation standards" appropriate to the political management of the state, including the ordered management of "change" between governments of differing political hues'.

In recent years, for example, the issue of 'transformational leadership' has emerged as a hot topic within the field of public management (Newman 2005). In Britain, the New Labour Government's White Paper, *Modernizing Government* (CM4310 1999) and its related policy documents (Cabinet Office 1999*a*, 1999*b*) placed considerable emphasis upon the capacity of executive leadership to help change the culture of 'risk aversion' that it considered endemic to the British Civil Service. Thus, the White Paper stated that officials must 'move away from the risk-averse culture inherent in government' and that this was to be achieved through removing 'unnecessary bureaucracy which prevents public servants from experimenting, innovating and delivering a better product'. As with a previous attempt to inculcate 'real qualities of leadership' among senior civil servants, in the *Next Steps* report (Cabinet Office 1988: para 35), quite what this meant in the British constitutional context, where ministerial accountability was still assumed to be a crucial constitutional convention, was not at all clear. At one level, encouraging all senior civil servants to become leaders and to take individual personal responsibility for their decision-making would make the accountability trail more, not less, complicated. With so many leaders among politicians and civil servants, where would the buck stop, exactly? Indeed, would not the distinction between these categories of person become somewhat blurred—and their respective 'responsibilities of office' compromised—if everyone is equally assumed to be a leader?

Throughout the Anglo-American world, governments have been busy preaching the virtues of enthusiasm as part of a search for more 'responsive' forms of public management. In Britain, the former Labour government's demands for 'delivery', combined with an often unsubtle distaste for the traditions of the civil service as the 'other governing profession', led it quickly to demand changes in the 'ethos' governing the conduct of public administrators. As the former British Home Secretary, Charles Clarke, put it, 'what I think we'd benefit from is a more effective managerial quality at the top, and I'd say put the "just do it" ethic in, is the change that's needed' (BBC Radio 4: 25/07/02). Once again, the civil servant as part of an institutional 'gyroscope of state' and bulwark against what Walt Whitman once described as 'the never ending audacity of elected persons' was to be reconfigured as a something akin to an enthusiastic, energetic 'yes-person'.

The consequences of the shift in style and emphasis for the civil service as a constitutional bureaucracy have become increasingly clear. The last three decades have witnessed a concerted attempt by governing parties in many different political contexts to strengthen their control over state bureaux. One aspect of this particular trend has been the erosion of the powers of centralized staffing agencies that safeguarded public service recruitment and promotions from political or official interference; strengthening ministerial control of top departmental appointments by removing the need to consult an independent staffing agency; substituting short-term contracts for security of tenure in top official posts, generating the general attitude that party-political governments should not have to tolerate obstruction or inertia from conservative bureaucrats, and should instead insist they were supported by enthusiastic advocates of their policies who would ensure that the latter were 'delivered' (Chapman 2004). In attempting to achieve these ends, however, politicians and their advisers have arguably weakened the legitimate role of officials in government by undermining the Weberian ethos of bureaucratic office (Parker 1993; du Gay 2000; Chapman 2004).

The tactic of increasing the use of external appointments to senior civil service positions, in particular, and especially the appointment of those with known prior policy enthusiasms, has given rise to two particular problems. The first is that of ensuring that standards in state service are maintained— that the obligations of office are lived up to; the second is that distinctions between office and self are not so blurred that the civil service becomes a politically partisan institution. In the United Kingdom, for instance, the political neutrality, or party political impartiality, of the British Civil Service, has flowed in no small part from its career basis (Bogdanor 2001; Chapman 2004). Career civil servants are expected to serve successive governments of differing party political hues. The key to being able to do this, as Weber indicated long ago, is to cultivate a degree of indifference to the enthusiasms of all political parties. Traditionally, at least, civil servants have been trained to conduct themselves in such a manner. Indeed, in Britain, as elsewhere, people with strong party political or single issue interests have—until relatively recently—been unlikely to be appointed to senior civil service positions, or to present themselves for consideration as candidates in the first place (Chapman 1988). As a result, civil servants have been likely to greet the panaceas of all political parties with caution. Inevitably, this leads them to embrace party political programmes with less fervour than party political enthusiasts would like. But this is part of their job, one assigned to them by the constitution. And in fulfilling this role they may be seen as servants of the state.

It is precisely the statist/constitutional role that is being affected by political and managerial demands for displays of 'enthusiasm' among civil servants, and which is evident in the growing number of external appointments to the senior echelons of the service. New recruits coming from outside—whether from commercial organizations or social enterprises—will generally lack the traditional patterns of experience, such as those gained by being a private secretary to a minister, which help inculcate in civil servants that very impartiality described by Weber. Moreover, someone recruited from outside the service by virtue of relevant knowledge and approved commitments is likely to arrive with all sorts of partisan baggage derived from their previous situation. That is almost inevitable if 'new' enthusiastic civil servants are expected to be cheerleaders for government, and act as committed champions for specific policies. It is not easy, however, for those same people both to fulfil such a role and at the same time to conform to traditional practices of subordination and lack of constitutional personality, their views being those of their minister, and not their own (Bogdanor 2001).

As Bogdanor (2001: 296) has suggested, it is not clear, therefore, how far outside recruitment to senior policy positions in the Civil Service can avoid the dangers of politicization or at least a degree of prior policy commitment, incompatible with traditional notions of 'political impartiality'. 'Politicization' is a loaded term—one deployed rather too flexibly perhaps. However, if suitably disaggregated, it is not without its uses. Certainly, it should not be seen simply to refer to a process by which civil servants are recruited, selected, or promoted on the basis of their political views. Even a politician as partisan as Margaret Thatcher denied taking political outlook into consideration when discussing civil service personnel issues. Instead, she was clear that she wanted a certain proactive 'can do' disposition to be at a premium among public servants—'drive and enthusiasm were what mattered' (Thatcher 1993: 46). However, the promotion of these latter qualities should alert us to another, less overtly party political, facet of the term 'politicization'. The term can also be used to refer to the willingness of officials to implement politicians' ideas enthusiastically (Stahlberg 1987). Put simply, politicization can refer to a civil service that reacts over-favourably to political signals, even though the officials personally or necessarily do not have a commitment to a specific political party or programme.

One of the problems about enthusiasms among civil servants is that office and self can become blurred, with committed champions coming to see the office as an extension of themselves, thereby effecting a confusion of public and private interests and identities. The American scholar Patrick Dobel (1999: 131) calls this 'zealous sleaze', a process whereby individuals come to view public office as an extension of their own will and ideological commitments—their enthusiasms. The introduction into state bureaux of people with prior policy commitments and established enthusiasms could therefore easily undermine the traditional obligations of office that frame the conduct of the Civil Service as an institution of government. Similar objections can be made to the proliferation of special advisers, especially when, as in some well-known cases in the United Kingdom, this category of actor has been allotted extraordinary powers to issue orders to civil servants, or has, through its gatekeeper role with ministers, effectively been able to negate the influence of civil servants in the area of advising on policy issues (Daintith 2002; Jones 2002; Oliver 2003; O'Toole 2006).

Well before the latest manifestations of the 'ethics of enthusiasm' and enterprise in government and public administration, the problems attendant upon the promotion of such capacities among officials was considered and foreseen by the Secretary to the Fulton Committee—perhaps the best known of the post-Second World War official investigations into the role and function of the British Civil Service. As a result of his career in the British Civil Service, and his reflections upon its constitutional role and purposes, R.W. Wilding had some interesting things to say about the place of enthusiasm in the professional ethic of the career public administrator. Writing in 1979, he argued that it was necessary for bureaucrats to 'distinguish energy from commitment; it is absolutely necessary to pursue today's policy with energy; it is almost equally necessary, in order to survive, to withhold from it the last ounce of commitment' (quoted in Chapman 2006: 6). For Wilding, as for Weber, enthusiasm for particular policies is dangerous for public administrators precisely because it means that bureaucrats become increasingly indistinguishable from politicians in that they too are encouraged to engage in 'partisanship, fighting, passion—*ira et studium*' (Weber 1994b: 330). If they act outside the limits of their office, or if the office itself becomes indistinguishable from another department of existence, bureaucrats will have ceased being bureaucrats and have become something else altogether. While it may never be possible to rid the term 'bureaucrat' of negative connotations, it is nonetheless the case that the disappearance of such a category of person would have profound and far from positive effects on many aspects of existence that we tend to take for granted.

How then, can they continue to live up to the obligations of their office? The abiding problem of 'enthusiasm' in administrative life is precisely the way in which it can effectively undermine what Weber and Wilding see as the virtues of the non-sectarian comportment of the bureaucratic person. In so doing, the ethics of enthusiasm run the risk of returning the administration of public life to the pursuit of private moral absolutisms, rather than, as Weber noted in his discussion of the moral economy of bureaucratic ethics, divorcing it from them.

The development of the bureaucratic ethos therefore furnishes the state with an important tool. The political positivities flowing from this bureaucratic ethos derive in large part from its imperviousness to particular sorts of enthusiasm. This does not preclude bureaucrats from pursuing their instituted purposes with energy, demonstrating rigorous dispassionateness, integrity, and propriety, including appropriate attention to criteria of efficiency, effectiveness, and economy (terms that only attain specific meaning in the context of specific tasks) in the conduct of official business. This commitment, however—to behaving constitutionally, within the confines of their office, as servants of the state—precisely excludes enthusiasm for particular policies.

As recent events in the United Kingdom have demonstrated, most notably, perhaps, those surrounding the decision to go to war in Iraq, enthusiasm for a particular course of action, combined with impatience with due process and the minutiae of bureaucratic record-keeping, can have the gravest consequences. While discussions of civil service reform might at first sight appear largely unrelated to the processes through which, and the manner in which, the decision to go to war with Iraq was made, there is much to be learned from seeing them in tandem, as a number of former senior civil servants have argued (Quinlan 2004; Wilson 2004). As Quinlan (2004: 125) has indicated, for example, the important inquiries by Lords Hutton and Butler into aspects of the Iraq saga painted a picture of the workings of government, including its politico-administrative 'condition', that was in many important respects remarkably disquieting. Norms and modes of conduct designed to assist in the seemingly innocuous objectives of enhancing 'delivery' and aiding 'responsiveness', for instance, had had some profound effects upon the capacity of the civil service to live up to its constitutional obligations. These changes, often apparently marked by an impatience with existing norms and modes of conduct, appeared to rest upon an insufficient understanding, (one might even say failure to understand) that existing patterns had not been developed without practical reason, and that departing from them might have serious costs that necessitated careful consideration beforehand. In particular, seemingly banal, 'old-fashioned' forms of bureaucratic administration turned out to play an important role in constituting the political landscape. Attempts to by-pass or transcend these forms of administration could therefore have some significant political as well as organizational costs (Wilson 2004; for a fuller explication of this point, see Byrkjeflot & du Gay 2009).

The antipathy towards enthusiasm inherent in the bureaucratic ethos has its own *raison d'être*. While it is easy to see how such an ethos can be viewed by politicians as a licence to obstruct, it was, until comparatively recently, generally considered indispensable to the achievement of responsible (as opposed to merely 'responsive') government, because it was seen to balance and even complement political will, making governance more effective in the long run.

As John Rohr (1998) has suggested, the bureaucratic ethos is in important respects necessarily one of unresponsiveness. The role accorded to governmental bureaux in many polities has been deliberately devised to insulate officials from the electoral process, or from the demands of 'special interests', for example, thus institutionalizing the very 'lack of responsiveness' that so many enthusiasts decry. And it has been so organized to serve a positive political purpose—to help preserve a modicum of stability, consistency, and continuity, in the face of the vagaries and experimental enthusiasms of partisan politicians, for instance. In this specific and limited sense, the bureaucratic ethos is a conservative one or better, perhaps, a *conservational* one. The bureaucratic comportment of the person embodies an acceptance, which no moral zealot can abide, of the irreconcilable diversity of human goods, and an awareness of the possible costs, moral and otherwise, of pursuing one end to the exclusion of all others. In this way, the bureaucrat tends to see in every controversial change to existing arrangements the possibility of important losses, as well as the opportunity for certain gains (Larmore 1987: xiv). Like the ethos of the Lawyer/Statesman described so eloquently by Anthony Kronman (1993: 161), the good bureaucrat 'is unlikely to be moved by that passion for purity which motivates the adherents of every great political simplification'. Programmes of radical change will be approached with a degree of caution unlikely to appeal to the enthusiast. Rather than being soulless, uncaring 'pen pushers', unelected policy wreckers, or unentrepreneurial 'automata of the paragraphs', as the *literati* (old and new) would have it, the bureaucrat's antipathy to enthusiasm can be seen to provide an important service to the state, and to make a crucial contribution to the long-range effectiveness of government.

Concluding Comments

The main argument of this chapter has been that, when applied to the office-based commitments of professional civil servants, contemporary political and managerial demands for increased 'responsiveness' and 'enthusiasm' associated with a 'post-bureaucratic' departure from the features of the bureaucratic ethos outlined by Weber, should be treated with considerable scepticism. As has been argued, the demand for higher levels of 'personal' involvement on the part of career civil servants in championing and delivering policies, and related demands upon them for increased levels of personal attachment to those policies has been a hallmark of some recent political and managerial initiatives in government. In the United Kingdom, one area where this has become more evident is in the practice of appointing to civil service positions people with known policy commitments whom governing politicians regard as 'one of us' in a way that they do not regard career civil servants. This does not imply that these enthusiasts are necessarily members of the same political party as their recruiting sergeants, but simply that they are advocates of particular policy programmes or solutions and are committed to seeing them delivered. At the same time, and not unrelated, there has also been a substantial increase in the number of so-called 'special advisers' operating in government, some charged with executive responsibilities, and once again exhibiting a more partisan approach to policy making and delivery than would be expected in a career civil servant (O'Toole 2006).

The consequences for the institutional and ethical integrity of the governmental machinery of this embedding of enthusiasm or 'partisanship' within the organs of the state need careful consideration. In their search for greater control over the state bureaucracy, politicians may well have weakened or undermined the important role played by the bureaucratic ethos—with its spirit of formalistic impersonality—in the responsible operation of a state and in the effective running of a constitution. When advocates of the 'ethics of enthusiasm' characterize governmental administration as an unreconstructed Weberian world of 'formal rationality', they forget that for Weber such an ethic of *Zweckrationalität* was not merely 'instrumental' or dependent upon arbitrarily given ends. Rather an ethos of formalistic impersonality—'without affection or enthusiasm'—was premised upon the cultivation of indifference to certain ultimate moral ends. This indifference was a remarkable, if ultimately fragile, achievement, requiring those subject to its demands to learn to take cognizance of the incompatibility between a plurality of enthusiastically held convictions about rival moral ends, and hence the consequences of pursuing one of them at the expense of the others. Seen in this light, formal rationality is not predicated upon an amoral instrumentalism, a wilful obstructionism or incapacity to 'deliver', but on what we might term a positive, statist, 'ethics of responsibility'.

☐ BIBLIOGRAPHY

Armbrüster, T. (2005) Bureaucracy and the Controversy Between Liberal Interventionism and Non-Interventionism, in P. du Gay (ed.), *The Values of Bureaucracy*, Oxford: Oxford University Press.

Barber, M. (2008) *Instruction to Deliver: Tony Blair, Public Services and the Challenge of Achieving Targets*, London: Methuen.

Bauman, Z. (1989) *Modernity and the Holocaust*, Cambridge: Polity Press.

BBC Radio 4 'Analysis', Miraculous Mandarins, Broadcast Date: 25.07.2002.

Blumenberg, H. (1985) *The Legitimacy of the Modern Age*, Boston, Massachusetts: MIT Press.

Bogdanor, V. (2001) Civil Service Reform: A Critique, *The Political Quarterly*, 73(3): 291–9.

Byrkjeflot, H. and du Gay, P. (2009) Bureaucracy: An Idea Whose Time has Come (Again), Paper presented to the 25th EGOS Colloquium, Barcelona, July 2009.

Cabinet Office (1988) *Improving Management in Government: The Next Steps*, London: HMSO.

——(1999*a*) *Vision and Values*, London: Cabinet Office.

——(1999*b*) *Civil Service Reform*, London: Cabinet Office.

Caiden, G. (2006) The Administrative State in a Globalizing World: Trends and Challenges, in Lind, N. S. and Otenyo, E. (eds) *Comparative Public Administration: The Essential Readings*, Elsevier, New York, 515–42.

Chapman, R.A. (1988) *Ethics in the British Civil Service*, London: Routledge.

——(2004) *The Civil Service Commission 1855–1991: A Bureau Biography*, London: Taylor Francis Routledge.

——(2006) The Ethics of Enthusiasm, *Public Money & Management*, January 5–7.

CM4310 (1999) *Modernising Government*, London: HMSO.

Condren, C. (2006) *Argument and Authority in Early Modern England: The Presupposition of Oaths and Offices*, Cambridge: Cambridge University Press.

Daintith, T. (2002) A Very Good Day to Get Anything Out We Want to Bury, *Public Law*, Spring: 13–21.

Dobel, P. (1999) *Public Integrity*, Baltimore: The Johns Hopkins University Press.

Du Gay, P. (2000) *In Praise of Bureaucracy*, London: Sage.

——(2005) Bureaucracy and Liberty. State, Authority, and Freedom, in P. du Gay (ed.) *The Values of Bureaucracy*, Oxford: Oxford University Press, 41–62.

Gordon, C. (1987) The Soul of the Citizen: Max Weber and Michel Foucault on Rationality and Government, in S. Whimster and S. Lash (eds), *Max Weber, Rationality and Modernity*, London: Allen & Unwin, 293–316.

Hamel, G. (2000) *Leading the Revolution*, Boston, Massachusetts: Harvard Business School Press.

Heckscher, C. and Donnellon, A. (1994) *The Post-Bureaucratic Organization: New Perspectives on Organizational Change*, London: Sage.

Hennis, W. (1988) *Max Weber: Essays in Reconstruction*, London: Allen & Unwin.

Hennis, M. (2000) *Max Weber's Science of Man*, Newbury, Berks: Threshold Press.

Hunter, I. (1994) *Re-Thinking the School*, Sydney: Allen & Unwin.

Jones, N. (2002) *The Control Freaks*, London: Methuen.

Kronman, A. (1993) *The Lost Lawyer*, Cambridge, Massachusetts: Harvard University Press.

Larmore, C. (1987) *Patterns of Moral Complexity*, Cambridge: Cambridge University Press.

Lind, M. (2005) *In Defence of Mandarins*, London: Prospect, October, 34–7.

Minson, J. (1993) *Questions of Conduct*, Basingstoke: Macmillan.

——(1998) Ethics in the Service of the State, in M. Dean and B. Hindess (eds), *Governing Australia*, Sydney: Cambridge University Press.

Mommsen, W. (1987) Personal Conduct and Societal Change, in S. Whimster and S. Lash (eds), *Max Weber, Rationality and Modernity*, London: Allen & Unwin, 35–51.

Newman, J. (2005) Bending Bureaucracy: Leadership and Multi-Level Governance, in P. du Gay (ed.), *The Values of Bureaucracy*, Oxford: Oxford University Press.

Oliver, D. (2003) *Constitutional Reform in the UK*, Oxford: Oxford University Press.

O'Toole, B. (2006) *The Ideal of Public Service*, London: Routledge.

Parker, R. (1993) *The Administrative Vocation*, Sydney: Hale and Iremonger.

Peters, T. (1989) *Thriving on Chaos*, Basingstoke: Macmillan.

——and Waterman, R. (1982) *In Search of Excellence*, New York: Harper & Row.

Quinlan, M. (2004) Lessons for Governmental Process, in W.G. Runciman (ed.), *Hutton and Butler: Lifting the Lid on the Workings of Power*, Oxford: British Academy/Oxford University Press, 112–30.

Ritzer, G. (2004) *The MacDonaldization of Society*, Thousand Oaks: Pine Forge Press.

Rohr, J. (1998) *Public Service, Ethics and Constitutional Practice*, Lawrence, Kansas: University of Kansas Press.

Saunders, D. (1997) *The Anti-Lawyers*, London: Routledge.

Schluchter, W. (1981) *The Rise of Western Rationalism*, Berkeley: University of California Press.

Stahlberg, K. (1987) The Politicization of Public Administration: Notes on the Concept, Causes and Consequences, *International Review of Administrative Sciences*, 53: 363–82.

Supiot, A. (2006) The Condition of France, *London Review of Books*, 28(11): 1–9.

Thatcher, M. (1993) *The Downing Street Years*, London: Harper Collins.

Turner, C. (1992) *Modernity and Politics in the Work of Max Weber*, London: Routledge.

Uhr, J. (1993) Administrative Responsibility and Responsible Administrators: An Introduction, in R.S. Parker (ed.), *The Administrative Vocation*, Sydney: Hale and Iremonger, xiii–xxiii.

Walzer, M. (1984) Liberalism and the Art of Separation, *Political Theory*, 12(3): 315–30.

Weber, M. (1930) *The Protestant Ethic and the Spirit of Capitalism*, London: Harper Collins.

——(1978) *Economy & Society* (2 Vols.), Los Angeles: University of California Press.

——(1989) Science as a Vocation, in P. Lassman and I. Velody (eds), *Max Weber's Science as a Vocation*, London: Unwin Hyman.

——(1994*a*) Parliament and Government in Germany under a New Political Order, in P. Lassman and R. Speirs (eds), *Weber: Political Writings*, Cambridge: CUP.

——(1994*b*) The Profession and Vocation of Politics, in P. Lassman and R. Speirs (eds), *Weber: Political Writings*, Cambridge: CUP.

Wilson, R. (2004) Discussion, in W. G. Runciman (ed.), *Hutton and Butler: Lifting the Lid on the Workings of Power*, Oxford: British Academy/Oxford University Press, 82–6.

2 Bureaucratic and Post-Bureaucratic Accountability in Britain: Some Sceptical Reflections

HARRO M. HÖPFL

> The difference between the traditionalists and the modernizers [in public administration]...is that the former use rose-tinted spectacles to view the past and grey-tinted glasses to look at the present, while for the latter the lens tints are reversed. (Christopher Hood, *The Art of the State*: 1998)

My argument will be that 'post-bureaucracy' as a concept or a reality raises the same issues of accountability as the 'old' bureaucratic forms of administration. Whatever may be the benefits of the New Public Management (NPM)—the guise in which 'post-bureaucracy' appears in the polity—resolving the issue of accountability is not among them. But there is no comfort in this for the defenders of 'traditional' bureaucracy and the old ways, and even less for 'democratic' accountability. Irrespective of its specific arrangements, accountability cannot 'deliver' all that is expected of it, and in particular it cannot dispense with trust. The problem in the end is *not* accountability, but: who is to be trusted?

In the British political tradition, bureaucratic or civil service[1] accountability cannot be discussed independently of 'ministerial responsibility'. The authorized version is that civil servants, organized into departments, are accountable to their own departmental superiors. These are in turn ultimately accountable to the 'permanent secretary', the apex of the civil service department's hierarchy. The permanent secretary is responsible to the department's political master, the minister. All this is 'internal accountability'. Ministers in turn are 'externally' accountable to Parliament for the work of their departments in accordance with the 'doctrine', 'principle', or 'convention'[2] of individual and collective ministerial responsibility. Civil servants as individuals or as departments, then, are *not* accountable to Parliament, except via their ministers; they have 'as such no constitutional personality or responsibility separate from the duly elected government of the day'.[3]

As regards *internal* accountability in the British Civil Service, or any bureaucracy, the accountability questions—who is answerable, to whom, for what, when, and how—seem to answer themselves. Civil servants are ordered hierarchically, and hierarchy can tolerate any number of subdivisions and levels of super- and subordination, provided they culminate in an individual or collective headship with ultimate authority (*plena* or *summa potestas* in the language of medieval hierocracy, 'sovereignty' in that of modernity). A distinguishing mark of 'modern' bureaucracy is that the duties, competence, and resources of every level of the hierarchy are specified in formal rules, and therefore it should be possible to identify who in any particular instance is responsible for what. The most senior bureaucratic hierarchs are legally and morally answerable to their political masters because, even though the euphonious British term 'civil *servant*' seems to have no precise Romance or Germanic equivalent, bureaucracies are everywhere 'ad*ministra*tions',[4] servants of the government, or state. *Ergo* bureaucracy is deemed to solve the problem of political accountability (e.g. Jaques 1990). This, however, is illusory, even conceptually. As the scholastic maxim says: equals cannot command equals. The relationship between those on the same rung of the ladder of super- and subordination therefore cannot be one of command and obedience or accountability, but must be one of negotiation and networking. The 'Mandarinate', the most senior civil servants, are in this position with respect to one another. The responsibility for their acts is therefore *not* covered by the straightforward accountability relations of hierarchy. And it is their collective *moral and professional* authority that confronts ministers, and diffuses the loci of responsibility.

Therefore, where (as in Britain) of administrative courts or direct 'democratic accountability' there are no, the *political* or *external* accountability of a civil service depends on the effective working of the 'convention of ministerial responsibility'.[5] Conventions unlike statutes are 'what is done', in both the descriptive and the normative sense, and so do not permit precise formulation. However, the commonplaces about ministerial responsibility are outstandingly threadbare. They require circumspect statement to have even minimal plausibility. Thus, UK government departments[6] may have five or more 'junior' ministers, all 'answerable' to Parliament. They are however usually headed by a minister of Cabinet rank, a 'secretary of state', with overall parliamentary accountability for a department. 'The accepted constitutional position where departmental fault is concerned [is that] the responsibility belongs to the Secretary of State and, whatever delegatory arrangements he might make with a junior minister, he cannot devolve ministerial responsibility' (Woodhouse 1994: 125). Practice and latterly government codes allow parliamentary select committees to summon senior civil servants to explain and justify the work of their departments, and therefore their own. Civil servants are, however, not liable to formal sanctions from such committees or from public inquiries, although adverse consequences for their careers may follow from their performances. What is more, it has been obvious for generations that no ministers can possibly be conversant with everything done in their department, still less in its satellites and dependencies. Ministers cannot morally be made accountable for what they *cannot* know about, only for what they *should* know about, a problematic but rhetorically fertile distinction. The possibility then arises that no one at all (minister or civil servant) will ever be held to account when responsibility is diffused, as it normally is.

Even with these qualifications, ministerial and therefore civil service accountability remains practically and theoretically incoherent. The convention represents the work of government as neatly compartmentalized between departments, each with a ministerial 'team' and a permanent secretary responsible for it, and ministers collectively ('the government' or, for devotees of archaisms, 'cabinet') as 'responsible' for the administration as a whole. This ignores everything known about the British political process: the complications introduced by the Cabinet Office, the Prime Minister's Office, and the various 'units' at Number 10; the role of permanent and *ad hoc* cabinet committees of ministers (which with their personnel are designated, and some of them chaired, by the Prime Minister[7]) or committees of civil servants, or both; the vast variety of administrative bodies (Hogwood et al. 2001); informal decision making by networking between prime ministers and individual ministers; the politics of departmentalism; and the ever-growing number of 'task-forces' or 'units' of the Blair and Brown governments that cut across departmental boundaries (departmental 'silos').

Party-political adversarialism, moreover, has long since meant prime ministers being held responsible by oppositions for everything. And why not. Prime ministers are entitled (though not always politically able) to take charge of policy, task allocation, and progress review. They appoint and dismiss all ministers (apart from Parliamentary Private Secretaries (PPSs)) and can also appoint or move the most senior civil servants. They can unilaterally establish, dissolve, or reorganize entire departments by fiat ('Order in Council'): Blair divided up the Home Office; Wilson combined the already enormous Health and Social Security departments; Mrs Thatcher separated them again, and abolished Heath's Central Policy Review Staff and the Civil Service Department. Until recently, the doctrine of ministerial responsibility also ignored the role of special advisers who have proliferated since the 1990s, but were well known long before: Wilson (1964–70) had Williams, Donaghue, and two 'Hungarian' economists; Mrs Thatcher had fewer than Blair and Brown, but more notorious ones. The nature of their accountability is far from clear even now. They are civil servants, but 'temporary' and not politically neutral—but then Cabinet Secretaries do not stand above the bear-pit either, Robert

Armstrong being a notable case in point; unlike civil servants they can be sacked by their political masters; the *Code of Conduct for Special Advisers*, 2009, does not assign them any right to issue instructions to civil servants, but requires them to cooperate with senior civil servants (s. 7). And so forth.

All this merely compounds the weaknesses of 'ministerial responsibility', whether individual or collective, which has been a staple topic of academic texts for more than a century (Fry 1969: 11, citing Sidney Low's 1904 warnings against complacency about it; Woodhouse 1994, 2004; Barberis 1997; Polidano 2000; Flinders 2001; *Individual ministerial responsibility* 2004). Given party-governments, a single member, simple plurality electoral system, and an all-pervasive tradition of adversarialism and winner-takes-all (the 'Westminster model'), 'parliamentary sovereignty' is a euphemism for executive dominance. 'Parliament' is not a single body capable of agency; when it for once acted thus, in dismissing Speaker Martin in May 2009, it was reckoned a marvel. The 'ultimate sanction' traditionally ascribed to 'Parliament' of dismissing a government is unusable, except by government backbenchers who have every reason *not* to use it: turkeys do not vote for Christmas. Defeats in the Commons, even on issues of confidence, do not require a government to resign. The idea that 'debate' or parliamentary questions can count as 'scrutiny' invokes a golden age of parliamentary orators addressing a spell-bound nation via a press reporting their every word. Parliamentary 'control of the executive' is now mentioned only in derision. The sole exception to Parliament's general debility is the select committees, sufficiently influential to have been subjected to sustained attempts at subversion by the party-leaderships.

As for *individual ministerial responsibility,* in the sense that an *individual* minister might fall victim to Parliament's sanctions for something his/her civil servants have done, there is nothing to support the idea. If 'the responsibility of individual ministers for their own conduct and that of their departments is a vital aspect of accountable and democratic parliamentary government' (*Individual ministerial responsibility* 2004: 2), this 'convention' cannot satisfy the requirement, in that it lacks the defining characteristic of a convention, namely *de facto* observance. It dates from the brief 'Golden Age' between management of the Commons by patronage before 1830, and by mass parties from the 1870s, an age that was 'golden' only to those who considered fragile and vulnerable governments a desirable state of affairs. For Tories or Peelites and Old Whigs, executive *dominance* was always the desideratum (Beattie 1995; Flinders 2001). The convention preserved plausibility while a sufficiently conscientious minister could supervise the work of the handful of clerks in his 'office' in intimate detail, or do it himself. These clerks could *not* possibly be held accountable by Parliament; accountability presupposes capacity for independent action and they had none.

As the size, scope, and complexity of the civil service increased remorselessly from the later nineteenth century until the 1980s (Greenleaf 1987), it became impossible for any individual minister, nowadays in post for perhaps a couple of years, to be familiar with most of what was being done in their department. Some ministers have not even known what they were responsible for; Marshall (1989: 128) nicely termed this 'diminished ministerial responsibility'. The handful of ministerial resignations for *departmental* 'errors' in well over a hundred years has *never* been an acknowledgement of a minister's responsibility for the work of civil servants. Sonorous reaffirmations of personal responsibility by Herbert Morrison in 1950 and George Brown in 1968 were made safe in the knowledge that there was no prospect of sanctions (*pace* O'Toole 2006: 194). The 'exemplary' resignations—Brittan was clearly *sacrificed* (Brazier 1997: 274)—of Sir Thomas Dugdale, Lord Carrington, and Richard Luce do not unambiguously exemplify anything (Marshall 1989: 130; Woodhouse 1994: esp. 87–106). And three episodes do not make a convention. Brazier describes the 'principle' as 'at best elastic', with ministers testing how far the scope of ways of avoiding resignation will stretch (1997: 261, 271, 275 ff).

Collective ministerial responsibility, the duty of ministers to speak and act as one, has even less plausibility as a convention of *constitutional* significance (i.e. as a supra-legal norm of proper conduct for office holders). The Commons Select Committees that have dealt with accountability have had nothing to say about 'collective responsibility' (Public Service Committee 1999; Public Administration Committee 2007). It functions exclusively as a party-political expedient demanded by adversarial politics; even Gordon Brown's *Ministerial Code* (2007: 2.1) invokes no higher purpose than 'maintaining a united front'. As Mackintosh summed up (1979: 533–5, expanding his already dismissive comments of 1962): '. . . just as individual responsibility operates when and where the Prime Minister and the majority of the Cabinet want it to operate, collective responsibility can be applied or waived depending on the convenience of these same politicians.' Individual and collective conceptions of ministerial responsibility have, moreover, been mutually contradictory ever since the advent of party-government (see Barberis 1997: 134). Ministers now depart to 'spend more time with their families' when prime ministers and their colleagues deem rallying round them the more politically costly option (Jennings 1959: 497; Mackintosh 1962: 493).

The fragile pegs on which civil service accountability hung before the NPM, then, were 'ministerial responsibility' to 'Parliament' and the public (or the media) for the work of departments, and 'internal' answerability of individual civil servants to their civil service superiors. Civil service 'disciplinary proceedings', and *a fortiori* judicial accountability, concerned gross incompetence, neglect of duty, or illegal or *ultra vires* actions. For *departmental* failures or incompetence there was no sanction at all; the Ministry of Agriculture (eventually MAFF, then DEFRA) has provided years of choice examples (Weir and Beetham 1999, index entry). *Individually,* career civil servants were not (and are not) dismissible for indifferent performance, although it arrested progress along the *cursus honorum* to a knighthood, a generous pension, and perhaps an executive directorship for their autumnal years. Moreover,

civil servants, except in the role of Accounting Officer, have no direct responsibility to Parliament. They are responsible to their minister. [The principle of ministerial accountability means that] when there have been mistakes as a result of civil service failures, the minister must demonstrate to Parliament that action has been taken to correct these mistakes and to prevent any recurrence . . . disciplinary proceedings taken against particular civil servants as provided for by the Civil Service Management Code . . . will not be initiated by the minister. Nor is it for Parliament to impose a penalty upon a civil servant since, constitutionally, officials are the servants of the Crown, i.e. of ministers, and not of Parliament.[8]

Constitutionally civil servants are, or were, merely the 'mouthpieces of their ministers', dictaphones, anonymous ciphers.

I have until now treated 'responsibility' and 'accountability' as interchangeable. They ought, however, to be distinguished. Uniquely, the English language itself makes the distinction.[9] Responsibility does not necessarily involve an answer to the question *to whom,* whereas accountability does. A 'responsible' driver, drinker, parent, or a person 'responsible' for an accident has certain duties in respect of something or someone; *to whom* if anyone they have to answer is an entirely separate and unrelated issue. My responsibility for our cat is unrelated to the existence of the RSPCA or laws against cruelty to animals. And I am not accountable to our cat.

A late eighteenth-century derivative from the medieval 'account' (*conto, compte,* or 'reckoning', *Rechnung*), accountability has always designated a relationship between an agent and an individual or corporate principal (Greenwood et al. 2002: 229). It is inherently and not contingently a moral concept, in that it connotes an agent's duty to render an honest account, and the principal's to judge fairly. Those owed accounts may, however, be unable to judge their validity, or to obtain redress. To remedy this, the clients of the professions in the United Kingdom, for example, have an appeal to some third party competent to judge the professionals' accounts, which is *in this respect* the accountor's 'principal' or superior: the disciplinary arrangements of the Law Society, the GMC of the BMA, or the Parliamentary Ombudsman for citizens vis-à-vis the civil service. Accountability moreover presupposes: some autonomy, discretion, freedom of manoeuvre on the part of the agent, otherwise there would be nothing to account for, and no point to the arrangement; an understanding of the terms of the relationship, whether explicit (contractual) or implied (in custom and practice); and an arrangement or procedure with some degree of formality, to comply with the natural justice requirements of a fair hearing and just judgement. Finally, accountability would be otiose if there were no sanction for accounts disclosing culpable misuse, or culpably incompetent use, of entrusted powers or resources. For this reason, the familiar interpretation of *ministerial* accountability as 'answerability' (e.g. Rogers and Walters 2004: 96) must fail: the duty to 'answer' is pointless unless there are sanctions for bad answers.

On this reading, what has no identifiable agent or author is either totally unaccountable, or accountable for only by imputation to some individual or collective agent, with the deeply suspect moral implications of collective or vicarious punishments, or scapegoating. However, with bureaucracy on the British pattern, any policy or administrative activity that is capable of generating controversy is unlikely to have a determinate, identifiable author. The same conundrum bedevils the *legal* (especially criminal) accountability of corporations, but the law can ignore moral considerations (Gobert and Punch 2003), whereas political accountability cannot. The constitutional orthodoxy provides for such situations by eliminating civil servants from *political* accountability altogether. This, however, demands the unsustainable pretence that it is ministers that are accountable 'for every stamp stuck on an envelope in Whitehall', according to Herbert Morrison's preposterous dictum (Barberis 1997: 135). Rightly derided by proponents of the NPM (Waldegrave, in Barberis 1996*a*: 182), this 'old myth' is still sometimes maintained, although it directly contradicts the overwhelming evidence about how policy is made (or 'emerges') and administration is conducted, as well as the moral premises of the accountability relationship. It can only be given a shred of plausibility by gratuitously attenuating accountability into 'answerability' (see above) or by converting all accountability into the 'collective responsibility' of governments, which in effect means the accountability of no one at all. Bureaucratic villains might of course still receive their comeuppance, but that depends on the vagaries of the internal politics of governments and parties, the transient preoccupations of the media and other indeterminate authors of the 'public agenda', the eccentricities of the British electoral systems, and occasionally on the courts or regulatory agencies, and not on the conventions and institutions meant to secure political accountability.

The wholly unsatisfactory state of affairs here was illustrated when the House of Commons Public Administration Select Committee, like the Treasury and Civil Service Committee long a credit to the House, once again agonized over the relationship between ministers and civil servants (*Politics and Administration*, 2007). Ignoring *collective* ministerial responsibility altogether, it pronounced that 'we are...fortunate to have a robust system of political accountability' (s. 83). Nevertheless, it concluded that, as with the 'boundaries of ministerial accountability, civil service accountability is far from clear' (s. 30); and that (contrary to the government's declared view) 'areas where a minister is personally responsible, and liable to take blame, and those in which he is constitutionally accountable' are not clearly distinguishable (s. 27). It found unpersuasive both the 'developing view' that ministers and civil servants should each be responsible for decisions which they have taken (s. 4) and Waldegrave's cliché, commended by the General Secretary of the First Division Association, that 'Ministers are accountable to Parliament; civil servants are accountable to Ministers' (s. 3).

The Committee thought 'extreme' the traditional distinction between 'politics' and 'administration' (ss. 53–4) and questioned the distinction between 'strategy' or 'policy' and 'delivery'. All the same, it regarded the Home Office 'compact' between ministers and civil servants (Appendix 1) as pointing the way to a more 'explicit public service bargain' (ss. 65, 67) despite the 'difficulty of clear demarcation of responsibility'. The Committee thought the problem about identifying what decisions were taken and by whom (s. 54) was a 'lack of transparency', rather than a conceptual issue about the nature of decision making in British politics, which it never discussed. Eventually (s. 68) it even desiderated 'full accounts of operational errors to Parliament', including admission of errors by civil servants, on condition that the current 'blame culture' was abandoned. This is equivalent to saying that there could be civil service accountability if the circumstances which require accountability did not arise. Without discussing civil service dismissals (which cannot 'now' be done by ministers, s. 30), the Committee limited 'accountability' of civil servants to giving honest (and ideally independent) answers to Parliament, without imputation of 'blame'. In short, it could not resist the logic of accountability, which demands identifiable agents with identifiable responsibilities and sanctions. This, however, is precisely equivalent to accepting the division between policy (or politics) and administration which it had rejected. How else could ministers or civil servants be held accountable for anything?

The appeal to *democratic* accountability presents itself as the answer to all these difficulties. Dispassionate consideration is vitiated by the status of democracy as the modern rhetorical trump card, an even more 'golden concept' than accountability (Bovens 2008: 225). However, democracy comes in many distinct versions: deliberative, civic republican, radical, 'people's', critical, participative/activist, anarchist/syndicalist/autonomist, 'discourse', 'agonistic', as well as constitutional/representative/pluralistic; none of them can vindicate a proprietary claim to the label. But *ex vi termini* none can dispense with the concepts of the *demos* ('the people') and rule or government (*kratia*). 'The people', or worse, the 'nation' or 'Society'—concepts that need book-length treatment (see Canovan 2005)—cannot conceivably conduct law-making, domestic and foreign policy, diplomacy or war, let alone administer courts, taxation, or the machinery of a social security system (i.e. 'govern'). The *demos/populus* could not even lead or administer the Greek *poleis* or the medieval *civitates* or *respublicae* with their miniscule citizenries, scant resources, and geographically restricted reach. The *populus Romanus* never attempted anything of the kind, even before it settled for a dole of 'bread and circuses'. 'Local' or 'devolved' accountability is in no better condition; sustained administration even of a parish or a student union is impossible without representation.

Allowing 'the people' an extremely restricted scope was not only the 'elitist' view of Weber, Michels, or Schumpeter but also that of Machiavelli, James Harrington, Rousseau, and John Stuart Mill and a host of lesser stars in the firmament of authorities for 'classical republicanism' and 'participative democracy' (*pace* Held 1987). Harrington (1656) was explicit that the popular element in his proposed 'model' of 'popular government' must confine itself entirely to 'resolve', choosing between the alternatives proposed to it by a senate of the prudent and morally authoritative, and selecting, in a very constrained process, the holders of public office to carry on the actual work of government (*Oceana* 1656). Rousseau could not logically eliminate the legislative supremacy of 'the people', despite his comprehensive (and thoroughly republican) distrust of how it would use it. But he assigned all initiative, policy, judicature, and administration to 'magistrates', and restricted the role of 'the people' even in legislation and in the election of magistrates as far as possible (Rousseau 1762, Bk. III, 1&6; 1755). 'Representative democracy', for its part, has always taken for granted a 'separation of powers' between 'the people', or rather the 'legislature' or 'representative', and the executive. John Stuart Mill, a former civil servant in the East India Company and, as a Benthamite at least in this respect, a devotee of administrative expertise, was careful to distinguish 'government' from 'executive functions' or 'administrative business', the latter a technical subject on which even politicians had nothing to contribute (1861, ch. 14).

As for the 'international community' as a possible *demos* (Mulgan 2003), or Mouffe and Laclau's idea that 'agonal' democracy could be anything except a recipe for civil war, or that 'emancipated' dependants of public services could have a 'negotiating' relationship with the agencies of the state (except via the NPM's 'charters', complaints systems, or marketization), these must be left over for another occasion and a more indulgent author.

Democracy, then, is at best—or, where popular selection of bureaucrats is envisaged, at worst—a way of designating and replacing the personnel of government, and possibly passing some verdict on its conduct. 'Police accountability' as the local 'democratic accountability' advocated by the Hard Left in the 1970s and 1980s, for example, meant subordination of the police to 'operational' control and direct appointments even to not particularly senior ranks by politicians/activists: this approximated Left aspirations to American worst practice.[10] 'Deliberative democracy' seems to be the best hope for combining democracy with judgement and justice (e.g. Dryzek 2002). Even so, no possible *policy*-role for a *demos* is possible without some distinction between policy and operations/administration. The actual conduct of government and administration must still be left to those who might know what they are doing, and who could conceivably be subject to sanctions, unlike the *demos*.

Accountability, like justifications and legal appeals, must certainly stop somewhere; unless the pyramid of accountabilities has an apex there is merely gridlock (a plurality of 'accounts' and no one to judge between them): a 'condition of mere nature' (Hobbes 1651: ch. 13). By the same Bodinian or Hobbesian logic of sovereignty, that apex must itself be *un*accountable. A *demos*, personated in some way, can possibly be that apex, and therefore by definition the ultimate judge of all accounts. But the criteria for inclusion in, or exclusion from, any *demos* are necessarily indeterminate, and given that a 'multitude is not naturally one but many' (Hobbes 1651: ch. 16, p.104), the *demos* will merely be what are, interpretatively, the representatives or agents of some popular majority, or plurality (Dahl 1989: ch. 9). And a democratic sovereign is just as 'arbitrary' as any other—arbitrary from *arbitrium*, judgement, will, or choice—that is, subject to no one else's judgement, will, or consent, the identifying feature of sovereignty (Bodin 1576/1586, Bk. I, ch. 10: 56). As sovereign and anonymous, 'the people' 'can do no wrong'. It is therefore no more to be trusted than any other sovereign, and accountability to a democratic sovereign does not begin to satisfy the moral and conceptual requirements of accountability identified earlier. It merely identifies a supreme hierarch, a locus of *power*.

The *New Public Management*, a term apparently coined by Christopher Hood (Hood 1989), has been presented as promising real civil service accountability, not only in Britain, America, and New Zealand, where it was first explored, but (in principle) in respect of any bureaucracy whatever. It designates an approach to 'public administration' that promises not only the efficiency, effectiveness, and economy that had previously eluded the public sector but also unprecedented accountability.

Its more radical critics take it as read that NPM is an ideological project, complicit with 'Thatcherism', and more generally 'managerialism' (as one for all: O'Toole 2006). It is not, however, any more 'ideological', 'Thatcherite', 'managerialist' to be concerned about the level and value of public expenditure, or to think that the public sector might learn from other organizations, than it is to take someone's word for it that all is for the best in the best of all possible bureaucratic worlds. Anthony King and Samuel Beer, prominent among academics voicing concern about British 'ungovernability' in the 1970s, were neither managerialists nor Thatcherites; nor were the scriptwriters for *Yes Minister*. It is *not* insignificant that before the 1980s British government departments literally did not even know their running costs (Fry et al. 1988: 437). Those receptive to NPM are not invariably more addicted to hyperbole than its critics, nor do they all share the 'hatred' of the Civil Service and its traditions attributed to Thatcher and her allies by, for example,

Plowden (1994: 3), himself an enthusiast for Fulton (*infra*). Much of the NPM consists of pragmatic responses to issues that had long plagued British (and other) governments, notably the control of public expenditure and the absence in the bureaucratic paradigm of any criteria for evaluating the effectiveness of the provision of public services (*infra*).

Nevertheless, both its exponents and its critics have been anxious to exhibit an overall rationale for the NPM. Its proponents formulate part of this rationale as a critique of 'bureaucracy', and even as a very abstract contrast between bureaucracy and 'post-bureaucracy' (Massey 1997). Their concept of bureaucracy, like the British Civil Service itself, corresponds broadly to the 'Weberian' ideal type fashioned by sociology, organization studies, and the management schools, and like them is in some respects a caricature of Weber. The 'Weberian' ideal-typical bureaucracy, like the British Civil Service,[11] is the career civil service: office as never a personal, alienable, or transferable possession; competitive admission by open examination; promotion on merit or seniority, in accordance with written performance evaluations by superiors (and for Weber, by formal examination); pensionable salary related to position in the hierarchy not performance; dismissal or demotion only by due process; conduct of business according to formal allocation of tasks, routines, and impersonal norms, with records for everything; hierarchical division of labour or specialization. The organization-studies 'Weberian' ideal type of bureaucracy, however, incorporates many attributes Weber ignored. He paid no attention to careerism, the 'office-politics' of bureaucracies, issues of personnel management and leadership (except insofar as *Beamten-herrschaft* compromised or replaced political leadership), or the perverse incentives typical of organizations with vast budgets and a numerous person-nel (the 'bureau-shaping' or 'bureau-maximizing' model).

Weber's own ideal type of bureaucracy elides 'utopian' (his unfortunate term) and dystopian standard features. It was not a *self-conscious* reinstate-ment of the *officium/persona* tradition,[12] but incorporated the cynical 'real-ism' of his time. He certainly attributed incomparable efficiency and a distinctive ethic to bureaucratic organization, derided the idea of 'parasites' and 'litterateurs' that socialism, romanticism, or revolution would transcend it, and denied that bureaucrats were capable only of routine tasks (Weber 1918: 153–5). Equally, however, he saw bureaucracy as likely to elude political control, by virtue of an expertise vastly superior to that of politicians and any other organizations except business enterprises, and as promoting its own collective self-interest, especially by official secrecy, due process to protect its members, and promotion by seniority, not ability (Höpfl 2006). On the financing and resource utilization of bureaucracy, aside from stressing its dependence on reliable state financing, he had nothing whatsoever to say.

The NPM critique of 'bureaucracy' combines many of the 'dystopic' fea-tures of the Weberian ideal type with elements of 'public choice' theory, the standard organization-studies critique of Weberian bureaucracy for lack of adaptability, the long-established managerialist tradition in civil service reform, and a marked predilection for market ordering mechanisms. It incorporates the concern with 'departmentalism', voiced by every serious British commentator on the civil service since the Northcote-Trevelyan Report of 1854,[13] but ignored by Weber, who did not deal with the coordination of multiple, relatively autonomous bureaucracies ('departments') coexisting within the same bureaucratic complex (*the* Civil Service). To this, 'post-bureaucracy' adds new and ostentatiously non-hierarchical concepts of organization and management, and a confidence that these will prove irresistible; possibly that they mark the advent of a new epoch (McSweeney 2006). 'Post-bureaucratic' organizations, public or private, are characterized by teamwork, task-groups, outsourcing, offshoring, role-flexibility, dispensing with command and obedience relations and hierarchies wherever possible (delayering), virtuality and the ICT and real-time communication it presupposes, networks, targets, benchmarking entrepreneurship and self-motivation, and in the public sector by value for money (Vfm), cost-units, targets, subordination of public service provision to 'consumer' not 'producer' interests, etc. (e.g. Massey 1997: 41; Christensen and Laegreid 2002: 269).

The only kind of *accountability* that at first concerned NPM was the aspired-to answerability of civil servants to *ministers* (Jenkins 2008); public accountability was something of an afterthought (Flinders 2001: 10). But Weber and the 'Weberian' paradigm offer no distinctive conception of accountability either. Weber counterposed the ideal politician characterized by 'vocation' (*Berufspolitiker*) with the ideal official (*Beamter*). The politician's duty is to take a stand, to lead (*Leitung, Führung*), and to conduct *Politik*, that is, both politics and policy; the official's task is dispassionate administration (*Verwaltung*) attending to 'official, firmly circumscribed tasks of a technical (*fachlich*) nature' (Weber 1918: 170–1/160; 1919: 330–1/414). This is exactly the same distinction as 'ministers decide/make policy and civil servants advise/administer/implement'; it also accords with the NPM's delimitation of the competence of ministers and civil servants as respectively 'policy' (or 'strategy') and 'operations', latterly 'delivery', a distinction already queried by the Treasury Select Committee and some prescient academics in 1988 (Fry et al. 1988: 442–3; for the now-orthodox critique, see O'Toole 2006). All these distinctions in turn are in many respects merely reformulations of the classic rationalist distinction between 'ends' and 'means', the principal meaning of 'rationality' in Weber, and are vulnerable to the same criticisms.[14] But some such distinction is inherent in the very terms 'civil service' and 'administration' (see note 4), which connote subordinate and conditional authority. The civil service ideals of impartiality, independence, objectivity, and probity simply designate the moral and intellectual spirit in which that subordination is to be practised. As Northcote-Trevelyan magisterially formulated it (1854: 3): 'duly subordinate…yet possessing sufficient independence, character, ability and experience to be able to advise, assist, and, to some extent, influence, those who are from time set over them'. Weber added some valuable observations about the 'sense of responsibility' (*Verantwortlich-keit*) of the *Beamter*, his professional ethic. This 'responsibility' entails civil servants giving the best advice they can, but carrying out their (political) super-ior's 'command' as if it were their own will, even when it contradicts their advice and professional opinion (Weber 1919: 177/330–1); the echo of the 'blind' obedience owed to their superiors by Jesuits was presumably inadvertent.

NPM aims at 'efficiency, effectiveness, and economy', or Vfm, in the provision of public services, and at entrepreneurial management, but has professed agnosticism about arrangements: what matters is what works, 'delivery'. Efficiency and Vfm in service provision in turn require comparators and criteria, about which the 'Weberian' ideal type and the old public administration were entirely silent.[15] NPM has tended to look for such comparators in the private sector, and to privilege markets (or analogues) and competition. Its abiding ambition is the state retreating from the role of direct provider of services wherever possible, though not necessarily by privatization. But its defining policy has been 'agencification', the 'Next Steps' programme initiated only in 1987/8, towards the end of Mrs Thatcher's tenure, developed by John Major, and continued ever since. Accountability acquired specification in NPM only with agencification.

The guiding maxims of NPM are that the best people should be chosen for jobs, subordinates should not get above themselves, and superiors should neither micro-manage subordinates nor leave them without adequate direc-tion and supervision. These are not *arcana imperii* that NPM or 'Thatcherism' claim to have discovered. Agencies ('hiving off') were proposed in the Fulton Report of 1968. Mrs Thatcher's insistence that the principal task of permanent secretaries and their immediate subordinates is management rather than policy advice, and that Oxbridge 'generalists' do not meet this bill, were both main planks of Fulton. The same views were absolutely standard on the Left, which also, albeit for different reasons, expected the mandarinate to try to subvert radical changes: Crossman, Castle, Plowden, still carrying the 'social democrat' torch (in Barberis 1996a), and obviously Benn (Pilkington 1999: 41–2) had long embraced root and branch politicization of the Civil Service, not merely importing special advisers.[16] In all these respects, the NPM's 'managerialism', like the Left's, is an endeavour to resubmit bureaucracy to political control. Christensen and Laegreid (2002: 273) rightly characterize it as 'a reform movement that to some extent seeks to revitalize the sovereign state' (i.e. the dominance of politicians). Its reforming agenda has to rely heavily on the civil service, but its critique of bureaucracy for empire-building and reform-resisting tendencies demands determined polit-ical direction and incessant civil service reform. It has therefore needed a distinction between ministers 'driving the reform agenda' by determining 'policy', 'strategy', 'frameworks', 'goals', 'objectives', 'benchmarks', etc., and civil servants responsible for 'performance', 'implementation', 'operations', 'delivery', etc. This distinction has been cashed out in any number of ways, some highly *dirigiste*, like the National Health Service (NHS) reforms from the late 1980s to those of Blair and Brown (Ham 2007). 'Agencification', however, attempts to render the distinction more precise in a quasi-contractual 'public service agreement', or 'framework document', specifying the respective roles of 'sponsoring' departments and the chief executives of 'delivery *agencies*', whose performance is audited and measured, and who are in this sense accountable. It potentially transcends departmentalism.[17]

Critics of NPM and of post-bureaucracy on the whole are not concerned to defend bureaucracy *per se*, or to endorse Douglas Jay's 1939 dictum that 'the gentleman in Whitehall really does know better what is good for people than people know themselves'. They tend rather to object to NPM triumphalism, sweeping assertions about the 'systemic disfunctionality' of bureaucracy as such (Alvesson and Thompson 2005: 486), post-bureaucracy's 'pretensions to universality' (Massey 1997), the rhetoric of an inexorable, epochal march ever onwards and upwards, and last not least its 'permanent revolution' (McSweeney 2006). Most critics see a return to the *status quo ante* as neither possible nor even desirable (Hood and Lodge 2006), though with some critics it is hard to decide, given their visceral antipathy to 'managerialism' and the private sector (e.g. Learmont and Harding 2004; O'Toole 2006). Few presumably yearn for the return of the Post Office's telecommunications monopoly (extended to mobile phones?), NHS paternalism, or mandarins regarding management as *infra dignitatem*. Such a reversion would not be the return of an *accountable* civil service anyway, because even NPM's severest critics admit that it had gone long before (O'Toole 2006: 178–9), if indeed it ever existed.

But whatever the substance of the failures and malign and/or unintended consequences imputed to the NPM, *as far as civil service accountability is concerned* they sum to no more than that NPM is liable to the same objections as the old public administration. A recurrent complaint ever since 1988 (Fry et al. 1988: esp. 443; Gains 2003: 7–8) has been that the NPM confuses loci of accountability, in that the policy/operations distinction provides politicians with a convenient way of passing the buck. Buck-passing, however, originated with Adam (*Genesis*, 3.12). The 130 or so Next Steps agencies that have *not* given rise to accusations of buck-passing, or have been turned around by ministerial intervention, seem to be regarded as beneath consideration: for example the DVLA, or the Passport Agency; Gains (2003: 9) notes the latter, but ignores that it has since ceased to be an issue. The Prisons Agency and the Child Support Agency are the anti-NPM *causes célèbres*, no doubt because they had *ministers* attempting to pass the buck (Pilkington 1999: 106; Rhodes 2000: 158; Greenwood et al. 2002: 247; Talbot 2002: 10–11; Gains 2003: 8–9; Plant 2003: 51–4; O'Toole 2006: 139–40). By contrast, Hogwood et al. (2001: 6–7) describe the Prisons Agency as 'an extreme and untypical example of ministerial involvement', and as 'pathological accountability'. The policy/operations rhetoric in fact works both ways: civil servants, especially managers or agency chief executives, can equally employ it in self-exculpation. They will always have justification for doing so, given the inveterate interfering[18] habits of all ministers, and New Labour's reversion to Old Labour *dirigisme* (Gains 2003: 12 ff). Derek Lewis, the Director of the Prisons Agency, in fact defended himself in precisely this way; Michael Howard emerged severely damaged by the episode. Buck-passing is therefore not an objection to ministers evading responsibility under NPM, but to *both* them and civil servants doing so, just as they had done before. Mrs Thatcher announced that *Next Steps* would leave ministerial accountability for the civil service unchanged. Some NPM advocates at its inception, on the contrary, promised improved accountability (Flinders 2001; Gains 2003). They were both right and both wrong.

As Barberis has said: 'the changes of the 1980s and 1990s have brought few if any completely new changes to traditional notions of accountability. In certain respects they may even offer opportunities to strengthen traditional mechanisms, though in practice they seem to have had the effect ... of exacerbating existing fault-lines' (Barberis 1997: 142). Just so. Accountability demands identification of who is responsible for what and to whom, and liability to sanctions, and NPM arguably does this in allocating responsibilities more specifically, and making civil service jobs less bulletproof. In principle, it might therefore *improve* the accountability of senior civil servants not only to ministers but also to Parliament.

Unlike 'Weberian' civil servants, executive agency chief executives are appointed by competitive recruitment, from a pool that extends beyond the career civil service. But in this they are now not unique: of the most senior civil servants, more than 60 per cent appointed in 2007/8 had come from outside the career civil service, 40 per cent from outside the public sector (*Recruitment* 2010). Agency CEs are on fixed-term contracts, can be dismissed for underperformance, and enjoy neither immunity nor anonymity. They are therefore vulnerable to sanctions, and thus accountable. They have become answerable to Parliament for their agencies, although the original intention was that it would be ministers, on the basis that executive agencies remained within departments (Gains 2003: 7). In terms of *internal* accountability, the agency model is extremely flexible, as New Labour's endless experiments in 'joined up' government demonstrate (James 2001; Gains 2003).

NPM, again, is charged with undermining the anonymity of civil servants, the confidentiality of their policy advice, and indeed their central role in advising on policy. This is in part by the interposition of special advisers, and by appointments to senior civil positions of people recruited from outside the career civil service. Special advisors, as anomalous temporary civil servants, obviously do compete with mandarins for the minister's ear, but career civil servants should be able to face such competition; 'servants of princes' faced much stiffer competition from *eminences grises*, confessors, courtiers, and even courtesans. I would have thought it much more likely that special advisers would go native. But the confidentiality of special advisers' advice is the same as the 'old' civil service confidentiality, except that in virtue of their high visibility and their status as mere creatures of their ministers, their advice is much more likely to becoming notorious, like Jo Moore's counsel in the wake of 9/11 that: 'It's now a very good day to get out anything we want to bury. Councillors expenses?', and they can be much more easily sacrificed to 'Parliament' and the media.

As for civil service anonymity the revised 'Osmotherly Rules' (*Departmental Evidence* 2005) and the Civil Service Code (2006: ss. 6, 13) still require civil servants to say nothing without permission, and to protect ministers against Parliament, just like the Armstrong Memorandum and the good old days. Enthusiasts for 'open government' (Weir and Beetham 1999: 10) can have no investment in either anonymity or its twin, 'confidentiality'. Both sit ill with 'transparency' and freedom of information. These in turn are rightly coupled with accountability: evaluating accounts presupposes knowing which questions to ask. Select committees and public inquiries have invariably sought to extend their access to 'persons and papers'. It has been many years since it was uncontroversial that 'confidentiality' must include what advice was given, or whole classes of advice, rather than simply who gave it (RUSI 1996). But departmental accounting officers (i.e. the permanent secretaries) of every department have been answerable to the PAC since the 1880s, and senior and middle ranking civil servants could long since be called to 'explain' their departments' activities to public enquiries and to select committees, and to suffer adverse career consequences; the Crichel Down and Vehicle and General Insurance cases are noted instances (O'Toole 2006: 117–18). The argument for 'confidentiality' rests on the supposed need to protect frank speaking between ministers and their civil servants, and on the inability of civil servants to defend themselves in public, or so the civil service unions claimed after Vehicle and General (ibid.: 120–6). They most certainly can and do defend themselves now. 'Speaking truth unto power' has never been risk-free, and willingness to do it depends on moral character, not on arrangements. 'Freedom of information' is, moreover, a mixed blessing. It can be misused: Blair apparently used the Foreign Affairs Select Committee's known enthusiasm for it as a way of ensuring the 'outing' of David Kelly without naming him (Tweedie 2004). Accountability simply is not the kind of good (like, say, visits to Italy) where some is good, more is better, and most is best of all.

In any case, diminished anonymity was already regarded as a *fait accompli* by civil service commentators in the 1970s and 1980s, who related it to media habits and especially the new select committees of 1980 and not to 'Thatcherism', that is, NPM (Johnstone 1977; Regan 1989). The Freedom of

Information Act, the St John Stevas multiplication of select committees, the increased insistence of courts and public inquiries on access to information, and Professor Peter Hennessy's unrivalled knowledge of Whitehall (he was a Whitehall correspondent for *The Times* from 1972 to 1984) have no obvious connection with NPM either. According to Regan (1989), senior- and middle-ranking civil servants positively relished 'non-facelessness'. Pilkington's contention (1999: 57) that after Westland 'it became almost routine for ministers actually to name particular civil servants as being to blame' is clearly exaggerated.

In sum, under NPM there is if anything *more* civil service public accountability than before. Parliamentary 'scrutiny', a function that only its select committees can perform, cannot extend to bureaucratic accountability unless civil servants can be required to disclose policy advice. How else could it be justly decided that a minister was ill-advised, and therefore potentially blameless, or well-advised, and therefore blameworthy? Public inquiries or commissions, however revealing (e.g. Scott, Hutton, Butler), cannot be the ordinary instrument of parliamentary scrutiny. But I cannot see how there can be improved scrutiny, and thus *public* accountability of civil servants, unless agency can be attributed to them; in other words, unless some distinction, however rough and ready, is made between what is and what is not their proper role. These distinctions can never be politically incontestable. But that is no more an objection to the NPM than it was to the old Public Administration. Assigning responsibility and blame fairly simply *is* a difficult matter.

Perhaps the weightiest charge against the NPM is that it has conduced to an erosion of morale in the civil service, and throughout the public sector. The 'perpetual revolution' in the public sector and a culture of (moving) targets and performance measurement that guarantees that whatever is done will never be good enough are certainly highly likely to damage morale. Specifically, NPM is said to have destroyed the old 'public service bargain' (*Ministers and Civil Servants* 2007) which *inter alia* involved lower salaries than putative private sector comparators, in return for a generous pension, job security, and non-cash benefits such as titles, social esteem, and above all the rewards of a job intrinsically worth doing. But this topic needs careful handling. The 'bargain' was eroding long before the NPM (Hood and Lodge 2006). And from the perspective of this essay, it must be insisted that there is no necessary relationship between morale and *accountability*. There can be full accountability and poor morale, or high morale and low accountability. No doubt the morale of the KGB deteriorated under *glasnost*. Moreover, any suggestion that public sector personnel *in general* have, or had, a morally superior 'public service' motivation is no more self-evident than the public choice, 'bureau-shaping', or *Yes Minster* rejoinder; civil service trade unionism, for instance, is not more *pro bono publico* than any other. In any event, *any* durable arrangement demands a structure of incentives and sanctions. There have been organizations that relied on terror to animate their members,[19] but none, not even religious orders, that relied exclusively on their zeal for the collective good. As the ancients said, 'rewards and punishments are the sinews of the commonwealth', and the same holds for any organization. NPM or post-bureaucracy and old style bureaucracy rank the efficacy of various combinations of incentives and sanctions differently, but each combination has its own perverse consequences. Open competition for top civil service posts may encourage institutional amnesia (Pollitt 2004), and advancement of those with 'can-do' attitudes prejudices the career chances of those with the Oake-shottian bureaucratic virtues of circumspection, respect for experience, and distrust of fashion and novelties (du Gay, this volume). But 'Weberian' bureaucracy for its part rewards Iagos, careerists, snag-hunters, and jobs-worths, and it is conspicuously invulnerable to *overall* constraint or sanctions.

NPM and post-bureaucracy share with the liberal tradition and the old public administration a common faith that well-contrived arrangements will secure the public interest. Isms like 'neo-liberalism' or 'managerialism', however, obscure an important distinction between them. For both the liberal tradition and NPM, policy and arrangements are most prudently predicated on the assumption that all men are 'knaves', or at any rate are likely to prefer their own interest to that of others (see Le Grand 2003). Both share the belief that well-designed arrangements can induce even knaves to do what is in the public interest, because it will coincide with their perceived self-interest. Bentham's proposals for the reform of legal procedure, the poor laws, prisons, and public administration are exemplary illustrations of 'institutional design'. Such arrangements will on no account allow bureaucracies free rein. Liberals and NPM agree that *competition* can overcome (to quote Herbert Spencer 1884) the 'resistance of officialism to improvements; as by the Admiralty when use of the electric telegraph was proposed, and the reply was—"We have a very good semaphore system"'. For liberals, markets or market analogues are paradigmatic arrangements for reconciling the private and the public interest, whether as undesigned 'spontaneous ordering' mechanisms, or as the deliberate design of 'marketization'. The NPM's equally strong faith in market or quasi-market mechanisms and competition is visible in, for example, the purchaser–provider split in the NHS, the *Next Steps* contracts, special advisers competing with career civil servants, open competition for civil service jobs, competitive tendering, outsourcing, pressure from clients or consumers on providers via 'charterization', and proxies for the impersonal judgements of the market such as audit, targets, objectives, and performance measures, 'payment by result', managerial autonomy, etc.

NPM and liberalism, 'neo-' or any other, however, fundamentally *dis*agree in one respect. For liberalism, even gridlock is preferable to the unconstrained exercise of power. Its preferred institutional arrangements, *checks and balances* or *the separation of powers*, are premised on this belief. (The private sector version of checks and balances is the Combined Codes of Corporate Governance (2003, 2006, 2008), designed to constrain corporate actors by arrangements and their self-interest to act only in ways that benefit the corporation.) Montesquieu, marvellously reworking Locke's *Two Treatises* and various Whig clichés in his *L'esprit des loix*, could not entirely resist the logic of sovereignty, but regarded sovereignty as nullified *de facto* even in modern monarchies, where monarchs are 'sovereign', by their dependence on the cooperation of 'intermediate powers'. Locke too had made the 'legislature' 'supreme' (he could not bring himself to say 'sovereign'), and allowed an 'executive' with prerogatives as necessary to political order, but attempted so to arrange matters that the holders of these powers could only act together or not at all. The Federalists, Montesquieu's most brilliant students, of course intended the separation of powers to produce cooperation and 'energetic' government, not gridlock, but were prepared to allow the latter in preference to arbitrary government.

NPM, however, is *not* predicated on distrust of *every* concentration of power. For NPM, well-designed arrangements mean that the choice between arbitrary power and potential gridlock does not have to be made. That, however, is illusory. NPM requires that bureaucracy is ultimately subject to *political* accountability and control, which in turn postulates a superior to whom accounts are due, and who is able to *control*. This is not checks and balances. The NPM and post-bureaucracy thesis is that efficiency and morale are not achieved by hierarchy and micro-management, but by 'empowering' staff, by self-motivation, networking, cooperation and negotiated understandings. The point of accountability and the policy/operations split for NPM is to reconcile ultimate *political* control and empowerment of staff. For such an arrangement to be viable, however, each party to it must trust the other. But if there were perfect trust there would be no need for accountability arrangements in the first place. The propensity to espouse accountability arrangements varies inversely with the existence of trust (Power 1997; O'Neill 2002), a truth perfectly illustrated by the recently discovered willingness of the House of Commons to be accountable and transparent about expenses. As trust has come to be in ever shorter supply in the polity, the salience of accountability has increased accordingly. Those (not least academics) at the receiving end of the proliferation of accountability arrangements are distinctly unenthusiastic about them, and no wonder: review, audit, cost units, efficiency savings, targets, benchmarks, payment by 'results', and all the rest have arguably undermined such autonomy as there was, perversely diverting ever increasing time and energy to the production of accounts, at the expense of the substantive activities of which these accounts are supposedly the narrative and justification.

Of late, it has been politicians of the right and the centre that have displayed particular distrust of bureaucracy, and therefore most enthusiasm for accountability arrangements, whereas previously it was the Left that denigrated the civil service (Plant 2003: 570).[20] But as has been argued earlier, accountability is a relationship of super- and subordination. There can be a ladder of judges of accounts, but accountability, like appeals procedures, must stop somewhere. And the ultimate arbiter of accounts must be *trusted*; arrangements, however ingenious their design, cannot alter this. Thus, accountability does not in fact eliminate the need to trust *someone*: at most it can displace the need for trust somewhere else.

Under NPM, the ultimate locus of the right to judge accounts almost invariably proves to be *politicians* (or their appointees), always ranked by the public near the bottom of any list of those most trusted. This in no way differs from the old public accountability, or 'democratic' accountability. Reed, for example, emphatically restates the impeccably social liberal belief that 'rules and mechanisms of accountability are essential to the protection of individual and collective choice' (in du Gay 2005: 137). This supposes that 'rules and mechanisms' (in other words arrangements) are a substitute for trust. Reed's further contention that bureaucracy is 'a necessary organizational and ethical precondition for defending and sustaining pluralist and interest group democracy in the workplace and beyond' demands both trust in bureaucracy and trust in the *demos*. Only a *virtuous* bureaucracy could even begin to serve this purpose, and even then only as a necessary and certainly not the sufficient condition for the protection of 'individual choice' and 'democracy'. It was precisely the residuum of bureaucratic *virtues* in the Third Reich (cited by Reed as an awful warning) that made it unspeakable from the point of view of its victims; they would have been better off if the *Deutscher Beamtentum* had been susceptible to bribery, or incapable of organizing an efficient transport system. And the 'individual and collective choices' of the *demos* may well be hostile to taxation, bureaucracy, 'human rights', workplace democracy and trade unionism, multiculturalism, foreign aid, immigrants, asylum seekers, 'scroungers', and to any number of other causes espoused by opponents of NPM. Constitutionality (the rule of law) and the safeguarding of individual rights are, *pace* Reed, premised on removing certain activities from the purview of government altogether (Dahl 1970), precisely because of *dis*trust of the *demos*.

Bureaucratic accountability thus requires trust in politicians, or bureaucrats, or both. 'Ministerial responsibility'—checks and balances—and 'democratic' accountability are predicated on *dis*trust of politicians and require a reliable Parliament. Parliament, however, is equally composed of politicians. Therefore, neither ministers nor Parliament can be the uncontested repositories of trust. For reasons outlined earlier, the *demos* as sovereign cannot be unconditionally trusted either. Nor, however, can the bureaucracy, whether as the old public administration or as the NPM. There are no arrangements or 'systems' that can *guarantee* that a public bureaucracy will be incorrupt and efficient, but also impersonal and objective, in Weber's term: *sachlich*. No accountability arrangement can immunize bureaucracy against careerism and cynicism. More important, a bureaucracy with an ethic of public service will inevitably be a *corps* with an *esprit de corps*. It will have its own traditions and custom and practice, departmentalism, and instincts of collective self-defence; civil servants owe their expertise to initiation into them. Any such bureaucracy, to the extent that it is genuinely a public service, will therefore *not* be mere servants of government, or 'Parliament', and still less of the *demos*, but will be to a considerable degree an unaccountable and (by definition) an unelected participant in the business of government. The more 'fit for purpose' it is, the less 'subordinate' it will be. Even supposing an improbable reversion to the old public administration, the old accountability would be no more a substitute for trust than the new. No accountability arrangement whatever can guarantee that either those rendering accounts or those judging them will be trustworthy.

⬚ NOTES

1. 'Civil Service' in Britain strangely excludes the Police (but not prison officers), the teaching professions, local government, the NHS, and much else that would count as part of the civil service in mainland Europe. Inclusion of these bureaucracies would merely strengthen my case.
2. These conceptually quite distinct terms are used interchangeably even by Marshall (1989: 1–2; on ministerial responsibility as a convention, e.g. Jennings 1959: 2, citing Dicey).
3. *Civil Service Management Code* (1993, incorporating the *Armstrong Memorandum*, reproduced in Barberis 1996*b*) p. 26; there is no reference to this in the 2009 version.
4. From *ministrare*, to serve. The same etymology implicit in 'a minister' is now safely dead and buried.
5. The complications introduced by judicial accountability, especially in conditions of judicial 'human rights' activism, are beyond the scope of this chapter.
6. British 'departments' have various names (*Office, Ministry*, the *Treasury*—which incidentally has *two* Cabinet ministers) and quite different identities. Some do not use the title 'secretary of state', some cabinet ministers have no 'department' and vice versa; see *Machinery of Government Reform*. 'Secretary' for senior office-holders, whether political or civil service, is from *secretarius*, a person who can be entrusted with secrets.
7. *Questions of Procedure for Ministers* prohibited disclosure even of which committees had made decisions (Brazier 1997: 262); James Callaghan in 1968 refused to tell Parliament which cabinet committees there were, and even ministers did not know; by 1987 only four had been officially identified (Seldon, in Rhodes and Dunleavy 1995: 126). Since John Major this information has been available on the Internet.
8. Bogdanor (1997: 76); much the same: S.E. Finer (1927: 67–8). 'Must demonstrate', 'mistakes', and 'initiated' are equivocal.
9. The Germanic, Romance including Romanian, and Slavonic languages all have only one word, which (apart from Slavonic—my thanks to my colleague Jerzy Kociatkiewicz) is etymologically equivalent to 'responsibility' (from *respondere* or *antworten*, to answer). Latin had only *officium*. For the relationship between accountability and responsibility, see Höpfl (in Höpfl 2008; Mulgan 2003; Bovens et al. 2008). For reasons given above, I dissent from Philp's otherwise impressive (2009) piece and, on this point, from Flinders (2001).

10. The youthfully radical Jack Straw, subsequently a no-nonsense Home Secretary, proposed in the early 1980s that all police officers above the rank of superintendent (a fairly junior grade) should be political appointees of local government. For this attitude applied to the mandarinate *de nos jours*, see the New Local Government Network's *Changing Whitehall's DNA* (2007), especially chapter 8.
11. Weber attached no paradigmatic significance to the British Civil Service, and seems to have noted neither Northcote-Trevelyan nor subsequent reforms. The culminating work of Warren Fisher (Pilkington 1999: 19–20) post-dates his most significant writings.
12. This is not to deny the value of du Gay's and Hennis's admirable work; there is, however, much in Weber that has nothing to do with it.
13. *Pace* Greenaway (2004), Northcote-Trevelyan's warnings about 'departmental views' are general, and Trevelyan, Treasury Under- (i.e. Permanent) Secretary, was always much concerned to ensure Treasury coordination of the whole civil service.
14. Specifically the NPM assumption that means-ends deliberation is applicable both to specific tasks—repairing a roof, launching a new enterprise or academic course, or a surgical or military operation—and to practices and institutions (Oakeshott 1962); the fallacy was vividly illustrated by the 1993 Sheehy Report's attempt to distinguish 'core' and 'ancillary' tasks of the police, and to rationalize policing (including promotion and salaries) as 'means' to the 'core ends'.
15. Treasury and PAC accounting has always been exemplary in eliminating fraud and malversation, but before NPM was entirely unconcerned with the *global* sums involved, which were a 'political' matter.
16. J.D. Kingsley (1944: 222, 304) was confident that 'the militant proletariat' and the 'planning state will require new types of civil servants: managers, accountants, consumer's counsels (*sic*) and economists', also 'men of push and go, energetic innovators and hard-driving managers. . . . above all it will require men (*sic*) wholly committed to the purposes the State is undertaking to serve'.
17. Unlike, say, the Treasury and the Prime Minister's Office of Civil Service Reform's firmly departmentalist *Better Government Services. Executive Agencies in the 21st Century*, 2001.
18. What counts as 'interference' is inherently problematic, given the indeterminable scope and character of ministerial responsibility. The precedent of ministerial interference in nationalized industries is often noted (e.g. O'Toole 2006: 142, 194); Fry et al. (1988: 434) records Herbert Morrison's fond hope that public corporations could combine 'the best of both worlds: business management and public accountability'.
19. Although as Hume observed (1741): 'The soldan of EGYPT, or the emperor of ROME, might drive his harmless subjects, like brute beasts, against their sentiments and inclination. But he must, at least, have led his mamalukes, or praetorian bands, like men, by their opinion'.
20. And also judges, ruling them out as alternative evaluators of political accounts as well. J.A.G. Griffith (1977) has been the *locus classicus* for 40 years. We hear less of this left orthodoxy than we did.

☐ BIBLIOGRAPHY

Ackroyd, S. et al. (2005) *The Oxford Handbook of Work and Organization*, Oxford: Oxford University Press.

Alvesson, M. and Thompson, P. (2005) Post-Bureaucracy, in Ackroyd, S et al. (eds), 2005, pp. 485–507.

Barberis, P. (ed.) (1996*a*) *The Whitehall Reader*, Buckingham: Open University Press.

——(1996*b*) *The Elite of the Elite: Permanent Secretaries in the British Civil Service*, Aldershot: Ashgate.

——(1997) *The Civil Service in an Era of Change*, Aldershot: Dartmouth.

Barker, A. (1998) Political Responsibility for UK Prison Security-Ministers Escape Again, *Public Administration*, 76(1): 1–23.

Beattie, A. (1995) Ministerial Responsibility and the Theory of the British State, in Rhodes, R. and Dunleavy, P. (1995), pp. 158–78.

Brazier, R. (1997) *Ministers of the Crown*, Oxford: Clarendon.

Bodin, J. (1576/1586) Six Livres de la République/ De Republica Libri Sex; relevant chapters translated in *Bodin on Sovereignty* (J.H. Franklin, ed.), Cambridge: Cambridge University Press (1992).

Bogdanor, V. (1997) Ministerial Accountability, *Parliamentary Affairs*, 50(1): 71–83.

Bovens, M. Schillemans, T., Hast, P.T. (2008) Does Political Accountability Work? An assessment tool, *Public Administration*, 8601, pp. 225–42.

Canovan, M. (2005) *The People*, Cambridge: Polity Press.

Changing Whitehall's DNA (2007) by Dick Sorabji for New Local Government Network at http://www.nlgn.org.uk/public/wp-content/uploads/changing-whitehalls-dna.pdf.

Child, J. and McGrath, R. (2001) Organizations Unfettered: Organizational Form in an Information-Intensive Economy, *Academy of Management Journal*, 44(6): 1135–48.

Christensen, T. and Laegreid, P. (2002) New Public Management: Puzzles of Democracy and the Influence of Citizens, *The Journal of Political Philosophy*, 10(3): 267–95.

Civil Service Code (2006) at http://www.civilservice.gov.uk/about/work/cscode/index.aspx.

Code of Conduct for Special Advisers (2009) at http://www.cabinetoffice.gov.uk/propriety_and_ethics/special_advisers/code/code.aspx.

Dahl, R. (1970) *After the Revolution*, New Haven: Yale University Press.

——(1989) *Democracy and its Critics*, New Haven: Yale University Press.

Departmental Evidence and Response to Select Committees (the 'Osmotherly Rules' 2005) Cabinet Office, at http://www.cabinetoffice.gov.uk/media/cabinetoffice/propriety_and_ethics/assets/osmotherly_rules.pdf.

Dicey, A.V. (1959) *Introduction to the Study of the Law of the Constitution* 10th edition, Basingstoke: Macmillan.

Donnellon, A. (1994) Defining the Post-Bureaucratic Type, in C. Heckscher and A. Donnellon (eds), *The Post Bureaucratic Organization: New Perspectives on Organizational Change*, Thousand Oaks, California: Sage, 14–62.

Dryzek, J.S. (2002) *Deliberative Democracy: Liberals, Critics, Contestations*, Oxford: Oxford University Press.

du Gay, P. (2000) *In Praise of Bureaucracy*, London: Sage.

——(ed) (2005) *The Values of Bureaucracy*, Oxford: Oxford University Press.

Finer, S.E. (1927) *The British Civil Service*, London: Fabian Society.

——(1956) The Individual Responsibility of Ministers, *Public Administration*, 34: 377–96.

Flinders, M. (2000) The Enduring Centrality of Individual Ministerial Responsibility within the British Constitution, *Legislative Studies*, 6(3): 73–92.

——(2001) *The Politics of Accountability in the Modern State*, Aldershot: Ashgate.

——(2002) Shifting the Balance? Parliament, the Executive and the British Constitution, *Political Studies*, 50(1): 23–42.

Flynn, N. (2007) *Public Sector Management*, 5th edn, London: Sage.

Fry, G.K. (1969) Thoughts on the Present State of the Convention of Ministerial Responsibility, *Parliamentary Affairs* 21 (September 1969), pp. 10–20.

Fry, G., Flynn, A., Gray, A., Jenkins, W., and Rutherford, B. (1988) Symposium on Improving Management in Government, *Public Administration*, 66(4): pp. 420–39.

Gains, F. (2003) Surveying the Landscape of Modernization: Executive Agencies under New Labour, *Public Policy and Administration*, 18(2): 4–20.

Gobert, J. and Punch, M. (2003) *Rethinking Corporate Crime*, London: Butterworths.

Greenaway, J. (2004) Celebrating Northcote-Trevelyan: Dispelling the Myths, *Public Policy and Administration*, 19(1): 1–14.

Greenleaf, W.H. (1987) *The British Political Tradition, Vol. III: A Much Governed Nation*, Methuen: London.

Greenwood, J.R., Pyper, R., Wilson, D. (2002) *New Public Administration in Britain*, 3rd edition, London: Routledge.

Greer, P. (1994) *Transforming Central Government*, Buckingham: Open University Press.

Griffith, J.A.G. (1977) *The Politics of the Judiciary*, Manchester: Manchester University Press.

Ham, C. (2007) When Politics and Markets Collide: Reforming the English National Health Service, Health Services Management Centre, University of Birmingham, at. http://www. hsmc.bham.ac.uk./publications/pdfs/Pol/Markets.pdf.

Harrington, J. (1656) *The Commonwealth of Oceana*, in J.G.A. Pocock (ed. and intro.), *The Commonwealth of Oceana, and: A System of Politics*, Cambridge: Cambridge University Press (1992).

Harris, M. and Höpfl, H. (eds) (2006) Organizations in the Age of Post-Bureaucracy, *Journal of Organizational Change Management*, Special Issue, 19(1).

Heckscher, C. and Donnellon, A. (eds) (1994) *The Post-Bureaucratic Organization*, London: Sage.

Held, D. (1987) *Models of Democracy*, 1st edn, Cambridge: Polity Press.

Hobbes, T. (1651) *Leviathan*, E. Curley (ed.), Indianapolis: Hackett, 1994.

Hogwood, B.W., Judge, D. and McVicar, M. (2001) Agencies, Ministers and Civil Servants in Britain, in *Politicians, Bureaucrats and Administrative Reform*, London, UK: Routledge, 35–44, at http://eprints.cdlr.strath.ac.uk/1797/.

Hood, C. (1989) Public Administration and Public Policy: Intellectual Challenges for the 1990s, *Australian Journal of Public Administration*, 48: 346–58.

——(1998) *The Art of the State*, Oxford: Clarendon Press.

——and Lodge, M. (2006) From Sir Humphrey to Sir Nigel: What Future for the Public Service Bargain After Blairworld?, *Political Quarterly*, 77(3): 360–8.

Höpfl, H.M. (2006) Postbureaucracy and Weber's "Modern" Bureaucrat, in Harris and Höpfl (eds), 8–21.

——(2008) The Critical Subject of Accountability, in D.M. Boje (ed.), *Critical Theory Ethics for Business and Public Administration, Part II.2*, Charlotte, North Carolina: Information Age Publishing.

Hume, D. (1741) Of the First Principles of Government, in *Essays Moral, Political and Literary*, 1741, at http://www.iep.utm.edu/h/humeessa.html.

Individual Ministerial Responsibility—Issues and Examples (2004) House of Commons Research Paper 04/31, 5 April 2004, at http://www.parliament.uk/commons/lib/research/ rp2004/rp04-031.pdf.

James, O. (2001) Evaluating Executive Agencies in UK Government, *Public Policy and Administration*, 16(3), pp 24–52.

Jaques, E. (1990) In Praise of Hierarchy, *Harvard Business Review*, 68(1): 127–33 (Jan/Feb 90).

Jenkins, K. (2008) Politicians and Civil Servants: Unfinished Business—The Next Steps Report, Fulton and the Future, *Public Administration*, 79(3): 418–25.

Jennings, S.I. (1959) *Cabinet Government*, 1st edn, 1936, Cambridge: Cambridge University Press.

Johnstone, D. (1977) Facelessness: Anonymity in the Civil Service, reproduced in *Parliamentary Affairs*, 1986, 39(4): 407–20.

Jones, C., Parker, M. and ten Bos, R. (2005) *For Business Ethics*, London: Routledge.

Judge, D. (1999) *Representation: Theory And Practice In Britain*, London: Routledge.

Kingsley, J.D. (1944) *Representative Bureaucracy*, Yellow Springs, Ohio: Antioch Press.

Learmont, M. and Harding, S. (eds) (2004) *Unmasking Health Management: A Critical Text*, New York: Nova Science Publishers.

Le Grand, J. (2003) *Motivation, Agency and Public Policy: Of Knights and Knaves, Pawns and Queens*, Oxford: Oxford University Press.

Machinery of Government Reform (n.d.) at http://www.nuffield.ox.ac.uk/Politics/Whitehall/MoGRPaP.doc.

Marshall, G. (ed.) (1989) *Ministerial Responsibility*, Oxford: Oxford University Press.

Mackintosh, J.P. (1962) *The British Cabinet*, 3rd edn, 1975, London: Stevens and Sons.

Madgwick, P.J. (1991) *British Government: The Central Executive Territory*, Hemel Hempstead: P. Allan.

McSweeney, B. (2006) Are We Living in a Post-Bureaucratic Epoch, in Harris and Höpfl (2006).

Massey, A. (1997) The British Agency Model of Government, in P. Barberis (ed.) (1997), pp. 38–53.

Mill, J.S. (1861) *Considerations on Representative Government*, in Mill, J.S. *Utilitarianism, Liberty and Representative Government*, A.D. Lindsay ed., London: Dent, 1957.

Ministerial Code (2007) Cabinet Office, at http://www.cabinetoffice.gov.uk/media/cabinetoffice/propriety_and_ethics/assets/ministerial_code_current.pdf.

Mulgan, R. (2003) *Holding Power to Account: Accountability in Modern Democracies*, Basingstoke: Palgrave.

Northcote-Trevelyan Report on the Organisation of the Permanent Civil Service (1854) at http://www.civilservant.org.uk/northcotetrevelyan.pdf.

Oakeshott, M. (1962) Rationalism in Politics, in *Rationalism in Politics and Other Essays*, Oxford: Oxford University Press, pp. 1–36.

O'Neill, O. (2002) *A Question of Trust*, Cambridge: Cambridge University Press.

Osborne, D. and Gaebler, T. (1993) *Reinventing Government: How the Entrepreneurial Spirit is Transforming the Public Sector*, New York: Plume.

——and Plastrik, P. (1997) *Banishing Bureaucracy*, Reading: Addison Wesley.

O'Toole, B. (2006) *The Ideal of Public Service; Reflections on the Higher Civil Service in Britain*, Abingdon: Routledge.

Outside Appointments to the Senior Civil Service (2009) House of Commons Public Administration Select Committee at http://www.parliament.uk/documents/upload/memosforweb14jul.pdf.

Philp, M. (2009) Delimiting Democratic Accountability, *Political Studies*, 57(1): 28–53 (March 2009).

Pilkington, C. (1999) *The Civil Service Today*, Manchester: Manchester University Press.

Plant, R. (2003) A Public Service Ethic and Political Accountability, *Parliamentary Affairs*, 56: 560–79.

Plowden, W. (1994) *Ministers and Mandarins*, London: Institute for Public Policy Research.

Polidano, C. (2000) The Bureaucrats Who Almost Fell Under a Bus: A Reassertion of Ministerial Responsibility?, *Political Quarterly*, 82(1): 177–83.

Politics and Administration: Ministers and Civil Servants (2007) House of Commons Public Administration Select Committee: Third Report of Session 2006–07, Volume I, at http://www.publications.parliament.uk/pa/cm200607/cmselect/cmpubadm/122/122i.pdf.

Pollitt, C. (2004) Bureaucracies Remember, Post-Bureaucracies Forget, *Public Administration*, 87(2): 198–218.

Power, M. (1997) *The Audit Society: Rituals of Verification*, Oxford: Oxford University Press.

Public Service Agreement 12: Improve the Health and Wellbeing of Children and Young People (2008) http://www.hm-treasury.gov.uk/d/pbr_csr07_psa12.pdf.

Recruitment (2010) External recruitment to the senior civil service, at http://www.parliament. the-stationery-office.com/pa/cm200910/cmselect/cmpubadm/241/24105.htm/

Regan, C.M. (1989) Anonymity in the British Civil Service: Facelessness Diminished, *Parliamentary Affairs*, 39(4): 421–34.

Rhodes, R. (2000) New Labour's Civil Service, Summing up Joining up, *Political Quarterly*, 7102, pp. 151–66.

——and Dunleavy, P. (1995) *Prime Minister, Cabinet and Core Executive*, Basingstoke: Macmillan.

Rogers, R. and Walters, R. (2004) *How Parliament Works*, 5th edn, Harlow: Pearsons Longman.

Rousseau, J.J. (1755) *De l'Economie Politique*, in C.E. Vaughan (ed.), *Rousseau: Political Writings*, Vol. I, Oxford: Blackwell, 1962.

——(1762) *Du Contrat Social*, in *Oeuvres Complètes*, Vol. III, Paris: Pléiade, 1966.

Royal United Services Institute (RUSI) (1996) Seminar on '*Is Public Access to Civil Service Advice Possible*', at http://www.cfoi.org.uk/pdf/polad96.pdf.

Spencer, H. (1884) The Sins of Legislators, in *The Man versus the State*, at http://oll.libertyfund. org/index.php?option=com_staticxt&staticfile=show.php%3Ftitle=330&Itemid=27.

Talbot, C. (2002) The Agency idea, sometimes old, sometimes new, sometimes borrowed, sometimes untrue, in Osborne, S., *Public Management: Critical Perspectives*, vol. v, pp. 3–21, London: Routledge.

Tweedie, N. (2004) Who should Shoulder the Blame for Kelly's Death?, *Daily Telegraph*, 27.1.2004.

Webb, P. (2000) *The Modern British Party System*, London: Sage.

Weber, M. (1918) 'Parlament und Regierung im neugeordneten Deutschland', and (1919) 'Politicals Beruf', both in *Weber: Political Writings*, Lassman, P. and Speirs, R. (eds.), Cambridge University Press, 1994 (First citation in text), and in *Politische Schriften*, Potsdamer Internet Ausgabe, at http://141.89.99.185:8080/uni/professuren/e06/a/a/ha/PS.pdf. (Second, corresponding German citation).

Weir, S. and Beetham, D. (1999) *Political Power and Democratic Control in Britain*, London: Routledge.

Woodhouse, D. (1994) *Ministers and Parliament: Accountability in Theory and Practice*, Oxford: Clarendon Press.

——(2004) UK Ministerial Responsibility in 2002: The Tale of Two Resignations, *Public Administration*, 82(1): 1–19.

3 New Lock, New Stock, New Barrel, Same Gun: The Accessorized Bureaucracy of Health Care

DAVID A. BUCHANAN AND LOUISE FITZGERALD

Coats, Knickers, Other Garments, and a Weapon

This chapter explores the proposition that the British National Health Service (NHS) has been subjected to so much change in the past two decades that the notions of bureaucracy in general, and professional bureaucracies in particular, no longer apply.[1] Have we seen the development of a new non-bureaucratic archetype? In a previous answer to this question, Kitchener (1999) concluded that, while the 'fur coat' of structures had changed, the 'knickers' of underpinning power relations were still intact. Has the past decade altered that picture? Or, switching metaphors from apparel to weaponry, are we looking at the hunter's rifle: 'I've replaced the lock, I've changed the stock, and I've bought a new barrel, but it's still my favourite old gun'.

Evidence for dramatic change in the archetype of the professional bureaucracy appears to be overwhelming. Funding is locally controlled by primary care trusts. Hospitals can achieve autonomy by applying for 'foundation trust' status. Monitor (2007), the foundation trust regulator, encourages foundation trusts to manage their clinical services as quasi-autonomous divisions, run by doctors, with their own business plans and budgets. Activity-based costing allows hospitals to determine which services are 'profitable', and which are not. Commercial programme and project management practices are encouraged. Hospitals can advertise and compete, adapting 'lean manufacturing' methods to streamline patient flows. The language of 'service reconfiguration' disguises health-care activities which in commercial organizations are known as mergers and acquisitions. Commercial discourse now pervades the health-care management conversation. Overturning hierarchical controls and rigid rules, an inevitable, progressive, and dynamic 'new public management' based on quasi-markets and networks appears finally to have been institutionalized (although the processes of government policy making do not seem to have changed much).

That is a selective picture. Now 60 years old, with 1.3 million employees in England, and with over 300 provider units (primary care, ambulance, acute care, mental health, community care), the NHS is old enough, large enough, and complex enough to display, from time to time, a variety of novel, innovative, maverick, deviant organizational arrangements and management practices. With running costs of over £2 billion a week, the service is also expensive enough to ensure constant media attention and political interference. Government ministers and members of Parliament become personally involved with single providers (proposed hospital closures routinely draw attention) and will pursue the cases of individual patients (perceived to have been wronged, for example, by being denied access to expensive treatments). Scrutiny and intervention lead inevitably to the imposition of new structures and controls. Consequently, a hunt for the 'old public management', in the midst of the allegedly new, in the shape of hierarchical structures and the proliferation of rules, is still productive.

Evidence for transformation and a fresh archetype relies on isolated experiments, transient innovations, and new labels which, returning to Kitchener's metaphor, are mere accessories—gloves, hats, scarves, wraps, jewellery. These adornments enhance the overall effect of the wardrobe, but they can be added and removed as required without compromising the basic outfit. In sum, the traditional archetype may not be in much danger. Changes to structures, labels, and discourse are not necessarily symptomatic of transformation. On the contrary, those visible and audible shifts effectively cloak stability in the underpinning frame.

Public sentiment shows an enduring attachment to an NHS, funded by taxation, and free at the point of delivery. Government ministers wishing to wreck their reputations and careers need only to appear to challenge these values. But this attachment is accompanied by the presumption that the system is wanting, lacking, failing. It is in this context that academic debate concerning 'new versus old' occurs; it is in the interest of politicians, healthcare managers, research academics, and the general commentariat to emphasize departures and innovations, the different and the new, to create an impression of the perception of transformation which is as significant as substantive change. The new enduring archetype is thus a socio-political construct, *the accessorized bureaucracy*. This is not form without substance. The accessories appear demonstrably to have improved the quality of patient care. Kitchener's knickers have not been dropped. For reasons discussed later, this may be cause for celebration, rather than concern.

What's in an Archetype?

Established in 1948, and vigorously resisted at the time by the medical profession, the NHS was underpinned by a set of core values: health care should be free to all, funded by taxation, based on need, and provide equitable access. While those values have been eroded at the margins (patients now pay for some specialist treatments), they are still widely endorsed. Policy and funding remain matters for government determination, which ensures constant political scrutiny and ongoing interference. The stream of non-negotiable top-down policy initiatives, particularly since the start of the twenty-first century, has been overwhelming.

If we accept those core values, we would presumably not want health-care decisions to be influenced by personal, emotional, irrational considerations. Weber (1947) defines the bureaucratic archetype as a rational and efficient mode of organization based on division of labour, written guidelines, a hierarchical role structure staffed by career professionals, and with authority residing in the position rather than the person. In practice, an organization may approach this 'ideal type' without displaying a full-blown version of the model.

A bureaucratic structure that performed well on criteria such as unity, coordination, precision, predictability, impartiality, organizational memory, and continuity across changes in government (Olsen 2006: 8) could be considered appropriate to an NHS. The services which the NHS provides, however, are often criticized for being fragmented, uncoordinated, confused, unpredictable, partial, and forgetful (Donaldson 2000). The idea that health care in Britain is *over*-bureaucratized and *under*-managed, rather than the opposite, is one that dates at least from the 1980s. The reforms introduced then are visible today in the clinical directorate structures of most acute hospitals, where a senior doctor and a general manager run their service in collaboration (a triumvirate sometimes with the addition of a senior nurse manager). The consultant typically holds a hybrid medical and managerial role with the title clinical director. As we will see, in the attempt to involve medical staff in management decisions, and overcome 'grey suits, white coats' stereotypes, the clinical directorate model has been reinforced more recently with the development of 'service line reporting' systems of clinical management, which put clinical directors and their teams in potentially more powerful decision-making and resource-allocating roles (Monitor 2007).

The term 'bureaucracy' is popularly associated with impersonal hierarchy, rigid rules, predictable procedures, and a pace of decision-making and change that would embarrass a glacier. Emphasizing the disadvantages of bureaucracy in a fast-paced world, theorists have consistently contrasted inflexible mechanistic systems with fluid organic systems (Burns and Stalker 1961), and plodding segmentalist cultures with innovative integrative cultures (Kanter 1983, 1989). Mintzberg (1979) argues that health care is a professional bureaucracy, in which rationality and efficiency are attended by powerful professional groups whose education and socialization processes allow them considerable degrees of freedom from management control. Change is potentially even more difficult in a professional bureaucracy as management cannot act or direct without the prior consent of their professional staff. From their research in Canadian hospitals, Denis et al. (2001) argue that it is difficult simultaneously to sustain a coherent strategy, internal support for the leadership group, and an effective response to external pressures. As this three-way alignment is fragile, change tends to be episodic, or sporadic, rather than smooth and continuous.

The concept of 'new public management' reflecting the neo-liberal ideology of right-wing governments signalled the import of flexible, adaptable, commercial 'bureaucracy-busting' quasi-market-based management principles into public sector organizations, including health care (Seddon 2008). Kitchener (1999) thus asks whether the idea of the professional bureaucracy remains useful in the face of these trends. Weber considered the concept of bureaucracy as an 'ideal type'—a sensitizing device highlighting features to which we should be alert, rather than a description of any actual organization. Referring to organizational forms, Kitchener uses the term archetype to refer to a distinctive interpretive framework, and identifies three: professional bureaucracy, quasi-market, and local networking archetypes.

Kitchener conducted comparative case study research in British hospitals between 1991 and 1995, based on over 100 interviews, observation, and archival material. The new public management in focus at the time related to a set of policies that included financial restraint, preference for market mechanisms, the adoption of private sector management methods, and increased control over professional work (see also chapter by Speed in this volume). The first quasi-market reforms date from the early 1990s with hospitals competing for service contracts with new commissioning bodies, which today are primary care trusts. Those combined policies were meant to improve the performance of the health-care system while reducing clinical autonomy. Kitchener argues that the quasi-market archetype is quite different from professional bureaucracy. The professional collegiate climate has been replaced by clinical directorates, which are in effect medical cost centres, in which doctors ostensibly manage themselves. The quasi-market form, for Kitchener, was thus a major challenge to the traditional professional bureaucracy. However, professional support for the quasi-market archetype was weak, leading to 'the co-existence of new structures and systems with a hybrid interpretive scheme that maintains established values and attitudes' (Kitchener 1999: 185). Traditional patterns of power and control were not affected. Medical staff dominated organization hierarchies, with doctors taking most of the clinical director posts, managing the budgets, and thus controlling most of the spending related to the delivery of clinical care. The clinical reaction appears to have been, 'we'll work with this, but we don't think it's legitimate or appropriate', and traditional values and practices were sustained, although formal structures and processes changed.

By the mid-1990s, most hospitals had adopted a clinical directorate structure with medical cost centres with their own budgets and business plans, encouraged to work within the quasi-market archetype based on the purchaser-provider split, which was designed to improve performance by stimulating competition. As clinical directors, some senior doctors assumed responsibility for large budgets. The annual budget for surgical services in a medium-size district general hospital could run to over £15 million, creating a significant management challenge for the clinical director who had no previous managerial education or experience. However, as professional ideology privileges the patient, and not the customer, many doctors were unhappy that managers could override clinical judgements on the basis of income generation and costs. The apparent commercialization of health care was thus deeply disliked by some, and clinical directorate structures did not always effectively integrate medical and managerial thinking. As might be expected, medical and other clinical staff resisted management intrusion on their autonomy, and regular (often voluntary) peer review remains one of the main quality control mechanisms. In other words, the concept and characteristics of professional bureaucracy had not been seriously disturbed by those quasi-market reforms, which maintained what Kitchener describes as a 'hybrid interpretive scheme' incorporating opportunism, maintained autonomy, hybrid roles, and professional self-monitoring.

The interpretive framework or archetype being formed by government policy in England towards the end of the first decade of the twenty-first century involves autonomous hospitals, locally controlled funding, intense centralized performance monitoring, patient choice, competition between providers, empowerment of local communities, patients, staff, and managers, clinical engagement in management work, and the further adoption and adaptation of private sector management methods such as service line reporting, process redesign, lean processes, and activity-based costing. (*Note*: The argument in this chapter concerns the service in England; the health services in Scotland, Wales, and Northern Ireland are much smaller, and operate differently.) However, these policies are often contradictory, encouraging competition while expecting collaboration, advocating leaner processes while prioritizing quality of care, granting autonomy while strengthening central audit and control. Another key component of this interpretive framework is constant policy-driven adjustment, tinkering, and refinement of structures, policies, regulations, and targets. While some of those features of the archetype leave the concept of professional bureaucracy intact, others resemble a quasi-market archetype, and Kitchener's conclusion of 'no change' may well have been overtaken by these more recent developments. This debate can either be expressed in terms of 'the current archetype' or, as Kitchener observes, in terms of hybrid forms more or less happily coexisting. We will explore some of the current evidence before revisiting this issue.

All Change Please

There appears to be a significant body of evidence to counter Kitchener's assessment (1999), pointing to radical transformation in the health-care archetype.

FOLLOW THE MONEY

Although centrally provided, funding is no longer centrally controlled, but is channelled through primary care trusts which commission services from their local acute and other providers (Marks and Hunter 2005). This is a major shift in power relations, from an acute, consultant-led service towards one that is driven by primary care organizations. The current fashion influencing primary care trust practice in this regard concerns the eleven principles of 'world class commissioning'. Principle 7 is 'Effectively stimulate the market to meet demand and secure required clinical, and health and well-being outcomes'. Principle 8 is 'Promote and specify continuous improvements in quality and outcomes through clinical and provider innovation and configuration'. Principle 11 is 'Make sound financial investments to ensure sustainable development and value for money' (Department of Health 2007a: 4). While paying attention to quality of patient care and clinical outcomes, these principles of commissioning also clearly echo commercial practice.

GO FOR AUTONOMY (OR GET TAKEN OVER)

Hospitals that are considered to be operating effectively can be granted 'foundation trust' status with considerable financial autonomy. Following Lord Darzi's *Next Stage Review* (Department of Health 2008), foundation trust status is a requirement for all trusts, and not an aspiration. But this implies a degree of freedom from central and even regional control. In early 2009, over twenty acute and mental health Trusts were warned that they were in danger of missing the end-December 2010 target to become foundation Trusts, and that as a result they could expect either radical restructuring or to be taken over by existing foundation trusts seeking to expand their businesses. The director of the Foundation Trust Network, Sue Slipman, explained that

'Either you focus on becoming a foundation trust or someone else will do it for you' (Gainsbury 2009).

BUSINESS WITHIN A BUSINESS

The foundation trust regulator, Monitor (2007), has encouraged trusts to develop 'service line reporting'. This is an internal management system which turns clinical services into quasi-businesses (sometimes called clinical business units) within the overall business of their trust. This in turn grants substantial decision-making autonomy to service heads, typically clinical directors, who are also senior doctors. This internal arrangement mirrors the relationship between Monitor and foundation trusts—manage the money and we will leave you alone. Anecdotal evidence from the early stages of this development suggests that medical staff have accepted this type of arrangement; doctors, who perhaps resisted the previous quasi-market reforms because of their commercialism, welcome the introduction of service line reporting and clinical business units because it returns decision-making power and responsibility from management directly to them. In addition, there are of course now more clinical directors who have some prior management experience, and younger consultants who are more willing to take on the role of clinical director which is seen as potentially influential.

IT REALLY IS A BUSINESS

Foundation trusts are now run as private sector businesses, with customers, suppliers, competitors, cost centres, strategic plans, and business development managers (who may hold board-level positions). The language of the Dr Foster Intelligence report (2006) on the information requirements and decision processes of 'the intelligent board' is striking in its commercial orientation. (Dr Foster Intelligence is an independent health-care market intelligence, research, and advisory body.) The report discusses the need to establish a 'dashboard' of performance indicators, identifying the income and costs associated with each business unit (i.e. clinical service) and making benchmark comparisons with competing trusts. The 'minimum data set' for informing strategic decisions includes information relating to market and business development, key trends and forecasts, strategic objectives, income and expenditure, cash flow, debtors, and gross margin by trading centre. Such key performance indicators and the accompanying advice relating to board roles and relationships would not be out of place in a private sector company boardroom. Under the terms of its foundation trust license, King's College Hospital in London has set up a wholly owned private subsidiary company to market its own home-grown activity-based costing software package to other hospitals. Some larger trusts have considered merging into even larger 'super-trusts' and, since April 2008, hospitals and primary care trusts have been allowed to advertise their services, including the use of direct marketing, and to seek sponsorship deals with private companies as part of the drive to encourage and improve patient choice.

TALK THE TALK

Following the previous point about running trusts as businesses, management plans and decisions are now typically couched in commercial discourse; business units, customers, competitors, marketing ('promotion of services'), cost allocations, margins, profitability, portfolio analysis, mergers and acquisitions and takeovers, and business development (Shepherd 2008). New facilities are implemented through private finance initiatives. These trends reflect values different from those that have inspired this publicly funded system for the past sixty years. Anecdotal evidence indicates that managers and senior medical staff welcome these developments, but others remain sceptical. There is evidence to suggest that these changes are creating new tensions (Sambrook 2005).

CUSTOMER IS KING

The policy of patient choice has been established, with funding following patients who, from April 2008, could choose any NHS-approved hospital for their treatment, thus reinforcing the quasi-market competitive status of health-care providers. Patients who are unable to find suitable treatment in Britain can travel to a hospital in another European country for treatment, at NHS expense. Patient and public involvement and patient choice have also become routine slogans. Foundation trusts must recruit 'members' from the local community and establish an elected board of governors from that lay membership. Governors are to contribute to defining trust priorities and strategy.

YOU'RE A LEADER TOO

'Clinical engagement in leadership' is another new slogan and a key dimension of Darzi's *Next Stage Review* of the NHS, putting renewed emphasis on management and leadership training and development for clinical staff in general, and for doctors in particular (Department of Health 2008). The desire to engage medical staff in management and leadership dates from the 1980s, and has thus achieved new urgency in current proposals, such as the 'medical leadership competency framework' approved by the Academy of Medical Royal Colleges (Hamilton et al. 2008; NHS Institute for Innovation and Improvement 2008). *The NHS Operating Framework for 2008/09*, noting that finance and waiting times were no longer major concerns, declares an 'ambitious new chapter' in the transformation of the service, focusing on patient safety, access, better health and reduced inequalities, improving the patient experience and staff satisfaction, and enhanced emergency preparedness; not a recipe for stability (Department of Health 2007b). These aspirations are to be achieved by empowering local management and staff and by reducing central direction. Funding does become a concern in 2009, as economic trends threaten to affect the health service budget from 2011, but the service is expected to meet those other care quality and access targets nevertheless.

NETWORK TEAMS AND DIFFUSED POWER

It is notable that several recent government reports emphasize the need for 'leaders' and 'leadership' in health care, shifting the focus from management in general, and from directive or autocratic management in particular, to 'soft' management (O'Reilly and Reed, forthcoming). This apparent shift in policy relates to two other trends: the development of networks to deliver 'joined up services' which mirror the needs of the patient pathway, and the establishment of quality frameworks as opposed to targets as a means of setting standards (and monitoring performance). The growth in the number of areas where networks are used has been considerable. Starting with the creation of cancer networks (Calman and Hine 1995), networks are now either recommended or mandatory in a wide range of fields such as services for women and children, and care for the elderly. Many of these services require the collaboration of acute and primary care services, or of health and social care.

Networks require a specific mode of management to be successful (Kelwell et al. 2002; Addicott et al. 2007; Ferlie et al. 2009), the evidence suggesting that networks are more effectively run by duos and trios of managers with complementary skills. These teams include clinical managers, or hybrids, that retain a clinical practice, so this is one route to engaging clinicians in management. In addition, these senior strategic skills are supported by 'distributed leadership' at other levels, and across the clinical professions, which helps to drive continuous improvements in front line services (Buchanan et al. 2007). Interestingly, in care of the elderly, the Department of Health has instituted the idea of Older People's Champions, where individuals opt to support standards of care (such as dignity, for example) for older people. This might be conceived as a process of mass mobilization such as that seen in social movements, where change is dependent, not on sole heroic leadership figures, but on 'multiple, multi-level, dispersed and networked leadership, including "everyday leadership" by frontline staff' (Bate et al. 2005: 35).

These shifts in the nature of leadership in health care might also be linked to the development of acronym-rich quality frameworks, notably the Improving Outcomes Guidance (IOGs) developed by the National Institute for Health and Clinical Excellence (NICE) and National Service Frameworks (NSFs) which engage more closely with clinical standards. The NSFs are often developed by and in consultation with clinicians, drawing on the latest research on the efficacy of standards and care pathways. The practicing clinician has great difficulty in rejecting these quality standards. Clinical managers thus rely on the credibility of the NSFs to legitimate changes to services using 'soft' management techniques of persuasion and peer pressure, supported by 'harder' deadlines and government dictats. Does this suggest that at last, after many misplaced attempts since the Griffiths report (DHSS 1983), doctors are now engaging with the processes of management and the implementation of change?

TOYOTA IN YOUR TRUST

'Lean thinking' methods have become de rigueur, and conferences and training programmes concerning applications in health care are now commonplace. The methods that are used to reduce costs, improve quality, and address problems in car manufacturing (Womack et al. 1990; Benders and Morita 2004) can be applied successfully to the management of patient flows through the health-care system. One hospital reduced the number of steps required to process a routine blood sample from 309 to 57. Using a 'lean' model, an Australian hospital is said to have increased capacity by 20 per cent while improving patient safety on the same budget, with the same staff and infrastructure (Lister 2006). Lean has thus become a key tool in the struggle for competitive advantage between health-care providers seeking to negotiate the best deals (in financial terms) with their commissioners. The issues involved in implementing lean methods are illustrated in Figure 3.1.

It is possible, therefore, to cite compelling evidence to support the view that a quasi-market archetype of health care is thriving. Faced with this evidence, Kitchener's conclusion, that professional bureaucracy was in no real danger, would perhaps no longer be warranted. We can argue instead that government policy, national organization structures and strategies, interorganizational collaborations, local leadership and management practices, everyday managerial discourse, and roles and attitudes among medical staff have changed to such a degree that an almost full-blown commercial archetype has evolved within the public sector envelope. Before accepting this view, however, we will consider evidence to the contrary.

Equating health care with the supermarket chain Tesco, Lister (2006) argues that inefficiencies and delays can be tackled with 'lean manufacturing' methods, developed by the car company Toyota, to overcome bottlenecks by reducing paperwork and the staff involved, and by removing unnecessary activities that do not add value. A process-mapping exercise by staff at Bolton Hospitals NHS Trust revealed that it took more than 250 interactions to discharge from hospital a patient with a complex medical problem (Jones and Mitchell, 2006: 12).

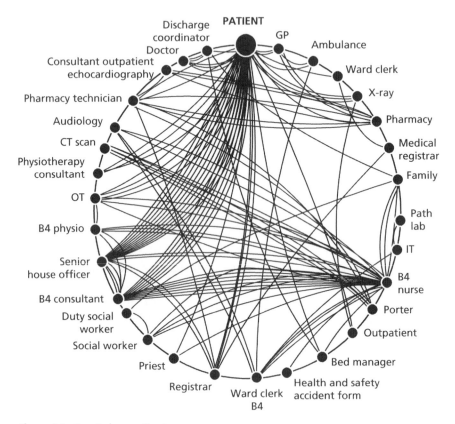

Figure 3.1. Toyota in your Trust

More of the Same

Has health care really been 'transformed'? The concept of organizational transformation has not been adequately defined and is rarely tested empirically. Ferlie et al. (1996: 94) identify and assess six criteria for judging transformation in health care. They conclude that, while there is evidence for transformation on some of these criteria, such as the introduction of new services and delivery models, there is much less evidence for a reconfiguration of power relationships, the development of a new ideology, or new interpretive frameworks. It is therefore possible to cite an equally compelling range of evidence to support the view that the NHS is increasingly hierarchical and rule-bound, and that doctors have strengthened their power base in these new structures, embedding more firmly the archetype of the professional bureaucracy. Although quasi-market pressures have generated local and interorganizational changes, these are counterbalanced by the continuing power of the Royal Colleges and other clinical professional bodies. In other words, it may be too early to claim that health care has been 'transformed'. What evidence is there for continuing bureaucratization?

KAFKAESQUE STRUCTURES

Foundation trusts, which ostensibly have greater autonomy in managing their affairs than non-foundation trusts, still sit at the base of the extended hierarchy of governance arrangements shown in Figure 3.2. Primary care trusts are responsible for commissioning care from secondary and tertiary providers who must therefore compete with each other for patient referrals from family doctors. Hospitals are performance-managed by their commissioning primary care trusts, which are in turn performance-managed by regional Strategic Health Authorities (of which there are ten in England). When things go wrong (waiting times targets for elective surgery are not being met, for example), Strategic Health Authorities and the foundation trust regulator, Monitor, can singly or together take direct action in relation to offending hospitals, and failures to comply with procedures or to meet national targets can lead to the dismissal of senior management.

The system also has a complex, overlapping, and confusing set of regulatory arrangements. In March 2007, *The Times* newspaper published a list of fifty-six inspection bodies each of which had a right to visit hospitals and other health-care providers, often without invitation or warning (Hawkes 2007*a*). If each of these bodies were to visit your hospital just once each year, then this would involve on average more than one inspection or audit a week, each requiring the time of managers and other staff, physical facilities, information, and accompanying paperwork. A report on 'removing unnecessary bureaucracy' by The NHS Confederation (2009: 2) cites, for example, the forty-seven 'core standards' for recruitment, training, and skill mix that are monitored by twenty-five bodies. These different bodies can, and do, ask for the same information, but in different formats, consuming even more administrative time, as providers have only limited rights to refuse these requests. These auditing and monitoring bodies merge and change their names and roles from time to time, simultaneously changing their information requirements, of course, and thus placing further burdens on providers.

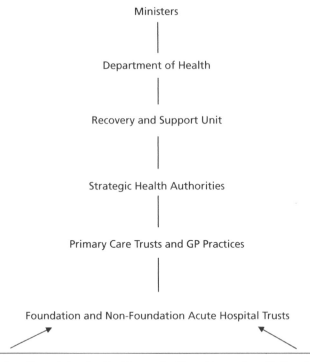

Ministers

Department of Health

Recovery and Support Unit

Strategic Health Authorities

Primary Care Trusts and GP Practices

Foundation and Non-Foundation Acute Hospital Trusts

Monitor; Commission for Healthcare Audit and Inspection; National Audit Commission; National Institute for Clinical Excellence; Health Select Committee; Public Accounts Committee; Clinical Networks; NHS Institute for Innovation and Improvement; Patient and Public Forums; Diversity Groups; numerous other regulatory bodies and inspection agencies

There are different forms of governance regulations cascading down through this structure standards, assurance frameworks, regulations, incentives, codes of conduct, and standing orders.

Figure 3.2. Health care governance structure

For example, in December 2008, the Care Quality Commission announced a change in its review policy in assuming, from April 2009, the responsibilities of the previous Healthcare Commission. In place of the 'annual health check', there would be 'periodic reviews', to identify problems and help to spread good practice. Assessments would be based on a combination of core standards, national priorities, financial management, and compliance with legislation. The performance of primary care trusts would be measured through (*a*) a 'world class commissioning assurance system', (*b*) performance against a 'vital signs indicator', (c) a value for money assessment (relying on a 'resources score' produced by the Audit Commission), and (d) 'an overarching framework spanning health and adult social care commissioning, to feed into the comprehensive area assessment' (Shantry 2008). Special topics would also be investigated, and in 2009 these were to include health inequalities, equality and human rights, and value for money. Different special topics would of course become the focus of attention in 2010, so preparatory and investigative work carried out in one year would not necessarily be relevant the next.

Seddon (2008), in particular, is convinced that the public sector in Britain today suffers badly from the regime of specifications, inspections, targets, and incentives to which it is subject. He highlights the waste incurred by employing people to develop 'guidance', and to devise standards, targets, and reporting schedules. Then there is the added cost of inspecting against specifications, involving more protocols, checklists, and of course training for the inspectors. On top of that, organizations spend considerable amounts of time and money preparing for those inspections. Noting that specialized consultancies have evolved to coach organizations on how to pass inspections, Seddon questions whether inspections have any impact on the organization's performance as viewed by the customer, client, or citizen. And where performance is assessed solely on compliance with standards and specifications with which people disagree, or find pointless, this leads to demoralization which represents another cost. Echoing the policy contradictions mentioned earlier, there is a difference of philosophy between performance management based on education and self-imposed professional standards, and performance management based on regulation and inspection. Seddon (2008: 195) observes: 'Talk to people who have been through an inspection and you will be struck by their sense of emptiness. They have been through all that preparation, worry, unhelpful bureaucracy and stress, only to be met by someone for a brief time who sat over them in apparently arbitrary judgement'.

The organizational complexity of the NHS can thus display a Kafkaesque quality. *The Times* newspaper, for example, became so excited about how 'red tape and a lack of leadership' was jeopardizing attempts to address childhood obesity in Britain that it published two of its own versions of a diagram originally produced by the National Audit Office, Audit Commission, and Healthcare Commission (National Audit Office 2006: 30), the first version appearing in February 2006 (on the front page, in colour), and the second in January 2007 (on an inside page, in black and white, shown in Figure 3.3). This pictures what the Audit Office called 'the current delivery chain', and the point of this, *The Times* observed, was to show that the national childhood obesity strategy was being delivered by five government departments, dozens of quangos, and hundreds of local bodies, whose various purposes and functions were unclear to each other and confused, thus making it difficult for them to work together effectively (Hawkes 2006, 2007b). The tangle of

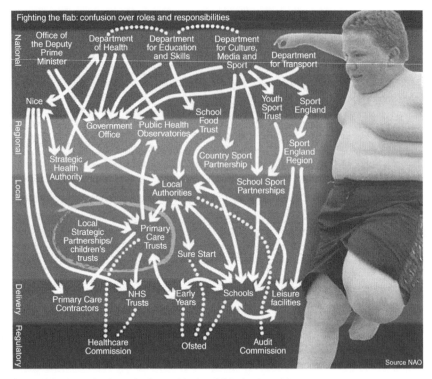

Figure 3.3. Organizations dealing with the child obesity crisis

bureaucracy was thus impeding progress in addressing a key dimension of national health-care strategy. The repeated failures of child protection in Britain have also been attributed, in part, to the complex organization structures and conflicting priorities of the various agencies, which do not share information or collaborate, leading to infant deaths (see Laming 2003, 2009, on the cases of Victoria Climbié and Baby Peter, respectively).

Foundation trusts appear to have been given an escape route from red tape in the autonomy that accompanies their status. Foundation trusts that meet their financial goals are 'rewarded' with lower levels of interference from the regulator, Monitor. Monitor encourages foundation trusts to manage their own businesses in a similar way. This is achieved by the introduction of service-line reporting structures, based on 'clinical business units' run by senior medical staff with appropriate dedicated professional management support (Monitor 2007). Clinical business units that meet their targets, including financial goals, will in turn be relatively free from management intervention, and many medical staff regard this development as a way to regain decision-making power previously lost to management, thus strengthening this dimension of the professional bureaucracy. There is other evidence for the continuing dominance of medical power. Sir Gerry Robinson, a private sector 'management guru', was sent into Rotherham General Hospital in Yorkshire in 2006 for six months, in an attempt to reduce waiting times. Echoing the findings of the Griffiths report (DHSS 1983), he observed the lack of effective management, noting that 'consultants are a law unto themselves' (BBC 2007). Recent research with a wider range of organizations confirms this finding (Fitzgerald et al. 2006), producing robust evidence of poor relationships within and between groups of doctors, which impact detrimentally on the processes of improving patient care. But while management were aware of these issues, they expressed the view that it was difficult to intervene, or they 'dared' not interfere. Two decades of change thus appear to have had little impact on this aspect of the professional bureaucracy.

MANAGING BY NUMBERS

The NHS Plan (Department of Health 2000) was a departure for the health service in many regards, but one of the most controversial innovations was the introduction of numerous and detailed measurable performance targets. An apocryphal (but plausible) tale has the chief executive of the service at the time debating the wisdom of this approach with the minister for health who simply kept repeating, 'there will be targets'. *The Plan* identified over 300 targets, most with deadlines. Waiting times, to see a hospital consultant, for diagnostic testing, and for treatment, were among the most politically sensitive and significant. The overarching aim of *The Plan* was to develop a patient-centred service. Lengthy waiting times had become a major source of public concern and complaint, and therefore became a key political goal as well as an operational focus. Targets have had opposing effects. On the one hand, many targets were regarded as politically inspired, with no clinical basis, thus diverting attention and resources from patients in need. On the other hand, the changes that were required in order to achieve those targets were responsible for numerous innovations and significant service improvements. A participant in one of our studies recently observed that, as a lead infection control nurse, she would probably not have been able to argue for the resources and actions required to reduce the levels of health care acquired infections (clostridium difficile and MRSA) in her hospital without the presence of closely monitored national targets (monitored by government and the media).

The Healthcare Commission published its first league tables in 2006 based on quality indicators in its 'annual health check', rating trusts as 'excellent', 'good', 'fair', or 'weak'. In 2008, the government's *Next Stage Review* (Department of Health 2008), led by a surgeon, Lord Ara Darzi, proposed new structures (polyclinics) and policies (emphasizing patient safety and quality of care), but promised 'no new targets'. Hospitals were nevertheless to be measured on patient satisfaction, which would affect their funding. However, within a matter of weeks, the Department of Health published on its website a range of over 400 'care quality indicators' or 'clinical quality metrics' (well, not 'targets' then) from which trusts could choose. This 'freedom' to select locally significant targets was of course accompanied by 'principles for indicator selection', and a briefing on 'the framework for measurement and improvement' complete with a four-tier 'quality pyramid' showing team, local, regional, and national evidence-based indicators or 'example products' (NHS Information Centre 2008). Towards the end of 2008, management briefings by staff from the foundation trust regulator, Monitor, indicated that, while hospitals were of course absolutely free to choose the indicators on which they wished to be measured, taking local considerations into account, they also made it clear that 'we would expect to see' indicators relating to safety, clinical effectiveness, and patient experience (the latter being a *Next Stage* priority). The NHS Information Centre report (2009) on 'indicators for quality improvement' is 600 pages long.

COMPASSION 2.0

Here is an iconic example of further bureaucratization under the guise of the radically new. Demonstrating how embedded the concepts of targets and measurement have become, in June 2008, the health minister used the occasion of a speech to the NHS Confederation to announce a new initiative, to measure the quality of nursing. The background to this initiative lay with concern that the emphasis on meeting targets, redesigning patient pathways, reducing waiting times, and treating patients more rapidly had led to a lack of concern with the 'human' aspects of care (Goodrich and Cornwell 2008). The *Next Stage* review proposed to measure quality of care, and one of the dimensions that is now politically fashionable concerns the display of 'compassion', defined here as, 'the human quality of understanding suffering in others and wanting to do something about it' (Youngson 2008: 2).

Has the health-care system become less compassionate? Youngson (2008: 4) observes that a nurse who pauses for 10 minutes to speak with a patient is more likely to be reprimanded than rewarded. However, as there are no hard data, the obvious response is to generate some, and thus to measure compassion. Thus, anxiety about the effects of focusing on too many targets leads inexorably to the generation of more targets. In June 2008, the Department of Health set out plans to develop metrics to assess the effectiveness and safety of nursing practice, including 'how compassionately care has been delivered', a process supported by the Royal College of Nursing, as this would provide recognition for the quality of nursing care, and benchmark work on individual wards. Indicators were to focus on three themes (Department of Health online News Distribution Service, 15 December 2008). Two of these concerned effectiveness (nutrition, managing pain, hygiene) and safety (falls, infection rates). The third concerned 'compassionate care', this time defined as 'measuring whether patients are treated with compassion, and whether they are kept informed of what is happening with their treatment'. The current workload and other pressures on nurses are also relevant to this initiative. Developments in health-care staffing have intensified nursing work. Health-care assistants have been employed ostensibly to relieve nurses from personal and non-clinical aspects of care. Consequently, nurses are now fully occupied with more difficult and stressful clinical tasks, with even less time for idle chatter with patients (Allen and Hughes 2002).

The initiative raises significant logistical and ethical questions concerning how the construct of compassion is to be measured, by whom, how often and where, and against what standards or benchmarks. The appropriate degree of compassion, however defined, may vary across contexts and between patients who may each have different views on what compassion involves and how much of it they want given their current condition and circumstances. And what is to become of the otherwise highly competent and effective nurse, doctor, or manager who apparently displays a 'compassion deficit'? Relatively trivial concerns such as these will doubtless be overtaken by the political pressure to find and implement a solution, leading to the publication of regular 'compassion league tables' in the national press in the near future.

In sum, complex national organization structures, national and local governance regimes, the burden of regulation and monitoring, the weight of targets and performance measurement, and the opportunities for medical staff to regain decision-making and resource-allocating power from management, in combination, suggest that the archetype of the professional bureaucracy remains intact, despite the many other adjustments that have been made to the system over the past decade or so. Kitchener's 'no change' conclusion (1999) continues to find support.

Living in Harmony

With evidence on both sides of the 'bureaucracy-busting, bureaucracy-building' debate, why must we settle for one or the other, rather than for both? While some commentators have focused on observing shifts from one holistic archetypal form to another distinctly different form, others recognize the coexistence of organizational archetypes.

Greenwood and Hinings (1988, 1993) are concerned to understand change with reference to 'design archetypes and tracks', defined as holistic organizational patternings or configurations. The meaning and coherence of these configurations are underpinned by 'interpretive schema'—the ideas, values, and beliefs of those who design and work within them. Tracks include inertia, aborted excursions, reorientations, and unresolved excursions. They argue that the track followed by an organization is a function of the degree of alignment or compatibility between structures and contingency constraints, the pattern of commitment to prevailing and alternative interpretive schemes, and the incidence of dissatisfaction of the interests of powerful groups. They identify two archetypes: corporate bureaucracy and heteronymous professional bureaucracy, and focus on change involving movement from one archetype to another. They assume 'archetypal coherence', or at least moves towards that condition. It may be especially problematic to achieve such coherence in a large heterogeneous organization such as the NHS which combines primary, acute, and tertiary care sectors.

In contrast, Cooper et al. (1996) discuss how archetypes change through shifts in discourse, with interpretive schemes jostling for supremacy. Critically, one archetype may not sweep away another, but one may be 'layered' on another. While the concept of 'layering' (Cooper et al. 1996) implies a degree of separation, those forms appear to be intertwined in a more complex and fluid manner. This argument challenging the notion of archetypal coherence is similar to Clegg's more dynamic concept (1981: 552) of superimposition or 'sedimentation' which also allows for unanticipated consequences and contradictions.

Olsen (2006: 18) thus argues that, 'bureaucracy is not *the* way to organize public administration, for all kinds of tasks and under all circumstances. Bureaucratic organization is part of a repertoire of overlapping, supplementary, and competing forms coexisting in contemporary democracies, and so are market and network organization'. He thus rejects the fashionable 'dinosaur scenario' in which the undesirable presence of obsolete bureaucratic organizational forms and their accompanying bureaucrats inevitably wither and disappear because they are incompatible with a complex, individualistic, rapidly changing society. Bureaucracy, market, and network forms have been seen as alternatives based on hierarchical authority, competition, and collaboration, respectively. These are simply different mechanisms for mobilizing resources while achieving rationality, accountability, and control. But Olsen (2006: 16) also observes that, 'In modern, pluralistic societies with a variety of criteria for success and different causal understandings, it is, however, unlikely that public administration can be organized on the basis of one principle alone. An administration that simultaneously has to cope with contradictory demands and standards, balance system coordination, and legitimate diversity organizationally and technologically is likely to require more complexity than a single principle can provide'. In other words the notion of convergence on a single homogeneous archetype is inappropriate.

It is helpful to remember that, while bureaucracy has become something of a hate term in contemporary popular discourse, the Weberian archetype has potential strengths, with regard to order, stability, predictability, standardization, and control. In a system where policy dictates equality of access, consistency of treatment, and standards of performance, a degree of bureaucracy could be considered to be desirable, if not essential (Leavitt 2005).

Bureaucracy is popularly associated with inflexibility. However, Briscoe (2007) inverts this view, showing how the temporal flexibility of professional service workers can be enhanced by intensifying bureaucratic processes. Temporal flexibility concerns the scope to adjust work schedules to accommodate personal circumstances, and the professional service workers that Briscoe studied were (American) primary care doctors. Professional service work is seen as temporally inflexible because it requires responses to the unpredictable needs of clients with whom professionals have specific personal relationships, and variable working practices make it difficult to hand a client on to a colleague. The processes that can increase flexibility in this context include managing client expectations by routinizing the 'service encounter', the use of rules, procedures, and decision protocols to standardize the handling of common conditions, and codifying client knowledge by developing knowledge management systems. This formalization of working practices, relying on rules and procedures, represents increased bureaucracy and hierarchical control. For many (not all) of the doctors in Briscoe's study, however, these constraints were offset by increased temporal flexibility, and the protocols were themselves flexible in response to circumstances, and not treated as binding. In sum, those organizational processes generate a more bureaucratic, and more flexible, workplace, and Briscoe concludes that this applies to professional services in general, not just medicine.

Nobody in the early twenty-first century is going to admit in public to being enthusiastic about bureaucracy. Commentators working with a narrative perspective (e.g. Czarniawska 1998; Buchanan and Dawson 2007) observe that power often lies with those who can tell a good story. Exploring 'New Labour' health-care policies, Morrell (2006) argues that the motifs of 'freedom' for Foundation Trusts, 'clinical governance' for staff, and 'choice' for patients are part of a narrative of inevitable progress and radical reform emphasizing emancipation, progress, and duty. These motifs, however, do not coincide with the empirical evidence. The 'freedoms' of Foundation Trusts are tightly constrained; 'clinical governance' is a clumsy and ambiguous concept directed more towards avoiding litigation than improving the quality of care; 'choice' of treatment locations is by definition based on inequality between providers (contrary to NHS core values), and requires access to adequate information and transport which many patients lack. Nevertheless, these motifs lend credibility and novelty to the government narrative—they produce a good story—which glosses over the tensions, ambiguities, and complexities that might compromise the espoused outcomes.

We can treat the question of 'archetypal' change as a matter for academic debate to be resolved with empirical evidence. But in health care in particular, the archetype concept needs to be understood as a socio-political construct which, over time, is formed and reformed at the various intersections between government policy, public expectations, the pronouncements of government and opposition ministers, and media accounts. There may be a process of gradual change, where discourses that were at first rejected are gradually accepted over time (Ferlie et al. 2009). What the health-care system is, or may be, therefore, is not always as significant or as influential as what the public, government, and media want it to be and to become. Viewed through this perceptual, narrative-based, aspirational lens, archetypal coherence cannot be taken for granted, or even expected, and the paths that an organization follows in this respect may be multiple, circular, layered, and sedimented, rather than singular and linear.

A Choice of Endings

This story offers a choice of three possible endings.

First, we can conclude that, while the process may be far from complete, and although pockets of bureaucracy remain, the quasi-market archetype of commercial health-care organization and delivery is now well established. This can clearly be seen in current policies (patient choice, independent treatment centres), structures (foundation trusts, commissioning), and in the thoroughly commercial discourse that colours the management conversation, strategic planning, board-level decision, and action. Arguments to the contrary rely on the selective use of evidence, on outliers, on the stubborn remnants of an outdated regime.

Second, we can conclude that, despite a string of policy interventions designed to establish internal competition in health-care delivery, the organizational archetype of the professional bureaucracy in health care is now more firmly embedded than ever. This can clearly be seen in current policies (targets, indicators, demands for compliance), structures (governance hierarchy, organizational proliferation), and in the overwhelming burden of regulation, audit, and review. Recent policy and structural changes, particularly relating to foundation trust status, external and internal financial monitoring, and the development of service line reporting systems around clinical business units, have served either to return power from management to medicine, or to strengthen the existing medical power base.

Third, we can conclude that different adapted forms of the quasi-market and professional bureaucracy archetypes coexist, both empirically, and in the narratives that are spun around the service. These archetypes are impure and unstable, lacking permanence and coherence, varying from place to place, fluctuating through time in response to the constantly changing mix of national policy, local priority, and the winds of fashion with regard to both medical and managerial practice. There is rarely an evidence base for shifts in government policy, thus contributing to the often dysfunctional combination of archetypal forms. However, this fluidity permits a range of different and credible narratives that serve the interests of their authors at different points in time, with different audiences.

We can see, therefore, a more or less traditional archetype 'accessorized' with the trappings (structures, processes, discourse) of modern commercial enterprise. But this should not be dismissed as a cynical conclusion, for a number of reasons. One is that the accessories have affected substance as well as form, for example, contributing to reductions in waiting times and rates of infection and to overall improvements in access to and quality of patient care (see, e.g. Nicholson 2009). A second reason is that the accessories, while shifting power in the system, have also increased transparency (activity levels, costs, clinical outcomes). A third reason is that while there are still multiple targets and constant performance monitoring, the nature of the targets themselves has changed. The slide from 'targets' to quality service frameworks is a subtle but significant movement. A final reason, moving beyond the perennial debate about 'private versus public' and 'market forces versus social responsibility' in health care, is that the accessorized bureaucracy may be a good solution.

IT'S THE SENTIMENT, STUPID

Given the depth of public attachment, it is essential that the service is *perceived* to be working well and improving. Governments have to be cautious about criticizing or attacking the health service, lest they be seen as (or perhaps more significantly, *reported* as) threatening to turn the system over to private sector providers. Any criticism, therefore, must be accompanied by a policy to rectify the deficiency. It is thus in the interest not only of politicians, but also of healthcare managers, research academics, and the media commentariat in general to be able to emphasize departures and innovations, the different and the new. In other words, the accessorized bureaucracy is the new archetype, the new interpretive framework which gives us a traditional, stable, and predictable system that is simultaneously characterized by innovation and radical change. If this approach meets the criteria of (*a*) sustaining public sentiment and the willingness to pay for the service through general taxation, (*b*) delivering a service that is perceived to be effective and subject to continuous improvement, and (*c*) limiting the threat to political careers, then this archetype could be considered appropriate and successful, and should perhaps be endorsed, not spurned.

☐ NOTES

1. We would like to thank Stewart Clegg, David Denyer, Martin Harris, Donna Ladkin, Colin Pilbeam, and an anonymous reviewer for their advice and comments on earlier drafts of this chapter. The gaps and flaws that remain, however, are the responsibility of the authors.

☐ BIBLIOGRAPHY

Addicott, R., McGivern, G. and Ferlie, E. (2007) The Distortion of a Managerial Technique? The Case of Clinical Networks in UK Health Care, *British Journal of Management*, 18(1): 93–105.

Allen, D. and Hughes, D. (2002) *Nursing and the Division of Labour in Health Care*, Basingstoke and New York: Palgrave, Macmillan.

Bate, P., Bevan, H. and Robert, G. (2005) *Towards a Million Change Agents: A Review of the Social Movements Literature*, Leicester: NHS Modernisation Agency.

BBC (2007) *Can Gerry Robinson Fix the NHS?* (three episodes, Monday 8, Tuesday 9, and Wednesday 10 January), London: British Broadcasting Corporation.

Benders, J. and Morita, M. (2004) Changes in Toyota Motors' Operations Management, *International Journal of Production Research*, 42(3): 433–44.

Briscoe, F. (2007) From Iron Cage to Iron Shield? How Bureaucracy Enables Temporal Flexibility for Professional Service Workers, *Organization Science*, 18(2): 297–314.

Buchanan, D.A. and Dawson, P. (2007) Discourse and Audience: Organizational Change as Multi-Story Process, *Journal of Management Studies*, 44(5): 669–86.

——Addicott, R., Fitzgerald, L., Ferlie, E. and Baeza, J. (2007) Nobody in Charge: Distributed Change Agency in Healthcare, *Human Relations*, 60(7): 1065–90.

Burns, T. and Stalker, G.M. (1961) *The Management of Innovation*, London: Tavistock Publications.

Calman, K. and Hine, D. (1995) *A Policy Framework for Commissioning Cancer Services*, London: Department of Health.

Clegg, S.R. (1981) Organization and Control, *Administrative Science Quarterly*, 26(4): 545–62.

Cooper, D.J., Hinings, B., Greenwood, R. and Brown, J.L. (1996) Sedimentation and Transformation in Organizational Change: The Case of Canadian Law Firms, *Organization Studies*, 17(4): 623–47.

Czarniawska, B. (1998) *A Narrative Approach to Organization Studies*, Thousand Oaks, California: Sage Publications.

Denis, J.-L., Lamothe, L. and Langley, A. (2001) The Dynamics of Collective Leadership and Strategic Change in Pluralistic Organizations, *Academy of Management Journal*, 44(4): 809–37.

Department of Health (2000) *The NHS Plan: A Plan for Investment, A Plan for Reform*, London: Department of Health.

——(2007*a*) *World Class Commissioning: Competencies*, London: Department of Health.

——(2007*b*) *The Operating Framework for the NHS in England 2008/09*, London: Department of Health.

——(2008) *High Quality Care For All: NHS Next Stage Review Final Report*, London: Department of Health (cmnd 7432).

DHSS (1983) *NHS Management Inquiry (The Griffiths Report)*, London: Department of Health and Social Security, Her Majesty's Stationery Office.

Donaldson, L. (2000) *An Organization With a Memory*, London: Department of Health/The Stationery Office.

Dr Foster Intelligence (2006) *The Intelligent Board*, London: Dr Foster Intelligence Unit.

Ferlie, E., Ashburner, L., Fitzgerald, L. and Pettigrew, A.M. (1996) *The New Public Management in Action*, Oxford: Oxford University Press.

——Fitzgerald, L., McGivern, G. and Dopson, S. (2009) *Networks in Health Care: A Comparative Study of their Management, Impact and Performance*, London: Draft Final Report to the National Institute for Health Research Service Delivery and Organization R&D Programme.

Fitzgerald, L., Lilley, C., Ferlie, E., Addicott, R., McGivern, G. and Buchanan, D. (2006) *Managing Change and Role Enactment in the Professionalized Organization*, London: National Institute for Health Research Service Delivery and Organization R&D Programme; www.sdo. nihr.ac.uk/sdo212002.html.

Gainsbury, S. (2009) 20 Trusts Set to Miss Foundation Trust Deadline, *Health Service Journal*, 12 February, www.hsj.co.uk/printpage.html?pageid=1988005.

Goodrich, J. and Cornwell, J. (2008) *Seeing the Person in the Patient: The Point of Care Review Paper*, London: The King's Fund.

Greenwood, R. and Hinings, C.R. (1988) Organizational Design Types, Tracks and the Dynamics of Strategic Change, *Organization Studies*, 9(3): 293–316.

————(1993) Understanding Strategic Change: The Contribution of Archetypes, *Academy of Management Journal*, 36(5): 1052–81.

Hamilton, P., Spurgeon, P., Clark, J., Dent, J. and Armit, K. (2008) *Engaging Doctors: Can Doctors Influence Organisational Performance*, London: Academy of Medical Royal Colleges and NHS Institute for Innovation and Improvement.

Hawkes, N. (2006) Children Grow Fatter as the Experts Dither, *The Times*, 28 February, 1.

——(2007a) Number of Inspections Choking Life out of NHS, *The Times*, 8 March, 24.

——(2007b) Government is Slammed for Dithering on Deadline to Curb Childhood Obesity, *The Times*, 25 January, 9.

Jones, D. and Mitchell, A. (2006) *Lean Thinking for the NHS*, London: The NHS Confederation.

Kanter, R.M. (1983) *The Change Masters: Corporate Entrepreneurs at Work*, London: George Allen & Unwin.

——(1989) *When Giants Learn to Dance: Mastering The Challenges of Strategy, Management, and Careers in the 1990s*, London: George Allen & Unwin.

Kelwell, B., Hawkins, C. and Ferlie, E. (2002) Calman-Hine Reassessed: A Survey of Cancer Network Development in England, 1999–2000, *Journal of Evaluation in Clinical Practice*, 8(3): 303–11.

Kitchener, M. (1999) All Fur Coat and No Knickers: Contemporary Organizational Change in United Kingdom Hospitals, in D.M. Brock, M.J. Powell and C.R. Hinings (eds), *Restructuring the Professional Organization: Accounting, Health Care and Law*, London and New York: Routledge, 183–248.

Laming, W. (2003) *The Victoria Climbié Inquiry*, Norwich: Her Majesty's Stationery Office.

——(2009) *The Protection of Children in England: A Progress Report*, London: The Stationery Office.

Leavitt, H.J. (2005) *Top Down: Why Hierarchies Are Here To Stay and How To Manage Them More Effectively*, Boston, Massachusetts: Harvard Business School Press.

Lister, S. (2006) Bloated NHS is to Receive the Tesco treatment, *The Times*, 15 June, 26.

Marks, L. and Hunter, D.J. (2005) *Practice Based Commissioning: Policy into Practice*, Stockton on Tees: Durham University Centre for Public Policy and Health.

Mintzberg, H. (1979) *The Structure of Organizations*, Englewood Cliffs, New Jersey: Prentice Hall.

Monitor (2007) *Guide to Implementing Service-Line Management*, London: Monitor: Independent Regulator of NHS Foundation Trusts.

Morrell, K. (2006) Policy as Narrative: New Labour's Reform of the National Health Service, *Public Administration*, 84(2): 367–85.

National Audit Office (2006) *Tackling Child Obesity: First Steps*, London: Audit Commission/ The Stationery Office.

NHS Information Centre (2008) *Next Stage Review Clinical Quality Metrics: Framework for Selecting Indicators for Engagement Process* (Phase 1), www.ic.nhs.uk/work-with-us/consultations/clinical-quality-indicators-survey (accessed 2 December 2008).

——(2009) *Indicators for Quality Improvement Report*, London: The Health and Social Care Information Centre.

NHS Institute for Innovation and Improvement (2008) *Medical Leadership Competency Framework*, Warwick: NHS Institute for Innovation and Improvement.

Nicholson, D. (2009) *The Year: NHS Chief Executive's Annual Report 2008/09*, London: Department of Health.

Olsen, J.P. (2006) Maybe It is Time to Rediscover Bureaucracy, *Journal of Public Administration Research and Theory*, 16(1): 1–24.

O'Reilly, D. and Reed, M. (forthcoming) Leaderism: An Evolution of Managerialism in UK Public Service Reform, *Public Administration*.

Sambrook, S. (2005) Management Development in the NHS: Nurses and Managers, Discourses and Identities, *Journal of European Industrial Training*, 30(1): 48–64.

Seddon, J. (2008) *Systems Thinking in the Public Sector*, Axminster: Triarchy Press.

Shantry, C. (2008) Annual Health Check to be Replaced with Periodic Reviews, *Health Services Journal*, 18 December, www.hsj.co.uk/printpage.html?pageid=1954203.

Shepherd, A. (2008) Finance: Make your Business Boom, *Health Services Journal*, 18 August, www.hsj.co.uk/printpage.html?pageid=1767141.

The NHS Confederation (2009) *What's It All For?: Removing Unnecessary Bureaucracy in Regulation*, London: The NHS Confederation and Independent Healthcare Advisory Services.

Weber, M. (1947) *The Theory of Social and Economic Organization* (A.M. Henderson and T. Parsons, trans.), Oxford: Oxford University Press.

Womack, J.P., Jones, D.T. and Roos, D. (1990) *The Machine that Changed the World: The Triumph of Lean Production*, New York: Macmillan.

Youngson, R. (2008) *Compassion in Healthcare: The Missing Dimension of Healthcare Reform?*, London: NHS Confederation.

4 Applying Soft Bureaucracy to Rhetorics of Choice: The UK NHS 1983–2007

EWEN SPEED

Introduction

Public sector health-care provision in the United Kingdom is a regime dominated by rhetorics and practices of choice.[1] The development of new management processes, originating in the Griffiths report (Griffiths, 1983), underpins much of the choice agenda. This chapter considers these processes of reform up to the National Health Service (NHS) 'next stage' review published in 2008. The Darzi review[2] (as it has come to be known) is dominated by two inter-related features. One of these is the principle of post-bureaucratic network governance, with more health-care decisions being taken at a local level, and with the empowered consumer/patient located at the centre of policy thinking. A second, related feature is a focus on quality and choice as the key determinants of effective clinical treatment. I will argue that the choice agenda has evolved cumulatively within a programme of health services reform that has been designed as much to limit the autonomy of professionals and increase control of health expenditure as it has been to empower consumers. This chapter identifies several distinct phases, or shifts of emphasis in the development of these reforms. Working within a broadly discursive frame of reference, the chapter considers the ways in which these shifts have affected service delivery within the NHS.

From 1983 onwards UK policy makers were committed to the idea that principles underlying private sector management offered an alternative, better means of organizing public services. The inherent assumption is that increased competition equals increased quality and efficiency, hence increased effectiveness. From 1990 onwards evolving market mechanisms introduced a range of new, and even more explicitly 'post-bureaucratic' ways of organizing health service provision.

This drive for effectiveness and efficiency in public services was neither new nor was it particularly noteworthy. What is remarkable is the way in which processes designed to engender or increase efficiency and effectiveness have been articulated as novel and distinct innovations (or technologies) aimed at improving 'the patient experience'. These different articulations point to some of the difficulties and sensitivities that successive UK governments faced as they reformed the NHS. Consideration of these processes also highlights the changing ways in which bureaucracy is used by governments as a command and control mechanism. In these efficiency drives, bureaucratic processes are simultaneously held up as either the answer to, or the cause of, perceived ineffectiveness and inefficiency.

Principles of choice and competition are held up as foils to inefficiency and they have been utilized by both the left and the right, in ideologically different ways. Notions of choice and competition have been rejected by the political left for going too far down a road of privatization and vilified by the right for not going far enough down that path. In this context, choice equals competition (or 'exit', cf. Hirschman 1970). Framing choice in this way gives primacy to the idea that the individual consumer is sovereign, and therefore the locus around which health care markets are constructed. Choice in a health-care context cannot, however, be regarded as the same order of choice that is so readily associated with neo-liberal economics. The choosing health consumer is constructed differently from the rational choice individual of economic theory. It is from *homo economicus* that discourses of responsibility and patient choice (as well as rights) come to supplant the citizen with the citizen-consumer. But patient choices are in practice limited in a number of ways: most importantly, patients cannot choose which treatment they receive. This is the domain of clinical practice into which principles of choice cannot be extended. Organizations such as the National Institute for Health and Clinical Excellence (NICE) might find themselves over-burdened with requests from patients for treatments which have not been clinically trialled. As such, this particular articulation of choice needs to be regarded as a secondary feature of these market mechanisms, rather than a constitutive component of the market itself. In other words, choice in the UK public health-care system is not based on free market principles, but is much more tightly delimited, and based primarily on choice of provider. In this context, the functions of the market cannot be read as accomplishing the simple provision of consumer choice. Quite how choice can be shown to fulfil a regulatory role is examined later in the chapter.

Another related problem is the nature of the reform process. A key development, discussed in the organizational studies and sociology of health and illness literatures, is the rise of the New Public Management (NPM) as the dominant approach to the organization of UK health care services. This marks the historical point at which principles of neo-liberalism entered the lexicon of UK health-care provision. Central to this project was the creation of new modes of managerialism, what Willmott (1993) describes as the prescription of corporate culture. Over the period from 1983 to 2007 there are a number of reforms that can be read as iterations, and indeed re-iterations, aimed at constructing 'exit' or competition mechanisms that operate in a public service context (most notably the market reforms contained in the 1990 *National Health Service & Community Care Act*). For the purpose of this chapter, the argument that I pursue is that neo-liberal public service reforms have been concerned with efforts to introduce effective exit mechanisms into monopoly provider organizations, such as the NHS. Their import is that they are the stick, rather than the carrot, that is held over health-care provision, as a means of effecting reform and controlling expenditure. It must be noted at this juncture that I do not intend to pursue this argument through a consideration of the economic data of financial returns and the like. The argument being presented here locates these processes and changes at a discursive level. The focus is on the ways in which processes and techniques of command and control can be extrapolated from policy frames that share a genealogical kinship with processes of NPM reform across respective UK governments from traditionally right and left wing positions.

The three key problematics considered in this chapter are (*a*) the creation of markets in health-care provision, which in turn, are predicated upon (*b*) a tightly de-limited conception of the choosing consumer, in turn predicated on (*c*) NPM reforms of public services.

A Caveat on Health Activism

Before going any further, I want to offer a caveat regarding health-care consumers, and more particularly health-care consumer groups. Many health activists—both in the United Kingdom and in the United States—have taken up the notion of the health-care consumer, and used it to demand more say in their treatment and generally to improve the services available to them. There are many who argue that the use of the term health-care consumer has its origins in health activism of the 1960s and 1970s (Kaufmann 1999; Tomes 2006). In the United Kingdom, there are many consumer groups that work to improve service provision, and by extension, the lives of service users

(Speed 2002, 2006, 2007). I do not want to criticize these organizations, the work they do or the progress they have made. However there is a clear need to consider the organizational implications that arise from the shift away from the traditional 'patient' (with citizen rights to medical treatment) to a health-care consumer whose entitlement to health care is predicated upon self-surveillance of their health behaviours.

Health activists have used the term 'consumer' to exploit new spaces that have opened up in the organization of health care, and it can be argued that some, though not all, consumer discourse in health care has been used by health-care activists—for example people in the psychiatric survivor movement—to counter the hegemonic dominance of the medical professions. Consumer discourse, in this context, can be regarded as part of a bottom-up movement with principles of empowerment and active participation at its core. The link between the NPM approach and the health activist approach is the complex issue of entitlement.

A Sense of Entitlement

Much has been written about the changing modes of citizenship, as we switch from citizens with rights to citizen-consumers with rights and responsibilities (Forster and Gabe 2008). The responsibilities of health-care consumers are evident in the manner in which the public have been encouraged, through successive public health campaigns, to drink sensibly, eat sensibly, take regular exercise, and stop smoking. The New Public Health (Petersen and Lupton 1996) agenda makes these 'lifestyle choices' the duty of the responsible health-care consumer, with the caveat that consumption must be controlled if they are to attain 'optimal' levels of health and well-being. The focus on making 'healthy' choices, coupled with the provision of tightly de-limited modes of choice in the provision of services invokes a discursive association between lifestyle choices, (responsible) consumption, and the market. Health and choice/choice and health become inextricably bound. The health consumer comes to expect choice, and even to demand choice from their provider. Regardless of whether this demand comes from the service user or from the state, in both instances it is the front-line professional that bears the brunt of the raised sense of entitlement.

It is not clear whether the consumer activists opened up the social space and this was exploited by the entrepreneurial bureaucrats of the state, or whether these health-care consumers were simply co-opted into a wider project of social change. However, this latter scenario is more persuasive when one considers the global rise of NPM and the central role that consumers of services have within that project. NPM is an elusive concept and one that tends to polarize opinion. Dunleavy and Hood (1994) describe NPM as a process aimed at making the public sector less distinctive from the private sector (in this context, NPM can be regarded as an attempt to redraw the boundaries of civil society, or more accurately, to shrink it, so that more aspects of civil society become tied to economic transactions). Dunleavy and Hood also describe NPM as a process of going 'down grid', reducing the extent to which discretionary power is limited by uniform and general rules of procedure (a de-regulation of bureaucracy). The chapter does not discuss these procedures in any great detail-but it does show how the three problematics noted above (see page 83) have impinged on the autonomy of health care professionals.

New Public Management in the UK NHS

The most visible early manifestation of NPM inspired reform in the UK health-care system is the 1983 *NHS Management Inquiry* report, compiled by the Deputy Chairman and Managing Director of Sainsbury's, Roy Griffiths. Other members of the team included a British Telecom board member, the Group Finance Director at United Biscuits, and the Chairman of Television South West (Edwards and Fall 2005). The Griffiths report coincided with a range of efficiency initiatives being implemented by Sir Derek Rayner including the early development of performance indicators (Bristol Royal Infirmary: 2001). High-profile figures from the UK private sector were given the job of creating new management structures (staffed by non-medical managers) where before there had been only self-regulation by professional groups.

Griffiths (1983: 11) argued that the NHS lacked 'a clearly defined general management function... By general management we mean the responsibility drawn together in one person, at different levels of organisation, for planning, implementation and control of performance'. The inquiry drew parallels with the world of business management, where managers were 'concerned with levels of service, quality of product, meeting budgets, cost improvement, productivity, motivating and rewarding staff, research and development and the long term viability of the undertaking' (Ibid.: 10). The Griffiths report marks a milestone in the move towards the managerialisation of clinical practice, but the initial target was not, indeed could not, be identified as such. The report notes the lack of "precise management objectives," (*ibid*. p. 10) and it also notes that "there is little measurement of health output," (*ibid.* p.10). Of those foci listed in the report, only the rather oblique nods towards the 'quality of product', 'productivity', and 'long-term viability' might be construed as indicating a concern with clinical practice. The emphasis is firmly on the managerial structures that surround clinical practice rather than clinical practice itself. The new managerial regime being proposed was concerned with prioritizing economic rather than clinical management (but with an implicit proviso that with budgetary control, clinical control was likely to follow, through measurement of health output).

For example, the report sets out a list of recommendations most of which are centred on the introduction of new management structures and controls. One such structure was the proposed Health Services Supervisory Board (HSSB) concerned with the 'determination of purpose, objectives and direction for the NHS, approval of overall budget, strategic decisions and receiving reports on performance and other evaluations' (Ibid.: 3). The report also called for the creation of a new NHS management board that would implement policies approved by the HSSB, control performance and 'give leadership to [the] management of the NHS', (Ibid.: 3). Here again, reference to clinical practice is notable by its absence; the emphasis is on developing an administrative bureaucracy that will operate in tandem with the medical bureaucracy. This strategy was central to the establishment of these processes, but as later events demonstrated, this focus on complementary hierarchies was not maintained. Griffiths also identified the need for management structures at district and regional levels. These organizations were entrusted with the task of embedding and sedimenting the requisite management processes at their respective levels. We see in this activity the disaggregation of separable functions (Dunleavy and Hood 1994). This disaggregation breaks treatment processes down into discrete quantifiable components, helping to ensure that the doctrine of (management by accounting) was spread nationally, regionally and locally.[3]

The levels of autonomy and independence enjoyed by British medical professionals at this time were relatively high. Harrison and Ahmad (2000: 132) characterise the system of management that was in place pre-Griffiths as one of multidisciplinary consensus management that was akin to the 'practice of diplomacy'. Doctors regulated their own members and responsibility for the budgetary consequences of clinical decisions lay with the region or with local NHS organizations, not with individual practitioners.[4] Any management roles that existed prior to Griffiths had very little influence over doctors and their clinical decision making; any regulation that mattered (i.e. clinical regulation) was done by personnel with a medical background. The Griffiths report changed this, creating the conditions of possibility for non-clinically trained personnel to engage in management practices (mainly budgetary practices) that had the capacity to affect clinical decision making, albeit in a non-clinical way. Griffiths introduced the idea that general managers would replace the previous consensual management approach.[5] Sheaff and colleagues (2003: 409) argue that NPM reforms in UK health care took the novel step of embedding the clinical self-regulatory mechanisms 'more fully within lay-controlled organisational structures'. The consensual management processes were sequestered from professional groupings and replaced by a lay management structure that was not dependent on clinical knowledge. Harrison and Ahmad (2000: 132) characterize this turn of events as a 'major defeat for the medical profession'. As such, Griffiths marks an epistemic break in the organization of UK health care. It marks an NPM-inspired attack on clinical autonomy, but it was an attack that did not cite clinical autonomy as its target. Rather it sets up a straw-man: the discourse of change and reform was couched in the rhetoric of clinical *performance* management, not clinical *practice* management; it is the lack of management structure that is the initial target. The creation of management positions in non-clinical roles means that initially they only manage non-clinical matters. At this time, it was only possible for the new level of managers to address (and re-construct) the bureaucratic framework within which clinical practice takes place; they could not change the clinical practices themselves. It is worthy of note that very few of the new managers came from a business background.

This creation of executive managers can be read a move away from a situation characterized by normative trust to a situation characterized by political control (Reed, 2001). The previous bureaucratic regime, predicated on management by consensus, may have been efficient and effective enough in relation to clinical practice, but it was hugely problematic in relation to fiscal practice. The blurring of the distinction between competing forms of bureaucracy—for example, professional versus managerial—can be understood as part of a longer term transition whereby the imposition of an external management culture initiates the process of full-scale NPM reform. This is what Dunleavy and Hood (1994) describe as an 'incubated' mode of reform, designed to control practice through budgets.

The new form of management introduced by Griffith was one that clearly set its limits such that it accomplished its goals whilst keeping all of the associated players in the game. To clarify: the history of reform in the NHS has long been characterised by running battles between the medical profession and successive UK governments. A committed and long-term campaign against the Griffiths reforms by the medical regulatory bodies would arguably have functioned to obviate or delay substantially any further NPM-inspired reforms. In the event, change had to be introduced incrementally, not just to keep everyone at the table, but to ensure that everyone stayed in the game.

Dunleavy and Hood (1994) identify five distinct criteria that have defined the shift from 'old public administration' towards 'new public management'. These are firstly, making budgets transparent for account-ing; secondly, re-conceptualizing organizations as characterized by low-trust transactions rather than processes of high-trust communitarian-ism—low-trust principal/agent transactions are much easier to manage; thirdly, disaggregating functions into quasi-market forms; fourthly, creating conditions for competition between public agencies; and lastly, de-concentrating provider roles and increasing exit/competition—rather than voice—options. The Griffiths report did not accomplish all of these substantive changes, but it did determine some vital 'conditions of possibility' for a distinctively new discourse of managerialism within the NHS. By 1988 the Griffiths reforms had only accomplished two of the five changes (transparent budgets and a move to low-trust transac-tions) noted by Dunleavy and Hood. However, the reforms established the preconditions that allowed the other three elements of reform to be introduced in subsequent years. In the first instance these reforms could only be introduced incrementally. By making the target of reform an administrative one, rather than a clinical one, it was much harder for clinical professionals to resist or contest these changes. As in other parts of the UK public sector, financial management emerges as a very substantial challenge to established professional norms and criteria of judgement.

These developments resonate strongly with Willmott's (1993) account of the management of culture as a key element of control in contemporary organizational life. The 'strengthening of corporate culture' is regarded by its advocates as a means of enhancing organizational performance by securing greater commitment and flexibility from employees. (Willmott 1993:515–516). The culture of management that was imposed on the NHS was based on externally generated atomistic targets and not on the extant norms of professional bureaucracy.

The NPM reforms of the initial Griffiths report (1983) created the struc-tural and discursive conditions for the second-stage changes that followed, most notably, the internal market posited by the second Griffiths report (1988). The introduction of the internal market mechanism can be seen as a key element linking the historic project of NPM reform to the emergence of the 'the choosing consumer' as a defining feature of contemporary UK health care.

The Fiscal Market

As noted above, the Griffiths report lead to changes that established some vital preconditions for subsequent phases of reform, but it was not until the publication of the 1990 *National Health Service & Community Care Act* that the idea of marketizing health care provision was enacted. The 1990 act emerged from a second Griffiths report published in 1988 and from a 1989 policy document entitled *Working for Patients*. The 1990 act sought to make fundmental changes to the disbursement of health care services. Its provisions can be equated with the third element in Dunleavy and Hood's schema—the idea that the allocation of resources should be regulated not by professional bureaucracies but by 'quasi markets' and the purchaser/provider split. The 1990 Act created the first internal market in UK health care.

Two key elements of these internal market reforms were (*a*) the creation of General Practitioner Fund Holders (GPFH) and (*b*) the creation of a market split between providers of services such as hospitals and general practitioners (GPs) and purchasers of services such as district health authorities (DHAs). Budd (2007) outlines the ways in which the statutory functions of purchaser and provider were separated by the NPM reforms. In the context of the 1990 Act, the expectation was that under programmes of Compulsory Competitive Tendering (CCT) providers would compete with each other for contracts from purchasers. Within this market mechanism, competition is localized between providers; that is, this mechanism is the sole exit mechanism in the market. The fundholders were given a budget with which they were entitled to purchase specified secondary care (i.e. hospital referrals or services) but not primary care services. That is to say, GPs could choose who to refer patients to for additional treatment, but they could not choose to purchase general 'first point of consultation care from other providers. In addition, GPFHs also had a prescribing budget (Harrison and Ahmad 2000). The point to note in the context of this chapter, is that GP fundholding was introduced on a voluntary basis. It was not imposed. Instead it was offered as an incentive—the incentive being that any 'under-spend' on the secondary care and prescribing budgets could be spent on the GP's own practice. At this time, GPs were self-employed doctors who were contracted to the NHS. The offer of a possible surplus with which to upgrade their practices was often too good to resist.

Whereas the 1983 Griffiths report created a group of exogenous managers, the 1990 reforms created a band of endogenous professionals who may have been more loyal to government reforms than they were to their fellow professionals.

Having successfully embedded principles of management, the reform of the NHS now impinged more directly on clinical practice, for it was here that savings could be made most readily. Incentivizing GP fundholders allowed a previously closed door to be opened to the steadily advancing creep of NPM reform. This move can be equated with Dunleavy and Hood's fourth criterion whereby provider roles are opened up to competition between agencies and to processes of competition between different groups, such as public agencies, firms, and not-for-profit bodies. A stated intention of the 1990 reforms was that they created a mixed economy of statutory and non-statutory providers.

The purchaser-provider split greatly increased the scope for competition (or 'exit'), the fifth of Dunleavy and Hood's defining criteria. Exit is only possible if there is somewhere else to go. Within the NHS, it is possible to exit, but there will almost always be a cost to the patient incurred by this exit. If the patient decides to go to another geographical area, then there are costs associated with getting to that area. If they decide to leave the NHS altogether, then there are the costs that need to be met for private provision, either directly or through private health insurance. Questions of where best to locate competition mechanisms were not directly addressed by the 1990 reforms and they remained unresolved for the remainder of that decade. The policy stated that '[m]oney must move with the patients so that hospitals which are efficient and effective, and attract more work, get the resources they need' (Department of Health 1989, section 11.11). A possible reading of this statement is that those hospitals that competed most effectively in the pricing and provision of services were likely to be those that attracted the most patients, since the policy equated volume of business with effectiveness and efficiency. Quite simply, the message appeared to be 'compete or die'.

The benefit to the patient is invoked as the key driving agent, but it can be argued that it was these new means of resource allocation, and not patient choice, that lay at the centre of this round of reforms. The competition or exit mechanism was constructed around the threat of sanction and not through the exercise of patient choice. The key point is that competition is located within purchaser organizations, and not within the grasp of patients.

This model can be categorized as an economistic 'command and control' model. The idea of money following the patients was supposed to be the exit mechanism, but the governance framework was ineffective because the system allowed local purchasers to manipulate it, so that some health and social services purchasers often elected not to compete and instead block-purchased packages of care. It was difficult for the state to invoke exit in a public service context, particularly when we consider the high degree of monopolization within the UK health-care system. Exit mechanisms are only effective if there is at least one *equivalent* alternative provider. One reason for the much trumpeted failure of the first internal market was its lack of an equivalent exit mechanism. Choice could not work effectively, or the precise locus of choice meant it was difficult to regulate. This was because, in practice, it was relatively easy for local organizations to collaborate as a means of obviating the possibility of exit.

These initial attempts at internal markets were characterized by competition over pricing (Le Grand 2003). Hunter (2006: 7) argues this was part of a concerted effort to move from a 'producer-led' to a 'user-driven' NHS. The NHS was re-structured such that resources were supposed to follow patients. All of this led to a dilution of power within professionally dominated health authorities. These changes instantiated an essentially bureaucratic means of securing change. Far from heralding a new era of the sovereign consumer, the 1990 reforms had the effect of pushing patients to the periphery as battles ensued over professional autonomy. These battles would continue across the second iteration of the market.

The Quality Market

The first internal market created the preconditions for what would follow, as evidenced in the new Labour government White Paper entitled *The New NHS: Modern, Dependable* (Department of Health, 1997). This document detailed how the NHS would be characterized by a system of integrated care, based on partnership—an early echo of principles of network governance—and 'driven by performance' (Department of Health 1997: section 1.3). The document also detailed how the previous government had 'wasted resources administering competition between hospitals' (section 1.3). An alternate reading of this process is that the previous regime's metrics had not worked; they were ineffective exit mechanisms that had been manipulated by colluding purchasers and providers.

The New NHS declared that the NHS internal market was dead. The 'new' NHS would be predicated not on market principles but on principles of quality. In his foreword Tony Blair stated that the legislation '...replaces the internal market with integrated care'. Similarly, Section 1.3 outlines how the '...internal market will be replaced by a system we have called "integrated care", based on partnership and driven by performance'. Section 1.4 outlines how '[a]bolishing the internal market will enable health professionals to focus on patients, making the NHS better every year. Individual patients...will get access to an integrated system of care that is quick and reliable'. This section continues with the statement that '[p]atients will be guaranteed national standards of excellence so that they can have confidence in the quality of the services they receive. Whilst there would be new incentives and new sanctions to improve quality and efficiency. The report also indicated that the purchaser-provider split would be retained. In an interesting discursive twist, one section of the report (entitled 'Keeping what works') announced that:

The Government will retain the separation between the planning of hospital care and its provision. This is the best way to put into practice the new emphasis on improving health and on meeting the healthcare needs of the whole community. (Department of Health 1997: section 2.6)

The 1997 White Paper replaces a fiscal metric with a quality metric. The split between providers and planners is an essential market mechanism (Budd 2007), so that far from being dead, it seems more appropriate to characterize the market as having been re-branded and extended. This extension takes the form of organizing principles based on a combination of fiscal metrics *and* quality metrics[6] (whereas the previous market was solely fiscal). An alternative to state provision (Dunleavy and Hood 1994) was created that incorporates the public into the arena of competition. The system underpinning the previous fiscal market meant it was only possible for competition to be located across providers. This proved ineffective as providers sought to undercut each other within the process of CCT. A market predicated on quality metrics meant that competition could be entended across both providers and purchasers. Purchasers were thus open to criticism, and those not meeting the normatively ascribed quality standards would be liable to sanction—both in terms of central funding and patient numbers.

In a critique of the *New NHS* plan, Dixon and Mays (1997) typify the four key changes enacted in the 1997 legislation. In a move redolent of Dunleavy and Hood's 'incubated' model of reform, the first change outlined by Dixon and Mays relates to the introduction of a unitary purchasing model, predicated upon primary care practitioners (essentially the creation of a cash-limited unified budget for providing primary health care and purchasing hospital and community care, within the Primary Care Group, PCG) (Harrison and Ahmad 2000). In terms of the relation between the previous and the new mechanism, the prior concession granted to GP fundholders is not rolled back,[7] but rather it is reined in, and reassigned under a new regulatory body, the PCG. The PCG marks a more collaborative approach than the GPFH agreement, but it is a collaborative approach that is much more tightly constrained by a prescribed and limited budget. The purchaser role is extended by a full scale adoption and application of Healthcare Resource Groups (HRG),[8] which were used to regulate clinical practice, via treatment costs, within a newly delimited context. This process makes the governance of clinical practice much more immediate as it breaks down all interventions into generic categories of resources and costs.

The second factor detailed by Dixon and Mays was a change in the role of District Health Authorities (DHA's). Whereas in the previous market these had been explicitly tasked with generating competition, they were now charged with regulating quality control activities. This development corroborates the idea that regulation has in fact been deepened and extended within the rhetoric of markets and competition. The DHAs were re-tasked with the job of extending the market into this new 'quality' arena, and this was underscored by the creation of the National Institute for Clinical Excellence (NICE; subsequently the National Institute for Health and Clinical Excellence) and the Commission for Health Improvement (CHI; subsequently Health Care Commission, and then Care Quality Commission). These organizations mark the third element of these reforms. NICE was designated as an 'Arms Length Body' (ALB) charged with drawing up national evidence-based guidelines on the costs and effectiveness of treatments. The CHI was responsible for overseeing the quality of clinical care, measured against national clinical governance guidelines, and tackling any shortcomings that arose. Again we see an extension of principles of bureaucratic regulation—again note that it is still not clinical regulation—into more areas of clinical practice. The nature of the relationship between ALBs and the main 'body' of government is evidenced in a review undertaken by the Department of Health. This review stated that ALBs have 'substantial independence from direction by the Secretary of State. Nevertheless, the Department remains sponsor' (Department of Health 2004: 8). Organizations such as NICE and CHI would have been unthinkable fifteen years previously, but the (incubated) model of NPM reform meant these organizations become possible, fourteen years after the Griffiths report created the original layer of non-clinical management. The fourth factor introduced in this legislation was a statutory duty of collaboration between NHS trusts and other NHS organizations, the integrated care framework mentioned in the White Paper.

The emphasis in all of these quality measures is on the standardization of clinical practice. The difference from the previous market is that the 'invisible fist' (Paton 2006) of the state has been extended into previously uncharted areas. The previous market sought only to regulate on the basis of cost and this proved ineffective. This second market proposed regulation based on clinical guidelines, marking a direct intervention into professional practice. In effect, this is a new mode of governance. It marks a fundamental shift in the state regulation of medical practice, and in a similar vein to the Griffiths report creating the conditions for the first internal market, this first New Labour iteration creates the potential for a fundamental re-conceptualization of exit in health-care provision. Quality allows the ineffective mechanism of the fiscal market to be redressed and redeployed.

The raising of quality standards is equated with raising efficiency, better budgetary controls—because quality is evidence based, and the evidence is based on a utilitarian conception of clinical efficacy (i.e. rationing)—and a plethora other performance indicators. The difficulty here is a discursive one. The quality agenda is promoted as being in the best interests of the patient, but a quality agenda predicated upon utilitarian clinical efficacy cannot be in the best interests of all the patients all of the time. Here the argument is not that rationing is avoidable, it is that the rhetoric of quality sequesters the issue of rationing away from the discussion. Quality measurement was depicted as a panacea for a reform-battered NHS. Drawing on the work of David Courpasson, the imposition of this new quality metric can be understood as a process of 'soft coercion'. Courpasson characterises this as a mechanism where '[O]rganisations have not renounced the use of coercion for governing', rather, he argues, 'they apply it through different media, whose power is systematically legitimised' (Courpasson 2000: 157). The quality metrics outlined here provide the framework for this mode of governance.

Reflecting on the 1997 'market', Le Grand (2003) stated that whereas previously competition had taken place over issues of pricing, in the 'new' market, the talk was now that price would be fixed and competition would depend only on quality. This position works to distance the new market from the old to construct it as something different, with a different set of metrics (although the bottom line, regulation of budget, remains the same). This argument finds a strong resonance in Courpasson's definition of soft bureaucracy according to which 'organisations are evolving towards an ambivalent structure of governance within which domination is not essentially exerted by means of, for example, violence, direct punishment or local hierarchical supervision, but through sophisticated management strategies' (Courpasson 2000: 142).

It is possible to regard the first NHS internal market, marked by efficiency, as a part of an 'older' type of bureaucracy, marked by punishment or hierarchical supervision. The second, quality-dominated NHS is characterized by internal markets, soft bureaucracy and new modes of managerial control. Whilst these developments would have real and signficant consequences throughout the NHS from the 1990s onwards, older modes of bureaucratic control were retained (see Buchanan and Fitzgerald, in this volume). The processes of clinical governance noted above offer an excellent example of this political and organizational hybridity. The notion of 'clinical governance' appears to offer this new means of control, but it is not apparent that the older practices of punishment and hierarchy have been fully revised. Commentaries such as those offered by Flynn (2002) and Sheaff et al (2003) argue that clinical governance is a policy designed to increase surveillance of health care professionals. Flynn asserts that 'clinical governance is another method of strengthening state control over quasi-autonomous professionals in a decentralised system' (Flynn 2002: 169). These manifestations of organizational hybridity contradict the ameliorist view of clinical governance propounded by the Department of Health. At its inception, clinical governance was described as 'a framework through which NHS organisations are accountable for continuously improving the quality of their services and safeguarding high standards of care by creating an environment in which excellence in clinical care will flourish' (Department of Health 1998: 33). Clinical governance is presented as an unalloyed good that can do nothing other than benefit service users. The deployment of quality and excellence as drivers of change, function to obfuscate the apparently secondary managerialist mechanisms simultaneously being put in place to ensure the highest attainable standards. But which of these of these aspects has more primacy for government?

In terms of presentation, it is only really possible to represent concerns with efficiency in one way, and that is how it will affect the public purse. The quality discourse is underlain by an unresolved tension between efficiency and quality of service. This discourse often proves to be highly effective initially, but there comes a tipping point at which the relative benefits of lower taxes are cancelled out by the emaciated condition of public services. At this point the efficiency discourse becomes problematic. The services may be much more efficient (i.e. cheaper to run) but they may also be failing to deliver an acceptable level of care. By invoking a quality discourse, albeit a reified form of quality, gains made towards efficiency can be maintained, whilst at the same time appearing to tackle the poor condition of the service, through focussing on quality rather than budget. A further appeal of a quality agenda, as far as the state is concerned, is that it becomes possible to discursively represent fiscal management in a number of different ways, for example under a rubric of choice.

The Choice Market

The extension of the parameters of the market was repeated in 2002,[9] when an additional metric was added, one that was predicated on the idea of patient choice. This choice metric can be read cynically as a move to strengthen the degree of competition (enacted through market mechanisms) across providers and purchasers, or more positively, as a means of opening up more and more aspects of care to patients. Choice, in this context, is intended to offer a fairer form of exit for an empowered service user (or consumer). If patients are unhappy with the service they can voice their concern and exit by seeking the same service from another NHS provider. This marks a definite shift away from the previous quality regime of 1997, in that now there is an additional voice element incorporated into the market; the creation of more voice mechanisms contradicts Dunleavy and Hood's fifth criterion. However, this contradiction presents no problem for government. It raises the question of whether this 'voice' option is better regarded as more of a regulatory than an empowering mechanism, or indeed whether it executes both these functions simultaneously, that is, it is both empowering for service users, whilst also performing a regulatory role on service providers, in which case it offers a win-win scenario for the state. The voice mechanism is secondary to the exit mechanism, such that voice is used as a means of producing competition (i.e. exit).

The rhetoric of choice is ubiquitous in the NHS, from 2002 to the present day. The discourses invoked are powerful ones—see Department of Health publications such as *Choice Matters: Putting Patients in Control,* or *Choosing Your Hospital,* or policies around direct payments, personalized budgets, choice at referral, *The Patients Charter,* or new digital means of service delivery such as *Choose And Book.* All of these elements of service provision are couched in discourses related to choice, and how it positively impacts upon the patient experience. However, these developments occured in a political context that was dominated by some highly particular constructions of patient choice. Le Grand, writing about the choice agenda, boldly states that 'the promotion of freedom of decision is a desirable end in and of itself' (2003: 77). Here the question is: for whom is it more desirable?

Patient choice is deeply problematic when viewed in the broader political and organizational context of the NHS. It is choice only in the sense that there is a range of alternatives, but these alternatives are limited. This is not to say there could be an unlimited choice agenda, but just as with the utilitarian notions of clinical efficiency evidenced in the quality market, the concept of limits or control are not features of the choice discourse as it is portrayed to patients—limited choice is not part of the livery. As originally laid out in the government policy documents (Department of Health 2002), the patient or consumer could be offered a choice of service, a choice of provider, a choice of time, and a choice of access. Within the choice agenda it is apparent that professional groups have retained control over diagnosis, and to all intents and purposes treatment (i.e. the professional domain). Quality and choice function as fundamental challenges to control over the evaluation of care, as well as control of the nature and volume of medical tasks.

So the question is how to typify this choice: what sort of choice is it? In order to answer this question it is necessary to address the idea of competition. One choice needs another choice to compete with; otherwise it is not a choice. Is it quality that determines choice? Services, providers, time, and access can all be read as characteristics of quality, and conversely also as characteristic of a discourse of health-care choice. Personal preference for non-invasive surgery may be the key determinant of choice in a health-care context, but the rubric of choice does not necessarily allow for that care component to be 'chosen'—control of diagnosis and treatment still rests with the physician.

Choice in the NHS is not choice as any lay person might conceive of it, but is perhaps better characterized as a very specific, non-fiscal, quality-dominated discourse. The standard of comparison here is choice in a free market, where the consumer is sovereign. The consumer is not, and indeed never can be, sovereign in a health-care market, and to suggest otherwise is disingenuous. Yet this is precisely the rhetoric put forward by key proponents of choice in health care (see Le Grand 2003, 2007). Patient choice is dressed up as a macro level principle that delivers improvements in service quality when it is more accurately characterized as a series of micro level mechanisms that have had the effect of diverting power away from UK healthcare professionals. The analysis that follows is focused on the next iteration of the marketisation discourse–the emergence of the 'choosing consumer' in the years after 2002.

Choosing Consumers

The conceptualization of patients as consumers, customers or clients offered UK policy makers a useful, and highly expedient means of extending the NPM programme of reform. The key component of both activist and statist applications of this discourse is the notion of consumer empowerment, but it can be argued that empowerment is fundamentally different in these two contexts and that these notions of empowerment are being used to pursue fundamentally different social and political projects. The statist view of the empowered consumer is at the heart of the post-bureaucratic notion, where 'flat hierarchies'[10] encourage the formation of local networks and consensus building dialogue (Grey and Garsten, 2001). It is at this point that the empowered consumer might become useful from the perspective of the state. From this perspective, invoking a post-bureaucratic paradigm, the empowered consumer has the potential to be both regulatory and emancipatory. This position asserts that the choice agenda is being used for purposes other than 'user empowerment'. Needham's (2002) account of New Labour's marketplace democracy argues that 'in almost all cases the term consumer is used in a context that implies something about the nature of the transaction, rather than simply being a synonym for the service user' (2003: 24). Needham demonstrates the ways in which New Labour politicians make the notion of the consumer synonymous with a shift towards high quality, diverse, accountable and individualised public services. This distinction between synonym and agent brings us back to the contradiction posed at the start of the chapter. Consumer as activist implies an element of resistance and a counterpoint to the passive discourse of the patient. Consumer as dupe can be read as an instrumental discourse used to counter medical autonomy; it is only by revoking the status of dupe that the consumer can begin to effect change and counter medical hegemony (see Speed 2007). Conversely, a patient is a citizen, who by right has access to health and welfare provision, provided via the welfare state. A consumer is a sovereign agent who has an entitlement to the best standard quality of care, provided via the welfare state. The consumer context is much more value-laden. The discourse of the healthy consumer also creates a new layer of responsibility; the imperative is for the consumer to follow guidelines on eating, drinking, exercise and other health related activities. The patient has no such responsibility: being passive objects of medical intervention, patients are discursively constituted as repositories of pathology (Armstrong 1984), who are treated by medicine when they are ill. Conversely, consumers are expected to take more responsibility for their health. Health is construed as a series of lifestyle choices, with the result that the debate on deeply rooted health inequalities is marginalised. Petersen and Lupton assert that these developments have created 'a moral climate of self-regulation' (1996: 22) which, when considered over a whole population, may create significant savings on health-care expenditure. The moral dimensions of this consumerism are considered in more detail below.

The Morality of Consumption

This new moralism works a number of ways. As already stated, it creates a climate of self-regulation amongst health-care consumers. It also makes processes of regulation much harder to resist amongst professional groupings. Any professional resistance leads to the rhetorical question of how any 'reasonable' professional could be opposed to reforms aimed at 'improving' the quality of the service or the choices available to end users. The first iteration of the market instantiated a fiscal effort to control expenditure. The second iteration of the market saw an expansion of that market into areas aligned to clinical practice. The third, choice led iteration of the market invokes a new morality of consumption. Grey and Garsten echo this point when they talk about customer rhetoric as 'providing a notion of moral community' (2001: 242). Consider this moralism as a dichotomy. Advocates such as Le Grand argue that choice must be at the centre of all public service provision, in order to make the patient/pawn the most powerful chess piece in the game. The following joint memorandum issued by the Public Administration Select Committee Inquiry into *Choice*, Voice, and Public Services highlight some of the ambiguities that pervade this third iteration:

User choice is an effective instrument for promoting quality, responsiveness, efficiency and equity in public services. It is in many cases more effective than alternatives, such as voice mechanisms. However, it should not be assumed that extending user choice is an option for all public services or that it is the principal determinant of reform. (PASC 2004, Executive summary)

There are also some reasonably stringent conditions that have to be met if choice is to achieve the aims of government policy. Good policy design is the key to extending user choice; undertaking such design is a key task of the current Government. (PASC 2004, Executive summary)

It is interesting to note that user choice is typified in the first paragraph as an 'effective instrument'. User choice, in this context, is not as Le Grand previously stated 'a desirable end in and of itself', but is represented as a policy tool, used for promoting management functions associated with quality, responsiveness, efficiency, and equity in public service reform. The second paragraph conveys a clear sense that user choice is being used instrumentally as a means to an end that is quite distinct from the empowerment of patients. Le Grand states that his vision of a public service would be one '... that treats the users of services as queens not pawns: that is, it would have user power at its base' (Le Grand 2003: 84); however, this assertion is qualified when he states that '... it would also have to incorporate mechanisms that avoid the overuse or over-provision of the service concerned, or the use of the service in such a way that damages either the user himself or herself or the wider society' (Le Grand 2003: 84). Whilst these qualifications are somewhat vague, they do cast a clearly discernable shadow of bureaucratic control over the 'empowered' user. This management principle is not communicated to the service user. The conception of choice offered is a naïve one. This naivety is not, however, countered at the point of interaction between provider and consumer. As the quotes from the select committee demonstrate, the policy is far from naïve about the conception of choice.

The choice agenda can be read as a further iteration or expansion of the regulatory market. It is an attempt to imbue the process of regulation with a moral component that extends its locus outside of the professional context, facilitating an ideological challenge to the principle of professional bureaucracy. It functions to raise the expectation amongst consumers, of how much they can be involved and what they can directly expect of *their* health-care provider (Laing and Hogg 2002 echo this point). Grey and Garsten show the ways in which the ethics of customer services 'offer the basis of predictability which is not organisationally specific, but which creates subject positions ("the professional manager" ...) that, if taken up, render individuals potentially controlled and controllable, predictable and hence trustworthy' (2001: 245). I would argue that this also applies to the choosing consumer. By delimiting the choice into manageable and predictable components, the invocation of the health-care consumer can be read as an attempt to further extend the principles of management and fiscal regulation out towards service users, applied through a normative framework of self-regulation.[11]

Conclusion

The years between 1983 and 2007 were a period of significant change for the NHS. An evolving discourse of marketization, quality and patient choice created a communicative and normative framework that gives moral primacy to the sovereign consumer. What Dunleavy and Hood characterise as a period of incubation wherein NPM reforms remain nascent is perhaps better seen as one in which certain conditions of possibility were established within successive iterations of the reform agenda. By 2002 UK healthcare provision was being shaped in fundamental ways by the idea of consumer choice. The hidden hand of the state was instrumental in shaping these developments. Policies advocated patient centredness whilst simultaneously contraining and controlling powerful professional groupings. The limiting of professional power and the expansion of patient-centredness may appear to mark a *quid pro quo*, where the (perceived) imbalance in power could be redressed. The problem, however, lay in the processes deployed to achieve this redress. Whilst power could be wrested from professionals, this power did not devolve to the service user. Successive Conservative and Labour governments have played a central role in mediating this redistribution. Organizations such as NICE function bureaucratically to give the appearance of distance between the decisions of government and the provision of services. New procedural mechanisms have been devolved to a variety of intermediary organizations whose workings have obscured the role of the state.

The discourses and processes outlined in this chapter mark not so much a change in notions of bureaucracy as a change in the discourses used to construct that bureaucracy. The purpose and function of the bureaucratic regime has remained constant through each iteration of the market. What has changed is the manner in which this target is pursued: the quarry remains the same, but the manner of the hunt has changed, and each iteration has moved closer to the object of pursuit. Put simply, these are new discourses for old processes.

The policy object of the health-care consumer and the legislative object of health-care choice are normative and moral discourses that function to domi-nate and regulate health professionals through less and less visible, but more and more pervasive command and control mechanisms. The choosing consumer becomes allied to a form of bureaucracy wherein quality and choice are the key moral imperatives. These processes mark the transformation of medicine from a self-regulating profession. Whilst having the appearance of a post-bureaucratic regime based on devolved network governance and empowered consumers, the new forms of control outlined in this chapter function in ways that assert strong, centrally regulated and highly normative state bureaucratic controls that are aimed first and foremost at controlling fiscal expenditure and professional practice. Concerns with placing the service user at the centre of the health-care provision are only a secondary concern within the transformations discussed in this chapter. These secondary concerns must be revisited if the stated goals of successive reform programmes are to be achieved.

⬚ NOTES

1. I would like to thank Joan Busfield, Martin Harris, Neil Serougi, and Rob Stones for their comments and assistance with this piece of work. I would also like to thank the anonymous reviewers for their comments.
2. For reasons of space, the Darzi review is not considered in the analysis presented in this chapter, although the principles identified are equally applicable to the Darzi review.
3. This potential was not fully realized until the introduction of Health Resource Groups (HRG) in the 1990 legislation.
4. Ellwood (2000: 23) characterizes the pre-1990s NHS as the world's 'largest single health care system'.
5. The consensus management approach was itself a development of reforms undertaken in the 1970s (see Harrison 1982).
6. These 'quality' metrics were also accompanied by the development of the National Refer-ence Cost Index, a key fiscal metric. The argument is not that fiscal principles underpinning the market mechanisms disappeared, rather that they were badged differently in each new iteration.
7. GP fundholding was abolished in 1999.
8. HRG is a group of health-related activities that have been judged to consume a similar level of resources (Benton et al. 1998).

9. However, as with the quality market of 1997, the choice market is also characterized by changing fiscal imperatives. This latest iteration is in the form of sustained reorganization of services around principles of 'Payment by Results', first introduced in 2000, aimed at linking the allocation of funds to hospitals to the activity they undertake (Department of Health 2009).

10. Whilst a flat hierarchy does not necessarily evoke an empowered consumer, discursively it is a different construction from the passive patient dependent upon the doctors' expertise.

11. The construction of a heightened sense of entitlement amongst consumers also provides a pragmatic justification for the expansion of Independent Sector Treatment Centres (ISTCs), that are legitimized as necessary to meet consumer demand.

☐ BIBLIOGRAPHY

Armstrong, D. (1984) *A Political Anatomy of the Body*, Cambridge: Cambridge University Press.

Benton, P.L., Evans, H., Light, S.M., Mountney, L.M., Sanderson, H.F. and Anthony, P. (1998) The development of Healthcare Resource Groups—Version 3, *Journal of Public Health Medicine*, 20(3), 351–8.

Bristol Royal Infirmary (2001) *Learning from Bristol: The Report of the Public Inquiry into Children's Heart Surgery at the Bristol Royal Infirmary 1984–1995*, London: Stationery Office.

Budd, L. (2007) Post-bureaucracy and Reanimating Public Governance: A Discourse and Practice of Continuity?, *International Journal of Public Sector Management*, 20(6), 531–47.

Courpasson, D. (2000) Managerial Strategies of Domination: Power in Soft Bureaucracies, *Organization Studies*, 21, 141–61.

Department of Health (1989) *Working for Patients*, London: Stationery Office.

——(1997) *New NHS: Modern, Dependable*, London: Stationery Office.

——(1998) *A First Class Service: Quality in the New NHS*, London: Stationery Office.

——(2002) *Delivering the NHS Plan: Next Steps on Investment, Next Steps on Reform*, London: Stationery Office.

——(2004) *Reconfiguring the Department of Health's Arm's Length Bodies*, London: Stationery Office.

——(2008) *Next Stage Review*, London: Stationery Office.

——(2009) *Payment by Results: Background and History*, http://www.dh.gov.uk/en/Managing-yourorganisation/Financeandplanning/NHSFinancialReforms/DH_077259 (accessed 12 May 2009).

Dixon, J. and Mays, N. (1997) New Labour, New NHS?, *British Medical Journal*, 315: 1639–40.

——Le Grand, J. and Smith, P. (2003) *Shaping the New NHS: Can Market Forces Be Used for Good?* London: Kings Fund.

Dunleavy, P. and Hood, C. (1994) From Old Public Administration to New Public Management, *Public Money and Management*, 13(3): 9–16.

Edwards, B. and Fall, M. (2005) *The Executive Years of the NHS: The England Account 1985–2003*, Abingdon: Radcliffe Publishing.

Ellwood, S. (2000) The NHS Financial Manager in 2010, *Public Money and Management*, 20(1): 23–30.

Flynn, R. (2002) Clinical Governance and Governmentality, *Health, Risk and Society*, 4(2): 155–73.

Forster, R. and Gabe, J. (2008) Voice or Choice? Patient and Public Involvement in the National Health Service in England under New Labour, *International Journal of Health Services*, 38(2): 333–56.

Grey, C. and Garsten, C. (2001) Trust, Control and Post-bureaucracy, *Organization Studies*, 22(2): 229–50.

Griffiths, R. (1983) *NHS Management Inquiry*, Department of Health and Social Security, London: Stationery Office.

——(1988) *Community Care: Agenda for Action*, London: Stationery Office.

Harrison, S. (1982) Consensus Decision-Making in the National Health Service—A Review, *Journal of Management Studies*, 19(4): 377–94.

—— and Ahmad, W. (2000) Medical Autonomy and the UK State 1975 to 2025, *Sociology*, 34(1): 129–46.

Heckscher, C. and Donnellon, A. (eds) (1994) *The Post-Bureaucratic Organization*, Thousand Oaks, California: Sage.

Hirschman, A. (1970) *Exit, Voice, and Loyalty; Responses to Decline in Firms, Organizations, and States*, Cambridge, Massachusetts: Harvard University Press.

Hunter, D.J. (2006) The Tsunami of Reform: The Rise and Fall of the NHS, *British Journal of Health Care Management* 12(1): 18–23.

Kaufmann C. (1999) An Introduction to the Mental Health Consumer Movement, in A.V. Horwitz, T.L. Scheid (eds) (1999) *A Handbook for the Study of Mental Health: Social Contexts, Theories, and Systems*, Cambridge: Cambridge University Press.

Laing, A. and Hogg, G. (2002) Political Exhortation, Patient Expectation and Professional Execution: Perspectives on the Consumerization of Health Care, *British Journal of Management*, 13: 173–88.

Le Grand, J. (2003) *Motivation, Agency and Public Policy*, Oxford: Oxford University Press.

——(2007) The Politics of Choice and Competition in Public Services, *The Political Quarterly*, 78(2): 207–13.

National Health Service & Community Care Act (1990) London: Stationery Office.

Needham, C. (2003) *Citizen-Consumers: New Labour's Marketplace Democracy*, London: Catalyst Forum.

Paton, C. (2006) *New Labour's State of Health: Political Economy, Public Policy and the NHS*, Aldershot: Ashgate Publishing Ltd.

Petersen, A. and Lupton, D. (1996) *The New Public Health: Health and Self in the Age of Risk*, London: Sage.

Public Administration Select Committee (PASC) (2004) *Choice, Voice and Public Services: Written Evidence*, House of Commons. London: HMSO.

Reed, M. (2001) Organisation, Trust and Control: A Realist Analysis, *Organization Studies*, 22(2): 201–28.

Robson, N. (2008) Costing, Funding and Budgetary Control in UK hospitals: A Historical Reflection, *Journal of Accounting and Organizational Change*, 4(3): 343–62.

Sheaff, R., Rogers, A., Pickard, S., Marshall, M., Campbell, S., Sibbald, B., Halliwell S. and Roland, M. (2003) A Subtle Governance: 'Soft' Medical Leadership in English Primary Care, *Sociology of Health & Illness*, 25(5): 408–28.

Speed, E. (2002) Irish Mental Health Social Movements: A Consideration of Movement Habitus, *Irish Journal of Sociology*, 11(1): 61–80.

——(2006) Patients, Consumers and Survivors: A Case Study of Mental Health Service User Discourses, *Social Science and Medicine*, 62(1), 28–38.

——(2007) Discourses of Consumption or Consumed by Discourse? A Consideration of What "Consumer" Means to the Service User, *Journal of Mental Health*, 16(3): 307–18.

Tomes, N. (2006) Patients or Health-care Consumers? Why the History of Contested Terms Matters, in R. Stevens, C. Rosenberg and L. Burns (eds), *History and Health Policy in the United States: Putting the Past Back in*, New Brunswick, New Jersey: Rutgers University Press.

Willmott, H. (1993) Strength is Ignorance; Slavery is Freedom: Managing Culture in Modern Organisations, *Journal of Management Studies*, 30(4): 515–52.

5 Network Governance and the Politics of Organizational Resistance in UK Health Care: The National Programme for Information Technology

MARTIN HARRIS

Introduction

Few now doubt that the new information and communication technologies (ICTs) are having a profound effect on the advanced industrial societies. Public debate on the social implications of these technologies has long been dominated by anti-bureaucratic currents of thought, and by the belief that private sector corporations should be seen as the primary locus of innovation (Castells 2000). Whereas in the early 1970s, Daniel Bell and other theorists of post-industrialism regarded both the bureaucratic form and the state as central features of technological society (Bell 1974; Kumar 1995; Mattelart 2003), the 1980s and 1990s saw a 'rolling back' of the state, as evidenced by privatizations and attempts to impose private sector norms on public sector organizations. In the Anglo-Saxon societies, these reforms were very substantially influenced by 'the New Public Management (henceforth NPM)' (Ferlie et al. 1996; Hood 1998; Ferlie and Fitzgerald 2001), a term that embraces some explicitly 'managerial' strategies of marketization, decentralization, and the imposition of standardized performance measures in the public sector (Ferlie et al. 1996; Hoggett 1996; Kirkpatrick and Martinez Lucio 1996; Farrell and Morris 2003). The 1990s also saw an increasing emphasis on the potential role of ICTs in transforming public sector bureaucracies (Heckscher 1994; Heckscher and Donnelon 1994; Cabinet Office 1999). Here the suggestion was that the 'old' models of public sector bureaucracy could be transformed by shifting from a paper-based bureau to digital databases and networks. More recent commentaries on 'digital era governance' (Dunleavy et al. 2006; Bloomfield and Hayes 2009) have become closely intertwined with the puta-tive 'end', or at the very least a substantial 'refurbishment', of the bureaucratic form (Reed and Courpasson 2004; Josserand et al. 2006; Harris 2008; Reed and Ezzamel 2008; see also chapters by Clegg and Reed in this volume). The shift from paper trails to virtual reality has in many countries been accom-panied by the privatization of data management as large 'systems-integrator' corporations have become primary providers of information technology (IT) facilities to large government bureaucracies (Dunleavy et al. 2006).

The rapid diffusion of ICTs across the public sector adds a substantial degree of complexity to an already complex landscape of public sector reform. Studies have revealed a variegated mix of organizational continuity and change, much of which has been directly mediated by public sector profes-sionals responsible for IT-based service delivery (Bellamy and Taylor 1998; Harris 2008; Smith et al. 2008; Bloomfield and Hayes 2009). In many cases, organizational change has assumed a distinctly utilitarian form that owes little to the dazzling surface effects of the new technology or to the transformative visions of 'digital era governance'. But although many of the changes asso-ciated with large-scale investment in IT can be attributed to rationalization and cost cutting in machine bureaucracies (Cabinet Office 1999; Curthoys and Crabtree 2003; Dunleavy et al. 2006), there is growing evidence that ICT and institutional reform provides the context for new forms of 'centra-lized decentralization' and organizational hybridity.[1]

Comment on the entanglement of ICTs, NPM, and new networked orga-nizational forms has often been long on speculation and short on analysis of particular institutional and organizational choices (Margetts 2007)—but the available evidence indicates that these technologies are more deeply impli-cated in the creation of organizational hybrids than has hitherto been recog-nized (Harris 2008; Bloomfield and Hayes 2009). Previous work also suggests that the question of ICT and public sector reform needs to be addressed at two distinct levels of analysis. At one level, ICTs offer new and more distributed modes of coordination and control—features that create a 'struc-ture of opportunities' that may reshape the core operations of public sector bureaucracies in a wide variety of ways. At a second level of analysis, 'net-worked' organizational forms have featured prominently in recent discussions of institutional reform (Klijn 2005; Meier and Hill 2005). Here the argument is that the core functions of the public sector can be managed by networks of actors (e.g. public/private sector partnerships and other manifestations of co-governance). These new forms promise more integrated ('joined up') forms of governing (Osborne 2000; Newman 2003; Pollitt 2003). Theoretical developments on the theme of organizational hybridization indicate that there is a need to go beyond the binary oppositions inherent in the idea of the 'post-bureaucratic' organization. Organizational hybrids are fundamentally Janus-faced, pointing on one hand to more open-ended and diverse organizational futures (Dent 1995; Courpasson 2000; Clegg and Courpasson 2004), and on the other to the fragmentation and dismemberment of public sector bodies.

These considerations are highly relevant to the ten-year National Programme for Information Technology (NPfIT) which is being currently implemented across the UK National Health Service (NHS). Launched in 2002 by the Blair government, this £12.4 billion initiative aims at delivering more effective and integrated forms of service delivery. Whilst the huge scale of the investment represented by the programme involves a commitment to capacity building and infrastructural development, the NPfIT has been adversely affected by a succession of project overruns, 'IT failures', and data security problems (NAO 2006). The Programme has, in addition, attracted criticism from the British Medical Association, and it has also been investigated by a House of Commons Public Accounts Committee (PAC 2007; Randell 2007).

This chapter examines some 'post-bureaucratic' organizational features that have emerged in the context of the NPfIT. It begins by examining the origins, policy context, and main features of the initiative. The second part of the chapter highlights some dilemmas of centralization, decentralization, clinical autonomy, and managerial control that have emerged as the programme has progressed. The chapter then shows how these aspects resonate with recent theoretical work on organizational hybridity, political resistance, and legitimacy in public sector settings. The case study analysis that follows shows the ways in which the technological and organizational changes that have been implemented under the auspices of the NPfIT are being played out at local level. The introduction of a patient administration system (henceforth PAS) was influenced by its 'bureaucratic' context of use, and by the 'networked' forms of governance exercised by the *Connecting for Health* (henceforth CFH) directorate. The broader picture of network governance revealed by the case reflects the fragmentation and 'drift' observed in other examples of large-scale infrastructural development (Ciborra et al. 2000). On one hand, the system appeared to embody the shift to the operating norms and procedures of the 'business process' perspective adopted by CFH. On the other hand, the new system bore the marks of locally articulated meanings and professional values. The concluding part of the paper draws out some broader theoretical implications of these findings.

Policy and Organizational Background to the National Programme for Information Technology

The last decade has seen a very substantial policy interest in the potential role of new ICTs in transforming the delivery of health-care services within the UK NHS (Department of Health 1998, 2000; Wanless 2002). The 1980s and 1990s saw steep rises in IT expenditure across the NHS—but many commentators noted that the quality of information provision has been subject to wide variations with particularly significant differences observed between Acute and Community Units. A 1998 report entitled *Information for Health* called for a more integrated approach that would combine the benefits of a national infrastructure with locally implemented innovations in patient care. The report identified some major benefits that could be expected to flow from contemporary advances in ICT, including electronic patient records (EPRs), seamless care for patients, with general practitioners (GPs), hospitals, and community services sharing information across the NHS information high-way, and more effective use of NHS resources for health planners and man-agers. The master theme of integration was reprised in the subsequent *NHS Plan* (Department of Health 2000). Whilst the *NHS Plan* expressed a policy commitment to large-scale investment in infrastructure, this was accompanied by a clear shift of emphasis in the preferred means to this end. Whereas the 1998 report on *Information for Health* made brief reference to 'supplier partnerships' (Department of Health 1998: 43), the publication of the *NHS Plan* advocated strategic outsourcing, increased involvement of the independent/private sector in shaping IT infrastructures, a competitive market model of health-care provision, and a 'customer relations' view of patients.

A subsequent review of information provision in the NHS was undertaken on behalf of Gordon Brown, the Chancellor of the Exchequer. *Securing Our Future Health: Taking a Long-Term View* (Wanless 2002) proposed centrally managed national standards for data and called for IT spending to be doubled. The Department of Health report on *Delivering 21st Century IT Support for the NHS—A National Strategic Programme* (Department of Health 2002) outlined the first steps towards establishing a programme of work that would underpin the NPfIT. Standards and architecture would be designed in common but major components of the national programme were to be 'selectively out-sourced' via a new NHS Information Authority, whilst Strategic Health Autho-rities (henceforth SHAs) were to be 'performance managed to ensure implementation' (Department of Health 2002: 13). Contracts amounting to £6.2 billion were awarded to a small number of consortia later that year. The United Kingdom was divided into five main geographical areas (these came to be known as 'clusters') that comprised a number of SHAs. Consortia lead by large systems-integrator corporations such as BT, Fujitsu, and Accenture would act as 'local service providers' (henceforth LSPs)—that is, as sole suppliers to each of the regional 'clusters'. The successful bidder would then have sole rights to supply systems across the whole spectrum of Acute, Community, and eventually Primary Care, irrespective of existing contractual obligations by local Trusts. Failure to comply with the new contracts meant that LSPs could levy charges from individual Trusts. Integral to the plan was a common 'functional and data architecture' that would ensure interoperability across the NHS. This infrastructure was to be provided by the national communications information highway known as the national data Spine. In 2005, the UK government created *Connecting for Health*, a new directorate responsible for coordinating the implementation of the NPfIT. At the heart of this Programme is the Electronic Care Records (ECR) Service, designed to make patient records available to clinicians, administrators, and GPs across the United Kingdom.[2] Other key applications include patient administration systems, *Choose and Book* online scheduling of appointments, and new picture archiving and communications (PACs) systems (PAC 2007; Randell 2007).

As noted earlier, the NPfIT has been dogged by project overruns and 'IT failures'. The widely reported 'data security problems' associated with the NPfIT have a particular significance in the context of the NHS where the loss of patient records has caused serious disruption and clinical risk (NAO 2006; Peltu et al. 2008). A 2009 NAO report, noting that the ECR Service is the key to realizing the benefits of the entire Programme, has argued that the current timescales set for ECR systems are 'unachievable' and that the timescales imposed by CFH raised unrealistic expectations that threaten to undermine 'user confidence' in the Programme (NAO 2009). The same report recommended that the NHS and its suppliers should work towards establishing timescales for NPfIT deployments that reflect the circumstances of individual NHS Trusts. 'Staff commitment' is now seen as the *sine qua non* for identifying and realizing the benefits of the Programme.

One of the recurrent themes in these commentaries is the idea that the large-scale and centralized approach of the initiative is at odds with the strong tradition of localism that exists in the NHS, and it is apparent that the creation of *Connecting for Health* has added complexity to an already complex and politically fragmented institutional landscape of health-care provision. Research on the earlier phases of the Programme indicates that CFH has encountered very substantial difficulties in aligning the diverse roles, responsibilities, and organizational interests that obtain across the network of local NHS managers (who act as budget holders for NHS Trusts), private sector IT firms (who act as LSPs for the five regional 'clusters' covered by the NPfIT in England and Wales), and the clinicians, administrators, and other 'end users' tasked with assimilating these systems into local work practices (Currie and Guah 2007). Research on the organizational implications of the Programme also highlights the tendency for the 'local' implementation of new IT systems to result in changes that differ markedly from the formal goals and performance criteria espoused by CFH. The broad thrust of this work is that over-centralization has unnecessarily constrained the local shaping of solutions associated with NPfIT.[3] Thus, Peltu et al. (2008) cite a series of examples demonstrating the imposition of rigid, inappropriate, and poorly specified systems on NHS Trusts,[4] the marginalization of existing IT systems, and numerous project 'workarounds' and local adaptations.[5] These authors also note the relatively low level of use of *Choose and Book* online booking systems and the frequent failure to enter clinical data into the electronic health-care record. In such cases, clinical staff may develop a variety of strategies for accomplishing their tasks.

Where NPfIT usage is growing, there is some evidence that new forms of work organisation are beginning to emerge. Offering patient choice by using *Choose and Book*, for example, is not just a role for the GP but involves other members of the practice. Getting clinical data into electronic records may also not be a task only for clinicians, as it may involve sharing tasks with administrative staff. (Peltu et al. 2008: 9)

These developments suggest that the NPfIT raises some familiar issues of organizational contestation that have emerged in relation to the new context implied by the 'digital reformation' of the NHS. Buchanan et al. (2007*a*, 2007*b*) argue that the centralized implementation of particular applications (e.g. patient booking systems) is fundamentally at odds with the traditions of professional autonomy that have characterized the NHS. Other studies have indicated that the centrally defined timescales adopted by CFH are seen by NHS managers and staff as inflexible and out of step with the specificities of local service delivery (Currie and Guah 2007; Eason 2007; Mark 2007). Further, this work suggests that local examples of good practice have on occasion been usurped and displaced by the imposition of NPfIT applications (Eason 2007; Peltu et al. 2008).

   Whilst there can be little doubt that the over-centralized nature of the Programme has constrained local users, there is a general paucity of work on the more fundamental questions of power, legitimacy, and accountability raised by the NPfIT. The broader institutional context of the Programme is one in which the existing practices of UK health-care professionals are being challenged both by the centralization of resources that has occurred under the auspices of CFH and the simultaneous devolution of local service provision to private sector contractors who are now charged with the task of delivering the requisite ICT infrastructures. The scale of the NHS is matched by its diversity, comprising as it does hundreds of individual Trusts providing acute hospital care, GP services, primary care, mental and community health care—each with different IT requirements and organizational legacies (Sauer and Willcocks 2007). The rationale for the NPfIT is that a national programme would standardize IT provision and eliminate variations in performance across disparate clinical and administrative systems. It is therefore richly ironic that the charge of 'variability' has been levelled at some of the LSPs involved in delivering the NPfIT. A consortium led by Accenture withdrew from the Programme in September 2006 (CFH 2007) and a service provider contract awarded to Fujitsu for the south of England cluster was cancelled in 2008. The delivery of iSoft's *Lorenzo* software (a core element in patient record and administration systems) has been subject to serious delays (CFH 2006). Media commentaries on the initiative highlight the issue of poorly specified systems and frequent delays in the national roll-out of the Programme have tended to obscure the more fundamental point that NHS Trusts have lost much of their power to influence IT procurement and project management. One major plank of the NPfIT has been to abandon locally embedded 'legacy systems' irrespective of perceived benefits, and introduce a single 'one-size-fits-all system' in each cluster. A second is to ensure that information from these systems can flow across different organizations and clusters via the nationally interoperable 'Data Spine', an information architecture. One NHS IT manager has argued that:

The 'one size fits all' approach of the NPfIT discouraged local development insofar as the more functionally rich local solutions became, the more difficult the task also became of justifying to clinicians their replacement with something that might be less useful ... The NHS was not over-burdened with money and therefore expenditure on systems and project resources that were not aligned to the NPfIT would eventually be seen as both wasteful and counter-productive. In these circumstances, local ICT innovation tended to be discontinued with a resulting loss of momentum for many ICT strategies and for those informatics professionals whose role changed from innovators to programme managers within a pre-defined set of parameters. (Serougi 2008)

The above brief account gives some sense of the scale and complexity of the NPfIT. There is a need for further research on the new forms of network governance that arise from the creation of CFH, and there is also a clear need for further research on the implementation of IT systems at local level, particularly those relating to EPRs. The next section provides a brief overview of some relevant theoretical perspectives and identifies some key themes that emerge from the case study analysis presented in part three.

Theorizing Bureaucracy, ICT, and Organizational Change in the Context of the NPfIT

The NPfIT, widely reported to be the world's largest civil IT project, offers a substantial challenge to social science research on the 'new interactive orders' (Kallinikos 2006) that are now being enacted in public sector settings. Academic work relevant to the issues noted in the previous section embraces a number of overlapping, but poorly integrated, perspectives on ICT and public sector reform. These include commentary on new 'networked' forms of governance in public sector settings (Rhodes 2000; Harris 2008; Hendricks 2009; Pollitt 2009), studies of user-driven innovation and organizational change in the NHS, and debate on the 'transformational' claims of technology as the basis for reform in the NHS (McNulty and Ferlie 2002; Bloomfield and Hayes 2009).

From 1979 onwards, UK public utilities were privatized and services were contracted out to the private sector. Where full privatization was not possible, the Thatcher and Major governments initiated programmes of public sector reform, introducing quasi-markets and a purchaser–provider split into the NHS (Hoggett 1996; Kirkpatrick and Martinez Lucio 1996). These policies were continued under New Labour. The NPfIT is rooted in the Blair government's drive to modernize the UK public sector (Cabinet Office 1999), and the initiative has been strongly influenced by the notion that IT can be deployed as a key element in New Labour's programme of 'Transformational Government' (Bloomfield and Hayes 2009). The NPfIT has thus emerged from a policy context in which the state no longer assumes sole responsibility for the management of complex institutional changes. This is broadly consistent with the view that there has been a shift away from hierarchy and bureaucratic rule-making towards new forms of governance based on 'networked' organizational forms (Rhodes 1994, 1997; Pierre and Peters 1998). Rhodes argues that 'governance' should be viewed as a historically significant development that now constitutes the defining narrative of British government (Rhodes 2000: 349). The advent of NPM,[6] and the shift 'from government to governance' has created a much more plural and fragmented pattern of service delivery than was the case in the era of centralized bureaucracies. Rhodes argues that the shift to 'governance without government' can also be equated with a much more fundamental 'hollowing out' of the UK state (Rhodes 1994, 2000), as when the NHS Executive 'migrated' policy making and operational management from the core operating departments of the Department of Health to newly created agencies. The fragmentation that followed has, according to Rhodes, 'created a greater need for coordination while greatly reducing government ability to coordinate' (Rhodes 2000: 350).

Current debates on network governance, 'agentification', and 'the contract state' have a strong bearing on the origins and subsequent development of the NPfIT. The decision to replace the NHS Information Authority with a new agency that would coordinate a network of private sector contractors who would in turn deliver the programme of work laid down by the NPfIT reflects a continuing policy commitment to the 'contract state' (Kirkpatrick and Martinez Lucio 1996). Whilst academic work on contractualization indicates that public sector bureaucracies have been substantially 'refurbished'

(Josserand et al. 2006; Clegg, this volume), a long line of commentators have questioned the 'epochalist' assumption that the public sector reforms underway since the early 1990s can be construed as a historically significant 'end' of bureaucracy. Thus, early commentaries such as those offered by Kirkpatrick and Martinez Lucio (1996) show that the widespread use of contracting in the UK public sector created a shift to more inflexible definitions of service and an increased use of financially driven understandings of how these services should be delivered. These authors also note that marketization allowed the provider economy to become more, rather than less, 'organized' as private sector firms have come to enjoy a near-monopoly status as service providers. These aspects have a particular relevance for the NPfIT. Whilst the initiative has been dominated by the language of consumer choice and markets, the award of single contracts to a small number of large corporations acting as LSPs has allowed IT provision to become much more concentrated than was hitherto the case, and the use of the network form has coexisted with the imposition of some highly centralized and traditionally 'bureaucratic' controls exercised by CFH. These features are analysed in more depth in the closing sections of the chapter.

Whilst the broad contours of New Labour's transformation agenda have a strong bearing on the reform of the NHS and other public sector organizations (Fairclough 2000; Rhodes 2000; du Gay 2003; Newman 2003), few authors have been able to relate these broader ideological currents to detailed empirical studies of ICT and institutional change in public sector settings (but see Ferlie and McNulty (2002) and Bloomfield and Hayes (2009) for two notable exceptions). Currie and Guah's study (2007) of the NPfIT postulates three major phases of development since the launch of the NHS in 1948. The era of professional dominance (1948–71) was followed by an era of managerialism (1972–97), and this was in turn succeeded by an era of market mechanisms lasting from 1998 to the present. These eras are 'infused with distinct institutional logics' that derive from the strategic dispositions and political interests of politicians, clinicians, and managers. The NPfIT has been designed and implemented by a plurality of bureaucracies, a feature that has made the political 'alignment' of particular roles and responsibilities within the programme particularly difficult (Currie and Guah 2007: 241). The political pressure for the programme to meet its targets has led to calls for more attention to be placed on engagement with local users (Hendy et al. 2005; NAO 2006), but Currie and Guah note that the initiative has been shaped by deep and fundamental political divides that have emerged as the institutional logics of public sector professionalism and self-regulation have clashed with those that prioritize corporate performance and efficiency (Currie and Guah 2007: 244).

Recent comment on the institutional changes now underway in the NHS has borrowed from archetype theory to highlight the 'sedimented' ways in which new organizational forms may coexist with professional bureaucracy. McNulty and Ferlie (2002, 2004) question the idea that public sector reform can be understood in terms of 'big bang' changes in large professional bureaucracies, rejecting the basic premise of 'transformational' change in favour of a much more nuanced view in which extant modes of organizing retain their viability and resilience (McNulty and Ferlie 2004: 1,389). This view of public sector reform is closely associated with the idea that change processes may be characterized not by fundamental transitions but by the coexistence of things otherwise seen as wholly distinct or incommensurate (Harris and Wegg-Prosser 2007; Bloomfield and Hayes 2009; Buchanan and Fitzgerald, in this volume). Moreover, the broad corpus of work on organizational hybridity (see e.g. Farrell and Morris 2003; Clegg and Courpasson 2004; Skelcher 2005; Harris 2008; Bloomfield and Hayes 2009; Courpasson and Dany 2009) corroborates the view that the new organizational forms now emerging in public sector settings are mediated by professional identities, roles, and responsibilities (Ferlie and Geraghty 2007). These features are likely to remain a key influence on newly 'hybridized' means of public service delivery, for example those that combine centralized control with decentralized modes of imperative coordination, or those that incorporate new mixtures of private and public enterprise.

The case study account presented in the next section focuses on two particular manifestations of organizational hybridity. The first is that the IT infrastructures now being constructed under the auspices of the programme are necessarily subject to contestation by diverse or 'heterogeneous' interests (see Ciborra et al. 2000; Bloomfield and Hayes 2009 for accounts of this in other settings). The second is that local contexts of IT deployment in NHS organizations are such that health-care professionals charged with managing particular applications may adhere to the formal project guidelines espoused by CFH, whilst following highly localized logics of action that differ significantly from those expressed by formal project goals and specifications (Buchanan et al. 2007a). This is cognate with recent work (Courpasson and Dany 2009) showing the ways in which alternative logics of empowerment entailed by post-bureaucratic regimes may be used by key employees to resist specific decisions and/or to take unplanned and sometimes unorthodox initiatives. Buchanan et al. (2007b) note that the local adaptations (or project 'workarounds' to borrow the term used by Eason 2007) observed in the context of the NPfIT may constitute a more significant and enduring source of organizational innovation than has emerged from the supposedly 'transformational' change management programmes that have hitherto dominated the reform of the NHS (Eason 2007; Buchanan et al. 2007a).

Methods, Data Gathering, and Fieldwork

The chapter has thus far highlighted the complex and inherently contested terrain represented by the NPfIT. The case study set out in the next section investigates a Patient Administration System (PAS)[7] that was adopted by an NHS Primary Care Trust ('Western PCT') and it relates the organizational consequences of the system to the broader context of the NPfIT and CFH. Data gathering was based on internal documentation provided by the Trust, participant observation of meetings, and a total of eighteen semi-structured interviews carried out with a range of personnel, including nurses, project management personnel, heads of services, and a Director of ICT. The identity and geographic location of the Trust has been concealed as have the identities of individual respondents.

CASE STUDY: PAS IMPLEMENTATION AT WESTERN PCT

Western PCT is an NHS Trust located in a large UK conurbation. The PAS was introduced between 2005 and 2008. The timing of the deployment was decided centrally by CFH in line with the requirements of the NPfIT. Whilst the LSP is responsible for the implementation of new information systems, individual Trusts and their ICT directors bear ultimate responsibility for ensuring that these systems are rendered fully operational and compatible with existing IT infrastructures. Recent attempts to investigate the sustainability of innovation in UK health-care settings have emphasized the role of antecedent context in framing the receptivity of clinicians to particular innovations (Dopson and Fitzgerald 2006). The PAS project was initiated in 2005. Prior to this the Trust had implemented a number of 'bespoke' IT systems, and experience of these had confirmed the need for meaningful engagement with clinicians and doctors in the design and development of these systems. The PAS had to be deployed in accordance with a schedule that was very substantially determined by contractual timescales, but the style of project management adopted was broadly participative and involved clinicians at all levels. Thus, one Senior Nurse asserted that:

Connecting for Health is very much a 'project orientated' approach, whereas we have tried a much more user-based approach here.

The PAS project team was assembled by the Trust's Connecting for Health Board. The board took the view that a single team (comprising approximately forty individuals) would introduce the PAS over a two-year period across a wide range of services provided by the Trust. This included a CFH programme manager, project managers charged with separate applications (PAS, Choose and Book, and electronic prescriptions), a training team, administrative support, a supporting ICT team supporting (alongside but not under the direct control of) the programme manager, and a 'business change' team providing change facilitators. Overall responsibility for the PAS project lay with the ICT director. The project manager created a 'Clinical Lead' (CL) position in 2005. The rationale for this was that engagement with local clinicians was seen as essential to the project. The CL post was filled by a nurse who acted as an internal consultant to the project management team. Internal documentation shows that the individual who occupied this post exercised a substantial degree of autonomy and discretion *vis-a-vis* the PAS project—however, the following comment from the CL highlights some 'non-negotiable' aspects of the project:

> This is about how do we get people from where they are now through the transition to the where we need them to be within the CFH programme. We have an edict from the government that they will have a PAS and this is the agreement which has been endorsed by the SHA...we have all had to put in our plans, they have all to be approved. There are penalties if you don't meet those targets, so how do we as an organisation move clinicians off an existing system and get them onto a new unfamiliar system amidst a set of timescale pressures that may ultimately compromise effective clinical engagement?

The management of medical care records in UK community health care has long been based on patients' records being held locally by patients themselves. Here the fundamental premise is that continuity is guaranteed where there may be a number of different services involved in the treatment of individual patients. These services are frequently co-dependent and maintaining the patient care record is thus critical to the quality and coherence of the service being delivered. The CFH agenda confronted the Trust with the task of managing the transition from paper based, locally held patient records to a electronic system that allowed these to be accessed, shared and distributed in fundamentally new ways. The pace of the changes undertaken and the need to engage with 'what it means for users and clinicians' presented particular challenges. Analysts of IT project implementation have long commented on the relative advantages of incremental approaches versus more comprehensive 'big bang' approaches. This was a significant dilemma for those managing the PAS project within the Trust. On one hand, adopting a 'big bang' approach meant that the various care services (the majority of which were 'co-dependent' with other services) would have to 'go live' at the same time. There were significant resource and cost implications in a simultaneous launch that involved managing the expectations of approximately 1,200 users working across a diversity of physical locations and health-care services. On the other hand, taking an incremental approach in which the PAS would be run in parallel with paper-based records for a period would create potential duplication, fragmentation, and loss of information—all of which involved substantial clinical risk. The task of mapping the flow between paper-based and electronic records created logistical problems in the short term. The CL took formal responsibility for the 'clinical governance' of the project. This involved assessing the ways in which the PAS could be aligned with existing patient care records and then identifying potential gaps in these records by engaging with different clinician groupings and mapping co-dependences in patient treatment.

The introduction of EPRs confronts health-care practitioners and policy makers with complex organizational choices centring on the question of who owns the data contained in such records, and who gains access to which aspects of the electronic record. The CL for the Western PCT CFH project noted that these questions would become more pressing as more sophisticated clinical systems were developed within the Trust. The system also posed organizational choices about how clinicians would inform patients about their care, how contact between clinicians and patients would be maintained, and how confidentiality could be assured. These issues were of considerable interest to clinicians and the CL for the PAS project noted that their resolution was key to gaining clinical confidence and 'buy in' to the project. These were identified as critical success factors that needed to be 'pushed back up the *Connecting for Health* hierarchy' as future work associated with the move from the patient-held record to an electronically shared record.

All of the interviewees who contributed to the study noted the ways in which the 'business process' perspectives adopted by CFH pervaded the implementation of PAS. This was corroborated by documentation on the implementation of Community PAS projects supplied to the Trust by *Connecting for Health* (CFH 2008). This documentation combined conventional project management approaches with 'reengineering' perspectives on organizational change.[8] The dominant idiom was overtly predictive and highly technicist, attributing particular outcomes to PAS. So, for example, the CFH documentation stated that:

care in the community will benefit from increased provider efficiency, shorter and fewer consultations, and increased capacity. (CFH 2008: 7)

PASs were also construed as organizationally straightforward and inherently positive for clinical practice. Thus:

Greater capacity and increased strategic planning capabilities will result in decreased waiting lists and shorter waiting times from referral to clinic and domiciliary appointments. (CFH 2008: 7)

Information about patients was gathered to support invoicing and the administration of the internal market between commissioners and providers. The clinician focus on patient outcomes and effective treatment was lost as the viability of the project was threatened by lengthy delays, and there was a growing perception that the system was dominated by concerns with productivity, internal markets, and consumerist notions of 'patient choice'. The Director of ICT stated that:

> The project suffered a 'mid-life identity crisis' as clinicians who had previously been well disposed to the *Connecting for Health* vision began to identify PAS with support for a trading hub rather than front line support.

The chapter has already noted the extensive comment on the rigidly specified timing of systems implementation across the NPfIT. The case study findings corroborate this but they also show that the schedules imposed by CFH could be disrupted by factors beyond the control of project management teams. One community service that had been due to go 'live' on the PAS experienced a sharp rise in workload following the award of new contracts from an NHS purchaser. The CL argued that the 'go live' date should be deferred by two months in order to see the resource implications of the new contracts for workloads and throughput. The argument was that the system would be deployed exactly as agreed in the contract with the LSP:

> RESPONDENT: Delaying the implementation wasn't going to have any impact on the overall programme, it had no impact on training, and we mitigated all the other risks. We were told 'the implementation will go live today regardless of the business impacts...' I refused and we didn't do it.
> INTERVIEWER: And this was accepted by the LSP?
> RESPONDENT: Yes, but I also had the backing of our board internally, they were fully supportive—for me it was about conflict resolution and we didn't resolve the conflict... it was an issue all the way through.
> INTERVIEWER: So would you say that your big issue with the project is not just its top-down management style but also maybe the ability to contest it?
> RESPONDENT: Absolutely, without a doubt
> INTERVIEWER: And that contestation is real?
> RESPONDENT: Very much so

The contract with the LSP had been signed on the basis that the CFH systems could be developed in ways that would offer 'seamless' service delivery between the assessment of a patient's needs and the care planning requirements for different services. The project planning documents outlined an expanding series of applications that would be deployed in successive phases or 'releases' following the initial PAS, each of which would enhance the functioning of the previous release. The second release, timed for early 2009, was keenly anticipated by the project team because it was expected to support much richer clinical documentation than was contained in the initial release. However, the second release proved disappointing. Care assessments and care plans were available in separate releases but the system was unable to transfer data between the two. This lack of integration caused immediate problems with clinician 'buy-in'. The Director of ICT noted that:

> Immediately you have a problem in the sense that you are compliancy-wise mandated to take these products, but you can't affect how they operate... Nobody

in their right mind would have an assessment dislocated from a care plan because if another person needs to see it [the care plan] they need to see what the assessment was.

The CL corroborated this view, stating that:

CL:There is a contractual obligation about what we take for the next part of the system, and there is an expectation we will take it in a certain order on a certain date. We had to go to a meeting with the SHA to discuss what was feasible in a certain part of the system, what we were going to get delivered to us. When I analysed it from a clinical perspective I didn't think that it was fit for purpose, so my recommendation has been that we don't take the first release, even though this might have all sorts of contractual obligation impacts. The ICT director has backed my recommendation because he doesn't think that it is fit for purpose either. I am sorry we signed up to the [*Connecting for Health*] schedule in the plan because we were told it was going to do X. We have now discovered that it offers much less and with some potential for clinical risk built in as a result...so we were saying [to the SHA] no, you need to sort out any contractual problems.

INTERVIEWER: so you were in effect defending the principle of flexibility and interpretation?

CL: Yes fully, and if it is not right for you as an organisation that flexibility has to be there... That should be fundamental, because otherwise you have to sign up to these projects with very little knowledge... You can't see the contracts, they are national and locked away, nobody knows what's in them, you get very scant information about what's in the product, because it is still in development— they haven't even built it yet, so you are taking a leap in the dark... a leap of faith about what you are going to get.

The CL described the implementation of PAS as a 'tortuous' process, noting the need to engage clinicians in IT projects 'on their own terms'. The implementation of PAS was a lengthy and typically 'episodic' process in which those responsible for managing the project were confronted by a series of technical, political, and logistical problems in the two years since PAS was first introduced. The CL also noted that:

We are getting into that upwards slope now on the change continuum; people are now starting to accept it.

Some of the evidence from Western PCT supports the idea that new forms of 'distributed change management' are emerging in the context of the NPfIT (Buchanan et al. 2007a, 2007b). Internal documentation provided by the Trust shows that the CL was given a broadly defined change management remit within the PAS project, but this was nevertheless framed by the tight deadlines and delimited by the 'business process' approach.[9] At the time of the fieldwork the CL and another member of the PAS project team had recently carried out a series of data quality investigations on the first release of the PAS. These were apparently satisfactory and had been presented to one of the PCT directors. Although these were expected to be 'a long journey' for the local clinicians and the service administrators, the CL noted that the project management team had learnt lessons about professional culture and empowerment from earlier setbacks. The Director of ICT noted that the Trust had made user engagement a priority:

> ...in order to offset the inevitable organizational fatigue that kicks in when delays and problems occur.

This case study investigation gives some sense of the complexity, ambiguity, and divergent interests associated with a single PAS as it was implemented under the auspices of the NPfIT and CFH. The centralized nature of the deployment contrasts strongly with the relatively open and participative approach adopted with the earlier system. However, the case also shows the ways in which the situated practices and professional identities of agents on the ground provided a reference point for processes of contestation and negotiation as the systems were imposed on local clinical practice. These aspects are explored further below.

Discussion

This chapter has located the NPfIT in the broader policy context of NHS reform, and it has also related the 'networked' logic of the Programme to contemporary theorizations of post-bureaucracy. The theme of organizational hybridity features prominently in the broader 'networking' logic followed by CFH and it is also clearly apparent in the micropolitics of PAS implementation. Our discussion of these aspects forms the backdrop to some brief theoretical reflections presented in the concluding section.

The NPfIT is rooted in a policy context in which central government no longer assumes sole responsibility for the management of complex institutional changes. The Programme has been designed and implemented around the divergent requirements of several different bureaucracies. The balkanized nature of the initiative finds its clearest expression in the failure of the CFH agency to align a complex range of 'heterogeneous' political interests and constituencies. The evidence presented in this chapter is consistent with the idea that the NPM has been accompanied by a substantial 'hollowing out' of the British state (Rhodes 2000). In the case of the NHS, control over operational management has been shifted from the Department of Health to newly created agencies. The fragmentation that has followed from this 'agentification' (Hood 1998) has created a greater need for coordination whilst reducing the ability of the Department of Health to coordinate its own operations (Rhodes 2000: 351). The decision to replace the NHS Information Authority with a new directorate that would coordinate a network of private sector contractors is consistent with the view that there has been a shift away from hierarchy and bureaucratic rule-making towards new forms of governance based on 'networked' organizational forms (Rhodes 1994, 1997; Pierre and Peters 2005). Public sector networks offer 'collaborative advantages' over traditionally bureaucratized, state-centred modes of governing (Castells 2000; Hendriks 2009).[10] These benefits include improved problem-solving capability, greater flexibility, and more efficient service delivery (Kikert et al. 1997; Rhodes 1997; Skelcher et al. 2005; Marcussen and Torfing 2007). However, the process whereby inter-organizational networks are formed is open-ended and may be realized in a manifold diversity of ways. The 'variable geometry' of these networks (see also Reed in this volume) means that they are compatible with both hierarchy and oligarchy.[11] Here the clear implication is that the 'collaborative', 'democratic', and 'open' qualities commonly attributed to 'networked' organizational forms should be understood as made and not given. Recent anti-foundationalist critiques have recognized the role of broader historical and contingent factors in conditioning public sector networks (Bevir and Richards 2009), challenging the epochalist idea that 'impersonal forces are driving a shift from hierarchy to networks' (Bevir and Richards 2009: 7).

The NPfIT has created a highly decentralized and variegated delivery structure that cuts across a variety of organizational, professional, and geographical boundaries. And yet responsibility for IT provision has been devolved to a small number of private sector corporations whose strategic interests have little or no relation to the need for more transparent or accountable provision of health care. The centralizing tendencies of the Programme have become more apparent as the autonomy of individual Trusts has been undermined by the contractual obligations owed to LSPs, whilst SHAs have imposed a plethora of controls based on performance management measures and quality audits. Networks have long been imbued with 'totemic' qualities of flexibility, openness, and low cost (Hill et al. 2000), but comparative work on public sector networks suggests they are inherently resistant to steering, difficult to combine with other governing structures, and prone to immobilisation by conflicts of interest. These features are clearly manifested in the existing research on the NPfIT (Currie and Guah 2007; Mark 2007) and they are corroborated by the case study findings presented in this chapter. The operating priorities of the LSP differed very markedly from those of Western PCT and the 'networked' forms of governance imposed by CFH appear to have created ambiguity and dissension over the definition of basic IT requirements, the timing of particular IT deployments, and the matching of IT specifications to local clinical needs.

Western PCT faced very considerable logistical and political challenges as it implemented the PAS. The case study evidence corroborates the view that centrally imposed timescales placed heavy demands on those responsible for the implementing of NPfIT applications within the Trust. Western PCT placed considerable emphasis on the management of stakeholders, but our interviewees made it clear that the timetabling of (the PAS deployment) (formally expressed in the CFH contract with the LSP) had seriously undermined the Trust's capacity for authentic engagement with users. The implementation process was, moreover, dominated by the highly mechanistic language of business process reengineering that construed the PAS as unproblematic and inherently positive for the organization of clinical practice. The CL responsible for managing the implementation of the PAS project expressed a strong commitment to the realization of the project whilst exercising selective forms of resistance when the timing and systems deployments exposed the Trust to clinical risk. These manifestations of organizational hybridity reflect the 'conflicting institutional logics' noted by Currie and Guah's study (2007) of the NPfIT and they also provide support for a 'sedimented' view of organizational change (McNulty and Ferlie 2004; Buchanan and Fitzgerald, in this volume).

Conclusion

Some clear indications of fragmentation and organizational hybridity have emerged from our case study analysis. The NPfIT combines concentration of power with a highly fragmented approach to coordinating IT procurement and infrastructural development. Responsibility for the specification, procurement, and deployment of IT systems has been abstracted from its local context, creating unintended consequences and the loss of 'tacit knowledge'. These aspects of the programme recall 'the politics of forgetting' observed elsewhere in the UK public sector (Harris and Wegg-Prosser 2007), and they bear out Pollitt's argument that restructuring, 'incessant change', and over-centralized investment in IT systems leads to a loss of organizational memory (Pollitt 2009). The NPfIT example indicates that this view of the 'post-bureaucratic' world might be further nuanced in line with recent work on the role of power and legitimacy in explaining institutional change (Suchman 1995; Gordon et al. 2009). This chapter corroborates the view that new IT systems may exacerbate clinical risk as patient records are transcribed to new systems. Vital information may be lost as new applications are introduced— and this is regarded as particularly hazardous where patient care is administered on the basis of co-dependent services. However, it was also apparent that the process of adapting these systems to local conditions and clinical needs offered an important opportunity for 'inscribing' the PAS in accordance with the situated practices and strategic dispositions of local actors (Hoskin and Macve 1986; Bloomfield et al. 1992; Cooper 1992; Kallinikos 1994).[12]

The PAS introduced at Western PCT emerged as a site of resistance and contestation. On one hand, the system symbolized the centrally determined shift to the new operating norms and procedures of the 'business process' perspective. On the other hand, it is apparent that NHS clinicians may revalidate extant professional practices as they inscribe these systems with locally articulated meanings and public sector values. Both aspects occur within a process of 'bureaucratic writing' that appears to be fundamentally Janus-faced and thus cognate with the idea of organizational hybridity. The theme of hybridity is also apparent at the broader institutional level. The award of single contracts to private sector IT suppliers has undermined the capacity of NHS Trusts to determine their own IT strategies, and there is a clear danger that IT expertise will become increasingly detached from clinical practice. Local actors may, however, resist the inappropriate or ill-timed imposition of new systems when these create unacceptable clinical risk, and the case shows that the 'recursive constitution of legitimacy' (Gordon et al. 2009: 32) acted as a contextual referent that allowed local actors to challenge the technicism and managerialism of the 'change management' agendas promulgated by CFH.

The discourse of the NPfIT postulated a radically new, entirely discontinuous movement towards an NHS whose modes of organization would be transformed by the rapid introduction of new information infrastructures. The seamless vision of a digital future offered by New Labour policy makers was, however, blind to the complex history and organization of the NHS. The disaggregation of IT provision has undermined, but not displaced, the power of clinicians and IT professionals to determine their own organizational futures. The 'transformational' rhetoric of the Programme sits uneasily with the underlying questions of power and legitimacy that have long dominated the institutional landscape of the NHS (Klein 2001; Webster 2002; Harrison and McDonald 2008). This landscape is being shaped, not by digital technology, but by continued political dissent and resistance as the values of NHS clinicians have clashed with the doctrinal imperatives of marketization, outsourcing and the 'contract state'.

⬚ NOTES

1. Debate on 'hybrid' political regimes and democratic hierarchies is centred on the question of how organizations may combine the centralized control and coordination of resources with the flexibility and creativity offered by agents (on the ground). Thus, Reed and Courpasson (2004) show that project managers may exercise considerable autonomy, but do so within a wider bureaucratic context of control. Hill et al. (2000) show that strategies of outsourcing by advanced manufacturers coincided with more centralized financial control of R&D activities. Bloomfield and Hayes (2009) provide an extended discussion of ICT and organizational hybridity in a UK public sector setting.

2. The current debate on EPRs centres on some politically contentious questions of who owns the data contained in such records, and who gets access to which aspects of the electronic record. These issues were noted in the 2006 National Audit Office report on the NPfIT (NAO 2006). A subsequent Department of Health report examined the implications of summary care records in the context of the UK national data Spine (Department of Health 2006).

3. The centralizing features of the initiative have attracted widespread comment. A 2007 House of Commons (PAC 2007: 6) argued that there was an urgent need for the UK Department of Health to improve communications with NHS clinicians. The British Medical Association recommended a programme of 'renewed engagement' with NPfIT users across primary acute and community units (BMA 2007).

4. Peltu et al. (2008) record that a number of London Mental Health Trusts found that the EPR systems offered by the LSP had been designed for use in acute hospitals, did not contain facilities to deal with certain aspects of mental health care. A data migration programme run by the Nuffield Orthopaedic Centre resulted in the loss of patient records. The implementation of a Patient Administration System at an NHS Trust in Kent was seriously delayed when it was found to be incompatible with the *Choose and Book* system.

5. Peltu et al. (2008) also cite the case of an accident and emergency department experiencing difficulties in inputting and accessing information to NPfIT terminals. Individual staff members found that using their smartcards slowed their work, and they 'worked round' the system by using a single card to operate the system.

6. A recurring theme in the debate on NPM and the future of the UK public sector has been constraints on public sector expenditure and the need to 'do more with less' (Hood 1998; Hoggett 1996; Rhodes 2000). Hoggett (1996) argues that the 'success' of conservative governments has been to move decisively towards a 'high output/low commitment' public sector workforce. This is consistent with the 'slow death' of the Keynesian Welfare State that followed from successive waves of fiscal crisis and retrenchment in UK public expenditure.

7. The NHS has used computer-based hospital patient administration systems since the late 1960s. PASs began to appear in community care settings during the 1980s and 1990s. These systems were frequently aimed at providing financial and activity data rather than health status data. The PAS referred to in this chapter reflects the next generation of systems now being implemented under the auspices of CFH. These systems are designed to support administrators and clinicians working in Primary Care settings, including community, child health, and general practice. Their functions include patient registration, referrals, caseload management, scheduling, and appointments. They also support a variety of administrative, reporting, and operations management activities.

8. The 'transformational' claims of the business process reengineering movement have been undermined by evidence that points to high failure rates and mundane forms of simplification and automation (Grint and Willcocks 1995; Knights and Willmott 2000).

9. The Western PCT evidence complements work by Buchanan et al. (2007a) on the change management processes associated with the introduction of patient booking systems in an acute hospital setting. These authors found that individuals from administrative, secretarial, clerical, and nursing backgrounds were being deployed in change management roles. The length of service, depth of organizational knowledge, personal credibility, and political sensitivity of these individuals emerged as important influences on the sustainability of particular innovations. These authors make the tentative claim that we may be seeing an alternative form of 'distributed change agency' based on the exercise of leadership that is 'more localized, more diffuse, more modest, and less visible' than traditional forms.

However, they also note that new and more distributed forms of change management are likely to coexist with top-down modes of coordination and control.

10. So, for example, in Castells influential account, the network enterprise is defined as 'a dynamic and strategically planned network of self-programmed units based on decentralisation, participation, and coordination' (Castells 2000: 178).

11. Hendricks (2009) shows the ways in which public–private partnerships in the Dutch energy sector were dominated by industry and government elites. Inter-organizational networks can thus be understood as 'both an opportunity and a threat to democracy' (Hendricks 2009: 1,009).

12. Bloomfield et al. (1992) argue that IT is apprehended through the deployment of various 'inscription devices' that operate as intermediaries between technology and its users. The various means of selecting, transcribing, and encoding bureaucratic records serve to construct as well as to describe the reality of organizational life.

☐ BIBLIOGRAPHY

Bell, D. (1974) *The Coming of Post-Industrial Society: A Venture in Social Forecasting*, London: Heineman.

Bellamy, C. and Taylor, J. (1998) *Governing in the Information Age*, Buckingham: Open University Press.

Bevir, M. and Richards, D. (2009) Decentring Policy Networks: Lessons and Prospects, *Public Administration*, 87(1): 132–41.

Bloomfield, B., Coombs, R., Knights, D. and Littler, D. (1992) *Information Technology and Organizations*, Oxford: Oxford University Press.

——Hayes, N. (2009) Power and Organizational Transformation through Technology: Hybrids of Electronic Government, *Organizational Studies*, 30(5): 461–87.

Bridges, J., Fitzgerald, L. and Meyer, J. (2007) New Workforce Roles in Healthcare: Exploring the Longer Term Journey of Organizational Innovations, *Journal of Health Organization and Management*, 21(4/5): 381–92.

British Medical Association (2007) *BMA Recommendations on the National Programme for Information Technology (NPfIT)*, London: British Medical Association.

Buchanan, D., Fitzgerald, L. and Ketley, D. (eds) (2007a) *The Sustainability and Spread of Organizational Change*, Oxford: Oxford University Press.

Buchanan, D., Addicot, R., Fitzgerald, L., Ferlie, E., and Baeza, J. (2007b) Nobody in Charge: Distributed Change Agency in Healthcare, *Human Relations*, 60(7): 1065–90.

Cabinet Office (1999) *Modernizing Government*, London: Stationery Office, Cm 4310.

Castells, M. (2000) *The Information Age: Economy, Society and Culture, Volume I, The Rise of the Network Society*, 2nd edn, Oxford: Blackwell.

Ciborra, C. and associates (2000) *From Control to Drift: The Dynamics of Corporate Information Infrastructures*, Oxford: Oxford University Press.

Clegg, S. and Courpasson, D. (2004) Political Hybrids: Tocquevillean Views on Project Organizations, *Journal of Management Studies*, 41(4): 525–47.

Connecting for Health (CFH) (2006) *Response to Media Reports about LORENZO Software Development*, Leeds: Connecting for Health (28 September), available at: www.connecting forhealth.nhs.uk/newsroom/media/lorenzo_statement_210806?searchterm=lorenzo (accessed 7 October 2009).

——(2007) *Changes to delivery of NHS National Programme for IT*, Leeds: Connecting for Health (28 September), available at: www.connectingforhealth.nhs.uk/newsroom/news-stories/npfit_delivery?searchterm=accenture (accessed 7 October 2009).

Connecting for Health (CFH) (2008) *Mainstreaming Information Management and Technology: Summary of Community PAS Benefits, Courtyard Group*, March 2008.

Cooper, R. (1992) Formal Organization as Representation: Remote Control, Displacement and Abbreviation, in M. Reed and M. Hughes (eds), *Rethinking Organization: New Directions in Organization Theory and Analysis*, London: Sage, 254–72.

Courpasson, D. (2000) Manageral Strategies of Domination. Power in Soft Bureaucracies: *Organization Studies*, 21/1. 141–61.

——and Dany, F. (2009) Cultures of Resistance in the Workplace, in Clegg, S.R. and Haugaard, M. (eds.), *Handbook of Power*, Sage: 332–47.

Currie, W.L. and Guah, M.W. (2007) Conflicting Institutional Logics: A National Programme for IT in the Organisational Field of Healthcare, *Journal of Information Technology*, 22: 235–47.

Curthays, N. and Crabtree, J. (2003) *SmartGov: Renewing Electronic Government for Improved Service Delivery*: The Work Foundation, London.

Dent, M. (1995) The New National Health Service: A Case of Postmodernism?, *Organizational Studies*, 16(5): 875–99.

Department of Health (1998) *Information for Health: An Information Strategy for the Modern NHS 1998–2005; A National Strategy for Local Implementation*, London: Department of Health, available at: www.dh.gov.uk/prod_consum_dh/groups/dh_digitalassets/@dh/@en/documents/digitalasset/dh_4014469.pdf (accessed 7 October 2009).

——(2000) *The NHS Plan: A Plan for Investment; A Plan for Reform*, London: The Stationery Office Ltd, available at: http://www.dh.gov.uk/en/Publicationsandstatistics/Publications/PublicationsPolicyAndGuidance/DH_4002960 (accessed 7 October 2009).

——(2002) *Delivering 21st Century IT Support for the NHS: National Strategic Programme*, London: NHS Confederation.

——(2006) *Minister Announces Taskforce for Electronic Records*, London: Department of Health Press Office.

Dopson, S. and Fitzgerald, L. (2006) *Knowledge to Action? Evidence-based Health Care in Context*, Oxford: Oxford University Press.

du Gay, P. (2003) The Tyranny of the Epochal: Change, Epochalism and Organizational Reform, *Organization*, 10(4): 663–84.

Dunleavy, P., Margetts, H., Bastow, S. and Tinkler, J. (2006) *Digital Era Governance: IT Corporations, the State and E-Government*, Oxford: Oxford University Press.

Eason, K. (2007) Local Sociotechnical System Development in the NHS National Programme for Information Technology, *Journal of Information Technology*, 22: 257–64.

Fairclough, N. (2000) *New Labour, New Language?*, London: Routledge.

Farrell, C. and Morris, J. (2003) The Neo-Bureaucratic State: Professions, Managers and Professional Managers in Schools, General Practices and Social Work, *Organization*, 10(1): 129–56.

Ferlie, E., Ashburner, L., Fitzgerald, L. and Pettigrew, A. (1996) *The New Public Management in Action*, Oxford: Oxford University Press.

——Fitzgerald, L. (2001) The Sustainability of the New Public Management in the UK, in K. Mclaughlin, S. Osbourne and E. Ferlie (eds), *The New Public Management, Current Trends and Future Prospects*, London: Routledge, 341–53.

——Geraghty, K.J. (2007) Professionals in Public Services Organizations: Implications for Public Sector 'Reforming', in E. Ferlie, L.E. Lynn and C. Pollitt (eds), *The Oxford Handbook of Public Management*, Oxford: Oxford University Press.

——McNulty, T. (2002) *Reengineering Healthcare: The complexities of Organizational Transformation*, Oxford: Oxford University Press.

Gordon, R., Kornberger, M. and Clegg, S. (2009) Power, Rationality and Legitimacy in Public Organizations, *Public Administration*, 87(1): 15–34.

Grint, K. and Willcocks, L. (1995) Business Process Reengineering in Theory and Practice: Business Paradise Regained, *New Technology Work and Employment*, 10(2): 99–109.

Harris, M. (2008) Digital Technology and Governance in Transition: The Case of the British Library, *Human Relations*, 61(5): 741–58.

——Wegg-Prosser, V. (2007) Post Bureaucracy and the Politics of Forgetting: The Management of Change at the BBC 1991–2002, *Journal of Organisational Change Management*, 20(3): 290–303.

Harrison, S. and McDonald, R. (2008) *The Politics of Healthcare in Britain*, London: Sage Publications.

Heckscher, C. (1994) Defining the Post-Bureaucratic Type, in C. Heckscher and A. Donnellon (eds), *The Post Bureaucratic Organization: New Perspectives on Organizational Change*, Thousand Oaks, California: Sage.

——Donnellon, A. (1994) *The Post Bureaucratic Organization: New Perspectives on Organizational Change*, Thousand Oaks, California: Sage.

Hendricks, C. (2009) On Inclusion and Network Governance: The Democratic Disconnect of Dutch Energy Transitions, *Public Administration*, 86(4): 1009–31.

Hendy, J., Fulop, N., Huchings, A. and Masseria, C. (2005) Challenges to Implementing the National Programme for Information Technology: A Qualitative Study, *British Medical Journal*, 331–6 (6 August).

Hill, S., Martin, R. and Harris, M. (2000) Decentralization, Integration and the Post Bureaucratic Organization: The Case of R&D, *Journal of Management Studies*, 37(4): 563–85.

Hoggett, P. (1996) New Modes of Control in the Public Service, *Public Administration*, 74 (Spring): 9–32.

Hood, C. (1998) *The Art of the State: Culture, Rhetoric and Public Management*, Oxford: Clarendon Press.

Hoskin, K. and Macve, R. (1986) Accounting and the Examination: A Genealogy of Disciplinary Power, *Accounting, Organization and Society*, 11(2): 105–36.

Josserand, E., Teo, S. and Clegg, S. (2006) From Bureaucratic to Post-Bureaucratic: The Difficulties of Transition, *Journal of Organizational Change Management*, 19(1): 54–64.

Kallinikos, J. (1994) Predictable Worlds: On Writing, Rationality and Organizations, in *Workshop on Writing, Rationality and Organization*, 21–22 March, European Association for Advanced Studies on Management, Brussels.

——(2006) *The Consequences of Information: Institutional Implications of Technological Change*, Cheltenham: Edward Elgar.

Kikert, W.J.M., Klinj, E., and Koppenjan, J.F.M. (eds.) (1997) *Managing Complex Networks: Strategies for the Public Sector*, London: Sage.

Kirkpatrick, I. and Martinez Lucio, M. (1996) Introduction to Special Issue of Public Administration: The Contract State and the Future of Public Management, *Public Administration*, 74 (1): 1–8.

Klein, R. (2001) *The New Politics of the NHS*, 4th edn, Harlow: Pearson/Prentice Hall.

Klijn, E.-H. (2005) Networks and Inter-Organizational Management: Challenging, Steering, Evaluation and the Role of Public Actors in Public Management, in E. Ferlie, L.E. Lynn and C. Pollitt (eds), *The Oxford Handbook of Public Management*, Oxford: Oxford University Press, 257–81.

Knights, D. and Willmott, H. (2000) *The Reengineering Revolution: Critical Studies in Corporate Change*, London: Sage Publications.

Kumar, K. (1995) *From Post-Industrial to Post-Modern Society*, Oxford: Blackwell.

Marcussen, M. and Torfing, J. (2007) *Democratic Network Governance in Europe*, London: Palgrave.

Margetts, H. (2007) Virtual Organizations, in E. Ferlie, L.E. Lynn and C. Pollitt (eds), *The Oxford Handbook of Public Management*, Oxford: Oxford University Press.

Mark, A.L. (2007) Modernising Healthcare—Is the NPfIT for Purpose?, *Journal of Information Technology*, 22: 248–56.

Mattelart, A. (2003) *The Information Society: An Introduction*, London: Sage.

McNulty, T. and Ferlie, E. (2002) *Reengineering Health Care: The Complexities of Organizational Transformation*, Oxford: Oxford University Press.

——— (2002) *Reengineering Health Care: The Complexities of Organizational Transformation*, Oxford: Oxford University Press.

——— (2004) Process Transformation: Limitations to Radical Organizational Change within Public Service Organizations, *Organization Studies*, 25(8).

Meier, K.J. and Hill, G.C. (2005) Bureaucracy in the Twenty-First Century, in E. Ferlie, L.E. Lynn and C. Pollitt (eds), *The Oxford Handbook of Public Management*, Oxford: Oxford University Press.

National Audit Office (NAO) (2006) *The National Programme for IT in the NHS*, London: National Audit Office, The Stationery Office (16 June), available at: www.nao.org.uk/publications / nao_reports/05-06/05061173.pdf (accessed 27 August 2010).

——— (2008) *The National Programme for IT in the NHS: Progress Since 2006*, London: National Audit Office, The Stationery Office, 16 May, available at www.nao.org.uk/ph/07-08/0708484. htm (accessed 27 August, 2010).

Newman, J. (2003) New Labour and the Politics of Governance, in A. Salminen (ed.), *Governing Networks*, Amsterdam: IOS Press, 83–99.

Osborne, S.P. (2000) *Public-Private Partnerships: Theory and Practice in International Perspective*, London: Routledge.

PAC (2007) *The National Programme for IT in the NHS*, London: House of Commons Committee of Public Accounts, London: The Stationery Office (11 April 2007), available at: www. publications.parliament.uk/pa/cm200607/cmselect/cmpubacc/390/390.pdf www.nao.org.uk/ pn/07-08/0708484.htm (accessed 7 October 2009).

Peltu, M., Eason, K. and Clegg, C. (2008) *How a Sociotechnical Approach can Help NPfIT Deliver Better NHS Patient Care*, Report to the British Computing Society Sociotechnical Specialist Group, available at: http://lubswww2/COSLAC/index.php?id=54 and http://www.bcs.org/ server.php?show=nav.9932 (accessed 7 October 2009), London: National Audit Office, The Stationary Office, 16 May, available at www.nao.org.uk/pn/07-08/0708484.htm (accessed 27 August, 2009).

Peters, B. G. and Pierre, J. (1998) Governance without Governments?, *Journal of Public Administration Research and Theory* 8: 223–44.

Pierre, J. and Peters, B.G. (2005) *Governing Complex Societies: Trajectories and Scenarios*, London: Palgrave McMillan.

Pollitt, C. (2003) Joined-up Government: A Survey, *Political Studies Review*, 1: 34–49.

——(2009) Bureaucracies Remember, Post Bureaucratic Organizations Forget?, *Public Administration*, 87(2): 98–218.

Randell, B. (2007) A Computer Scientist Reactions to NPfIT, *Journal of Information Technology*, 22: 222–34.

Reed, M. (2005) Beyond the Iron Cage? Bureaucracy and Democracy in the Knowledge Economy and Society, in P. du Gay (ed.), *The Values of Bureaucracy*, Oxford: Oxford University Press.

Reed, M., Courpasson, D. (2004) Introduction: Special issue on Bureaucracy in the Age of Enterprise, *Organization*, 11(1): 5–12.

——Ezzamel, M. (2008) Introduction. Special issue on Governance in Transition? Emerging Paradigms and Practices for the 21st Century, *Human Relations*, 61(5): 595–6.

Rhodes, R.A.W. (1994) The Hollowing out of the State, *Political Quarterly*, 65: 138–51.

——(1997) The New Governance: Governing without Government, *Political Studies Association*, 44(4): 651–67.

——(2000) The Governance Narrative: Key Findings and Lessons from the ESRC's Whitehall Programme, *Public Administration*, 78(2): 345–64.

Sauer, C. and Willcocks, L. (2007) Unreasonable Expectations—NHS IT, Greek Choruses and the Games Institutions Play around Mega-Programmes, *Journal of information Technology*, 22: 195–201.

Serougi, N. (2008) Connecting for Health—An Analysis of the Context and Impacts of Major Technology in the NHS, seminar paper to the Essex University department of Health and Human Sciences, May 2008.

Skelcher, C. (2005) Public-Private Partnerships and Hybridity, in E. Ferlie, L.E. Lynn and C. Pollitt (eds), *The Oxford Handbook of Public Management*, Oxford: Oxford University Press, 347–70.

——Mathur, N. and Smith, M. (2005) The Public Governance of Collaborative spaces; Discourse, design and democracy, *Public Administration*, 83(3): 573–96.

Smith, C., Valsecchi, R., Mueller, F. and Gabe, J. (2008) Knowledge and the Discourse of Labour Process Transformation, Nurses and the Case of NHS Direct for England, *Work, Employment and Society*, 22(4): 581–99.

Sorensen, E. and Torfing, J. (2007) *Theories of Democratic Network Governance*, Basingstoke: Palgrave McMillan.

Suchman, M. (1995) Managing Legitimacy: Strategic and Institutional Approaches, *Academy of Management Review*, 20(3): 571–610.

Wanless, D. (2002) *Securing Our Future Health: Taking a Long-Term View*, London: HM Treasury, available at: www.hmtreasury.gov.uk/Consultations_and_Legislation/wanless/ consult_wanless_final.cfm (accessed 7 October 2009).

Webster, C. (2002) *The National Health Service: A Political History*, Oxford: Oxford University Press.

6 Bureaucracy under Siege: On Information, Collaboration, and Networks

JANNIS KALLINIKOS

Introduction

The convergence and gradual solidification of the socio-technical changes associated with the diffusion of information over the last few decades are establishing a new socio-economic environment in which information-based tasks and services acquire central importance. Information and the technologies and artefacts by which it is produced penetrate deep into the social fabric, mediating a wide range of new cultural impressions and promoting novel modes of living, acting, and communicating. At the same time, these developments impinge upon the production apparatuses of modern societies, redefining the nature of organizations and the structural scaffolds upon which organizational operations have been crafted since the consolidation of the present regime (e.g. Castells 1996; Sassen 2001; Webster 2002).

The cultural and technological shifts that characterize the present age have frequently been tied to the diffusion of networks as organizational arrangements for producing goods and services, an idea that has been articulated as a compelling claim by (Castells, 1996; 2000; 2001). Just a decade after Castells' seminal contribution (1996), this idea has been given a new push by Benkler's influential portrayal (2006) of the *collaborative arrangements* that mark the production of information-based goods and services, for example, open-source software production and Wikipedia. Benkler's key claim is that these developments instantiate a mode of producing goods and services that no longer needs to rely on the institutional framework of markets and corporations. *Social production*, as he refers to it, is the joint outcome of several developments, among which figure (*a*) the publicly available and non-rival nature of much information, (*b*) the diffusion of information resources across the population, (*c*) the distinctive character of computational technology, and (*d*) the low capital necessary to sustain network associations over the Internet. Combined with the circumvention of property rights (through e.g. GNU/ GPL), these conditions give rise to distributed, modular, and flexible arrangements of collaboration by which the accomplishment of information-based products or services can be pursued.

Whether, and the extent to which these arrangements will change the prevailing institutional landscape associated with markets, corporations, and property rights remains an open question. Most probably, they will not. Or, as the ongoing debate on collaboration suggests (Von Hippel 2005; Tapscott and Williams 2006), they will be consolidated into the prevailing institutional framework bringing along important changes. Irrespective of how things may turn out, the fluid patterns of collaboration that social production occasions do epitomize important cultural and technological shifts. In this respect, Benkler's claim is indicative of a growing awareness associated with these developments. Similar ideas have been around for quite a while and key parts of Benkler's claim owe much to scholars such as Lessig (2002), Raymond (2001), Von Hippel (2005), Wenger (1998), and others.

The claims that tie social production to the prospect of an entirely different organizational order, marked by openness and flexibility, are closely associated with the fact that these collaborative arrangements cross the divide between the social and the economic. In so doing, collaboration transforms sociality into an important source of productive capacity and innovation. In conventional accounts of networks that divide is never really questioned. In Castells' account of informational capitalism, for instance, networks are predominantly seen as organizational arrangements that seek to bypass some of the rigidities of the prevailing institutional framework and accommodate the commercial and coordinative possibilities mediated by the new technologies of computing and communication (see Castells 1996, ch. 3, 2000, 2001, ch. 3).[1] By contrast, the concept of social production transcends that divide, suggesting that Internet-based communities and associations (often no more than informal and episodic) can become powerful producers of information-based goods and services. Online *sociality* can under specific conditions become a potent productive force, thus challenging the rigid institutional boundaries that modernity constructed around the pursuit of *economic* versus *social* objectives. The diffusion of information and the cultural orientations with which it is associated establish a new socio-economic environment, a habitat, as it were, in which the line between working and living, producing and consuming become increasingly blurred.

In this chapter, I am concerned with the prospects of social production and the developments with which it is associated, in a context that takes the institutional complexity of the modern social arrangement[2] more fully into account. Benkler (2006, ch. 4), along with many others, attributes the dominance of corporations to the high capital requirements of industrial production and the prevailing regime of property rights. According to this view, concentrated systems, of which corporations are a case *par excellence*, require high fixed costs necessary to establish and run them successfully, and the motivational structure (profit seeking and appropriation) that the prevailing regime of property rights helps set in place. The concentration of resources, which the collaborative arrangements of social production challenge, is thus predominantly attributed to the economics of production and the institutional framework (power, corporations, and property rights) within which production takes place.

Corporations are certainly economic institutions and their rise and institutional dominance are bound up with the economics of production and the prevailing regime of property rights (Roy 1997; Perrow 2002; Heugens 2005). It would be foolish to claim otherwise. Yet, the organization form which corporations by necessity assume (i.e. formal organization) stretches beyond the interpretive horizon of capital requirements and property rights. The pursuit of economic goals which corporations exemplify takes place within normative and regulative frameworks that reflect the solidification of cultural orientations and the negotiating outcomes of interests and power over a long historical period. Such frameworks constrain, shape, and, to a certain degree, constitute all those operations by means of which profit is pursued. Corporations are accordingly economic and social units at the same time. Unless one sees the normative and regulative edifice of modernity as a secondary and irrelevant epiphenomenon, something important gets lost when the understanding of corporations is exclusively framed in economic terms.

In what follows I first present the key ideas that make up the claim of social production and outline some of the organizational and institutional implications that are associated with it, as these have predominantly been formulated by Benkler (2002, 2006). I then make an effort to place the understanding of the current developments within the wider context of modernity. In so doing, I give due consideration to the organizational innovations that have been brought about by the diffusion and embeddedness of the modern social arrangement and the establishment of organizations as formal entities, distinctively different from physical persons. Thus construed, the similarities and differences of formal organizations and the collaborative arrangements of social production are cast into new light. In the last section of the chapter, I therefore attempt to discover the thread that runs through these developments and to reflect on the nature of social and organizational changes currently underway.

Social Production and Collaboration

Social production epitomizes the linking of *individual contributions* and *collective engagements* in new ways that are made possible by the cultural orientations associated with the diffusion of information and the technologies by which information-based goods and services are produced and disseminated. Internet-based collaboration demonstrates that the establishment of collective arrangements and the pursuit of collective goals (e.g. Wikipedia) can be dissociated from the steady and regular supply of individual inputs (e.g. a contribution to Wikipedia). This is an important organizational innovation that breaks with the concentrated nature of organizations (place, fixed work schedules, amassing of resources) and the *bounded* and *hierarchical* forms of governance by which goods and services have commonly been produced since the consolidation of the capitalist mode of production. An organization such as Wikipedia or Flickr, for instance, is no longer dependent on inputs delivered in fixed time schedules by a finite and well-defined number of individuals who are employees in the standard sense of the term. While the steady and comprehensive supply of inputs is critical for the system, it does not really matter who provides these inputs, when, and under which conditions. Social production then coincides with the establishment of loose collaborative networks in which individuals can join the pursuit of collective goods in variable patterns that shift considerably in intensity, commitment, and durability. A new paradigm for constructing collective arrangements is thus emerging.

While many factors converge to support the diffusion of such collaborative arrangements in which individuals are loosely tied to collective pursuits, two among them are worth mentioning (Benkler 2006; Kallinikos 2006b). These are:

1. the highly *diffused character of computational resources and information* across the population, and
2. the distinctive nature of computation as technology; more particularly the *modular and granular nature* of information systems and processes, which are composed of smaller and easily aggregated or dissolvable subtasks and routines that admit fine-grained and individualized initiatives.

The highly diffused status of information and communication resources (computers and computer-based artefacts) across the population gives individuals the opportunity to undertake a wide range of activities and execute a substantial range of information-based tasks and operations that have not been possible before. Despite important differences between economic classes that become even more substantial in the context of global inequalities (Avgerou 2002), a significant and growing number of individuals across the globe are able to acquire the necessary resources to accomplish a wide range of information tasks over the Internet. The relatively low cost of supporting this individualized possession of computational resources contrasts sharply with the substantial capital investments necessary to build up and operate firms and organizations under those conditions commonly associated with modern industrial capitalism and scale economies.

According to this view, the construction of organizations as *bounded, hierarchical, and concentrated systems* is predominantly driven by *the economics of production* and the high costs that the establishment of economic organizations incurs. By the same token, it is associated with the institutionalization of a regime within which *property rights* can be asserted. This last offers individuals with access to certain resources a degree of institutional protection against the risks implied by the establishment of economic organizations. By contrast, those that lack the necessary resources to pursue such an objective have to subordinate themselves to the fixed work schedules and the hierarchical forms of governance necessary to operate the system. The high capital requirements for establishing economic organizations then combine with the prevailing regime of property rights to drive the construction of concentrated organizational arrangements in which the majority of individuals are tied to the system in wholesale, inflexible, and, if one wants to go a little bit further, unequal terms (Clegg et al. 2006). A system of social subordination ensues from these differences that limits a deeper division of labour and may stifle creativity and freedom of expression.

The conditions epitomized by the growth of the Internet and the diffusion of computational resources across the population substantially lowers the capital requirements for establishing and maintaining associations and are thus important drivers behind the emerging patterns of collaboration. These claims constitute what I would call the *economic–technological* explanation of social networks and social production. Left on their own, these claims provide the necessary but not the sufficient conditions for the emergence and diffusion of social production and the association networks by which it is sustained. Resources must themselves be divisible, amenable to unbundling, and, crucially, freely distributable across space and time. Industrial plants, for instance, are often made up of bundled resources and tightly coupled operations that drive concentration and the construction of large systems, quite independently of the capital requirements and the proprietary framework to which they may be tied. Information and computational resources and operations differ in this respect and the analysis of the distinctive character of computation adds to the claims advanced so far an explanation of social production in *technological* and *cognitive* terms (Benkler 2006; Kallinikos 2006b).

The accomplishment of information tasks may acquire distributed forms by virtue of computational operations being *modular* and considerably *granular*. Modularity concerns the packaging of operations in relatively independent modules that allow for operational adequacy within a larger network of functional interdependencies. Granularity refers to the minute and piecemeal character of information-based operations that make up batches and modules. In this respect, granularity recounts the analytical status of information-based operations and their procedural character. Being digital, rather than analogue, technological information is granular by its very nature (Borgmann 1999; Kallinikos 2006*b*), yet different batches or modules can exhibit varying granularity in the sense of being composed of more or less inclusive steps or bundled operations. Open-source software production usually requires working on batches of code while Flickr, Wikipedia, or YouTube may admit more fine-grained operations such as minor revisions and smaller uploads or downloads.

Thus viewed, computation provides the premises for constructing a techno-cognitive universe in which a fine-grained division of labour prevails. Larger tasks can generally be broken down to smaller units and undertaken and executed in different times and with varying intensity by a widely dispersed population of individuals, as is often the case with open-source software production. Or, to refer to another context, contributions to Wikipedia can be made in one blow or in a piecemeal fashion that fits the time availability or other conditions of the contributing individual. Similarly, videos, pictures, photos, or scientific chapters can be uploaded/downloaded from or onto corresponding websites and virtual associations, massively or in smaller doses, in regular intervals or in an episodic fashion.

The granularity and modular character of information and computational tasks therefore dispense with an important technical precondition (i.e. the bundled, indivisible character of resources) behind the emergence of concentrated systems. By disentangling resources and uncoupling them from their attachment to particular locations and people, computation offers a new technological paradigm of resource dispersion, recombinability, and distribution. This is clearly evidenced by the spectacular diffusion of service outsourcing within the traditional regime of markets and corporations (Kallinikos 2006*b*; Clegg 2007). Coupled with the freely and publicly available nature of information and the diffusion of computational resources across the population, the decomposable character of information-based tasks and operations establish the conditions for the emergence of new modes by which individuals can be tied to complex and aggregate ventures.

The modular and granular nature of information and the ability to transact and communicate over the electronic medium have been instrumental in unbundling work processes and distributing work over sites and organizations long before the recent advent of open collaborative networks. The relative processes have accordingly been observed and studied by many scholars (see e.g. Schmidt and Bannon 1992; Ciborra 1996; Wellman et al. 1996; DeSanctis and Monge 1999; Knorr-Cetina and Bruegger 2002; Hinds and Mortensen 2005). However, studies of this kind have for the most part focused on the investigation of patterns of work, interaction and collaboration occurring within finite and relatively well-defined populations of individuals, often embedded in particular institutional settings. Such a research orientation differs substantially from the open character of the collaborative transactions that social production occasions (Iannacci 2005). It is the open and *non-determined* nature of the population of participating individuals that enable the different patterns of social production to emerge. While not everyone actually participates in the collaborative arrangements of social production, anyone can potentially do so. In this respect, Internet-based collaboration stretches beyond the coordinative template of tasks and operations usually associated with distributed work and interaction.

The open collaboration over the Internet that coincides with social production is certainly dependent on the fine-grained and modular division of labour which computation as technological paradigm provides. However, open collaboration is a social project made, *inter alia*, possible through the construction of a navigable information sphere and the social choices this inevitably implies (Bowker and Star 1999). The developments that render open collaboration over the Internet feasible are crucially dependent on the ability to cross the cultural boundaries of text, sound, and image (Kittler 1985; Jenkins 2006) and the different semiotic traditions (e.g. writing, filming, composing, or arranging) developed around them over the years, as the outcome of strong technical and institutional compartmentalization. In this respect, the Internet and the ensemble of technologies by which it is supported occasion the construction of a techno-cultural universe in which such diverse activities and skills as those associated with the production of text, image, and sound are rendered technically interoperable (Borgmann 1999; Manovich 2001; Kallinikos 2006b, 2009). Without the possibility of technologically crossing that cultural space smoothly, the prospects of social production and open collaboration would have been considerably truncated. Far from being a technical project alone, the navigable infospace that coincides with media convergence results from cultural predilections and economic and political bargaining by means of which the patchwork of systems, technologies, and information sources underlying the Internet is rendered interoperable (Bowker and Star 1999; Hanseth 2004; Pollock and Williams 2009). It is poignant in this respect to recall that much of the navigability of the Internet and the possibility of exchanging information is contingent on the degree to which information-based products and cultural artefacts remain shared resources, free from the restrictive bounds of copyright and other property-related matters. As the fight over the institutional environment of the Internet demonstrates, huge interests currently coalesce in their effort to substantially delimit the free circulation of information and information-based culture (see e.g. Lessig 2002; Benkler 2006; Zittrain 2006).

The Institutional Matrix of Modernity

The innovative character of the collaborative networks of social production are most clearly shown in the *highly personalized terms* by which individuals are able to contribute to collective pursuits. Internet-based collaborative networks accommodate the varying proclivities of individuals, their time availability, and motivation brought together in scalable arrangements that are no longer dependent on the steady supply of individual inputs. Individual contributions vary not only among individuals but also between different life situations, stages, or projects of the same individual. Such flexible and shifting involvement in collective value-producing pursuits would seem to contrast rather sharply with the concentrated nature of organizations and the enduring and strictly scheduled patterns of employment underlying them.

The tendency to contrast social production with formal organizational conceals a deeper layer of relations that is essential to the adequate understanding of Internet-based collaboration and its prospects. The stereotypical depiction of formal organizations as concentrated, monolithic, and inflexible does not do justice to the complexity, subtle character, and adaptive capacity of this institution, evident in the substantial transformations it has undergone over time. Seen from a larger time perspective, formal organizations represent an historically innovative mode of fashioning membership that makes individual participation in the organization contingent and variable at the same time as it subjects it to regulations of various kinds. As a matter of fact, the regulative frameworks that govern formal organizations reflect, *inter alia*, the need to shape the premises of individual participation in the organization rendered contingent and variable, as the outcome of the progressive detachment of social life from the invariable bonds of *gemeinschaft* and the normative regulation they afford (Gellner 1983, 1995; Luhmann 1998). Let me elaborate.

The constitution of formal organizations as institutional entities presupposes the establishment of an operational sphere, a jurisdiction, within which an organization is assigned the responsibility to operate, according to standards, laws, and regulations that render such responsibility accountable (Weber 1978). Formal status cannot be assumed unless an organization has been assigned, through legal[3] or political processes, responsibility to operate within a particular area (e.g. an industry, government department, health care, education, the church). This applies as much to state agencies and corporations as to trade unions, professional associations, or voluntary organizations. To assign jurisdiction to a collective unit, as opposed to physical persons, and render it legally or politically accountable, it is necessary to institutionally separate its collective status from the persons and things to which it could be related (Roy 1997; Kallinikos 2004, 2006b). Obvious as it may be, it is nonetheless worth stressing that formal organizations are not natural but institutional (reified) entities, that is, *contrived social regimes established by human, collectively based decisions to serve particular purposes.* Thus conceived, formal organizations are a qualitatively different species from all other manifestations of organized order found in nature and made popular over the last decades by complexity science.

An inevitable consequence of the institutional separation of the collective status of an organization from physical persons and things is that individuals are admitted into the organizational system not as full-blown persons but as *social categories, specializations,* or *roles* (employees but also owners and managers), on the basis of formal or socially certified criteria provided by education, professional ability and experience, or access to resources as in the case of corporations. Organizations, *qua* institutional entities, are not populated by flesh and blood people. Such a claim may be hard to accept in view of the massive presence of people in organizations, and the entanglement of abilities with personal characteristics and social or ideological identifications, so typical of human beings (Walzer 1983). And yet, modern organizations as institutions are made possible by what Searle (1995) calls institutional facts entailing the contrivance and imposition of a set of relations and functions upon more primary social or natural entities (Kallinikos 2006b). The abstract social maps formal organizations instantiate are clearly manifested in the fact that individual jobs and positions are, within the lifetime of an organization, frequently assumed by a number of individuals. The impersonal order that rules formal organizations, together with the pervasiveness of routines and standard operating procedures, are the inevitable outcome of such an abstract conception of social relations (Meyer and Jepperson 2000).

To conceive and construct organizations this way, it is necessary to render social relations mobile and adaptable to contingencies and, thus, free from the invariable bonds of kinship, fixed social stratification, or other non-negotiable social (not natural) attributes of individuals, characteristic of premodern social arrangements.[4] In this regard, formal organizations are inseparable from the establishment of modernity, its cultural predispositions, and socio-political arrangements (Gellner 1983; Kallinikos 2006b). Placed in this context, formal organizations should be understood not only as instrumental but also social and political institutions (in the broad sense the term 'political' carries). Much of their distinctive operative profile derives from an amalgamation of sheer functional prerequisites with key polity concerns and the effort to align the pursuit of efficiency with key values of the modern social arrangement, for example, accountability, meritocracy and impartiality, transparency and universalism (Beck 2000; du Gay 2000, 2005; Kallinikos 2006a, 2006b). The safeguarding of these values has been inextricably bound up with the establishment of a rational–legal framework (opposed to tradition and personal charisma) of organizational governance that since Weber (1947, 1970, 1978) has been known as bureaucracy.

In thus describing formal organizations, I do not want to deny the social and economic practices, occasionally pervasive (e.g. family business, political patronage), that have persisted alongside the prevailing institutional matrix of the modern social arrangement. Nor do I wish to underestimate the social skills, techniques, programmes, or schemes by which these abstract ideals, principles, and cultural orientations are turned to reality (see e.g. Walzer 1983; Hasselbladh and Kallinikos 2000). The practices by which formal organizations are made accountable and the personnel policies and procedures by means of which organizations seek to address the principles of meritocracy, transparency, and impartiality in hiring and promotion entail a variety of subtle and elaborate operations. Distributed among different agents, these operations are undeniably subject to the local interpretation and, not infrequently, deliberate manipulation of the regulative frameworks in which they are ingrained. But my purpose here is primarily to paint in brush strokes the prevailing institutional matrix in which formal organizations, and corporations as a subspecies of formal organizations, are embedded. Principles are, alas, turned to reality by social practices but such a state of affairs does not deny the decisive role principles play in shaping these practices. The institutional matrix of which formal organizations are part and parcel is essential to constituting them as collective entities of a distinctive, historically embedded kind, and for shaping their operations.

The institution of property rights is undeniably a critical component of that framework but it does not exhaust its multivalent constitution and institutional coverage. The separation, for instance, of ownership from management that coincides with the institutional prevalence of the corporation (Chandler 1977; Roy 1997) reflects the same cultural developments of unbundling the construction of institutional entities and processes from real persons and things (Giddens 1990; Meyer and Jepperson 2000). The same holds true for authority and the ways in which modern hierarchy (as opposed to fixed stratification) operates. The formal nature of modern organizations is part and parcel of the effort to produce general principles and standards for constituting and regulating social relationships in such stringent, goal-oriented collectives. Employees, civil servants, professionals, owners, managers are all constructed social categories, institutional roles whose involvement in the organization is legally based and regulated. It is of utmost importance to uphold these claims, given the character of many recent developments (including those associated with social production) away from the forms of membership which formal organization has historically occasioned.

Organizing Logics: Stratification versus function

The regulative order ruling formal organizations is closely associated with the contingent and variable forms which individual involvement in organizations acquires as the inevitable outcome of the relations I have sketched in the preceding section. While relying on standardized job categories and skill profiles, the formal status of collective institutional entities is nonetheless an essential medium of social pliability and institutional flexibility (Pottage 1998; Meyer and Jepperson 2000; Feldman and Pentland 2003). By detaching individual involvement in the organization from personal predispositions and the invariable bonds of community and tradition, formal organization renders it potentially pliable, adaptable to the contingencies it addresses, and therefore variable. Placed in this context, the individual/organization relationship entails an element of choice on both sides, that is, the organization and the individual. Even though individuals may be driven to join an organization by a variety of compelling reasons (e.g. employees for reasons of subsistence) that may leave in practice little space for choice and freedom (Perrow 1986, 2002; Clegg et al. 2006), it should, at least in principle, be possible to do otherwise. Without the availability of such an option, we are brought back to social arrangements of a premodern type and patrimonial type that ties individuals' involvement in the organization to invariable individual and social characteristics (Weber 1947, 1978).

Contingency, choice, and formality are therefore tied together in ways that may not be evident at first glance. Formal status reifies organizations and separates them from the whims and dispositions of various organizational stakeholders. By the same token, individuals are admitted to the organization *qua* occupational roles rather than *qua* persons (in the sense of psychological and existential wholes), which makes them less dependent on the organization. Against this background, it comes as no surprise that hiring or appointment in formal organizations assumes a *contractual* status that renders individual participation *specific, time-limited*, and *revocable*. The contract is a legal and functional medium at the same time. It provides the means for making the hiring or appointment of personnel contingent on functions or tasks that incumbents are expected to perform in the organization. Hiring or appointment is always task or function driven and therefore specific. It is also revocable, at least in principle (for various reasons, including the violation of duties), and, for that reason, time-limited. Revocable individual involvement in the organizations most clearly epitomizes the separation of duties from personal characteristics and social identifications and fulfils various objectives among which figure the frequent renewal of manpower, the reconfiguration of roles, and the updating of skill profiles in the organization. At the same time as they address the goals of efficiency and environmental adaptation, the terms of the contract and the standards and principles governing appointment, and promotion aligns organizational practices to the wider institutional environment of the modern social arrangement.

Thus defined, organizational membership is predicated on the aforementioned distinction between the person as a whole and the band of the vocational roles or duties the person may assume in her lifetime, a condition with far-reaching social and political implications well understood by Weber (1947, 1978) and Simmel (1971) but largely overlooked these days. The distinction of the person from the vocational duties and the concomitant non-inclusive organizational involvement of individuals make modern formal organizations quite a different species from patrimonial systems, army or work barracks, prisons, religious sects, or any other kind of organization (e.g. family business) or practice (e.g. economic or political patronage) in which the basic principle of *contingent* and *non-inclusive membership* characteristic of an open, non-coercive society is suspended (Walzer 1983; Kallinikos 2004, 2006*b*). These observations make clear the restrictive interpretive horizon on which the understanding of corporations as predominantly economic entities is based.

Formal organization and the distinctive nature of the membership model on which this institution is based cannot fully be appreciated apart from the shift of the social order away from the principle of *stratification* to that of *function* coinciding with the establishment and institutional embeddedness of the modern social arrangement (Luhmann 1995; Heller 1999). Stratification is premised upon hereditary social relations (kinship and class belongingness) and, for that reason, binds social arrangements to non-negotiable individual characteristics that rule out social mobility and deeply constrain adaptability and the pursuit of alternative courses of action (Weber 1947, 1978; Gellner 1983). Function, on the other hand, is the accomplishment of education, training, and learning and, for that reason, changeable and renewable. As with the individual involvement in the organization, the hierarchical order of functions that is ubiquitous in formal organizations is time-limited and crucially revocable. Modern hierarchy is of an altogether different order than stratification derived from non-negotiable social characteristics. By shifting the principle of social organization to function, the modern social arrangement supercedes some deeply entrenched impediments (e.g. tradition and stratification) to social adaptation and change.

Social organization based on function and set free from the dictates of rigid cultural principles and non-negotiable social attributes needs extensive and detailed regulation. Hiring and appointment principles and procedures, promotion and career paths, reward systems, authority and decision-making principles all reflect the construction of a governance regime that encodes legal and cultural norms and principles. Corporations are no doubt economic institutions that must satisfy the imperative of profit. But this is a goal statement and not a statement of the legal and cultural conditions (legitimacy) under which such a goal has to be accomplished. Small wonder that means and ends are often related to one another and, in this respect, the economic nature of corporations makes them different from public agencies and other types of organizations (see e.g. Hannan and Carroll 1992; Carroll and Freeman 2000). And yet, corporations are public not private entities. The so-called private sphere of the economy is in fact a public sphere. Similarly to public agencies, the operations of corporations are for this reason regulated by a complex regime of rules, laws, and socially legitimated modes of conduct. Such a regime provides the framework of rights and obligations that govern the individual/organization relationship and is, at the same time, an important vehicle for shaping behaviour and expectations in the corporate workplace. Such a portrait of modern formal organizations entails admittedly strong elements of an ideal depiction that contrasts with the ruthless practices of power and the relentless pursuit of profit (Perrow 2002; Clegg et al. 2006). This ideal description recounts widely diffused cultural and normative orientations against which these practices may be judged as non-conformant to the legitimate social order of democratic societies, ruthless or socially insensitive, as the case may be. The portrait of formal organization I draw provides the legal framework and the yardstick by means of which such practices can be critiqued, brought to court, and eventually corrected and held accountable.

The constitution of modern formal organizations on a contractual basis has accordingly deep cultural roots that invoke a particular and historically unique understanding of collective entities and the ways individuals are involved in them. The dissociation of the function(s) an individual can perform in the context of work from other personal and psychological predispositions of that individual that are the outcome of lifelong and not easily changeable experiences and structures of motivation occurs for the first time in history in the social arrangement we call modernity. As Hirschman's work (1977) on 'the passions and the interests' suggests, such an understanding of being human goes back to the Scottish enlightenment and a long-standing cultural struggle to shape instinctually based, passion-driven acts by a model of being a person that put tempered, mildly calculative modes of human conduct at a premium. Ultimately, the dissociation of the person from the function furnishes the behavioural model of neutral proceduralism governing modern formal or bureaucratically constituted organizations that Weber describes as '*Sine ira et studio*, without hatred or passion and hence without affection or enthusiasm' (Weber 1947: 340).[5] Formal organizations are indeed the social technology through which the separation of vocation from other aspects of a person's life and personality is instrumented in massive scale. No matter how fragile and incomplete it may remain in practice, this dissociation is a normative milestone in modernity. It is intimately tied to the dynamics of the modern, social arrangement and the requirements for regulated but, in principle, unbounded social and geographic mobility of people and resources across strata and contexts (Luhmann 1995, 1998; Heller 1999).

Crossroads

The ideas put forth so far suggest a mutually reinforcing relationship between the culture of modernity, the institutional framework it fashioned, and the constitution of modern organizations as formal, bureaucratic systems. The contingent, variable character of the organizational involvement of individuals is the key to understanding formal organizations and the entire framework of relations that celebrates individuality, meritocracy, and freedom (du Gay 2005). How can we relate these ideas to the concept of social production and the proposition that social networks epitomize an alternative model of value creation that exhibits considerably more individual variation and freedom than what has been hitherto the case?

Social production refashions the terms by which individuals are involved in organizations in the direction of an informal, shifting, and (online) transaction-based model, which no longer relies on occupational categories nor distinguishes between owners/managers versus employees. Such models seem, as Benkler and others suggest, to expand the bounds of individuality and enhance freedom. In bypassing the constraints associated with the institutional embeddedness of formal organizations, the forms of collaboration social production occasions hold the promise of liberating individual membership in collective pursuits from the elaborate web of institutional relations in which it has been embedded in modernity. In a perhaps analogous fashion to that of formal organization and the ways it sought to break away from the tight bonds of a stratified, fixed, and hardly negotiable social order, social production-driven models of collaboration seek to suspend the restrictive power of the regulative regimes that have governed social relations in formal organizations.

Social development is of course never as linear and monocausal as such an account seems to suggest. Laws and regulations are certainly associated with the negotiating power of the social groups whose affairs they seek to govern but they cannot straightforwardly be deduced from the power differentials of these groups. In sketching the institutional matrix in which formal organizations in general and corporations in particular are embedded, I have been at pains to show that such a matrix is the outcome of social and cultural concerns, some of which celebrate equality, freedom, and individual sovereignty. Socio-cultural concerns of this sort are not straightforward derivatives of power. Modern regulative regimes have grown out of a large range of contingencies and entailed considerations that to a certain degree have given expression to the ideal of a fair social order (Walzer 1983) laying down the premises upon which social relationships should be predicated. In this respect, regulative regimes restrict but protect too.

Table 6.1 presents a schematic and descriptive account of some of the key claims I put forward in this chapter. I would like to use the relationships depicted in the table as the reference point in my brief effort to summarize and assess, *sine ira et studio*, the nature of the social changes associated with the refashioning of formal organizations over the last few decades (Castells 1996, 2001; DiMaggio 2001), of which social production (Benkler 2006) seems to be a highly interesting and relatively recent manifestation.

The table depicts three epochal forms of organization (patrimonial systems, formal organizations, collaborative networks) and the distinctive features (membership type, social relations, source of legitimacy, and spatio-temporal model) underlying each of them. The first three of these features are indissolubly bound up with one another while the fourth (spatio-temporal model) is subject to variation and should therefore be seen as a tendency. Professions, for instance, are species of formal organization that draw on concentration and distribution at the same time. Similarly, premodern or early modern commercial networks that were based on friendship, kinship, or patronage and other invariable social characteristics utilized a spatio-temporal model of dispersion. It is though a distinctive feature of collaborative networks to rely on distribution, both in terms of geographical dispersion and also in terms of a division of labour that moves away from the principles of succession and sequentiality. In this respect, collaborative networks are inimical to concentration and cannot exist apart from the distributed nature of the tasks with which they are associated. To the degree that distribution relies on the simultaneous execution of tasks in a population of dispersed individuals, it transcends the meaning of dispersion *qua* geographical feature and tends to become a mode of organizing collective pursuits.

The relationships depicted in Table 6.1 stretch over an extended timescale that covers the last two or three centuries and thus invoke a developmental trajectory of a sort. But such a trajectory should not be understood in terms of succession. The diffusion of the collaborative arrangements of the type discussed in this chapter may challenge but do not replace formal organizations. At least this remains to be seen. In a sense, collaborative networks entail the return to some of the features distinctive of patrimonial systems (see e.g. Tilly 2001). In yet another sense, they epitomize the fusion of bureaucratic principles with social relations of an informal or peer-based nature (e.g. Piana 2009). Indeed, the claim of a post-bureaucratic age in which key bureaucratic principles are transformed, bent, or reconfigured as a means of addressing the demands of the current age has been around for some time. While occasionally tied to the diffusion of information and communication technologies and

Table 6.1. Systems and logics of organization

	Patrimonial systems	Formal organizations	Collaborative networks
Membership type	Inclusive, non-negotiable, irrevocable	Non-inclusive, regular, revocable	Non-inclusive, episodic
Social relations	Stratification, fixed social order	Function and expertise-based formal role systems	Peer-based interactions
Legitimacy source	Tradition	Law and normative orders, expertise	Online sociality, expertise
Spatio-temporal model	Concentration	Concentration	Distribution
Examples	Traditional rural production, family business, political or economic patronage	Public agencies, corporations	Open-source software production, collaborative knowledge development

the cognitive and behavioural habits they introduce (e.g. Kallinikos 2006*b*; Harris 2008), the transformation of or drift away from bureaucracy has commonly been associated with one or another aspect of what I have here referred to as the institutional matrix of modernity (see e.g. Heckscher and Donnellon 1994; Fukuyama 1997; Courpasson and Reed 2004; Greenwood and Lawrence 2005; Newman 2005; Walton 2005; Olsen 2008). The ideas I pursue in this text suggest, however, that the transformation of bureaucracy and the organizational template to which it has given rise may occur via the less conspicuous route that entails the redefinition of the terms by means of which people are involved in collective pursuits. Bureaucracy (formal organization) is the particular type of social entity in which the coupling of individual goals and collective pursuits assumes the form of the contract, regulated by an elaborate regime of rules, laws, and regulations. Part of this regime is certainly associated with the institution of property rights and the power consolidation that allows public agencies to operate as the extended arm of the state. The open and transient nature of the bond underlying the online collaborative arrangements social production occasions challenges the contractual nature of organizations and, thus, represents a specific case of the wider shift away from bureaucracy characteristic of the present age.

From a certain point of view, social networks provide a complement rather than a full-fledged alternative to standard, proprietary modes of producing goods and services and the structural scaffolds associated with formal organizations. It is quite probable that key elements of the collaborative arrangements associated with social production will be assimilated in the established framework of markets and corporations, as cases like Flickr, YouTube,

Facebook, and the for-profit customization/implementation of Linux attest.[6] Popular management books (Anderson 2006; Tapscott and Williams 2006) outline scenarios in which open forms of collaboration become a widespread practice within the proprietary framework of markets and organizations. Management fads come and go, and no more than an indicative value should be attributed to these claims. While difficult to predict the organizational implications of these developments, it would seem nonetheless reasonable to conjecture that once introduced into the existing framework for running concentrated systems (corporations and public agencies), collaborative practices may bring along important changes. The massive invasion of the relatively well-defined jurisdictional space of formal organizations by relations of an entirely different type significantly erodes the contractual terms by which they are constituted as social entities and the rationalized regime of governance (e.g. assignment of responsibilities, accountability, and control) underlying the monitoring of their operations (Newman 2005; Contini and Lanzara 2009; Piana 2009).

A more radical take on these matters could suggest that social production and the open and fluid collaborative arrangements it occasions are just the beginnings of a long-wave change. The diffusion of social production could go as far as to obliterate the institutional logics separating economic and social life, public activities from private initiatives, and formal organizations from informal associations. The challenge of these distinctions, so characteristic of the modern social arrangement, occurs via the medium of coupling individuals to collective pursuits in new ways. In this process, the dissociation of the function (or the organizational role) from the person is given a new twist. The contractual relation, as analysed above, constructs a bond, an institutional receptacle, as it were, that shapes expectations, rights, and obligations. The contract recognizes an open future (the need to change the terms of the contract if it is found inadequate) at the same time as it constructs a stable present. Shifting and changing as it may be, the contractual basis of individual involvement in organizations presupposes a minimum of predictable relations by means of which expectations are fashioned and individual contributions are monitored, rewarded, and held accountable.

Social production seems to dispense altogether with the contract understood in these terms. In its place, it inserts a fragile and transient network of interacting individuals tied together by online exchanges. The stability of the missing contract is counterbalanced by the permanent nature of the technological arrangements, a minimal set of rules concerning individual contributions, and the control rationalities associated with user authentication/identification procedures (Deleuze, 1995). This is undeniably a flexible and much more open form of coupling but it is the one that is based on much thinner social ties.[7] Despite the aura of collaboration, peer-reviewing, and online sociality that is associated with social networks, a closer look suggests that the key element in social production is no longer the social relation but the online *transactional exchange*, made possible by the construction of an open bond and an invitation addressed to anyone. One could certainly invoke here the historical analogy of the shift between strong and weak ties that the transition from small, locally based communities to large social aggregates (nation states) signified. Social networks are primarily transactional machines. Relations are ephemeral and extremely functional. A proper understanding therefore of the social networks of collaboration and the organizing logic they promote must entail their assessment against the background of the wider institutional relations I have tried to summarize in this chapter. Is 'freedom just another word for nothing left to lose'?

Placed against the thick institutional framework of corporate capitalism, the restructuring potential of the developments brought about by social production, Web 2.0, and the Internet may be seen as a frivolous and transient episode. But it is reasonable to assume that they are not. Important technological, cultural, and economic changes, some of which I have outlined in this chapter, are constructing a new socio-economic habitat. The relationships I have described are better appreciated if related to the current and comprehensive informatization of social and physical relations that tends to produce an affluent universe of electronic tokens, a profusion of signs set free from any pretension to describe or represent reality (Kallinikos 1995, 2006*b*; Borgmann 1999). As suggested earlier in this chapter, the diffusion of information across the social fabric is not just a technological fact. It constitutes a destination (one among several) of a long cultural journey (Goody 1986) that bespeaks the prevalence of artifice over reality, and the dominance of representation over what once might have been thought as its origin (Lyotard 1984). The modular and granular nature of information is the outcome of this virtual and pliable universe. The unbundling of resources, the penetration of the social fabric by all sorts of information services, and the circulation of information in larger social and geographic space are all closely associated with the comprehensive informatization of reality.

Another group of changes that suggest distributed collaboration as something more than a fleeting episode in the history of capitalism relates to the key claim made in this chapter concerning the premises by which the bond between the individual and institutions is reconstituted. The developments associated with the growing involvement of information in social life vastly expand users' points of contact with the world and produce a wide range of electronically constituted interfaces whereby individuals are coupled with social pursuits in shifting and transient forms (Manovich 2001). Under these conditions, a new post-bureaucratic regime takes shape. Collaborative arrangements of a shifting and transient nature increasingly diffuse, while the standard bureaucratic form is massively invaded by short-lived projects that defy its specialized, rule-based, and enduring forms through which individual contributions have been admitted to formal organizations.

Concluding Remarks

I have sought in this chapter to review the ideas about social production and assess the validity of the proposition concerning the institutional significance of the collaborative arrangements with which it is associated. There is little doubt that open, fluid, and shifting collaborative, Internet-based groups increasingly cluster around the development of new services and the creation of value by means of exchanging and reshaping information. Many of these collaborative arrangements break with the enduring schedules characteristic of traditional organizations and their considerably denser social space. In their place they introduce loose, piecemeal, and transient ways of connecting individuals to organizations, relations that address the temporary and shifting nature of many of the projects that increasingly underlie contemporary life. While representing the confluence of several cultural and economic developments, these trends have been made possible by the technological breakthroughs that have occurred over the last few decades. Two among them seem to have been crucial: (*a*) the distinctive nature of the computational paradigm as this is reflected in the modular and granular nature of information, and (*b*) the diffusion of information-processing resources across the population.

These developments are intimately tied to the institutional matrix associated with corporations and more general formal organizations in modern times. I have therefore sought to revisit and reconstruct not only the complex but also the subtle character of this matrix. I have claimed that the defining characteristic of formal organizations (bureaucracies) coincides with the contractual basis of individual participation in the organization that represents a historical break with inclusive forms of involvement. The terms on which individuals join work organizations in modern times are *negotiable*, concern *specific contributions* or functions that the individual is expected to perform, are time bound, and, crucially, *revocable*, even in cases that may entail lifetime employment. The contractual nature of individual involvement in organizations is associated with wider cultural orientations concerning individual freedoms and the operations of social institutions (du Gay 2005). Formal organizations operate within a complex regime of rules, laws and regulations, and socially legitimate modes of conduct. These provide the framework of rights and obligations that govern the individual/organization relationship and are at the same time an important vehicle for shaping expectations in the workplace.

The degree to which this edifice is seriously challenged by the trends associated with social production and the collaborative arrangements it engenders is, of course, an open question. There are plenty of signs suggesting that these changes are far from transient and episodic (Benkler 2006) and, crucially, indicative of wider shifts that betray a drift away from formal organization (bureaucracy) as the dominant organizational template in modernity. For some time now, the core operations of a growing majority of formal organizations have increasingly been invaded by a variety of specific projects clustering around tasks of limited duration in which participants gather and disband rapidly after project completion (Castells 2000; Newman 2005; Clegg 2007; Contini and Lanzara 2009). Perhaps, as Lyotard (1984) perceptively saw more than thirty years ago,[8] temporary relationships increasingly erode the relatively stable social fabric of modernity and become the currency of the age. A hybrid organizational landscape is taking shape in which many constraints on the free flow of people and resources are lifted. Corporations, but even more so public agencies may increasingly come to resemble open public squares where each can stroll, sample the wares, and have refreshment—a new agora, perhaps? The collaborative arrangements of social production are part and parcel of this wider institutional landscape in the making and its double-edged nature. Their prospects are certainly dependent on the open character of an information habitat that is currently being shaped by struggles over digital copyright and other impediments to the free exchange of information (Lessig 2002; Benkler 2006).

☐ NOTES

1. Castells (1996, 2001) no doubt extends the concept of network to the operations of the state and to global civil movements. Yet, the understanding of online community as a potent productive force and the conception of social production as a mode of producing goods and services as analysed by Benkler (2006) have escaped him. The same applies to research on networks conducted within the tradition of organizational sociology and organization studies (see e.g. Powell 1990, 2001; Ahuja 2000).
2. Following Agnes Heller (1999), I will throughout this text deploy the singular form 'the modern social arrangement' to refer to modernity as a distinct cultural and institutional formation.
3. Recall that the corporation is a legal entity.
4. As a matter of fact, the birth of the individual in the modern sense of the world is inextricably bound up with these values and the identification of individuality on the basis of acquired rather than inborn or socially non-negotiable (e.g. stratification) characteristics (Heller 1999).
5. See Paul du Gay in this volume.

6. A $25 billion industry in 21 October 2008, Linux Foundation, http://www.linuxfoundation. org/en/Main_Page (Accessed 14th March 2009).
7. The rules governing individual contributions to the collaborative projects of social networks have been widely debated. As the case of Wikipedia suggests, they are subject to change with stricter regimes replacing the terms by which individual contributions took place in the early stages of the encyclopedia. It is reasonable to conjecture that the more important a social network is becoming, the stronger the stakes that develop around it and the greater the need for some form of regulation (see e.g. Terdiman 2009). Regulation, however, does not need to lead to centralization (see e.g. Forte and Bruckman 2008).
8. Lyotard's book was published in France in 1978.

☐ BIBLIOGRAPHY

Ahuja, G. (2000) Collaboration Networks, Structural Holes and Innovation: A Longitudinal Study, *Administrative Science Quarterly*, 45(3): 425–55.

Anderson, C. (2006) *The Long Tail*, London: Random House.

Arrow, K. (1974) *The Limits of Organization*, London: Norton.

Avgerou, C. (2002) *Information Systems and Global Diversity*, Oxford: Oxford University Press.

Barley, S.R. and Kunda, G. (2004) *Gurus, Hired Guns, and Warm Bodies: Itinerant Experts in a Knowledge Economy*, Princeton, New Jersey: Princeton University Press.

Bauman, Z. (2000) *Liquid Modernity*, Cambridge: Polity.

Beck, U. (2000) *The Brave New World of Work*, Cambridge: Polity.

Benkler, Y. (2002) *Coase's Penguin or Linux and the Nature of the Firm*, www.arxiv.org.

——(2006) *The Wealth of Networks*, New Haven, Connecticut: The Yale University Press, also freely available in www.benkler.org.

Borgman, A. (1999) *Holding On to Reality: The Nature of Information at the Turn of the Millennium*, Chicago: The University of Chicago Press.

Bowker, G. and Star, S.-L. (1999) *Sorting Things Out*, Cambridge, Massachusetts: The MIT Press.

Carroll, G.R. and Freeman, M.T. (2000) *The Demography of Corporations and Industries*, Princeton, New Jersey: Princeton University Press.

Castells, M. (1996) *The Rise of Network Society*, Oxford: Blackwell.

——(2000) Materials for an Explanatory Theory of Network Society, *British Journal of Sociology*, 51(1): 5–24.

——(2001) *The Internet Galaxy*, Oxford: Oxford University Press.

Chandler, A.D. (1977) *The Visible Hand: The Managerial Revolution in American Business*, Cambridge, Massachusetts: Harvard University Press.

Ciborra, C. (1996) *Groupware and Teamwork: Invisible Aid or Technical Hindrance*, London: Wiley.

Clegg, S. (2007) *Something is Happening Around Here But I Do Not Know What It Is, Do You Mr. Jones?*, https://www.lse.ac.uk/collections/informationSystems/newsAndEvents/2007events/ clegg2.pdf.

——, Courpasson, D. and Phillips, N. (2006) *Power and Organizations*, London: Sage.

Coase, R. (1937) The Nature of the Firm, *Economica*, 4: 386–405.

Contini, F. and Lanzara, G.F. (2009) *ICT and Innovation in the Public Sector*, New York: Palgrave.

Courpasson, D. and Reed, M. (2004) Special Issue on Bureaucracy in the Age of Enterprise, *Organization*, 11(1): 5–12.

Deleuze, G. (1995) Postscript in Control Societies, in G. Deleuze (ed.), *Negotiations*, New York: Columbia University Press.

DeSanctis, G. and Monge P. (1999) Introduction to the Special Issue: Communication Processes for Virtual Organizations, *Organization Science*, 10(6): 693–703.

DiMaggio, P.J. (2001) *The Twenty-First Century Firm*, Princeton, New Jersey: Princeton University Press.

du Gay, P. (2000) *In Praise of Bureaucracy: Weber, Organization, Ethics*, London: Sage.

——(2005) *The Values of Bureaucracy*, Oxford: Oxford University Press.

Feldman, M.S. and Pentland, B.T. (2003) Reconceptualizing Routines as a Source of Flexibility and Change, *Administrative Science Quarterly*, 48(1): 94–118.

Fligstein, N. (1990) *The Transformation of Corporate Control*, Cambridge, Massachusetts: Harvard University Press.

Forte, A. and Bruckman, A. (2008) Scaling Consensus: Increasing Decentralization in Wikipedia Governance, in *41st Hawaii International Conference on Systems Sciences*, Waikoloa, Big Island, Hawaii, January 7–10.

Fukuyama, F. (1997) *The End of Order*, London: Centre for Post-collectivist Studies.

Gellner, E. (1983) *Nations and Nationalism*, Oxford: Blackwell.

——(1995) *Conditions of Liberty: Civil Society and Its Rivals*, London: Penguin.

Giddens, A. (1990) *The Consequences of Modernity*, Cambridge: Polity.

Goffman, E. (1961) *Asylums*, London: Penguin.

Goody, J. (1986) *The Logic of Writing and the Organization of Society*, Cambridge: Cambridge University Press.

Granovetter, M. (1985) Economic Action and Social Structure: The Problem of Embeddedness, *American Journal of Sociology*, 91(3): 481–510.

Greenwood, R. and Lawrence, T.B. (2005) The Iron Cage in the Information Age: The Legacy and Relevance of Max Weber for Organization Studies, *Organization Studies*, 26(4), Special Issue.

Hacking, I. (1999) *The Social Construction of What?* Cambridge, Massachusetts: Harvard University Press.

Hannan, M.T. and Carroll, G.R. (1992) *The Dynamics of Organizational Populations*, Oxford: Oxford University Press.

Hanseth, O. (2004) Knowledge as Infrastructure, in C. Avgerou, C. Ciborra and F. Land (eds), *The Social Study of Information and Communication Technology*, Oxford: Oxford University Press.

Harris, M. (2008) Digital Technology and Governance in Transition: The Case of the British Library, *Human Relations*, 61(5): 741–58.

Hasselbladh, H. and Kallinikos, J. (2000) The Process of Institutionalization: A Critique and Reappraisal of Neo-institutionalism in Organization Studies, *Organization Studies*, 21(4): 697–720.

Heckscher, C. and Donnellon, A. (1994) *The Post-Bureaucratic Organization*, London: Sage.

Heller, A. (1999) *A Theory of Modernity*, Oxford: Blackwell.

Heugens, P. (2005) A Neo-Weberian Theory of the Firm, in The Iron Cage in the Information Age: The Legacy and Relevance of Max Weber for Organization Studies, *Organization Studies*, 26(4): 547–68, Special Issue.

Hinds, P. and Mortensen, M. (2005) Understanding Conflict in Geographically Distributed Teams: The Moderating Effects of Shared Identity, Shared Context, and Spontaneous Communication, *Organization Science*, 16(3): 290–307.

Hirschman, A. (1977) *The Passions and the Interests*, Princeton, NJ: Princeton University Press.

Iannacci, F. (2005) *The Social Epistemology of Open Source Software Development: The Linux Case Study*, PhD Thesis, London: Department of Information Systems, London School of Economics and Political Science.

Jenkins, H. (2006) *Convergence Culture: Where New and Old Media Collide*, New York: New York University Press.

Kallinikos, J. (1995) The Architecture of the Invisible: Technology is Representation, *Organization*, 2(1): 11–140.

——(2003) Work, Human Agency and Organizational Forms: An Anatomy of Fragmentation, *Organization Studies*, 24(4): 595–618.

——(2004) The Social Foundations of the Bureaucratic Order, *Organization*, 11(1): 13–36.

——(2006a) The Institution of Bureaucracy: Administration, Pluralism, Democracy, *Economy and Society*, 36(4): 611–27.

——(2006b) *The Consequences of Information: Institutional Implications of Technological Change*, Cheltenham: Elgar.

——(2009) On the Computational Rendition of Reality: Artefacts and Human Agency, *Organization*, 16/2: 183–202.

Kitler, F. (1985) *Gramophone, Film, Typewriter*, Stanford, California: Stanford University Press.

Knorr-Cetina, K. and Bruegger, U. (2002) Global Microstructures: The Virtual Societies of Financial Markets, *American Journal of Sociology*, 107(4): 905–50.

Lessig, L. (2002) *The Future of Ideas: The Fate of Commons in a Connected World*, New York: Vintage.

Luhmann, N. (1995) *Social Systems*, Stanford, California: Stanford University Press.

——(1998) *Observations on Modernity*, Stanford, California: Stanford University Press.

Lyotard, J.F. (1984) *The Postmodern Condition: A Report to Knowledge*, Manchester: Manchester University Press.

Manovich, L. (2001) *The Language of New Media*, Cambridge, Massachusetts: The MIT Press.

March, J.G. and Simon, H.A. (1993) *Organizations*, 2nd edn, New York: Willey, originally published in 1958.

Meyer, J.W. and Jepperson, R.L. (2000) The 'Actors' of Modern Society: The Cultural Construction of Social Agency, *Sociological Theory*, 18: 100–20.

Mintzberg, H. (1979) *The Structuring of Organizations*, Englewood Cliffs, New Jersey: Prentice-Hall.

Newman, J. (2005) Bending Bureaucracy: Leadership and Multi-Level Governance, in P. du Gay (ed.), *The Values of Bureaucracy*, Oxford: Oxford University Press.

Olsen, J.P. (2008) The Ups and Downs of Bureaucratic Organization, *The Annual Review of Political Science*, 11: 13–37.

Perrow, C. (1986) *Complex Organizations: A Critical Essay*, New York: Random House.

——(2002) *Organizing America: Wealth, Power and the Origins of Corporate Capitalism*, Princeton, New Jersey: Princeton University Press.

Piana, D. (2009) *Judicial Accountabilities in New Europe. From Rule of Law to Quality of Justice*, Aldershot: Ashgate.

Pollock, N. and Williams, R. (2009) *Software and Organizations*, London: Routledge.

Pottage, A. (1998) Power as an Act of Contingency: Luhmann, Deleuze, Foucault, *Economy and Society*, 27(1): 1–27.

Powell, W.W. (1990) Neither Market nor Hierarchy: Network Forms of Organization, in B. Staw and L. Cummings (eds), *Research in Organizational Behaviour*, Greenwich, Connecticut: JAI Press, 295–336.

——(2001) The Capitalist Firm in the Twenty-First Century: Emerging Patterns in Western Enterprise, in P.J. DiMaggio (ed.), *The Twenty-First Century Firm*, Princeton, New Jersey: Princeton University Press, 33–68.

Raymond, E.S. (2001) *The Cathedral and the Bazaar*, 2nd edn, Cambridge: O'Reily.

Reed, M. (2005) Beyond the Iron Cage? Bureaucracy and Democracy in the Knowledge Economy and Society, in P. du Gay (ed.), *The Values of Bureaucracy*, Oxford: Oxford University Press.

Roy, W.G. (1997) *Socializing Capital: The Rise of the Large Industrial Corporation*, Princeton, New Jersey: Princeton University Press.

Sassen, S. (2001) *The Global City*, Princeton, New Jersey: Princeton University Press.

Schmidt, K. and Bannon, L. (1992) Taking CSCW Seriously: Supporting Articulation Work, *CSCW*, 1(1–2): 7–40.

Searle, J. (1995) *The Construction of Social Reality*, London: Penguin. Simmel, G. (1971) *On Individuality and Social Fonus*, Chicago: The University of Chicago Press.

Sinha, K.K. and Van de Ven, A.H. (2005) Designing Work Within and Between Organizations, *Organization Science*, 16(4): 389–408.

Tapscott, D. and Williams, A.T. (2006) *Wikinomics: How Mass Collaboration Changes the World*, New York: Portfolio.

Terdiman, D. (2009) Wikipedia Community Grapples with Changes, *CNET News*, 26 August 2009.

Tilly, C. (2001) Welcome to the Seventeenth Century, P.J. DiMaggio (ed.), *The Twenty-First Century Firm*, Princeton, New Jersey: Princeton University Press, 200–9.

—— (1998) *Work Under Capitalism*, Boulder, Colorado: Westview Press.

Von Hippel, E. (2005) *Democratizing Innovation*, Cambridge, Massachusetts: The MIT Press, also available at http://web.mit.edu/evhippel/www/.

Walton, E.J. (2005) The Persistence of Bureaucracy: A Meta-Analysis of Weber's Model of Bureaucratic Control, *Organization Studies*, 26(4): 569–600.

Walzer, M. (1983) *Spheres of Justice: A Defense of Pluralism and Equality*, New York: Basic Books.

Weber, M. (1947) *The Theory of Social and Economic Organization*, London: Free Press.

——(1970) *From Max Weber*, in H. Gerth and C. Wright Mills (eds), London: Routledge.

——(1978) *Economy and Society*, 2 Vols, in G. Roth and C. Wittich (eds), Berkeley, California: University of California Press.

Webster, F. (2002) *Theories of the Information Society*, London: Routledge.

Wellman, B. and Haythornhwaite, C. (2002) *The Internet in Everyday Life*, Oxford: Blackwell.

——Salaff, J., Dimitrova, D., Garton, L., Gulia, M. and Haythornhwaite, C. (1996) Computer Networks as Social Networks: Collaborative Work, Telework and Virtual Community, *Annual Review of Sociology*, 22: 213–38.

Wenger, E. (1998) *Communities of Practice*, Cambridge: Cambridge University Press.

Williamson, O.E. (1975) *Markets and Hierarchies*, New York: Free Press.

——(1985) *The Economic Institutions of Capitalism*, New York: Basic Books.

Zittrain, J. (2006) The Generative Internet, *Harvard Law Review*, 119 (May): 1974.

7 'Meritocracy' Versus 'Sociocracy': Personnel Concepts and HRM in Two IT/Management Consulting Firms

MATS ALVESSON AND DAN KÄRREMAN

Introduction

It is a truism that knowledge workers are the most important resource in knowledge-intensive firms (KIFs). But what happens when the most important 'resource' consists of something that cannot be owned, only hired; cannot be perfectly controlled, only persuaded; and has wants, agendas, and aspirations of its own? This chapter discusses and compares the ways in which two KIFs deal with this conundrum. The firms are broadly similar on a number of key dimensions—industry, the age and educational attainment of their 'core' employees, type of work, and client base—but highly diverse in their management and organizational patterns. This chapter develops the idea of the *personnel concept*, and shows the value of this concept for understanding the diversity of organizational–personnel linkages in knowledge-intensive settings such as IT/management consultancy work. The idea of a personnel concept captures an organization's basic conceptualization of the kind of employees (i.e. senior managers and possibly broader groups) it wants to attract, the mix of rewards and other benefits it offers to its staff, the motivational basis for the employee–employer relationship, and an active shaping of the motivational-identity orientations of employees through Human Resource Management (HRM) and other arrangements. In organizations where highly competent personnel represent a key resource, the personnel concept influences how the organization is structured. It is also a significant theme in organizational cultures.

The idea of the personnel concept emerges from the perception that different firms seem to work with different models of the employee, which in turn underpin different ways of structuring HRM practices. In what follows we briefly explore these themes before outlining the key attributes of the personnel concept. We then present two contrasting case studies that substantiate and illustrate the value of the concept.

The Significance of Attracting, Developing, and Retaining Qualified Personnel

As Maister (1982) writes, professional service firms (PSFs) compete in two markets simultaneously: the 'output' market for their services and the 'input' market for attracting and keeping an expert workforce. These markets are closely related: a loss in one may affect the other. In KIFs it is vital to attract qualified personnel and to secure loyalty, commitment, and motivation (Meissner 1993; Löwendahl 1997; Boxall & Steeneveld 1999; Alvesson 2000, 2004; Newell et al. 2002). In consultancy firms, in which personnel are the most significant resource, technical competence is obviously vital, but motivation, commitment to the employer, and the social networks of the employees are also important. Key attributes of such firms, such as market reputation, client contacts, and codified knowledge, all depend on qualified personnel. The departure of middle and senior personnel may weaken or sever ties with clients, thus undermining the trust that underpins an industry in which the quality of its 'products' cannot be investigated prior to purchase (Alvesson 1993; Clark 1995; Broshak 2001).

Management consultancy is a 'knowledge-intensive' sector in which firms attract and retain qualified personnel by offering high salaries and other financial benefits, career prospects, satisfying work, and a positive organizational climate. Whilst attractive partnership or shareholding arrangements are common in law and accounting (Greenwood and Empson 2003), this mode of governance is not peculiar to them, and elements of the partnership model may be found in some KIFs. In many KIFs, there are ambitious attempts to create environments and attitudes that result in the development of socio-emotional ties between employees and the company (Kanter 1983; Van Maanen and Kunda 1989; Kunda 1992; Alvesson 1995; Grugulis et al. 2000). These environments may be contrasted with those that focus on narrowly instrumental rewards such as pay rises and promotion (Alvesson and Lindkvist 1993).

It could be argued that the circumstances in which KIFs operate will combine to create isomorphic pressures that would have the effect of minimizing the variation between them. This is corroborated by Boxall and Steeneveld (1999), who found very similar HRM practices across a sample of New Zealand engineering consulting firms. However, other studies (e.g. Starbuck 1993; Robertson et al. 2003) report interesting variations both in relation to specific HRM practices (rewards, education, promotion options) and with regard to a number of more broadly defined aspects such as 'business concepts', management style, organizational culture, and organizational structure. All these factors have significant implications for understanding what we have called the personnel concept, and it is to this that we now turn.

On Personnel Concepts

The idea of a 'personnel concept' emerged in the course of our research on issues of leadership, organizational culture, and control that affect the management of KIFs. We have derived insights from the surrounding literature on the managerial regulation of identity (Knights and Willmott 1989; Grey 1994; Alvesson and Willmott 2002), organizational culture (Smircich 1983; Alvesson 2002), and 'people management' (e.g. Kunda 1992; Robertson 1999; Greenwood and Empson 2003) within KIFs. The 'personnel concept' refers to the company's conceptualization of the kind of employees it wants to attract; the mix of rewards and other benefits it offers to its employees; and the ways in which the motivational-identity orientations of employees may be shaped by HRM strategies and other cultural means. The personnel concept of a firm also establishes a basis for communication—explicit as well as implicit—as played out in HRM rituals, leadership acts, and socialization processes. It encompasses a model of the (ideal) employee and provides an input to, and a point of reference for, a more or less integrated system of ideas and practices for recruiting, retaining, producing, and exploiting employees in KIFs. The personnel concept is thus an element of organizational culture—how senior and other organizational members create meanings around people, work, and motivation. As such it puts its imprint on, and is affected by, a variety of cultural manifestations in organizational life.

The personnel concept we present here is not intended to incorporate or summarize 'everything' about people management and motivation. It draws attention to the underlying assumptions and beliefs that can guide the interpretation of how various actors in an organization think about employment relations. Personnel concepts can be more or less distinctive, and they can be more or less powerfully communicated, internally and/or externally.

There is now a wide diversity of perspectives on the basic relation between organizations and their employees, and it is important (given this diversity) to indicate the originality and added value of the 'personnel concept'. Analysts of HRM have borrowed heavily from McGregor's contention (1960) that behaviour in organizations can be understood with respect to strongly contrasting 'theory X *versus* theory Y' constructions of employee behaviour. This polarized view has been reproduced and sustained by those who distinguish between 'soft' and 'hard' HRM systems (Tyson 1995), and by those who contrast high- and low-commitment organizations (Watson 2004; Legge 2005). Soft or high-commitment HRM is characterized by long-term relationships, caring, and personal development. Hard or low-commitment HRM is about exploitative and short-term relationships. These broad distinctions say little about the nuances in how organizations (i.e. their dominant coalitions and managerial elites) view their employees. This chapter argues that high-commitment HRM strategies can vary considerably, and it shows how we can conceptualize and understand some of this variation. Before presenting case study findings, we briefly review some existing work that has a bearing on our thinking about the personnel concept.

The idea of a psychological contract has been deployed in a number of different ways (Guest 1998). According to Morrison and Robinson (1997: 229), 'a psychological contract is commonly defined as an employee's beliefs about the reciprocal obligations between that employee and his or her organization'. Others use the term to refer to the deals or mutual expectations that exist between a company and its employees (e.g. Hendry and Jenkins 1997). Irrespective of the exact definition, the notion of a psychological contract is focused primarily on how individual employees perceive their obligations to the organization (Rosseau 1998). The idea of a psychological contract is thus relatively narrow in scope, and as such fails to capture the ways in which organizations can develop structures and overall employment conditions that are attractive and motivating. Other commentators have referred to organizational logics and 'HRM bundles'—interrelated and internally consistent sets of HR practices (MacDuffie 1995; see also Bowen and Ostroff 2004). MacDuffie, focusing on manufacturing firms, includes in an HR bundle both work systems and policy issues, such as recruitment and hiring, remuneration, status differentiation, and training. Here the focus is on the specific arrangements and practices that facilitate flexible production, rather than a more precise concern with the attraction, retention, and utilization of highly motivated personnel. Some analysts of HR policy (e.g. Tyson 1995) refer to formal personnel policies, whilst emphasizing the broader role of values and attitudes of management in determining the precise character of the personnel function. Tyson (1995) identifies this distinction with McGregor's theory (1960) X and Y assumptions.

We have developed the 'personnel concept' in ways that relate closely to HRM strategy, but we offer a more precisely situated view of how particular groups of employees can be attracted and stimulated to work. Normann (1983) uses the term 'personnel idea' to refer to how firms may identify and attract a particular segment of the labour market in a novel way, for instance when groups with limited options (e.g. retired people or unskilled house-wives) are recruited into low-paid service work. However, Normann does not address psychological wants, motives, and work identities, or the specific organizational and HRM arrangements that can be developed to attract and steer these. Legge (1999) discusses images of employees in the corporate world and in social science, on the basis of 'marketplace' and 'community' conceptualizations. The values associated with the former are individualism, free choice, and economic rationality, whilst communitarianism is grounded in collectivism, social consensus, and social rationality (including social bonds and loyalties). Legge argues that there are five major images of employ-ees: as customers, resources, commodities (market-based), team, and family (community-based). This conceptualization helps to illuminate the ideas that employers have of their employees and can thus be seen as analogous to our understanding of the personnel concept. Some of these images may indeed be ingredients in personnel concepts, but they are extremely broad and Legge does not connect them to specific implications they may have for organiza-tion–employee relations. As with many other attempts to link HRM to broader firm policies, Legge highlights two sharply differentiated dimensions—economic/social or soft/hard. We argue that such a polarized approach fails to get a purchase on the firm-specific, situated aspects of organization-al life illustrated by the personnel concept.

Method

The two cases reported here were not pre-selected for any specific analytical purpose, but were chosen as potentially valuable sites that offered excellent access for gathering data about a wide range of organizational issues that are germane to the KIF. Our research on 'Big Consulting' generated interest-ing comparisons with 'CCC', a company that we had studied some years previously. These case study accounts are based on forty to fifty interviews, and on participant observation of internal meetings, educational activities, and recruitment processes. Interviews were conducted with managers, part-ners, 'middle level' project leaders, and junior consultants. The interviews (typically lasting around 90 minutes) were loosely structured so as to allow space for the ideas, experiences, and perceptions of interviewees. Salient themes include leadership and the role of managers, motivation, organiza-tional structures, control systems, and cultural values. The two case studies allow us to contrast two radically different sets of employment ideas and practices. Our use of the term *organizational structure* refers to the social forms, systems of control, divisions of labour, roles, and standards (Mintzberg

1983) that we encountered during the course of the research. Our use of the term *culture* refers to systems of value and meaning (Geertz 1973; Smircich 1983) and to the particular values, artefacts, and emotions (Schein 1985; Van Maanen and Kunda 1989; Alvesson 2002; Martin 2002) that emerged during our data gathering within the two organizations. Following Ortner (1973), we concentrate on 'key symbols', that is, on phenomena that are crucial and meaningful to informants. The HRM function, and its role in conditioning specific patterns of recruitment, reward, compliance, and training, features prominently in each of the two cases.

Presentation of the Cases

Our two case study examples ('Big' and 'CCC') have many common features. Both are consulting firms combining management and IT (Big's assignments include more management and strategy). Both firms employ mainly younger people, with an average age of around 30 years. More than 80 per cent of these employees work as consultants. The market for both firms was expanding at the time of the research and both firms were experiencing a shortage of qualified candidates, a factor that was cited (in both cases) as a major constraint on expansion. Consultancy projects are routinely undertaken within client organizations, with the result that consultants often have more contact with the client's personnel than with their colleagues in the 'home' company. Both companies emphasize a strong work ethic, and those who have been absent from work may be expected to work overtime in order to compensate for lost revenue. Neither company pays for overtime. Both firms are highly distinctive, with a strong identity and image. Whilst Big is part of a multinational firm employing more than 25,000 employees worldwide, the operations of CCC are largely confined to Scandinavia. (Both firms employ approximately 500 people in Scandinavia.) Big reflects the partnership system that characterizes many large PSFs in accounting and management consulting (Greenwood and Empson 2003). The Scandinavian office of Big operates as a partnership that is also an autonomous part of a much larger federation. CCC was, at the time of the study, owned mainly by its founders. Whilst Big is a partnership (Löwendahl 1997), it is also highly integrated (Cooper et al. 1996; Greenwood et al. 1990). Both firms are strongly oriented to profit, growth, and marketing. Big differs markedly from CCC in terms of its hierarchy and its instrumental approach to career development and motivation. Big is the more 'up-market' of the two firms, charging very high fees for strategic management consultancy. CCC fees are less expensive, and the firm concentrates mainly on IT consultancy.

TECHNOCRATIC MERITOCRACY AT BIG CONSULTING LTD.

Big Consulting specializes in management consultancy, but with an emphasis on the development and implementation of administrative and technical solutions to organizational problems. Its projects are often relatively large, frequently involving dozens of people. Its employees often experience very long working days—many of our respondents stated that they frequently worked 60–70 hours per week.

The research carried out at Big reveals a striking dominance of instrumental rationality, as indicated by the emphasis on predictability, standardized measurements, and transparent decision making. Big Consulting's strongest competitive advantage centres on its capacity to deliver 'the solution' on time (a rare phenomenon, particularly amongst IT consultant firms) and its particular work procedures.

Customers see us as providers of competence, but also as resources in pushing. They know that we go in there with high motivation, a willingness to work hard. They also expect us to contribute with new thoughts and ideas. But somehow it feels as though not many expect us to come as the real experts and contribute the fantastic, brilliant ideas that will revolutionize the world...This is more a matter of hard work and producing sufficiently good ideas and drive and to see that things get in their place. And it becomes increasingly a matter of getting things straight. (Manager)

The upside, as indicated, is that the firm delivers the goods. The downside is that other important matters get crowded out, such as developing close and lasting relationships with customers. Thus, one manager told us that:

Big is good at taking on a task and making sure it is accomplished on time—very result oriented. It is a bit American in its culture in that way, you meet a lot of groups...and it sometimes clashes with the culture of Scandinavian firms. I do think we as a company have a culture of being extremely focused on delivery and perhaps not understanding...as much on building relationships with other firms.

A consultant described Big 'as the McDonalds amongst management consulting': a predictable and reliable but hardly innovative or surprising company. The capacity to deliver is facilitated by the extensive use of standardized methodologies, and a marked tendency to recycle earlier solutions.

Organizational Structure

Big is organized as a matrix, with a market (or industry) leg and a competence leg. The key unit at Big Consulting, however, is the project team. Thus, management control in Big Consulting is tightly focused on team management. Projects are carefully contracted, designed, and monitored. Senior management demands high-profit margins and employees are generally inclined to achieve these. The composition of project teams varies over time, partly because of the variation in the duration of particular projects, and partly because employees are allotted more senior project roles as their careers develop. One consequence of this 'team focus' is that the individual is typically seen as a rather insignificant organizational resource. On one level the individual is highly visible in the organization: it is the individual who is evaluated, rewarded, and punished. But on another level, the individual is hardly visible at all and is viewed as exchangeable and easy to replace. Thus, one senior manager stated that:

We enter as a group. We are perhaps not individuals but work more as a group. We always work in teams and it is not the particular individual that makes it good.

The use of a similar model for the design of the company and the same methods plus the same courses means the fostering of a culture that is extremely strong… making it possible for me to go to USA and be productive within a day.

Q: Does this mean that people are exchangeable?

Yes, I think so. It may be a bit of a problem because in our knowledge company and personnel there are people who do not want to be exchangeable.

Despite the *ad hoc* nature of consulting work, the organizational hierarchy of Big is highly formalized, with several career steps and associated designated job titles (from analyst and consultant, to manager, senior manager, and then partner). People on junior levels experience the hierarchy as very strong, with respondents stating that they have little contact with partners, feel small compared to them, and do not know what the partners do. On the other hand, most people see the hierarchy as a functionally useful feature that enables a productive division of labour. There are no overt status symbols (such as office space reserved for partners). Job titles are seen as reliable indicators of competence, and Big employees respect and comply with the formal hierarchy of the company.

Bureaucratic structures—in the form of standards, rules, and procedures—are pronounced. There are rules for dealing with most issues, for example, elaborate lists of criteria for appraisals and dress codes. However, the bureaucracy is not viewed as a repressive or constraining but as an enabling (cf. Adler 1999) feature of the organization, and employees told us that they have discretion in terms of complying with or sidestepping the rules and standards. The formal *control systems* are also elaborated and play an important role. Interviewees report that 'almost everything in Big is measured and evaluated'. There are frequent appraisals and rankings of employees, attitude surveys, measurements of various business results, and careful monitoring of the progress and budget situation of projects. There are no less than ten controllers employed in the Swedish part of the firm.

Organizational Culture

As noted earlier, the *cultural values* of Big revolve around instrumental rationality. There is a collectively strong desire to perform well, sometimes referred to as a 'culture of delivery'. Consultants emphasize the way knowledge management provides cultural guidance. Knowledge sharing is one important aspect of the organizational culture: there is a widespread willingness to help each other with advice and the sharing of experiences. Informants say that they can phone people that they have never met and be quite sure that they will receive at least some support. The dress code is strict. Organizational members typically wear grey suits, blue or white shirts, and conservative ties. The company has, however, made some attempt to loosen the company dress code, apparently because it can produce disbenefits in recruitment and in some client relations.

Young people, in particular, frequently experience the dominant culture of Big as somewhat impersonal, even if this is counterbalanced by their experience of working within a project team:

There is impersonality here in the office. There is a personal side, and that is in projects where you are living very close with people in the project for a long time. (Consultant)

HRM

Recruitment and selection are standardized and formalized. Big aims at a homogeneous workforce. Almost all Big employees are high-performing business administration or engineering graduates from the larger Scandinavian universities. The company attempts to profile itself as a demanding, but richly rewarding, place to work. Recruitment interviews emphasize the high demands on employees: on being flexible, able to travel a lot, and, at times, to work long hours. 'Big' ranks high in student polls of the most rewarding Scandinavian employers.

The firm rewards the employees well in monetary terms and offers quick and predictable promotion, that is, new titles and more responsibility in combination with assessments and rankings. These assessments affect the speed of promotion as well as pay rises. People are eager to get promoted. Often a few months more or less in the time promotion takes is viewed as important. Organizational members emphasize the firm's strength in developing, assessing, and promoting its employees. Employees talk about a 'feedback culture'. Formal appraisals take place several times per year for younger employees, less frequently for senior employees. Much attention is paid to rankings and promotions. Low rankings and promotions below medium time frames are clear signals that people must improve or ought to consider leaving the firm.

There is an 'up-or-out'-system. It is not brutal. People are not sacked because they fail in a project. But over a longer period, in one way or another, these people disappear. (Partner)

Big assists people in leaving. These employees typically have no problem finding a good job, but partners are also eager to place them in senior positions, partly to ease the transfer, but also in order to foster collaborative networks of ex-employees who are also potential clients. As the ex-employees know Big and their methods well, cooperation is often smooth. Big exercises 'exit management' (Alvesson 2000).

Considerable resources are invested in training and development and many opportunities are made available. The frequent assessments are seen as a triggering element. Courses, workshops, competence groups, the conscious and systematic use of new assignments for developing purposes mean that Big can claim to offer excellent development opportunities. The hierarchy combined with teamwork is also considered to be an effective way of developing young people through being able to cooperate with and learn from more experienced people. The hierarchy can thus, from a personnel concept perspective, be seen as facilitating competence development.

The Personnel Concept at Big Consulting

Big Consulting appears as a strongly profiled company with a distinctive style and a strong image amongst students, employees, and customers. The personnel concept of Big strongly emphasizes high wages, rapid promotion, titles, competency development, and high status in an internationally well-known organization that emphasizes competence and prides itself on meritocratic ideals. It makes high demands on its employees. It encourages self-discipline and a strong drive to perform and deliver. The firm targets young, adaptable, high-performing, and compliant individuals who value job status and monetary rewards. It appeals to the career- and development-oriented person. It offers differentiation, promotion, and hierarchy as key elements in its employment practices and organizational structure. The intensive use of HRM systems and procedures, as well as the careful monitoring and measurement of various outcomes, including fine-tuned hierarchical differentiation, exerts considerable control. These controls not only focus on behaviour and results but also shape the subjectivity of employees. Those not adapting or fitting in tend to leave: the up-or-out logic is strong.

MANAGERIALLY ORCHESTRATED SOCIOCRACY AT CCC

CCC was established as the market for IT consulting work and bespoke software development expanded rapidly. The company undertakes a broad range of projects that may vary in scope from one consultant employed for a very short period to a dozen people employed for a year or more. The CCC business concept combines expertise in IT, knowledge management, and consultancy on firm strategy, although the strategic component is in practice rather slight in most projects. Consultants are encouraged to establish contact with senior managers of clients: 'This is our strength, this is what we are good at', as one consultant emphasized. Technical qualifications are important, but these tend to be downplayed in favour of interpersonal skills and sociability. CCC emphasizes cooperation, work climate, establishing close contact with clients, negotiation of shared understandings and expectations, project leadership, and knowledge of the client's business situation. Thus, as one consultant told us:

I don't believe we are any better [than other companies] from a purely technical point of view. We are better at some things. And that is precisely the fundamental business concept: management and computer development. But we are no better at computer development [than other companies], perhaps worse in some cases. But on the management side—our way of handling customers—that's where we are better.

The company was founded by three people who are viewed as charismatic by CCC employees. The founders have gradually decreased their involvement in the company in recent years, leaving a gap behind them that is still felt by many of their co-workers. The leadership style established by the company founders, the selective recruitment of personnel from their professional networks, and rapid growth have all facilitated a positive organizational climate and a strong sense of community within the company.

Organization Structure

CCC is organized in the form of subsidiaries with a maximum of fifty employees. The subsidiaries have a relatively high degree of independence; integration is accomplished through corporate culture and the adoption of a common leadership style by company managers. The subsidiaries are viewed as the key units of the firm. When a subsidiary grows and employs over fifty people, it is divided into two. This organizational structure can be seen as a mechanism for the distribution of responsibility in a growing market and also serves to facilitate community, reduce hierarchy, and make it possible for the subsidiary manager to maintain close contact with subordinates.

The CCC managers we interviewed emphasized the non-hierarchical, egalitarian aspects of the company, and we were told that the company only has two organizational levels: subsidiary managing director and consultant. The hierarchical elements of CCC are in fact slightly more extensive: the management team of a subsidiary typically comprises a deputy manager and a group of senior consultants, even if all visible status symbols are minimized. We observed a limited focus on formal *systems*, structures, and procedures, reflecting strong beliefs in normative (cultural) control. Senior managers devoted considerable time and effort to developing and implementing values, meanings, and emotions in order to produce the requisite employee orientations and behaviour.

Organization Culture

Cultural forms of control are emphasized at CCC. Shared values, beliefs, meanings, and emotions are viewed as crucial to company success, and many organizational activities are devoted to producing, reproducing, and developing these elements of the culture. The dominant view is that the success of a given project is contingent on how social relations are managed, both within the project group and in relation to the client's management and operative personnel. The managerial group is well-integrated—an outcome of selective recruitment and frequent management conferences that often have a rich social content. One interviewee, comparing her experience of CCC with that of previous workplaces, said there was very little conflict and competition between CCC managers.

CCC managers also assume that the well-being of employees directly influences the quality of their work. A slogan expresses 'fun and profit' as overall values. The CEO emphasized the firm's ability to create a positive work climate, stating that 'if there is one thing that we are good at it is this, we are damned good at this'. This is viewed as affecting commitment and work cooperation.

The culture is based on a 'we-feeling' and loyalty. There is a strong group pressure to help out. Many employees felt that they should work a little harder at CCC.

The value ascribed to the social can be illustrated by the way office space is allocated in the corporate building. Personnel are seated closely together (something like 25 per cent of all consultants may be working in CCC's headquarters building on any given day); the social areas within the firm's premises are spacious and aesthetically appealing. The top floor of the company is designed as 'a home' that comes fully equipped with a TV, sauna, and kitchen. There is also a piano bar. The company also sponsors an art club, a choir, courses in navigation, and other activities. Communication aids such as white boards are used to stimulate discussion. The absence of straight corridors and the variety in the colours and paintings on the walls and floors (e.g. of clouds) stimulate personal involvement and creativity. The location of top management on the first floor, close to the reception, expresses availability and equality. Social activities are used to celebrate the idea that the company invests substantial resources in its people.

HRM

Given the identity of the firm as a 'people company' (as one of the founder expressed it), it is perhaps surprising that there is very little attention to formal personnel strategies or procedures for dealing with HRM issues in the organization. CCC has no personnel manager or function. A senior manager told us that 'the personnel are far too important for us to have a personnel manager', thus implying that personnel management was a primary concern of all subsidiary managers. HRM practice can thus be seen as an outcome of the culture. Personnel are often recruited internally and often join the firm from a secondary role in an existing subsidiary. These individuals can, if viewed as successful, become subsidiary managers after some time. New managers are mentored by senior managers. Shared values and meanings therefore lead to similar HRM practices.

Recruitment in CCC is done selectively. Many of the employees and managers were a part of the contact network of the three founders—who knew a lot of people—and were consequently personally known to the founders from earlier workplaces or other situations. For CCC, social criteria carry a substantial weight in recruitment. The organization looks as much at people's sociability as at their technical competence. Whilst there is considerable diversity in terms of educational background, two-thirds of employees have a university degree. Employees have the opportunity to veto applicants for consultancy and managerial posts. 'In CCC they don't employ managers that can't become friends with their co-workers' (Manager).

The vocabulary of motives at CCC highlights social and downplays instrumental rewards. As one manager said to a group of newcomers, 'I never persuade anybody to start here through offering a high wage or prevent anyone from leaving through it'. Whilst this may not hold true in all cases, it does illustrate the ways in which the recruitment and retention of personnel is informed by espoused company values.

Consultants note a certain discrepancy between the fees charged to clients and the employee salaries—'this is not a high-wage company'—but say that they are satisfied with less-than-optimal wages because the company offers them so many other benefits. As one consultant remarked, 'this company does not pay top bucks. The reason for staying is that you have fun together. We have a good team in our subsidiary'. Community feeling and having fun around and in the job thus act as a kind of glue, making people feel highly committed to their work and the company.

We have a great team here at this company. We have a lot of fun together. I have some critical views about CCC but I really enjoy myself a lot. I would find it hard to imagine moving over to another job. It's a lot of fun here, both professionally, and as far as I am concerned, personally. I have made an enormous number of friends through CCC. I'm very happy here. (Consultant)

At the same time, work at CCC is perceived as similar to that undertaken in most other firms. People experience a discrepancy between everyday work conditions, 'special' social events, the symbolism of the corporate building, and other more extraordinary activities. 'Sometimes it even irritates us' (consultant). Nevertheless, the company has been remarkably successful in terms of employee retention. Staff turnover is below 10 per cent per annum, low in comparison with other employers of young metropolitan employees. The emphasis on the social side of work at CCC is not matched by a commensurate emphasis on training. Some of our respondents complained about the lack of training opportunities. Training is restricted to a one-week introduction to the CCC 'project philosophy' and to occasional one-day conferences.

The Personnel Concept at CCC

CCC's personnel concept is closely integrated with the organizational culture. The company offers a strong sense of community that includes and involves even the most senior people. 'At CCC every consultant expects to be able to have a beer with the CEO' (Manager). CCC claims to integrate business ideals with 'having fun'. The experience of being part of a progressive and original firm, participation in social events, a strong community, and friendships are important parts of the CCC package. This is viewed as a successful strategy for the creation of strong organizational commitment and a positive service climate, making the consultants good at collaborating and easy to sell and re-sell to clients. The company targets people that value community more than career and titles, and being more attracted to a variety of organization-sponsored and orchestrated social events than maximum pay. The typical CCC employee is informal, social, communicative, and strongly interested in contributing to the 'positive' work climate. The founders and top management prioritize cultural control on the understanding that this will compensate for a certain looseness in technical and formal control.

Discussion: A Tale of Two Personnel Concepts

There are, as we have now seen, far-reaching differences between our two firms in competence, management style, structure, organizational culture, and HRM principles. These are summarized in Table 7.1.

Big emphasizes the attraction and retention of qualified graduates, of whom a number will reach partner level in due course, and maintains a good balance between seniors and juniors (Maister 1993). By contrast, CCC fosters the development and maintenance of the organization's social glue, through supporting an organization-based social identity, facilitating retainment and smooth cooperation. Big can thus be understood as a *meritocracy*

Table 7.1. Contrasting personnel concepts in two knowledge intensive firms

Big Consulting	CCC
Analytic skills, formal relations with customers. Organizational structures and controls	Social competences and people skills. Personal and business relationships with customers
Systems and structures more important than leadership. Emphasis on project methodology	Leadership relatively important. Business concept loosely tied to work practices
Employees express mixed feelings about senior partners	Systematic cultivation of strong positive feelings towards senior partners
Elaborated hierarchy, tight financial controls, emphasis on knowledge management and recycling of 'solutions'	Downplayed hierarchy, relatively loose financial controls, informal sharing of experiences
Technocratic orientation: validation of technical expertise	Human relations orientation: technical expertise downplayed
Emphasis on systems and procedures. Culture of 'delivery' and knowledge-sharing	Strong emphasis on cultural values and ideas. 'Community' approach to client support
Formal dress codes and neutral/impersonal artefacts. Formal evaluation of staff performance. Motivation through promotion and financial reward	Relatively informal dress codes and expressive artefacts. Informal evaluation of staff performance. Motivation through experience of community and 'having fun'

that places a key emphasis on differentiation, whilst CCC is primarily a *community* that puts an overwhelming emphasis on integration.

Following Legge (1999), it could be argued that Big has much to offer its employees in terms of pay, conditions, and status. CCC employees, on the other hand, are rewarded by means of 'community' benefits. The two companies are nevertheless characterized by some substantial overlaps and similarities. Big has social activities (skiing and travel opportunities), whilst CCC pays its employees comparatively well (even though employees note the discrepancy between charging clients relatively high fees and paying wages that correspond to the industry average). Both firms provide a variety of 'surplus offerings', whose purpose is to attract and retain the loyalty of capable employees whilst positively affecting relationships with clients. These aspects have a key bearing on how employees interpret their organization and construct a rationale for their employment (Salancik and Pfeffer 1978). A CCC interviewee remarked that his previous workplace was socially oriented, but that this was not systematically communicated and managed in the manner adopted by CCC.

The brand presence and image of large management consulting companies are such that management does not have to be too sensitive about the personnel issues of people at junior levels. One case study account noted that there is 'never a shortage of hopefuls eager to join the ranks', so the partners have 'over the years developed a callous and cavalier attitude to personnel management' (Akehurst 1994: 192). Far-reaching rationalizations of work procedures are thus possible and this may partly explain the willingness of Big employees to be treated as 'resources'. Grey has argued that people may view work-related *sacrifices* as *investments* (Grey 1994). This view is salient amongst younger Big employees. In CCC, employees are less long-term oriented and expect more *instant gratification*. Its managers act positively to facilitate the institutionalization of the company (Selznick 1957) as a flat, original, funny, friendship-oriented, and personal organization. The company is viewed as 'special' and as more progressive than most others.

The personnel concepts of the two firms interact with the 'core business' and link the two markets which PSFs must consider: the labour and the client markets. The personnel concept is also closely related to how work is structured. Big recruits very junior people, who form the bulk of the large-scale projects. The very large intake of young consultants calls for relatively well-structured project management and monitoring by more qualified people, producing a strongly asymmetrical pattern of employee relations (Werr and Stjernberg 2003). It also calls for compliant and learning-oriented people. In Big the highly structured approach to HRM and organizational structures can be seen as promoting a technocratic orientation in projects. Big employees sometime complain that they are perceived as 'square' and not so good at establishing close relations with clients, but they are focused, hardworking, effective, and reliable.

CCC's managerially led community strongly influences its client relations. HRM and the management of the consultant/client interface are connected. In CCC the approach to its personnel is seen as directly reproduced in its relationship to the market and in project work. As a senior consultant put it:

The company succeeds in making [its own] people feel happy with the company and then they also feel better in the work they are doing and then the job is also performed a bit better and then our customers also become happy.

The personnel concept adopted by the two firms affects their respective output markets. In service work, and in particular in professional service work, with complex interactions and substantial exposure to 'internal' orientations and the workplace climate of clients, HRM issues attain added significance compared to manufacturing. In order to represent the company in a relatively uniform way, and to contribute to its image, management aims to standardize employees through the promotion of values and the selection, retainment, and regulation of selves. Whilst a distinctive personnel concept may be productive, it may equally be perceived as reducing the variety of what is offered to clients. It is important to strive for harmony and mutual reinforcement of corporate image, organizational identity, and organizational culture (Hatch and Schulz 2002; Alvesson 2004). The personnel concept can be seen as a selling proposition, employed in both markets. In order to attract job candidates, a distinct profile and a clear and attractive employment package is called for. When approaching the client market, presenting a distinct view on personnel issues and a specific logic in respect of key consultant competencies and orientations also works as a sales device: it sharpens corporate profile.

Although Big and CCC operate in the same market, or at least in markets with considerable overlap, they have been able to develop two very different personnel concepts. This is at odds with the idea that most organizations operate under strongly isomorphic conditions. There are many different ways to organize work in people-intensive firms, and there is also space for a set of values and beliefs to put their imprint on organizations. As price competition and rationalization are not central, there is a fairly wide spectrum of ways in which the employment situation can be defined in terms of wages, careers, and community. There is management discretion, and different management philosophies can make a difference. The ideas and values of the entrepreneurs of CCC certainly played a role for the firm and its distinctive character. One can also assume that the Scandinavian market—and culture—influences CCC in particular ways. Here equality and downplaying of hierarchy is often celebrated. Big, as part of a very large US-dominated firm, is less sensitive to the cultural specifics of Scandinavian management and workforce values.

Framing the Corporate Citizen—The Personnel Concept and Aspirational Control

The analysis that has been offered here suggests that the personnel concept is deployed in ways that shape and control the orientations and identities of employees. In this sense, it provides a means for managers to exercise 'aspirational' control (Alvesson and Kärreman 2007). This form of control combines the encouragement of identification with a corporate identity perceived as attractive, support for a recognized skills set, the realization of particular objectives and rewards, and compliance with a specific normative order. It is exercised by linking a specific identity to a particular career/employment idea and prospect. Aspirational control is likely to emerge whenever distinct and clear-cut career trajectories are articulated, since these raise the possibility of 'provisional selves' (Ibarra 1999) as employees identify with 'what one wants to become'. Aspirational control typically subtly disciplines and normalizes, through attribution, classification, and ranking mechanisms (e.g. Foucault 1976, 1980; Townley 1993; Grey 1994; Covaleski et al. 1998). It also shifts agency to the target of control, thus converting the individual into an accomplice, through confession-like mechanisms such as self-evaluations and career coaching. This is very strong in Big, but less pronounced and also different in CCC, where the emphasis on employee satisfaction and community encourages a strong sense of 'wanting to do something for the company'. Here aspirations are less about linking identity with a future state of being (a possible self, i.e. sense of one's self in the context of the aspired/ imagined forthcoming identity, see Markus and Nurius 1986), and more about fitting in and being a full member of the corporate collective.

Aspirational control thus involves efforts to connect particular images and preferred identities to work positions and, sometimes, career trajectories. Attempts to exercise aspirational control may not only be supported by material means, such as salary packages and access to facilities (such as office space and car pools), but also by collective rewards such as pleasant social events. However, its main point of entry lies in the perceptual and ideational dimensions. Thus, an effective HRM strategy succeeds not only in providing satisfying conditions that bind the 'right' people to the organizations through rewards (widely defined), but also 'binds' the identity of people to the conditions and rewards that are offered. Personnel concepts refer to holistic, integrated, ambitious, and therefore powerful ways of controlling labour.

Identity regulation—the process through which companies offer convincing input into, and constraints on, how people see themselves—involves shaping people so that they define themselves in line with organizational standards (Knights and Willmott 1989; Kunda 1992; Alvesson and Willmott 2002). Thus, Big produces employees that are career-oriented, competitive, efficient, self-improving, rational, and hardworking. CCC produces employees that are social, non-competitive, positive ('don't criticise if you don't have a constructive alternative!'), hardworking, and friendly. The personnel concept marks out the prototypical employee, the template for how people can assess themselves and others. An organizational structure based on a clear definition of the employee is likely to produce this employee through 'truth creating' practices, wherein employees become 'normalized' and standardized in accordance with the definitions and ideals of organizational elites (see Foucault 1980; Townley 1994).

Through organizationally guided or reinforced constructions of oneself— as Social Man, Intrinsically Motivated Woman, or Career Woman—organization, identity, and motivation form a configuration in which various elements mutually define each other. One example is how organizational hierarchies lead Big employees to define themselves and others through career levels, speed of promotion, and titles. CCC employees are 'normalized' as positive (non-critical), friendly, and loyal individuals who are prepared to forego high wages or training in favour of community. Our point is not that this is bad—there are benefits for employees as well as employers and clients—but it is worth noting that the ability to shape work identities means that management is in effect defining the 'normal' employee, thus undermining autonomy and resistance.

Conclusion

The two cases presented in this chapter show some highly distinctive variants in organizational structure and HRM. We have used the personnel concept to describe and understand this variation, and the chapter has developed a framework for 'deeper thinking' about organizational–personnel links. We have also sought to go beyond the legacy of 'Theory X and Theory Y' (McGregor 1960). The personnel concept encourages an interest in the firm-specific and unique attributes of the organization, offering a more robustly sociological account of employee relations than does the notion of a psychological contract (e.g. Herriot et al. 1997; Guest 1998). Whereas the latter typically draws attention to individual perceptions of mutual obligations, the personnel concept refers to the underlying assumptions and situated practices that underpin organizational cultures.

The personnel concept refers to the organizational arrangements, benefits, and identity constructions that have most bearing on the recruitment, retention, and motivation of personnel. The concept highlights the ways in which work identities are constructed and it also contributes to understanding the exercise of aspirational control (Alvesson and Kärreman 2007). The emphasis on subjectivity and culture differentiates the personnel concept from the idea of 'HRM bundles' (MacDuffie 1995) or the strength of the HRM system (Bowen and Ostroff 2004).

Many, probably most, firms do *not* enact a distinct or ambitious personnel concept, as the term is used here. For organizations offering 'only' fair pay, safe working conditions, secure employment, and conventional control mechanisms with no 'extras', the concept may offer little added understanding. Many firms seek to minimize costs rather than maximize commitment (Pfeffer 1994), and the diversity of many organizations' workforces makes it difficult to work with a single or overall personnel concept. In most firms, only a core group of employees, sometimes small in number, are seen as vital to competitive advantage (Purcell 1999), and by no means all organizations have the capacity to think through how they conceive their (prototypical) employee. But organizations that seek to develop a competitive advantage through the competence and motivation of their personnel may benefit from the development of a strongly articulated personnel concept. Substantial advantages may accrue to those firms that develop unique (or at least firm-specific) organizational resources that are difficult to copy (Barney 1986; Pfeffer 1994; Löwendahl 1997). This diversity sustains innovation and variation as firms seek to combine different combinations of personnel and competence as they address the exigencies of particular input (labour) and output (client) markets.

Distinct and broadly articulated personnel concepts may facilitate the direction and integration of human resources (cf. Löwendahl 1997), but they may equally foster conformity and reduced flexibility in the criteria of employment, promotion, and reward. People with the 'wrong' personalities may not be employed, and those who are not fully attracted by what is offered may be inclined to leave. Studies of other organizations in the consultancy field have shown that there is considerable variation in both organizational identities and the links between organizations and their employees (Alvesson & Robertson 2006; Alvesson & Empson 2008). This indicates that, at least within this sector, the concept is of some general relevance. In this chapter we have concentrated on KIFs, but the framework presented may also be relevant to a wider set of organizations that may choose to follow ambitious and innovative employment practices.

⬚ BIBLIOGRAPHY

Adler, P. (1999) Building Better Bureaucracies, *Academy of Management Executive* 12(4): 36–47.

Akehurst, G. (1994) Brownloaf-MacTaggart—Control and Power in a Management Consultancy, in D. Adam-Smith and A. Peacock (eds), *Cases in Organizational Behaviour*, London: Pitman.

Alvesson, M. (1993) Cultural-Ideological Modes of Management Control, in S. Deetz (ed.), *Communication Yearbook*, Vol. 16, Newbury Park, California: Sage.

——(1995) *Management of Knowledge-Intensive Firms*, Berlin/New York: de Gruyter.

——(2000) Social Identity and Loyalty in Knowledge-Intensive Firms, *Journal of Management Studies*, 37(8): 1101–23.

——(2002) *Understanding Organizational Culture*, London: Sage.

——(2004) *Knowledge Work and Knowledge-intensive Firms*, Oxford: Oxford University Press.

——and Empson, L. (2008) The Construction of Organizational Identity, Comparative Case Studies of Consulting Firms, *Scandinavian Journal of Management*, 24: 1–16.

——and Kärreman, D. (2007) Unraveling HRM: Identity, Ceremony, and Control in a Management Consulting Firm, *Organization Science*, 18(4): 711–23.

——and Lindkvist, L. (1993) Transaction Costs, Clans and Corporate Culture, *Journal of Management Studies*, 30: 427–52.

——and Robertson, M. (2006) The Best and the Brightest. The Construction, Significance and Effects of Elite Identities in Consultancy Firms, *Organization*, 13(2): 195–224.

——and Willmott, H. (2002) Producing the Appropriate Individual. Identity Regulation as Organizational Control, *Journal of Management Studies*, 39(5): 619–44.

Barney, J. (1986) Organizational Culture: Can It Be a Source of Sustained Competitive Advantage?, *Academy of Management Review*, 11: 656–65.

Broshak, J. (2001) Do the Actors Make the Play? Individual Mobility and the Dissolution of Interorganizational Relationships, Chapter presented at the 2001 Academy of Management Annual Meeting, Washington.

Boween, D. and Ostroff, C. (2004) Understanding HRM-Firm Performance Linkages: The Role of the Strength of the HRM System, *Academy of Management Review*, 29(2): 203–21.

Boxall, P. and Steeneveld, M. (1999) Human Resource Strategy and Competitive Advantage: A Longitudinal Study of Engineering Consultants, *Journal of Management Studies*, 36(4): 443–63.

Clark, T. (1995) *Managing Consultants*, Buckingham: Open University Press.

Cooper, D., Hinings, B., Greenwood, R. and Brown, J. (1996) Sedimentation and Transformation in Organizational Change: The Case of Canadian Law Firms, *Organization Studies*, 17(4): 623–47.

Covaleski, M. et al. (1998) The Calculated and the Avowed: Techniques of Discipline and Struggles Over Identity in Big Six Public Accounting Firms, *Administrative Science Quarterly*, 43: 293–327.

DiMaggio, P. and Powell, W. (1983) The Iron Cage Revisited: Institutional Isomorphism and Collective Rationality in Organizational Fields, *American Sociological Review*, 48: 147–60.

Foucault, M. (1977) *Discipline and Punish*, New York: Vintage.

——(1980) *Power/Knowledge*, New York: Pantheon.

Geertz, C. (1973) *The Interpretation of Cultures*, New York: Free Press.

Greenwood, R. et al. (1990) P2-Form Strategic Management: Corporate Practices in Professional Partnerships, *Academy of Management Journal*, 33(4): 725–55.

——and Empson, L. (2003) The Professional Partnership: Relic or Exemplary Form of Governance?, *Organization Studies*, 24(6): 909–33.

Grey, C. (1994) Career as a Project of the Self and Labour Process Discipline, *Sociology*, 28: 479–97.

Grugulis, I., Dundon, T. and Wilkinson, A. (2000) Cultural Control and the Culture Manager: Employment Practices in a Consultancy, *Work, Employment and Society*, 14(1): 97–116.

Guest, D. (1998) Is the Psychological Contract Worth Taking Seriously?, *Journal of Organizational Behaviour*, 19: 649–64.

Hatch, M.J. and Schultz, M. (2003) Bringing the Corporation into Corporate Branding, *European Journal of Marketing*, 37: 1041–64.

Hendry, C. and Jenkins, R. (1997) Psychological Contracts and New Deals, *Human Resource, Management Journal*, 7(1): 38–44.

Herriot, P., Manning, W. and Kidd, J. (1997) The Content of the Psychological Contract, *British Journal of Management*, 8: 151–62.

Ibarra, H. (1999) Provisional Selves: Experimenting with Image and Identity in Professional Adaptation, *Administrative Science Quarterly*, 44: 764–91.

Kanter, R.M. (1983) *The Change Masters*, New York: Simon and Schuster.

Knights, D. and Willmott, H. (1989) Power and Subjectivity at Work, *Sociology*, 23(4): 535–58.

Kunda, G. (1992) *Engineering Culture. Control and Commitment in a High-Tech Corporation*, Philadelphia, Pennsylvania: Temple University Press.

Legge, K. (1999) Representing People at Work, *Organization*, 6(2): 247–64.

——(2005) Human Resource Management, in S. Ackroyd et al. (eds), *Oxford Handbook of Work and Organization Studies*, Oxford: Oxford University Press.

Lowendahl, B. (1997) *Strategic Management in Professional Service Firms*, Copenhagen: Copenhagen Business School Press.

MacDuffie, J.P. (1995) Human Resource Bundles and Manufacturing Performance: Organizational Logic and Flexible Production Systems in the World Auto Industry, *Industrial and Labor Relations Review*, 48(2): 197–221.

Maister, D. (1982) Balancing the Professional Service Firm, *Sloan Management Review*, Fall: 15–29.

——(1993) *Managing the Professional Service Firm*, New York: Free Press.

Martin, J. (2002) *Organizational Culture*, Thousand Oaks, California: Sage.

McGregor, D. (1960) *The Human Side of Enterprise*, New York: McGraw-Hill.

Morrison, E. and Robinson, S. (1997) When Employees Feel Betrayed: a Model of How Psychological Contract Violation Develops, *Academy of Management Review*, 22(1): 226–56.

Newell, S. et al. (2002) *Managing Knowledge Work*, Basingstoke: Palgrave.

Normann, R. (1983) *Service Management*, Chichester: Wiley.

Ortner, S. (1973) On Key Symbols, *American Anthropologist*, 75: 1338–46.

Pfeffer, J. (1994) *Competitive Advantage Through People*, Boston: Harvard Business Press.

Purcell, J. (1999) Best Practice and Best Fit: Chimera or Cul-de-Sac?, *Human Resource Management Journal*, 9(3): 26–41.

Robertson, M. (1999) *Sustaining Knowledge Creation within Knowledge-Intensive Firms*, Diss., Warwick Business School.

——Scarbrough, H. and Swan, J. (2003) Knowledge Creation in Professional Service Firms: Institutional Effects, *Organization Studies*, 24(6): 831–57.

Rousseau, D. (1998) The 'Problem' of the Psychological Contract Considered, *Journal of Organizational Behaviour*, 19: 665–71.

Salancik, G.R. and Pfeffer, J. (1978) A Social Information Processing Approach to Job Attitudes and Task Design, *Administrative Science Quarterly*, 23: 224–53.

Schein, E. (1980) *Organizational Psychology*, Reading, Massachusetts: Addison-Wesley.

Scott, R. (1995) *Institutions and Organizations*, Thousand Oaks, California: Sage.

Selznick, P. (1957) *Leadership in Administration—A Sociological Interpretation*, New York: Harper & Row.

Smircich, L. (1983) Concepts of Culture and Organizational Analysis, *Administrative Science Quarterly*, 28: 339–58.

Starbuck W. (1993) Keeping a Butterfly and an Elephant in a House of Cards: The Elements of Exceptional Success, *Journal of Management Studies*, 30(6): 885–921.

Townley, B. (1994) *Reframing Human Resource Management*, London: Sage.

Tyson, S. (1995) *Human Resource Strategy*, London: Pitman.

Van Maanen, J. and Kunda, G. (1989) Real feelings: Emotional Expression and Organizational Culture, in B.M. Staw and L.L. Cummings (eds) *Research in Organizational Behaviour*, Vol 11, Greenwich, Connecticut: JAI Press.

Watson, T. (2004) HRM and Critical Social Science Analysis, *Journal of Management Studies*, 41: 447–67.

Werr, A. and Stjernberg, T. (2003) Exploring Management Consulting Firms as Knowledge Systems, *Organization Studies*, 24(6): 881–908.

8 Post-Bureaucratic Manufacturing? The Post-War Organization of Large British Firms

STEPHEN ACKROYD

In Britain extensive and various bureaucracies developed in the public sector and for this reason the state and bureaucracy are securely linked in the public mind.[1] The extent to which large British firms were, at any time, bureaucratically organized is easily exaggerated however, and contemporary firms have developed in ways largely unaffected by a supposedly bureaucratic past. Although some very large firms emerged in Britain in the twentieth century, these firms lacked highly developed bureaucratic features—even in the years between 1945 and 1975 when they reached the apogee of their integration. This chapter will argue that the UK manufacturing sector remains locked into a long-run pattern of industrial underdevelopment and decline. The origins of this decline can be found not in any objective features of the competitive environment but in a highly distinctive British pattern of exceptionalism that emerged from the strategic choices of UK managerial elites. From their first establishment, large British firms not only lacked centralized direction, they also lacked the integrated and unitary structures suggested by the classic models of bureaucracy (Weber 1968; Mintzberg 1979, 1993).

Many factors militated against the development of centralized and bureaucratized private firms in the United Kingdom. Manufacturing, begun on a relatively small scale in the early phases of the industrial revolution, was driven by the activities of small proprietors whose businesses were often located in close proximity to each other, giving rise to the emergence of what would later be identified as 'industrial districts' (Marshall 1890). These were characterized by the geographic concentration of small firms in the same trades. High production volumes were achieved through pooled output based on the widespread use of subcontracting. There were processes of aggregation, but these were often partial and incomplete. Some industries developed holding company structures that were in fact thinly disguised cartels. Heavy investment on single sites, controlled by a developed

administration, was relatively unusual. With the exception of the bulk che-
micals and oil-refining industries, there was little approximation to the scale
of industrial investment found in the United States or Germany. Even today,
amongst British companies producing and marketing products, only the
scale-intensive pharmaceutical and oil industries include global corporations
that are capable of competing with their German and Japanese equivalents.

In recent decades, and particularly since 1995, the British manufacturing
sector has declined rapidly. Large manufacturing firms remain, but these are
much fewer than might be expected and they show no marked tendencies
towards growth. As recently as 1985, half of the top 200 largest British firms
could be classified as manufacturing companies (see Table 8.1). Twenty years
later the proportion had dwindled to around 15 per cent. These firms are
typically embedded in loosely coordinated and decentralized corporate structures that offer a very substantial degree of autonomy to operating units. To
describe them simply, very large British manufacturing companies can only
be considered 'large' when considered in aggregate, comprised as they are by
numerous subsidiary companies or affiliates.

As has been suggested, such features emerged historically and key continuities include a marked shortage of a large and formally qualified managerial
cadre and a relatively high ratio of productive to administrative employees.
Whilst these features can be understood in terms of 'hybrid' admixtures of

Table 8.1. Types of manufacturing firms amongst the largest 200 British companies for selected years 1970–2006

	1970 number	% of all firms	1985 number	% of all firms	1996 number	% of all firms	2006[a] number	% of all firms
1. Old staples (metals and cloth)	13	6.5	9	4.5	3	1.5	0	—
2. Complex products (cars, planes, ships, engines)	16	8.0	13	6.5	4	2.0	2	1
3. Related manufacturing groups								
3(a). Retail manufacture: food, drink, tobacco, clothing, other domestic consumption goods, paper packaging, etc.	42	21.0	38	19.0	25	12.5	15	7.5
3(b). Diverse engineering	19	9.5	24	12.0	18	9.0	13	6.5
3(c). Building materials	5	2.5	10	5.0	7	3.5	4	2
4. Conglomerates	0	—	5	2.5	6	3.0	0	—
Total	95	47.5	99	49.5	63	31.5	34	17

[a] Figures for 2006 take into account four 'losses' resulting from takeovers and mergers amongst the largest firms and three changes of category. Also included for 2006 are seven new entrants—three into 3a, three into 3b and one into 3c.

bureaucracy and other modes of coordination and control (Alvesson and Thompson 2004), care must be taken not to exaggerate the extent to which bureaucracy is fundamental to these structures. The corporate structures detailed in this chapter arise from the particular policies, strategic objectives, and values enacted by the managerial elites that have successively controlled UK manufacturing enterprise. The chapter will argue that British manufacturing firms were never markedly bureaucratic, and they have moved successively further away from this pattern in recent years. Whilst it is possible for managerial elites to make changes in strategy and structure, they are constrained by pre-existing patterns of organization and modes of workplace organization. Accordingly, the chapter details the historical development of the largest UK manufacturing companies. Change can only occur on the basis of what has gone before, and the chapter argues that successive elites have been responsible for changes that have taken British manufacturing industry in some specific directions rather than others.

Three Stages of Large Firm Development

The post-war development of the large British manufacturing firm can be divided into three distinct periods, each of which is characterized by a particular type of strategy and pattern of organization. Later in this chapter the strategy that is held to be characteristic of the dominant contemporary firms in these sectors at different periods will be given extended consideration. But, before that, as a prelude, all three stages in the development of firms will be briefly outlined as follows:

- Firstly, in the period 1945–70 there was the development of large firms seeking to be dominant in chosen domestic markets and the emergence of associated strategies aimed at firms becoming *dominant national firms* (DoNFs). These firms typically aimed to monopolize the home market within their chosen industrial sectors and they extended their operations into selected international export markets (well-known examples are BMC, Courtaulds, Imperial Tobacco, Metal Box, and Pilkington). Few firms of this type successfully established national monopolies, and there were contradictory trends of industrial policy that at times promoted and at times discouraged such developments. Many firms remained incomplete amalgamations of former competitors and they were often very inadequately incorporated within a single firm. It was not unusual for constituent firms to be allowed operational autonomy. This suggests the possibility of tensions occurring between factions at senior levels within companies that were difficult to resolve in favour of national priorities.

- Secondly, in the period 1970–95 the leading firms largely gave up the goal of domination at national level, becoming instead more diversified in their activities and more motivated by profit-making. As such, their strategy involved taking on new challenges and moving into new areas of production and markets, including overseas markets, where there were good opportunities for profitable operation. We may label these companies as *diversified international manufacturing firms* (DIMFs) because their activities became more diverse, relatively small scale in any one location but widely distributed (obvious examples can be found in the policies and practices of GEC, GKN, BTR, TI Group, Hanson Trust, Williams Holdings, and numerous others). Such firms often adopted a predatory attitude to the assets of other firms and groups, which they would take over to incorporate or 'sell on'. In such companies a range of businesses—sometimes covering diverse industrial sectors—were combined. Businesses adopting strategies of this type ranged from those whose aim was simply to be highly profitable business groups assembled from acquisitions from almost any sector, to those that developed the practice of buying and selling companies alongside more orthodox business plans. Conglomerates such as the Hanson Trust or F. H. Tomkins were matched by many firms that followed similar policies of takeover as important additions to their other activities (BTR, TI Group). Some large manufacturing firms continued to dominate their chosen industrial sectors (GEC, GKN) whilst following a more diverse pattern of investment, sometimes buying speculatively into new industries. All of the above companies managed their constituent plants in the absence of detailed control over local operations. They followed a common policy of prioritizing profit generation over growth.
- Thirdly, in the period 1995 to 2006, there has been widespread profit-taking that has frequently entailed the selling-off of companies to foreign owners or the dispersal of business groupings. However, these years have also seen the emergence of a new type of large business that is more concentrated in terms of the range of business activities it undertakes at any one time. A common feature of such companies is the policy of reproducing profitable businesses in as many mature markets as possible. For this and other reasons, the assets of such firms tend to be parcelled out into many subsidiaries, joint ventures, and other affiliate companies. These large and extensively 'disaggregated' UK manufacturing concerns are identified here as *capital extensive firms* (CEFs) (see also Ackroyd 2002). This type of organization and its associated business strategies will be considered more fully in the final sections of the chapter. In common with the earlier dominant organizational types, the CEF lacks centralized structures and is constituted by numerous legally and functionally separate businesses coordinated by means of information technologies. The subsidiaries and affiliates of these companies may easily number

in the high hundreds. The CEFs, like the DIMFs before them, have substantially abandoned the strategy of acquiring assets within particular industrial sectors. Firms in this category occupy strategic positions in carefully selected global supply chains and they also follow changing opportunities for profit-making afforded by the buying and selling of subsidiaries. These firms are not highly committed to particular countries, locations, or industrial sectors.

The distinctive strategy of the DoNFs is that of being, or aspiring to be, the leading player in the home market. This gives way to a general strategy adopted by DIMFs, in which the goal of dominating particular home markets becomes much less central. This second period is characterized by strategies of diversification—initially to reduce exposure to competition—combined with profit-taking from the reorganization, repositioning, and the subsequent resale of acquired firms. The strategy of diversification and profit-taking that emerges (very strongly in the case of the true conglomerates) means that firms become more variegated as they seek out profitable activities in new markets. This strategy of diversification and repositioning then gives way to a new pattern, more focused in terms of its main lines of business activity, that may be identified as the CEF. Such firms are even more marked by the number and small size of their constituent parts, and by their willingness to move into and out of proximate business activities in pursuit of profit. These CEFs are structured in ways that make them less exposed to capital risk, and they are capable of repositioning themselves through the buying and selling of other businesses. Their success derives from their ability to locate and occupy advantageous positions in global supply chains.

The idea that changes in firm strategy are tightly linked to changes in corporate structure is reminiscent of Chandler (Chandler 1962, 1990). The research presented in this chapter does not, however, corroborate the idea that the 'M' form of company (or its evolutionary developments) is adopted on the basis of its inherent efficiencies, or that this form offers a viable way of thinking about the structure of UK manufacturing corporations. The implicit functionalism of Chandler and the neo-Chandlerians (Chandler and Deams 1980; Channon 1982; Whittington and Meyer 2002) places the burden of explanation on managerial rationality, paying little or no attention to the strategic predispositions that shape managerial responses to the exigencies of particular local and national contexts (Pettigrew 1985). The approach favoured in the present analysis is an essentially historical one in which changes of policy are ascribed to changes in ideas and priorities of the groups that have exercised strategic control of UK manufacturing companies. The three-part typology presented above reflects changes in the control of UK manufacturing firms and their distinctive objectives. Control of firms by a nationalistically inclined elite gives way to much more opportunistically inclined corporate executives who are also usually large shareholders. This, in turn, gives way to the control of companies by profit-orientated international financial elites. The latter group is not strongly committed to manufacturing businesses that do not yield high returns to their shareholders. Consequently, the size of the remaining large firms (measured by their assets) has tended to shrink, as value has been appropriated and redistributed. Many UK manufacturing firms have been liquidated, sold into foreign ownership, or taken over by private equity interests.

Aspiring to Dominate National Markets (1945–75), or the Rise and Decline of the DoNFs

In Britain, many manufacturing firms of national importance emerged in the period 1945–75, even if the process of consolidation was discontinuous and uneven. The evidence shows that manufacturing capacity became increasingly concentrated as the process of consolidation gathered pace. This led to the emergence of national organizations enjoying oligopoly or even monopoly in their home markets, particularly in the case of firms operating in a narrow sector or having specific products. Leading examples include GEC, whose experience will be discussed more fully below; Pilkington, the glass-maker and BICC, the cable-maker. In addition, there were many firms primarily producing goods for consumer markets (such as Cadbury, Imperial Tobacco, Bass, and Tate and Lyle) that expanded through a combination of merger and acquisition to occupy very strong positions in home markets.

The annual number of firms disappearing as separate entities due to takeover and merger between 1961 and 1975 was more than 500 in most years (Hannah 1983). Whilst a high proportion of British manufacturing capacity came under the control of a relatively small number of companies, many weak and/or small regional firms remained as constituent parts of loosely federated firms. Thus, despite the fact that the acquisition and merger of manufacturing firms accelerated in the decades following the Second World War, many of the advantages of mass production were foregone. By the late 1970s, the United Kingdom exhibited the highest industrial concentration of any advanced manufacturing economy (Chandler and Deams 1980). According to Hannah (1976: 216), the share of net output produced by the 200 largest British firms rose to more than 40 per cent by the end of the 1960s. Williams et al. (1983: 32) suggest that the percentage was even higher in the 1970s, with the 100 largest companies accounting for around 50 per cent of manufacturing output and employment. But this concentration did not necessarily lead to efficient production.

Many companies could be used to illustrate the formation of national companies in the 1950s, 1960s, and early 1970s. The difficulties faced by these firms were often challenging; however, two interesting examples will be considered briefly here. A general point to make is that the major companies that emerged during these years grew through piecemeal acquisition and merger rather than through investment. For this reason, although undoubtedly large, emerging companies were often incapable of producing in very high volume at low prices. They achieved market dominance through the removal of competition. Concentration often brought together existing plants into common ownership, but this did little to encourage the planning of major new investments in production facilities. One of the most successful firms to emerge as a significant national player in this period was the (British) General Electric Company (GEC). The managing director of GEC, Arnold Weinstock, bought out a number of small companies and then, in two major coups, took over both its major rivals, English Electric and Amalgamated Electrical Industries in 1967 and 1968, respectively. Whilst these rivals were much larger than GEC, they were judged to be lacking in dynamism and the major shareholders allowed their takeover with the encouragement of the UK Government. The result was an extremely large electrical manufacturing firm that produced a wide range of products from radio and television sets to electric traction and electrical generation equipment. GEC also acquired capacity in heavy engineering and aerospace engineering. The path to growth through acquisition and merger meant that even the strongest of the emerging national firms comprised many activities in many plants that produced a very wide range of products. Such firms were far from being organizations of the Ford type, featuring the efficient mass production of standardized items.

The British car manufacturing industry exemplifies the inherent difficulties of forming effective national firms through mergers. Whereas companies such as Ford and Volkswagen utilized very large, horizontally integrated, and centralized manufacturing plants coordinated by a developed bureaucracy to produce a limited range of models, the UK automobile industry faced huge difficulties in realizing this type of production. Nothing approaching the pattern of US Ford was ever developed—even by the Ford Company itself when it began large-scale operations in Britain. Austin, the largest car producer in Britain in the 1930s, never produced more than a fifth of the numbers of the Ford plant at River Rouge. In most years during the 1930s, Ford's Rouge complex accounted for more than five times the units per annum than was produced by the entire UK automobile industry. British component manufacturers, such as Dunlop and Lucas, were significantly larger than even the largest car producers. However, in line with the general trends noted above, the British car industry had become increasingly concentrated by the end of the 1960s.

There were, in fact, several attempts to create national car companies after the Second World War and, here again, a distinctively British pattern of merger and acquisition produced what were, on paper at least, large manufacturing groups. Leyland Motors, the commercial vehicle producer, acquired the car-producing firms Standard-Triumph and Rover, and was profitable in the 1960s. A similar group combining the commercial producers Guy and Coventry Climax with the luxury car makers Jaguar and Daimler had been brought together under the leadership of William Lyons of Jaguar. However, the UK industry had difficulties in meeting domestic demand for cheap but serviceable small cars. Competition from European producers was beginning to make itself felt. The largest British car producers, Austin and Morris, were initially bundled together with several smaller companies— including MG, Riley, and Wolsley, in a series of mergers. But after the dust settled, the resulting British Motor Corporation (BMC) failed to develop as an effective volume producer of cars. Though large in the sense of owning the firms that supplied 70 per cent or so of British car production, BMC failed to achieve the required economies of scale because it lacked suitably large, integrated production facilities. Inadequate investment at almost all of its main production sites was, by 1965, only a few years after its formation, leaving the group with disappearing profits. The groups that grew up around Jaguar and Leyland continued to use more traditional small batch production methods. These firms were also under-capitalized and utilized high numbers of skilled workers to produce their products, but this was deemed workable insofar as their main products (luxury cars and commercial vehicles) could only be manufactured using traditional methods. The much larger BMC group offers a contrasting example. Finding itself competing against highly capitalized foreign competitors in the mass market for small cars, BMC could not continue with traditional production methods.

As is well known, rather than confront the problem of finding large new pools of investment capital, BMC, with the active assistance of the UK government, merged with the other major vehicle groups. Thus, after a merger between BMC and Jaguar group, British Motor Holdings (BMH) was formed in 1966. The effective takeover of BMH by Leyland in 1968 then created the British Leyland Motor Corporation (BLMC). Consistent with the desire to produce a national car-producing company supposedly large enough to meet international competition on a roughly equal basis, all the British eggs were now in one basket. Obviously these final mergers produced a very large combined group, but it had many production sites and a huge range of products. Drastic rationalization of production capacity and major capital investment were now essential for survival. But the problem of how to raise sufficient capital and to apply this to the efficient production of small cars was never solved. From this point onwards, the survival of the British-owned car industry depended on the fortunes of one company. In 1970, when BLMC reached its high point of output, two main production sites and several ancillary factories struggled to turn out more than 800,000 units with a product mix of seven or eight different models. In the same year, Ford produced 2.5 million units in the United States alone, though Ford was itself in difficulties by this time. Volkswagen produced over one million Beetles in its German plants, and many more in overseas plants and under license. The VW Company achieved this whilst planning and investing for the production of the Beetle's successor, the VW Golf, which, in time, achieved even higher volumes of sales than the Beetle.

British car manufacturing firms are of considerable interest insofar as they shed light (admittedly in a somewhat extreme form) on many of the problems that have beset UK industry considered more generally. The problem was how to develop efficient firms at a national level capable of beating whatever competition there was for the home market, whilst developing the capacity to expand overseas. Firms depended on being able to dominate their home market, sales from which would subsidize this expansion. With the exception of bulk chemical production and oil refining, however, where there were high levels of investment in a new plant, there was a general failure to procure sufficient capital. In chemical and oil production the tradition of small owner-managed firms described at the start of this chapter did not exist. By contrast, the dispersal that characterized British industry represented a considerable internal challenge to those seeking to undertake concentrated capital investment. Where executives responsible for production at different sites retained some influence on the main board of a company (as was the case in many British companies with their federated structures), proposals for consolidated investment could and did attract resistance from opposed managerial factions. Sectional interests often worked against the general good even when government backed the endeavour. Investment in technically advanced sectors became increasingly capital intensive and these investments were often difficult to justify within the standard estimates for return on capital propounded by UK accountants. In many industries the only source of capital for the scale of investment required for effective production was the stock market, which often regarded proposals for large-scale industrial modernization with extreme scepticism.

The above considerations shed some light on the difficulties experienced by UK manufacturing in the years down to 1975. The obstacles to the development of 'Fordist' production methods were legion: in addition to the problem of acquiring capital for investment, there was the problem of where to locate such investments, what production sites to develop, and which products to prioritize within particular strategies of market development.

Diversified, Low Technology Manufacturing (1975–96): Emergence of the DIMFs

The years between 1975 and 1996 saw a comprehensive restructuring of UK manufacturing. This period also gave rise to a new type of manufacturing organization that moved further away from the integrated pattern of production that typified the United States and the other advanced industrial economies. For a time it looked as if British manufacturing might develop its own distinctive trajectory of development, but the period culminates in the beginnings of precipitate decline. Even as late as 1985, however, the fate of the large UK manufacturing firm was far from obvious. As Table 8.1 shows, the number of companies producing complex products, such as cars, ships, and planes had fallen slightly, whilst the firms that comprised the 'old staple' industries on which the industrial basis of the British economy was founded, were disappearing fast. However, many of the highly capitalized manufacturing firms established after the Second World War—GEC, GKN, British Aerospace, and Rolls Royce—were apparently very strong indeed. GEC and GKN were amongst the very largest British firms at this time. Though such firms may have been few in number, those that remained were seen by many as, potentially at least, world-beating organizations. The Thatcher decade (1979–90) saw a precipitate decline in the numbers employed in manufacturing. But the 1980s can also be viewed as a time of organizational restructuring as UK manufacturing firms slimmed down their administration, particularly at the centre, outsourcing many of their services. The period of absolute decline in manufacturing capacity begins later, during the 1990s.

During the course of 1975–85, it became clear that many British manufacturing firms could hold their own at home, but found it difficult to grow into world-class firms operating on a global scale. One important issue was the unwillingness or inability of firms to invest heavily enough to ensure dominance in their chosen home markets. Because they were unable to do this, their ability to expand their product base for export and move into sustained growth was compromised. Even the numerous large firms that produced mainly for domestic consumption (line 3a in Table 8.1)—whose use of technology was relatively undemanding of capital and whose proximity to their markets gave them obvious advantages over foreign competitors— seemed unwilling to expand. The fate of formerly successful, highly capitalized, large companies is of particular interest here. These companies simply did not invest sufficiently to allow them to compete for world markets. Thus, although the early prosperity of GEC came from the manufacture of radio and television sets, in the medium term the company progressively withdrew from such activities. Rather than undertaking significant investment likely to yield good results in five or seven years, GEC saved its profits in the form of cash reserves, which soon became embarrassingly large. By 1982, GEC's reserves had become a 'cash mountain' of more than £1 billion. This was a Company that was content to earn interest at the bank rather than undertake significant R&D or risk capital in major investments. Comparable foreign firms—particularly, Japanese producers such as Mitsubishi Electric and Sony—moved rapidly into British and other markets for consumer electronics, establishing a strong pattern of export-led growth. By the mid-1990s, the leading German and Japanese electronics and engineering firms were capitalized at a level nearly twice that of GEC (Ackroyd and Procter 1998).

By contrast with the export-led strategies of their overseas counterparts, the UK national manufacturing firms played a low-risk game and concentrated on maintaining their domestic positions. In the period 1970–95, GEC and GKN dropped from their relatively high positions in the firm rankings (respectively, 9th and 12th) to become the 17th and 90th largest firms.[2] Both firms grew in value, but their wealth did not accrue from new investment raised, and nor did it derive from the reinvestment of earnings in volume. What growth there was is revealed as extremely modest when the figures are corrected for inflation. Arnold Weinstock became renowned for his risk aversion, his reliance on tried and tested but low technology manufacturing methods, and his policies of strict cost control. Whilst GEC continued to produce some technically complex products, GKN had never been a technically advanced firm,[3] its main output being steel fabrications of different sorts and, of course, fixings (nuts, bolts, and screws). GKN's main revenues came from supplying standard products to many other companies. For many other large British companies, a high proportion of growth derived from the acquisition of other companies in similar areas of business, thus reproducing the practices on which the company had originally been founded.

The British manufacturing firms that made the running during this period were those that made acquisitions. The elites controlling these companies had long understood that profitability could be effectively secured in the process of acquisition. This was undertaken primarily to achieve the consolidation of a business, but, from the second half of the 1970s, there was a shift in general strategy. The sale of acquired firms, previously seen as a minor activity, arising mainly when a company had obtained assets that were deemed inappropriate (as in many cases of major acquisition), was superseded by business policies that prioritized the systematic acquisition, reorganization, and selling on of undervalued firms. Such policies did not develop fully formed overnight. Some firms continued to buy and sell companies as a way of adding to their income whilst viewing these activities as ancillary to their main business. Thus, companies (such as GEC) that continued to see themselves as DoNFs typically sold acquired companies when these lay outside their main areas of operation. On the other hand, numbers of growing businesses developed a new slant on these practices. These firms focused exclusively on extracting value from acquired assets, typically choosing to retain the most profitable of the businesses they acquired irrespective of their sector. Successive takeover and resale exercises meant that these firms became much more plural and diverse in their basic constitution. Indeed, a new kind of manufacturing firm (usually described as a 'conglomerate') rose rapidly to prominence at this time. The most successful were BTR, The Hanson Trust, and Williams Holdings. Established firms perceived these thrusting upstarts as significant rivals, notwithstanding the increasing penetration of domestic markets by foreign producers. For one thing, aggressive British firms posed a direct threat to more traditional firms insofar as they appeared lacking in dynamism, and certainly the latter firms performed poorly by comparison in the years down to 1996. In these circumstances, firms that did not reorganize and change their growth strategy were likely to become takeover targets. In the period now under consideration, GEC and GKN generally stuck to their established business plans, and, as we have seen, moved sharply down the size rankings. BTR and The Hanson Trust (both noted for their active acquisition policies) moved smartly in the opposite direction from being, respectively, 307th and 356th to become the 6th and the 11th largest UK firms. Such firms could only grow in this spectacular fashion by acquisition and this could only be sustained for a limited period. Often, as the general appetite for takeover grew, relatively small but aggressive acquirers would undertake reverse takeovers, acquiring much larger groups judged to have lost momentum or direction. In cases where the incumbent executives in control of the target companies no longer had clearly espoused ambitions (domestic or otherwise), the money-making imperatives followed by the acquiring firms rapidly became the preferred and sanctioned outlook for investors. Executive pay, for the first time, generally came to include stock options as an important element of remuneration packages.[4]

As substantial investors themselves, the leaders of these new companies had different aspirations from the earlier, more patrician generation of UK business leaders. The controlling executives of rising firms were not always the founders of their firms, though many, like James Hanson and Gordon White were both. However, as stockholders, the new breed of British executives increasingly accepted the paramount importance of making profit, and of returning value to shareholders. Only insofar as profit-making was held to be beneficial to firms (whose owners would presumably be mainly British) could the motivation for ambitious growth be construed as nationalistic.[5] The main point to note is that many firms undertaking manufacture became more diverse as the acquisition of firms became a central plank of business strategy. In line with this new tendency towards diversity, industrial concentration began to level off by the 1980s; during that decade, divestment activity also became obvious (Shutt and Whittington 1987: 16; Wright et al. 1989: 116; Chandler 1990). Whilst the 1980s saw inefficient manufacturing stripped out and closed down, businesses were also rationalized with a view to making them more efficient. Management buyouts (MBOs) became popular for the first time, as parts of these rationalized firms were sold to incumbent managers.

As Table 8.1 suggests, there was no shrinkage in the absolute number of large British manufacturing firms in the years from 1970 to 1996. The demise of UK manufacturing begins towards the end of this period, at which point we see the final decline of the old staple industries—textiles and metal manufacture—on which the industrial revolution in Britain was based. Although significant national monopolies were achieved in these sectors, growth in world capacity for production was such that export markets became increasingly crowded. British firms producing complex manufactured products—cars, ships, planes, engines, etc.—followed a parallel trajectory of decline that derived from their failure to dominate their respective domestic markets. By 1996, the only very large firms that continued to manufacture complex products were leading defence suppliers whose revenues were sustained by lucrative military contracts and special relationships with the state. These firms were also rapidly diversifying their businesses into related services, such as the maintenance and efficient utilization of their products. The picture of precipitate decline is mitigated by the emergence of a small number of huge conglomerates that developed through aggressive acquisition policies. What are called 'related business groups' emerge as a major feature of the UK corporate landscape during this period. Large engineering companies hold their own in terms of absolute numbers whilst diversifying their business activities.

Dismembering the Titans, 1996–2006: The Emergence of the CEF

The most recent period that we now consider involves another marked change of direction, reflecting a change of outlook amongst the elites controlling large British manufacturing companies. There was little organic growth in British manufacturing in the years down to the mid-1990s, and what growth there was occurred through acquisitions. After 1995, however, commitment to growth was itself increasingly in doubt, and the practice of taking significant capital out of companies and distributing it to shareholders and the executive cadre became widespread. Growth based on investment in manufacturing capability—especially high technology capability—was almost entirely absent. Significantly, for the subject of this volume, in addition to downsizing, there was yet more emphasis on paring down administration, and a very marked tendency for head offices to regulate the activities of retained subsidiaries only lightly—

mainly by monitoring key performance indicators. Constituent firms were, in most other respects, simply left to their own devices.

There is little doubt that this period saw a sharp contraction in the net worth of many of the largest British firms. In the years 1996–2006, the median value of the 200 of the largest British companies grew by only 30 per cent in money terms, a figure that is insufficient to counter the effects of inflation during that decade. If we take out of the reckoning the small number of companies that underwent substantial growth in this period—none of which can be counted as large manufacturers—we find a significant reduction in the average capitalization of Britain's remaining large firms. The top ten companies on the London market in 2006—comprised of banks, oil, minerals, and pharmaceutical companies—were capitalized at an average of around 120 billion US dollars. These firms can be regarded as being in a league of their own. In late 2006, the largest fifteen British firms were worth more than all of the next 185 in terms of their total capitalization. Given that many of the largest manufacturing firms are in the lower half of the size rankings, there is clear evidence of shrinkage in manufacturing as well as some other sectors. In the period after 1996, growth all but ceased amongst manufacturing firms, and it is doubtful whether there was much continuing commitment to manufacturing amongst the controllers of such firms.

The evidence suggests that there was a systematic withdrawal of British capital from the ownership of publically traded manufacturing firms between 1996 and 2006.[6] The sale of businesses no longer deemed central to the core activities of companies was vigorously pursued as a policy; this often included dispensing with *all* manufacturing activities (and not merely those which were no longer deemed essential). As Table 8.2 indicates, only twenty-five of the sixty-three companies that remained active in UK manufacturing in 1996 survived with broadly the same main business until 2006. Almost all of these firms shrank in size, some of them radically, and the levels of their manufacturing activities were frequently reduced. As Table 8.2 indicates, eight firms in the 1996 manufacturing group moved out of manufacturing altogether, though they remained in business as large public companies. Examples here are: the former engineering group, Bunzl, which becomes a supply and logistics company; Invensys (formed out of a merger between the giant engineering firms, BTR and Siebe) was converted into a control systems and design company; and Whitbread which, no longer a producer of beverages, became a hotelier and food retail provider as the owner of Premier Inns and the Costa Coffee chain. No less than eleven of the largest publically traded manufacturing firms in 1996 were broken up and sold off by 2006. Examples here include Arjo-Wiggins, Hillsdown Holdings, Caradon, and Glynwed. We might also include GEC-Marconi in this category. The formerly huge electronics company, GEC (considered earlier as an example of a DoNF), had crashed into spectacular bankruptcy by 2005.[7]

It is true, of course, that many of the parts of formerly large companies that are broken up continue trading as smaller, independent companies.

Table 8.2. Fate of 1996 large manufacturing companies by 2006[a]

	Number	%	Firm types and examples
Still in broadly the same business and still in the top 200 firms. (However, reduced dependency on manufacturing sales is universal.)	25	42.4	Most numerous type of firm is retail-related manufacturers (food, drink, tobacco, household goods, e.g. Diageo, Cadbury, BAT). Also nine or so engineering firms mostly quite small.
Changed business type—still involved in some manufacturing	3	5.1	Various firms including Rexam (formerly Bowater); Elementis (formerly Harrison and Crossfield).
No longer manufacturing	8	13.6	Various firms including Whitbread, Booker, Bunzl, Invensys, etc.
Split up, greatly downsized or completely re-focused	11	19.6	Many diversified and old firms (e.g. Courtaulds), conglomerates voluntarily broken up and re-focused; also some others, such as United Biscuits, Hillsdown Holdings, etc.
Acquired by foreign owners/private equity	12	20.3	Many focused co's and building materials groups (e.g. BOC, Pilkington, Corus, British Plaster Board, etc.)

[a] Total is fifty-nine not sixty-three, as four firms are lost by mergers between firms in the study. Nor does the table include any new firms that were qualified for inclusion in 2006, as in Table 8.1.

Obviously also, a large company that moves out of manufacturing sells what it can of its factories and plants as going concerns. Thus, break-up and sell-off does not necessarily reduce the level of manufacturing in the economy. On the other hand, these processes often led to the loss of manufacturing capacity because some plants were unable to find a buyer, the products being more cheaply procured by outsourcing—especially from overseas. However, the key point is that the owning elites in British business seem to have decided, more or less *en bloc* by the beginning of the new century, that there was no longer significant profit in manufacturing and there was thus little point in owning manufacturing assets. Perhaps the most compelling evidence for this is the frequency with which apparently viable large companies were sold off to foreign buyers. There was a willingness to sell British firms combined with a distinct lack of interest by other British firms in acquiring them. Thus, as Table 8.2 shows, no less than twelve of the sixty-three largest manufacturing companies in British public ownership in 1996 had been sold to foreign buyers by 2006. Almost every company considered by the research on which this chapter is based was in danger of being sold if the price was judged to be right. Examples of firms sold abroad include some of Britain's most technically sophisticated and effective manufacturing companies. High-profile examples include: BOC (which must now be thought of as a German gases company), Pilkington (now a Japanese-owned glass company), British Steel (which, after a merger with a Dutch metals firm and a change of name, now belongs to an Indian private company). Ready Mixed Concrete

(RMC) is part of a Mexican cement and civil engineering group, and British Plaster Board, along with two other major producers of building materials, was sold to French Interests. Lucas, the electronics components firm and, most recently, all the defence companies previously owned by Smiths Industries were sold to US interests. A high proportion of the assets sold in this way are now controlled by private, rather than public, companies and few are quoted on London markets.

The glass-making firm, Pilkington, is one of a number of companies whose history nicely illustrates the changes in the outlook of corporate elites in recent years. Unusually for a British company, Pilkington was always technologically advanced. However, it remained tightly under family control until a relatively late stage, only floating as a public company in 1970. Its access to capital was limited as a private company, and though it clearly achieved dominance in its main national markets, it was unable to undertake much overseas expansion or to retain its technological lead in any area beyond the manufacture of flat glass for the main glass market. Depending as it did on flat glass, however, the company's main customers were the building trade and car makers, both of which were vulnerable to downturns in the business cycle. Fluctuating sales and profitability exacerbated the problem of raising capital, and hindered Pilkington's expansion. Fatefully, the company opted for earning royalties from licensing its float glass technology to major competitors, rather than entering the main overseas markets directly. Despite this income stream, the variable profit performance of the company made it vulnerable, and there were two serious takeover bids. The first of these, by BTR in 1987, became the subject of intense political debate at the national level and was bitterly contested by glass workers and local communities. The initial takeover offer by Owen Green of BTR was rejected out of hand, but was successively improved upon. However, the bid was successfully resisted in the end. The board viewed Pilkington as a technically advanced organization, arguing that the company was simply not big enough and/or diverse enough to offset profit fluctuations arising from the business cycle. Both of these problems could in principle be rectified, and the incumbent management won the ideological battle on this basis, even if the means of achieving high profitability would have been much more obvious had the company been absorbed into a suitably well-capitalized DIMF. The executive group at Pilkington took the view that BTR was a low-technology company run by accountants who were motivated primarily by short-term considerations of profit-making. In this critique they were essentially correct. Ownership of Pilkington by BTR would not have solved the problem of capital supply needed for expansion. Pilkington may well have become a more profitable company with a smaller number of employees—but it would have remained under-capitalized and incapable of expansion. After beating off the BTR assault, Pilkington put more effort into expansion overseas and opened plants in the growing markets of Latin America and South-East Asia. The firm also diversified into optical glass products and contact lenses, albeit with little success. Pilkington's main rivals—St Gobain and Asahi—were members of large business groups that were capable of sheltering their glass-making subsidiaries in the downturn of the business cycle. The recession of the early 1990s found Pilkington once again extremely vulnerable to takeover. World demand for flat glass turned down sharply and many industry commentators argued that the company was inefficiently managed with, according to the available figures, by far the weakest ratio of profit per employee of any major glass-making firm. These commentators also noted the strength of the trade unions in the United Kingdom and the patrician attitudes of UK management. In line with the then fashionable concept of focusing on core businesses, the peripheral interests of the company were sold during the 1990s, and the company was re-focused on its core business of flat glass production. With the retirement of Pilkington family members from the board in 1995, and the appointment of a 'new broom' Italian chief executive in 1997, the scene was set for a massive cost-saving exercise. Not only would the last 'non-core' businesses be sold off, but staff numbers and operating costs in the remaining core assets would be cut to the bone. By 2002, the Company had experienced a period of vigorous slimming down. It employed just over half of the staff and its turnover was lower than ten years previously.

By 2003, Pilkington was effectively up for sale. After protracted negotiations, it was sold in 2005 to the former licensee of its float glass technology in Japan, Nippon Sheet Glass (NSG). Pilkington was at this time the second or third largest flat glass manufacturer in the world, whilst NSG stood at tenth in the industry rankings. As a subsidiary of a Japanese industrial group, however, NSG had no difficulty in raising the necessary capital to buy its much larger rival. But perhaps the most interesting point is the ideological line taken on the proposed takeover by Pilkington's senior management. The contrast with the furore surrounding the 1987 takeover attempt by BTR could not have been sharper. There was little or no public debate on the ultimate fate of Pilkington, and the tone of the media coverage was distinctly muted. The board was consistently of the view that the company—obviously—would have to be sold. The reasons given were that the company was not profitable enough and, whilst they had obviously done their best, the production managers were simply not up to the task of managing efficiently in the prevailing market conditions. The board dragged their feet longer than was expected by industry analysts, and NSG's initial offer was significantly improved in the process. However, NSG was already a substantial shareholder of Pilkington (25 per cent) at the time of the bid, and many of the existing executive team retained their jobs when the takeover was completed, suggesting there was actually little hostility; the takeover was basically welcomed.

Certainly nobody—no industry analyst or journalist—ever suggested that this world-leading business should not be sold. There was no support for the view that the company belonged as much to the community of glass-makers (or for that matter to Britain) as much as it did to its shareholders. The incumbent managers showed no interest in continuing to manage the company, and the United Kingdom thus lost one of its prime technological assets. The analysis that follows in the remainder of this section suggests that the Pilkington story was by no means a unique one.

By 2006, only twenty-five large British firms remained active in broadly the same areas of manufacturing that they had occupied in 1996. To this group we can add seven firms that had some involvement in manufacturing as they entered the top 200 largest firms in this period. Before embarking on the next part of our discussion, the reader should note that the retreat from manufacture during this period is even more marked than the number of firms listed in Table 8.2 might indicate. Almost universally, the boards of manufacturing companies (even those that remained in the same business) took action aimed at reducing diversification. Typically, they undertook re-focusing exercises, selling off 'non-core' assets, and almost all reduced manufacturing capacity as they did so. There are some extreme examples of such withdrawals. One of the most remarkable examples is that of Invensys, which as we have seen was created from a merger of BTR and Siebe, both of which were heavily engaged in traditional engineering activities. In less than ten years, Invensys reinvented itself as a systems design firm that outsourced its manufacturing.

In the 1980s, 'make or buy' studies had become commonplace, but, as has been argued in an earlier paper, outsourcing decisions often favoured domestic suppliers (Ackroyd and Procter 1998). During the 1990s, UK firms were increasingly likely to subcontract manufacturing to overseas suppliers. Firms that could not easily outsource from foreign suppliers included a small group of major defence contractors (for whom there would be security considerations arising from international outsourcing) and a few high technology producers. In addition, a number of retail-related manufacturing groups (category 3a in Table 8.1) have retained their manufacturing capability, in large part because their proximity to their principal markets and established brands has allowed their low technology production base to put potential competitors at a disadvantage. In 2006, there were fifteen companies in this category, comprising 45 per cent of the large firms in the manufacturing sector, concentrated in food (e.g. Cadbury-Schweppes—since sold to Kraft, Associated British Food), drink (e.g. Diageo, Scottish and Newcastle—since sold to InBev), tobacco (e.g. British American Tobacco, Imperial Tobacco), and household products (e.g. Reckitt-Benckiser). Many divisions of these companies were, however, slimmed down as subsidiaries (their brands rationalized) or they were sold off. These strategies were squarely aimed at realizing value to be returned to shareholders.

For those companies that remained in high-technology manufacturing (i.e. firms in category 2 and some in 3b, Table 8.1), there was a marked shift towards reducing dependency on this activity. The remaining two large companies producing complex high-technology products (Rolls Royce and BAE), progressively shifted the balance of their activities towards servicing and away from manufacture. In the last decade, RR has developed a global servicing and 'aftercare' capability. The Company now offers engine servicing and repair almost anywhere in the world and is no longer dependent on new engine sales for its revenue stream. Indeed, industry analysts suggest that RR is ill-prepared for competing in the market for new engines.[8] Similarly, BAE has progressively shifted more resources into servicing and design activities (particularly those relating to land-based weapons systems), and can now be counted as a generic defence contractor rather than an aircraft producer. The changes in the company's name illustrate its general direction of travel. British Aerospace (B.Ae.) was renamed as B.Ae. Systems after acquiring shipbuilding assets and defence equipment capability from GEC. The change of name also indicates a shift towards the design, manufacture, and provision of logistical support for turnkey weapons systems. Most recently the company has become known as BAE, as its remaining interests in civil aircraft production were disposed of following the sale of its shares in Airbus and EDS. The Company is now a defence contracting firm, producing ships (mainly submarines), tanks, guns, and munitions as well as fighter aircraft. As with Rolls Royce, the company now earns a huge amount of revenue from servicing aircraft and other hardware. Revenues from land-based weapons supply and servicing exceeded £6 billion in the financial year 2007–8, suggesting that the Company has moved a long way from producing aircraft as its main source of revenue.

Structural Characteristics of the CEF

The changes in the activities of major UK companies that have occurred in the recent past have clearly been considerable. The tendency for corporate executives to focus on selected high-margin activities, and to take value out of companies, was often taken to extreme lengths. The 'hollowing out' of UK manufacturing has involved realizing value wholesale by splitting large groups up so that they no longer qualify as large firms. On the other hand, some very large firms remain in business. These have some distinctively new structural features, and it is to these that we now turn.

The main structural feature of what we will term the CEF is its dispersed character. The basic model that has been outlined in previous work (see

Ackroyd 2002, 2009). Similar models developed by others—see Prechel 1997; Zey and Swenson 1999) describe US firms. The label 'extensive' given to the CEF refers to the manner in which a firm's assets are parcelled out into numerous and often quite small packets—200–400 subsidiaries are common. Whilst the geographical reach of these firms is often global in scope, their dispersed character sets them apart from the integrated corporate structures that predominate outside the Anglo-Saxon societies. A company worth £3–5 billion operating between 300 and 500 subsidiaries has an average investment in any one place of £10 million—an almost negligible sum measured by the standards of today's transnational corporations. This new type of firm exhibits few of the features that one would associate with concentrated assets and centralized power, and their presence is easily overlooked if one's model of a big business is a centralized bureaucracy. These firms cannot, strictly speaking, be counted as large entities, and it is difficult to get a sense of their scale unless they are considered in aggregate. Few people have heard of renamed companies Elementis, Invensys, Meggitt, or Deageo.[9] But the aggregate value of these large enterprises are comparable in scale to that of some small countries[10] (De Grauwe and Camerman 2002).

The CEF's head office, although clearly still a centre of power, is typically very small when measured as a proportion of total staff. Prestigious head offices have passed into obsolescence, and there is no attempt to exert direct control over the detailed activities of subsidiaries. Indeed, there is typically no highly developed capacity for centralized control within the CEF. Head offices undertake sophisticated financial monitoring and review, but financial responsibility for the profitable use of assets in particular locations is extensively decentralized. Planning and service innovation functions are also decentralized. The precise division of responsibilities between centre and periphery is variable. Where there is a standard product or 'product plus service' package, parent corporations often restrict their activities to the replication of successful practices across their major markets. On the other hand, a great deal of autonomy is frequently encouraged, and where there are transferable benefits in terms of business processes, any improvements (and/or capacity for savings) are disseminated through all the subsidiaries. What we see here is best described as a 'loose/tight' pattern of 'centralized decentralization' (Hill et al. 2000 examine this form of control in specific relation to R&D) in which there is careful monitoring of key performance indicators, but otherwise loose surveillance of activities. There are normally legal and financial firewalls between centre and periphery, such that assets of subsidiaries are accounted for as part of company equity but, on the other hand, subsidiaries are legally separate entities. Hence, there is no likelihood of an entire business group haemorrhaging cash as a result of a liability incurred in one part of its operation.

As the interest in, and capacity for, direction from the centre has diminished, the social and economic distance between the core and periphery of the typical UK corporation has increased enormously. Staff at the periphery are very unlikely to have been recruited by the centre. Hierarchies have become increasingly discontinuous, and the top executives and strategic managers of CEFs are members of a very exclusive, self-perpetuating, internationalized elite. In the last thirty years the ratio of top salaries to the pay of the lowest level employees in the FTSE 250 has widened from an average of nine times to an average ratio of more than sixty times. It has become increasingly difficult to separate the interests of corporate executives from those of large share-holders as executives have themselves become substantial shareholders. Investors have, moreover, become increasingly dependent on the complicity of executives, and an increasing proportion of company earnings and assets have been commandeered by the top executive cadre.

In a prescient essay Sabel (1991) suggested that manufacturing companies might strategically reposition themselves in the medium term through the buying and selling of subsidiaries. Whilst the restructuring that occurred during the 1990s may be seen as a throwback to the opportunism of the conglomerate era, the trading of subsidiaries has become a defining feature of today's CEFs. In the period down to 1996, selling assets became more impor-tant as companies undertook divestment and re-focusing, often for purely defensive reasons. Viewing these practices ten years on, it is apparent that there has been a great deal of strategic change in the intervening period. Some companies have redefined themselves by moving from one industrial sector into another. The manner in which Invensys, the successor to Siebe and BTR, has been converted from a traditional engineering firm to a software and strategic services provider is a case in point. Bunzl has undergone broadly the same type of transformation, whilst Whitbread and Bass abandoned brewing and drinks manufacturing to become publicans, hoteliers, and restauranteurs. As we have seen, many companies have reduced their exposure to manufacturing and moved into servicing. Perhaps most significantly, strategic change has involved shuffling the portfolio of subsidiary companies. The frequent buying and selling of subsidiary companies is the primary means of structural flexibility in the CEF.

The disaggregated structure of British manufacturing industry meant that UK firms were well-placed to exploit the properties of global supply chains as these emerged in the 1990s. A key objective is to identify, occupy, and dominate lucrative niches whilst participating in global manufacturing pro-cesses. Put simply, this involves identifying key positions in value chains and then acquiring the assets required in order to provide the requisite services or product/service combinations. Control is realized within particular spheres of influence, as companies identify services and goods that tie their business partners into medium-term trading agreements. Disaggregation limits the need for in-house R&D, whilst costs are defrayed by increasing the number of longer term partners and joint venture arrangements. The structural flexibility of the CEF also allows for what might be called 'defensive man-oeuvring' in the face of threats from hostile investors or equity funds (e.g. when non-core subsidiaries are sold off in order to realize shareholder value). Other defensive measures include: manipulating share prices by means of artificially high dividend payments, 'share buyback' schemes, or the selling of assets that are then leased back to the parent corporation. This defensive manoeuvring encourages information closure and secrecy. Firms that engage in these manoeuvres are often reluctant to provide information on their strategies and they routinely put out misleading signals about their intentions.

Conclusions

The chapter has highlighted the cultural embeddedness of UK manufacturing industry and its distinctive patterns of organizing. This sheds some much-needed light on the imputed shift to 'post-bureaucratic' modes of organizing in the specific case of UK industry. Fragmentation and disaggregation, far from representing an emergent new paradigm, are in fact long-standing and endemic features of British industrial organization. Whilst a number of large UK manufacturers emerged to become DoNFs in the twenty-five years after the Second World War, these firms lacked the centralized direction and unitary structures suggested by classic models of bureaucracy. Many of these companies were incomplete amalgamations of former competitors and they were often very inadequately incorporated within a single corporation. During the period of initial rationalization (1975–85), administrative overheads were further stripped out and lean production was widely instituted. The percentage of people employed by UK manufacturing industry fell precipitately from something like 40 per cent to around 25–20 per cent. From the mid-1980s onwards UK manufacturing was extensively reorganized and the managerial elites in control of the sector presided over a strategic withdrawal of capital from the sector. Where manufacturing has continued, it has followed an under-capitalized, low-technology path to its present, much-diminished state. The emergence of the diversified low-technology firms between 1985 and 1995 saw manufacturing employment stabilize at around 20 per cent. In the last ten years, we have witnessed a further systematic withdrawal of capital from large manufacturing firms. By 2006 domestic manufacturing employment stood at around 10 per cent of the working population.

The years since 1995 have seen the emergence of a new type of UK-based 'capital-extensive' firm. These firms have ceased to operate in their original industrial sectors and now occupy strategic positions in a number of selected global supply chains. They are run by an increasingly internationalized cadre of shareholding managers whose long-term commitment to particular countries, locations, or industrial sectors is minimal. Whilst these firms may appear large when considered in aggregate, they are typically comprised of relatively small subsidiary companies that are governed in accordance with 'loose/tight' models of management. Whilst this mode of governance confers a very substantial degree of operating autonomy on local management, culturally based constraints on the availability of capital have long inhibited the technological capabilities of UK industry. The institutional landscape of this British exceptionalism—based on radically 'disaggregated' firm structures—derives not from the exigencies of markets or functional requirements, but from the values, policies, and strategic objectives of UK managerial elites.

☐ NOTES

1. British central government developed a centralized administrative apparatus relatively early. Following the reform of the civil service in the middle of the nineteenth century, centralized ministries manned by formally qualified and increasingly numerous civil servants, developed over the following hundred years. During the twentieth century, home-spending ministries, in particular, grew in importance; and, with consolidation of the welfare state, the trend was given a considerable boost in the thirty years immediately following the Second World War. Because the organizations to deliver health care, education, pensions, and social services of various kinds had to deal extensively with central government, they being directed, regulated, assessed, and to a considerable extent funded by the central state, they were also bureaucratically organized. It is not an exaggeration to say that the new welfare administration (established between 1945 and 1975) became an extension of the pre-existing bureaucratic state machine.

2. Firm rankings are drawn from *The Times* 1000 for appropriate years.

3. However, GKN briefly owned Westland Helicopters in the 1990s.

4. Some large business groups, of which BTR and Williams Holdings are prime examples, also retained their identity as manufacturing groups. Their controlling executives saw what they were doing as building large—if somewhat diverse—manufacturing businesses. BTR's acquisitions were mainly manufacturing companies or companies with some manufacturing capacity. The majority of such acquisitions were retained. The acquiring company would apply tough, uniform procedures to the manufacturing processes of the firms it bought. Key objectives were to cut waste by rationalizing the production processes that were central to the firm's activities. However, also important for them was the removal of unnecessary overheads including, significantly for this discussion, bureaucracy and other head office costs. Although led by an accountant in the person of Owen Green, the top team of executives at BTR almost uniformly had deep experience of manufacturing. BTR executives utilized some standard techniques to pare down costs of production. This management also specialized in taking on business that employed relatively low technology requiring low levels of reinvestment. It ran each business as a separate entity for which the costs were carefully monitored (Cowe 1993: 237). BTR did not sell businesses very readily except when they were far outside the traditional activities of the Company. By regular acquisition, therefore, BTR became a truly massive, diversified group of manufacturing companies by the late 1980s. It

owned several hundred manufacturing companies by this time, and although it was thought of as an engineering company and classified as such its range of activities was much wider.

In some respects the orientation of rising manufacturing businesses such as BTR was not so very different from the stance increasingly adopted by the established large companies of this period, as they increasingly distanced themselves from the old policy of national dominance. Arnold Weinstock of GEC is on record as saying that 'the key to successful manufacturing is to contract to produce products at a high unit price—and then ruthlessly drive down the costs of production'. Owen Green, CEO of BTR, appears to have believed much the same thing. For both Weinstock and Green, ideas about how to manufacture effectively did include the notion that new technology (requiring high investment from which the return would not be immediate) was the key to success. However, the interests of the conglomerates in manufacturing were more and more conditional and expedient even than the outlook of Owen Green. Conglomerates such as The Hanson Trust and F.H. Tomkins, both amongst the most profitable British firms in the 1980s and into early 1990s, also put together large business groups based on manufacturing activities—broadly conceived. These firms bought up relatively unprofitable medium sized and large British groups and rationalized them. Gordon White, for many years joint managing director of Hanson, used to evaluate takeover targets on the basis of their balance sheets alone. He boasted that he never visited many of the companies that he bought (Cowe 1993: 297). He clearly had little interest in what the companies he acquired produced, so long as they met his criteria as potential acquisitions. Nevertheless, most of the companies the conglomerates acquired included manufacturing operations, and these were usually given sustained attention after acquisition to make them profitable.

It was rare it was rare for an unprofitable business to be simply stripped out for its asset value and closed down. More typically, businesses would be pared down and made profitable by disposing of non-core activities and the costs associated with production in what remained would be driven down. In these respects the conglomerates acted in ways that were indistinguishable from more conventionally focussed manufacturers like BTR and GKN. What made the conglomerates different was the high proportion of their operating profits accrued from selling on the businesses they acquired and rationalized. It was often possible for acquiring companies—simply by selling on some of the businesses bought—to realize more than the sum paid for the acquisition as a whole (Diggle 1990). In 1986, for example, Hanson acquired the Imperial Group for £2.5 billon. The Company recouped this huge sum, however, in a short time through a series of sell-offs of subsidiaries. The group retained the tobacco business of the Imperial Group, which it had, in effect, acquired at no cost. The refocused tobacco business was made much more profitable than it had been before, making a win–win for Hanson shareholders. To illustrate the point about increasing diversity, however, suffice it to say that by the time of the acquisition of Imperial Group, Hanson Trust already owned businesses producing bricks and building materials, batteries and clothing, not to mention various foodstuffs, paper flowers, and cosmetics. Similarly, Tompkins, the purchaser of Smith and Wesson and Rank-Hovis-MacDougal, was regularly described as 'the guns to buns conglomerate'. Thus, the UK conglomorates retained businesses that were highly diversified and often completely unrelated. It need hardly be added that there were few synergies in their corporate activities. There was little to be gained from integrating their activities, and such companies had even smaller head offices, and fewer centralised functions than those considered thus far.

5. The Hanson Trust did indeed 'wrap itself in the flag'. For some time its advertising featured the British and US flags tied together accompanied by the strapline: 'A Company from over here, that is doing rather well over there'.

6. This is corroborated by evidence on recent corporate change amongst large US firms. Lazonick (2005) refers to a policy shift from the retention and reinvestment of profit to one of downsizing the corporation and redistributing value (see also Lazonick and O'Sullivan 2000; O'Sullivan 2000).

7. After the long-awaited retirement of Arnold Weinstock, a new senior management team sold off GEC's aerospace interests to B.Ae. in 1999, and undertook a strategic realignment exercise into telecommunications in 2002–4 adopting the name Marconi in the process. The repositioning was both badly timed and poorly conceived, and the company collapsed financially. The remnants of the company were finally sold overseas in the winding up process.

8. Rolls Royce has not undertaken the research and development necessary for the production of a new generation of large engines to replace the RB211 and its derivatives, though it has developed a new generation of smaller aero-engines as part of its joint venture with BMW.

9. Only 5 per cent of students in recent MBA classes at Lancaster University could identify one or more of these companies and fewer could give a good account of their activities.

10. Controversy continues concerning how far GDP (the main measure of a country's wealth) is comparable with company turnover. The original facile comparisons of companies and countries have been considerably revised, but the generalization here remains defensible.

⬜ BIBLIOGRAPHY

Ackroyd, S. (2002) *The Organisation of Business*, Oxford: Oxford University Press.
——(2009) The Re-Organisation of Manufacturing and the Emergence of a Flexible Economy in the UK, in Skorstad and Ramsdal (eds), *Flexible Organizations and the New Working Life*, Farnham: Ashgate, Chapter 9.
——Procter, S. (1998) British Manufacturing Organization and Workplace Industrial Relations: Some Attributes of the New Flexible Firm, *British Journal of Industrial Relations*, 36(2): 163–83.
Ahrne, G. (1990) *Agency and Organisation*, London: Sage.
Alvesson, M. and Thompson, P. (2005) Post-bureaucracy?, in S. Ackroyd, R. Batt, P. Thompson and P. Tolbert (eds), *A Handbook of Work and Organization*, Oxford: Oxford University Press.
Anderson, S. and Cavanagh, J. (2000) *A field Guide to the Global Economy*, New York: New Press.
Chandler, A.D. (1962) *Strategy and Structure*, Boston: MIT Press.
——(1990) *Scale and Scope: The Dynamics of Industrial Capitalism*, Boston: Harvard University Press.
——Deams, H. (1980) *Managerial Hierarchies: Comparative Perspectives on the Rise of the Modern Company*, Boston: Harvard University Press.
Channon, D. (1982) Industrial Structure, *Long Range Planning*, 15(5): 3–17.
Courpasson, D. (2000) Managerial Strategies of Domination: Power in Soft Bureaucracies, *Organization Studies*, 21(1): 141–61.
Cowe, R. (1993) *The Guardian Guide to the UK's Top Companies*, London: 4th Estate.
De Grauwe, P. and Camerman, F. (2002) How Big are the Big Multi-National Companies?, <http://www.econ.kuleuven.acobe/ew/academic/intecon/De Grauwe>.
Diggle, B. (1990) *Hanson*. An unpublished report by the Credit-Suisse. First Boston Bank, London: First Boston.
du Gay, P. (1996) *Consumption and Identity at Work*, London: Sage.
—— (ed.) (2005) *The Values of Bureaucracy*, Oxford University Press.
Hannah, L. (ed.) (1976) *Management Strategy and Business Development*, London: Macmillan.

Hannah, L. (1983) *The Rise of the Corporate Economy*, Methuen: London.

Harrison, B. (1994) *Lean and Mean: The Changing Landscape of Corporate Power in the Age of Flexibility*, New York: Basic Books.

Heckscher, C. and Donnellon, A. (eds) (1994) *The Post-Bureaucratic Organisation, New Perspectives on Organisational Change*, London: Sage.

Hill, S., Martin, R. and Harris, M. (2000) Decentralisation, Integration and the Post Bureaucratic Organization: The Case of R&D, *Journal of Management Studies*, 37(4): 563–85.

Hirst, P. and Zeitlin, J. (1989) Flexible Specialisation and the Competitive Failure of UK Manufacturing, *Political Quarterly*, 60(2): 164–78.

Jones, B. (1989) Flexible Automation and Factory Politics: the United Kingdom in Current Perspective, in P. Hirst and J. Zeitlin (eds), *Reversing Industrial Decline*, Oxford: Berg, pp. 95–121.

Lazonick, W. (2005) Corporate Restructuring, in S. Ackroyd et al. (eds), *The Oxford Handbook of Work and Organisation*, Oxford: Oxford University Press, Chapter 24.

——O'Sullivan, M. (2000) Maximizing Shareholder Value: A New Ideology for Corporate Governance, *Economy and Society*, 29(1): 13–35.

Marchington, M., Grimshaw, D., Rubery, J. and Willmott, H. (eds) (2004) *Fragmenting Work: Blurring, Organizational Boundaries and Disordering Hierarchies*, Oxford: Oxford University Press.

Marshall, A. (1890) *Principles of Economics*, London: Macmillan.

Mintzberg, H. (1978) Patterns in Strategy Formation, *Management Science*, 24(9): 934–48.

——(1979) *The Structuring of Organizations, A Synthesis of Research*, London: Prentice-Hall International.

——(1993) *Structure in Fives: Designing Effective Organizations*, London: Prentice-Hall.

O'Sullivan, M. (2000) *Contests for Corporate Control: Corporate Governance and Economic Performance in the United States and Germany*, Oxford: Oxford University Press.

Pettigrew, A. (1985) *The Awakening Giant*, Oxford: Blackwell.

Piore, M. and Sabel, C. (1984) *The Second Industrial Divide: Possibilities for Prosperity*, New York: Basic Books.

Prechel, H. (1997) Corporate Form and the State: Business Policy and Change from the Multidivisional to the Multilayered Subsidiary Form, *Sociological Inquiry*, 67(2): 15–74.

Procter, S. and Ackroyd, S. (2000) Strategies for Flexibility: Technology-Centred and Labour-Centred Flexibility in UK Manufacturing, *International Journal of Manufacturing Technology and Management*, 1(4/5): 366–80.

Sabel, C. (1991) Moebius Strip Organisations and Open Labour Markets: Some Consequence of the Reintegration of Conception and Execution in a Volatile Economy, in P. Bourdieu and J. Coleman (eds), *Social Theory for a Changing Society*, Colorado, Westview Press.

Shutt, J. and Whittington, R. (1987) Fragmentation Strategies and the Rise of Small Units, *Regional Studies*, 21(1): 13–23.

Sklair, L. (2001) *The Transnational Capitalist Class*, Oxford: Blackwell.

Thompson, P. and Alvesson, M. (2005) Reconfiguring Bureaucracy at Work, in P. du Gay (ed.), *The Values of Bureaucracy*, Oxford: Oxford University Press.

Weber, M. (1968) *Economy and Society*, London: Bedminster Press.

Whittington, R. and Mayer, M. (2002) *The European Corporation: Strategy, Structure and Social Science*, Oxford: Oxford University Press.

Williams, K., Williams, J., and Thomas, D. (1983) *Why Are the British Bad at Manufacturing?*, London: Routledge.

Wright, M., Chiplin, B. and Coyne, J. (1989) The Market for Corporate Control: The Divestment Option, in J. Fairburn and J. Kay (eds), *Mergers and Merger Policy*, London: Oxford University Press.

Zey, M. and Swenson, T. (1999) The Transformation of the Dominant Corporate Form from Multidivisional to Multisubsidiary, *The Sociological Quarterly*, 40(2): 241–67.

9 **Under Reconstruction: Modern Bureaucracies**

STEWART CLEGG

Introduction

Modern bureaucracies are under reconstruction. First, bureaucracy no longer being 'modern', those organizations formerly known as bureaucracies are seeking to become 'post'- bureaucratic, and second, as the ecology of the dot.com boom indicates, newly founded organizations often strive not to be bureaucratic. What, precisely, constitutes the post-bureaucratic is less clear. Often, the post-bureaucratic is defined in terms of hybrid new organization forms.

In this chapter I shall argue that bureaucracy, far from being superseded, is becoming embroiled in complex processes of hybridization (du Gay 2000; Courpasson and Reed 2004). To understand post-bureaucracy today, we need to see bureaucratic organizations through a dialectical lens, one that sees them as simultaneously decomposing and recomposing. Decomposition takes us to the world of supply chains and outsourcing, of which the phenomenon of call centres is probably the most pertinent example. Recomposition takes us into the world of new organizational forms. In the former, there are some very familiar politics of surveillance and control; in the latter there are more innovative developments that centre on the replacement of the central figure of the bureaucrat with that of the project leader, and the central life experience of the occupational career followed largely in one organization being replaced by that of the individual's management of projects. The politics of the project are the testing ground for elite reproduction. But first, a little prehistory...

Bureaucracy and Empirical Studies of Organizations

Bureaucracy is 'the primary institutional characteristic of highly complex and differentiated societies' (Landau 1972: 167), epitomizing 'the modern era' (Blau and Meyer 1971: 10). Its greatest theorist was Max Weber (1978), who foresaw that future states and organizations would be in step with the rhythms of bureaucracy irrespective of whether a capitalist or socialist drumbeat.

Weber's conception of bureaucracy was one aspect of his overall attempt to understand the features of Western civilization through the process of rationalization. For Weber, rationalization signifies increasing use of calculation to master phenomena and things through the domination of rules and instrumental systems. Weber's insight was that in a social context, such as an organization, the process of bureaucratization entailed by the rationalization process results in a diminution of freedom, initiative, and individual power. People would be expected to become obedient objects, trapped in the 'iron cage', enhancing the power of the machine as a tool. The cage is the metaphorical instrument of dominant authority within which bureaucracy appears as a system of legitimate power 'over' its members, neutralizing all potential sources of countervailing power.

In situations of bureaucratic rule, the domination of bureaucratic leaders is fundamentally based on knowledge. 'Bureaucratic domination means fundamentally domination through ... technical knowledge ... [and] ... knowledge growing out of experience in the service' (Weber 1978: 225); thus, knowledge is directly related to power expressed in terms of length of service, disciplinary formation, and progression through a career structure. It is, indeed, a situation of power/knowledge. One way of reading Weber's account of bureaucracy is as a treatise on the formation of a particular type of moral character bounded by an emotionally strong sense of duty as a vocation. The type was captured in terms of a mastery of technical rationality.

Weber's ideas about bureaucracy were transmitted through the methodology of ideal types. Weber's account of bureaucracy was not a representation for all seasons, an essential and eternal characterization of a functionally necessary social form. As Weber conceived them, ideal types were hypothetical, not a reference to something normatively ideal, but to an ideational type serving as a mental model that can be widely shared and used because analysts agree that it captures some essential features of a phenomenon here-and-now. The ideal type does not correspond to reality but seeks to condense essential features of it in the model so that one can better recognize its real characteristics when it is encountered. It is not an embodiment of one side or aspect but the synthetic ideational representation of complex phenomena from reality.

Later, Schutz (1967) was to take issue with one aspect of Weber's approach to ideal types: were they a construct by the analysts or were they the analysts' account of the constructs in use by the members of the research setting in question? For Schutz it was not clear whether Weber's ideal types, in their basis in social action, were a member's category or one that belonged to analysts. He thought that the construction of types out of the concepts of everyday life should be such that they were grounded in the member's usage. Once they were refined by an analyst, the risk was that they became somewhat dissociated from everyday usage; they could become reifications that related unreflexively to the evolving grounds of their own existence.

The history of the concept of bureaucracy is an example of the slippage that Schutz feared could occur. Bureaucracy had been identified by Weber with constructions that were widely known in common and shared amongst elite German echelons; these, in turn, were subsequently taken to be the literal depiction of the bureaucratic phenomenon wherever and however it might subsequently have evolved. Thus, a historical conception of bureaucracy, identified with top managerial prerogative in German state organizations, initially defined what bureaucracy was taken to be. Increasingly, as the concept was translated into post-Second World War empirical social science, Weber's concern with bureaucracy as a tool of technical rationality was replaced with the narrower conception of efficiency (Pugh 1966). The cultural, historical, political, and economic analysis which Weber (1978) pioneered, the institutional context, within which his conception of bureaucracy was embedded, was overshadowed. What was lost was the institutional character of bureaucracy.

Weber regarded bureaucracy as both an institution and an organization form. Institutionally, he focused on the ethos of bureaucracy, the specific character of the bureaucrat, and the experience of things being done according to rule rather than caprice. Recent writers such as Fligstein (1990, 2001) and above all, du Gay (2005), focus on these institutional aspects. Kallinikos (2006: 20) observes that the institution of bureaucracy is an 'outcome of complex cultural and social developments. These reflect, among other things, the institutional embeddedness of property rights and the employment contract and the legal and socio-political processes for assigning jurisdictions and laying out the rules of accountability in democratic societies'. Thus, all specific contexts in which bureaucracies flourish would be bureaucratic in their own way.

Because the ideal type was a construct from a highly specific place and time, it would have been odd for later and different realities to correspond to it. Nonetheless, some sociologists made such comparisons. When writers such as Gouldner (1954) investigated organizations, they compared the realities they found with the type that they had inherited. However, since the type was always an imaginary and synthetic construct from a specific place and time, doing so is not an immediately sensible activity. It ends up privileging the subjectivities of those members whose everyday usage first grounded the construct. The type becomes reified. It takes on a life of its own. The analysts' casting of the ideal type sets it in concrete long past its use-by date.

How current constructions necessarily relate to the different circumstances in which other members' constructs occurred might raise questions about the foundational limits of the initial conception, and why it should so frame and circumscribe debate. It might, but for a long time it rarely did. In the 1950s, bureaucracy became the object of critical attack on a dehumanized world in which the bureaucratic machine was seen to be destroying emotions and individualities in pursuit of efficiency (Gouldner 1955). Such views were hardly novel; for instance, Marx (1867) had explored them in *Capital*, nor was the most important point that Weber had left out the unintended consequences of the internal working of a concrete bureaucracy (Merton 1940; Dubin 1949; Gouldner 1955; Crozier 1964).

Weber's famous ideal type of bureaucracy became widely used as the basis for case studies (Selznick 1949; Burns and Stalker 1961; Selznick 1949). Later bureaucracy was both heralded by, and then seen as superseded in, taxonomic approaches to organizations (Pugh and Hickson 1976). These saw the ideal type elements, abstracted by Weber with respect to German nineteenth-century bureaucracy, become the definitive features of a functionalist conception of organization structure as an essential form, determined in its particular patterns by specific local contingencies, such as size or technology. Conceptualized as a set of stable structural arrangements emerging from a composite of variables that denote bureaucratization, such as standardization, formalization, and so on, the essence of bureaucracy became frozen as organization structure, rather like a liquefied jelly that could be poured into different moulds to set, and thus produce different shapes as variations on the essential 'jellyness' of the essence. The contingencies—of size, technology, environment, and even something imagined as 'national culture'—provided the moulds.

The focus on bureaucracy as an organization form, rather than as an institution, has been pervasive in organization theories. On these criteria, concrete organizations may be seen as more or less bureaucratic in their characteristics, depending on how they are rated on the measures taken to denote the dimensions of bureaucracy. Martindale (1960: 383) suggested that we should 'compare different empirical configurations, not empirical configurations and types' as any specific type is always historically bounded and 'destined to be scrapped'.

Martindale's (1960) advice was not widely heeded in organization theory. For several authors, analysing bureaucracy did not involve consideration of whether or not it actually existed but only examining the concrete conditions that might enable us to situate such and such organization somewhere along an abstract continuum (Gouldner 1954). For instance, Hall's study of the degree of bureaucratization, following in the footsteps of Bendix (1956), tended to confirm that 'bureaucracy in general may be viewed as a matter of degree, rather than of kind' (Hall 1963: 37). With the characterization of bureaucracy as a matter of dimensions, and the collection of data on them, the typology became taxonomy. The characteristics abstracted from Weber and other writers were taken to be constitutive categorically shared features that bestowed family resemblances on all organizations. If all efficient bureaucracies were alike, every inefficient bureaucracy would be inefficient in its own way, one might say. Epistemologically, subsequent analysis became caught in a historical cul-de-sac of ever-diminishing returns as contingency scholars sought to defend the essentially conceived ontological structure of the underlying configurationally moulded model against all comers. The work of Lex Donaldson (1996) is the exemplar of such tendencies, work that misses the essential institutional features of bureaucracy in the search for contingent universalisms.

By standardizing the requirements of role performance and formalizing the process of role taking, recruitment and appointment, the bureaucratic organization became the vehicle through which jobs became potentially available to anyone who fulfilled requirements of the job specification. It is through the very separation of the role from the person that such an availability can be rendered possible, and an employment contract signed that makes the term of the agreement legible and enforceable at law. (Kallinikos 2006: 135–6)

What it is difficult to grasp from empiricist approaches to bureaucracy conceived as a bundle of formal organization characteristics, captured as variables, is bureaucracy's role as a constitutive element of modernity. Bureaucracy provided a novel way of orchestrating the individual–organization relationship through an organization form premised on the ethical values of universalism and meritocracy, one that was necessarily concordant in its rational legal form with the emergence of universalism and meritocracy (Kallinikos (2006: 135).

Criticisms of Bureaucracy

To oppose bureaucracy is to oppose a particular conception of modernity as rational, legal, meritocratic, and universalistic. Such criticisms came increasingly into focus from the 1980s onwards. Much of this criticism was banal, criticising actually existing bureaucracies in terms of abstracted and utopian standards of efficiency. Utopias always have their own horrors to unfold—it is in the nature of the genre, one might say (Ten Bos 2000). Actual bureaucracies rarely achieve the efficiency that might be attributed to them in any pure state; rather than setting up an ideal, abstracted type, as the standard measure of efficiency and then proclaiming, dolefully, on the ruination of things in the present, a less utopian way of proceeding might be found. Rather than seek the utopian perfection of a pure bureaucratic type, perhaps one should instead search for forms of hybridity that actual organizations adopt, as their designers and social constructors seek to make sense of templates and times. In other words, rather than dismissing actual bureaucracy as inefficient when compared with its ideal type, wouldn't one be better employed in looking at the ways in which the actualities of bureaucracy are socially constructed in specific locales?

Bureaucracy, construed as an ideal type, has been seen as the source of much of what is wrong in the contemporary world. Recent history has been replete with rallying cries against fundamental errors said to emanate from the bacillus of bureaucracy. It is a culture that, seemingly, must be terminated with extreme prejudice. Critics of public sector management regard bureaucracy as something that must be 'banished' (Osborne and Plastrik 1997); government must be 'reinvented' (Osborne and Gaebler 1992). The reason is simple: bureaucracy is said to be inefficient. In the popular view, as du Gay (2000) or Pugh (1966) point out, bureaucracy is synonymous with inefficient business administration, pettifogging legalism, and red tape. For critics, demolition of bureaucratic systems will further efficiency: 'Employee empowerment does not mean every decision in the organization must be made democratically or through consensus' (Osborne and Plastrik 1997: 227). Empowerment will foster effectiveness, not egalitarian and universalistic values. These institutional attributes must be sacrificed in the name of efficiency.

Perversely, in the private sector, other critics are more enamoured of democracy than efficiency because the attributes of bureaucracy 'are maladaptive when massive change, environmental dynamism and considerable uncertainty are the norm' and there is a 'growing asymmetry of power between the managerial agents in charge of them [the mega global firms] and most other groups in the society, including consumers, employees, and members of the local communities in which the firms' operations are located' (Child and McGrath 2001: 1136–1140). The hierarchical configuration of power and the multiplication of different stakeholders mean that power and representation must be seen from different perspectives. Power within the bureaucratic apparatus fails to reflect the representation of interests to which it should attend.

Heckscher and Donnellon (1994) and Ashcraft (2001) suggest that entrepreneurially oriented organizations must try to base their efficiency and legitimacy on a different model of commitment of members, supported by a strategy of decentralization of authority and the granting of empowerment. Empowerment and the question of morality are relevant to post-bureaucratic trends. At the core of these trends is the idea that the person in role should be replaced with the enthusiastic participation of the whole person, wholly committed, to the courses of action chosen. The emergent notion of post-bureaucratic organization has very significant similarities to that of an empowered democracy. Its central concept has been suggested to be that 'everyone takes responsibility for the success of the whole' (Heckscher 1994: 24). Therefore, such organizations must develop informed consensus amongst their members, rather than relying on authority and hierarchical supervision. Above all, they must try and involve the whole person, rather than merely those aspects of the person invested in a given role. The development of agreement, it is said, has to be situated in interactive settings where the gathering of information increases collective power. Organizational politics in post-bureaucracies will be characterized by the use of influence and persuasion rather than power exercised through command and control.

The most salient implications of post-bureaucracy are conceived as political: they concern relationships between individual members, and between members and their organization, the nature of power and authority, the conception of equity instead of equality, and, above all, the existence of flexible and permanent dialogues concerning the rules of action. In some respects there are echoes of earlier ideal types, such as Rothschild-Whitt and Whitt's (1986), Rothschild-Whitt's (1979) collectivist organization, and Lazega's (2000) collegial organization, that were constructed in opposition to bureaucracy.

At the core of the politics of these post-bureaucracies, it is often argued, is a new conception of trust. Trust is a crucial resource in post-bureaucratic settings because everyone must believe that the others are seeking mutual benefit rather than maximizing personal gain (Heckscher 1994: 25). Leadership is not exercised through complex systems of rules but via guidelines for action, which take the form of principles, 'expressing the reasons behind the rules' (Heckscher 1994: 26). Hence, the rules are not simply taken for granted, with all the attendant economies of action, but have to be elaborated on an *ad hoc* case-by-case basis. Internal social processes decide who decides, the decision-making power not being derived from official rank but from the nature of the problems at hand. A deliberative and interactive structure is supposed to come from the necessary fluidity of internal relationships. Post-bureaucracies are 'networks of relationships based on specific performances and abilities (. . .) people one can "work with" on particular projects rather than "live with"' (Heckscher 1994: 55). What is sought is the 'substitution of normative identification with the organization for the purely utilitarian traditional employment nexus' (Child and McGrath 2001: 1,143). The traditional bureaucratic commitment 'We will take care of you if you do what we have asked', once premised on the celebrated balance of inducements and contributions (March and Simon 1958), seems now to be a dead letter (Heckscher and Applegate 1994: 7), they suggest.

What is demanded today by bureaucracy's critics, especially the more extreme such as Peters (2003), is total commitment and complete trust by the member in their organization and the subsumption of their identity to that of being an organization member *in toto*. They want to overthrow bureaucracy both substantively and in principle. Bureaucracy should be replaced with a new kind of total institution in which energized team members commit themselves wholly to the goals of the organization. Tom Peters proselytizes constant revolutionary change in *Re-imagine! Scorecard and Revolution Planner* and treats such a revolutionary approach as a process for sudden intuitive leaps of understanding, or epiphany, to combat the hardening of metaphorical managerial arteries in bureaucratic structures.

Kallinikos (2006: 141) captures the thinking behind these revolutionary slogans very clearly. While bureaucracy may be seen as too inward looking, too concerned with its own procedures, with doing things according to rules, this critique 'understates the fact that extreme concern with external contingencies and adaptability in the long run hollows out social systems (as they hollow out individuals) from the inside'. These hollow men and women of the corporation would be driven wholly by events, by contingent demands, and their commitment and involvement in responding to them, rather than by detached behaviour in role that enables the actor to achieve some distance from the minutiae of everyday organizational necessity. Such detachment in role is one of the old-fashioned verities that the new revolutionaries would smash in order to achieve post-bureaucracy.

Peters (2003) accentuates a 'Them and Us' mentality. The dualism is presented as an imperative to managers to unleash organizational change programmes with which to pursue a witch hunt within their organizations. The whole emphasis stresses that managers should seek out and label what are the old and smash them—'out with the old' and 'in with the new': new work context, new technology, new organization, new customers, new markets, new work, new people, new management.

A cult of personality is entailed in the Peters process. Peters is quite explicit about this; for him, the masses are confused and unable to find direction unless they have charismatic leaders able to project their egos in a cult of extraordinary personality. The confusion of the masses is a thesis that requires the antithesis of a great leader to lead them to the sunny uplands of a new synthesis:

I think the Iacocca thing, the Peters and Waterman thing, the Robbins thing, the [Ken] Blanchard thing, and the Hamel-Porter thing is a very specific reaction of a whole lot of people who are confused by all the shit that's going down. When people are confused, they want people on white horses to lead them. Obviously it didn't have to be me and Bob, and Blanchard and [John] Naisbitt and Porter and so on, any more than it had to be Iacocca and Ted Turner. But it had to be. (Postrel 1997)

What is being struggled against is also personified in a cult of personality. In order to give shape to the struggle against bureaucracy, Peters identifies it with a specific reactionary figure and ethos. The figure is Robert McNamara and the ethos is that of the Harvard Business School. Peters is on frequent record as saying that his whole life has been a struggle against the legacy of Robert McNamara, which he saw as having become the essential *de facto* wisdom of the Harvard Business School, setting the pace for large American enterprise in the post-war era. 'Start with Taylorism, add a layer of Drucker-ism and a dose of McNamaraism, and by the late 1970's you had the great American corporation that was being run by bean counters'.[1] McNamara and Harvard merely represented the tip of an iceberg. Opposing them was not enough. Bureaucracy had to be smashed and new organization forms emerged from its ashes.

The valorization of the charismatic leader in a cult of personality, who leads, guides, and governs, not according to rules, but according to convic-tions, is the most worrying aspect of the whole post-bureaucracy package. Hollowed-out men and women following the enthusiasms of the moment, as these are filtered through the convictions of their leaders and which they are supposed to enact with trust, as empowered and totally committed indivi-duals, begin to look worryingly like the inmates of total institutions (see Clegg et al., 2006, chapter 6). Nonetheless, as Kallinikos (2006: 145–6) suggests, they increasingly people the scenarios of contemporary HRM (Human Resource Management), a vocational discourse that targets the individual as a 'psychological unity', seeking to minimize the friction between the character of the person and the needs of the roles that they fulfil organizationally, allowing the expansion of work and professional concerns into the lifeworld that was once held secure outside the role of the bureaucrat. At its core, the new post-bureaucracy seeks a totalizing creep into and envelopment of an increasing part of the organizational member's lifeworld in a manner that would, from the perspective of bureaucracy as an institution, be seen as corrosive or destructive. New technologies, in particular, make this attempted takeover easier to accomplish. We turn now to a presentation of some of the characteristics of the new organizational forms that are seen to be replacing bureaucracy. We shall address these in terms of the dialectics of decomposition and recomposition.

Decomposing Bureaucracy

Behind the rhetoric of revolutionary change, there is often a technological determinism. The major external fact in speeding up organization change in recent times has been the Internet and associated information and commu-nication technologies (ICTs). The Internet enables speedier, more efficient, and cost-effective access to resources and customers and a different set of ownership, location, and organizational capabilities than was possible just a decade before. Contrast Amazon with a traditional book retailer.

Kallinikos (2006) argues that digital technologies allow tasks that were previously embedded in the 'fixed space' of traditional organizations (for example accounting, inventory management, production operations, or financial management) to be dissolved and recomposed as 'informatised' modules or services (Kallinikos 2006: 96). Computer screens have become the altars of the new secular religion of change. As secularized religions go, that of the digital devotees is fairly apocalyptic and a little messianic. There was a past, irrevocably broken with through the advances of digital technologies, and there is a bright sunlit future, a veritable New Jerusalem, just out of reach but visible through the miasma of the imperfect here-and-now. Only more devotion to newer and better digital technologies, an utter commitment requiring more dollars and tithes on the altar plate, can clear the present miasma. Digital technologies are implicated in an historic shift dissolving bureaucratic organizations. The New Jerusalem will be a robust, almost Quaker, Protestantism, not a Catholicism, with its attendant hierarchy and bureaucracy. Post-bureaucratic individuals, lost in the lonely existence of their souls, digital virtuosi all, will communicate with their Organizational Master, or at least, the Master's disciples, in a wholly unmediated and direct way. No priests, no bureaucrats—just believers and their digital devices, the only artefacts the new religious virtuosi need.

We should, perhaps, pause—are not all utopias, however beautifully glimpsed, false dawns? Digital technologies may be mapping paths to the future but they are no yellow brick road. While the way is pointed to the wizardry of radically changed organizations made virtual (Kallinikos, 2006: 100) by the 'dematerialization' of work processes and more 'inclusive' organizational designs, something else may be happening. What is mapped out is a deconstruction of the scalar and career elements of bureaucracy for all but the elites. New entrants must learn to compete and win if they are to pierce into the inner sanctum of the bureaucracy that remains. Not for them the golden chains, unless they can be seen to triumph in and make themselves a value proposition for the elites (Kallinkos, 2006: 109).

New technologies are often seen as foreshadowing wonderful things. Even old technologies were once new. In the nineteenth century, the typewriter was a profound mechanical invention. It speeded up clerical and recording systems that had been based on hand-writing. In Weber's view (1978), the typewriter directly contributed to the creation of modern managerial bureaucracies. The computer vastly extends the capabilities of the keyboard, even while retaining many of its apparent features, but its digital capabilities also transform the possible nature of organizational design.

Almost every organization today is awash with e-technology and software. Most of the tools that are bought are not revolutionary in their managerial impact; they merely enable managers to do what they would have done anyway but do it better and faster. The new tools are based on technological innovations that drastically change the hardware used to produce a good or service. For instance, e-mail replaces and speeds-up the postal system or search engines such as Google replace and speed-up the reference library; yet, as Beauvallet and Balle argue (2002) argue, revolutionary new technologies do not necessarily produce managerial revolutions. What digital technologies can do is to deliver business as usual much faster. Basic e-technologies, such as e-mail, websites, and search engines can be used effectively to obtain office productivity improvements. They make it possible to generate new channels for communicating with customers, suppliers, and staff. The digital revolution not only enhances service productivity but can transform what were once broadcast models of distribution—from a few centres to many customers—into narrow-cast communication where there are a great many points of distribution and reception—think of Limewire and downloads or favourite blogs. Additionally, and perhaps most importantly, digital technologies make extended supply chain operations feasible and reliable.

The major advantage of digital technologies for business and organizations are their virtual possibilities for disaggregating existing designs. Increasingly, organizations are able to segment activities that are critical to their competitive advantage and to specialize elsewhere those that are not. The non-core functions, such as back office accounting, telemarketing, or programming are outsourced to parts of the world where the wage is one-third to one-tenth the cost in the home market, dramatically reducing operating costs and increasing competitiveness.

Outsourcing is not a new phenomenon: in major production industries such as automotives, the outsourcing of initially non-core and latterly core functions and services has been progressively used since the 1930s (Macaulay, 1966). However, services outsourcing, although common for some time in specialist areas such as advertising and legal services, increased dramatically from the mid-1990s. The outsourcing of sectors such as IT and Telecommunications and Business Processing occurred with the dawning of advanced digital telecommunications services that facilitated the availability of this option. The imperative to outsource—as distinct from the opportunity to do so—was a result of other dynamics that occurred in parallel with the digital age, primarily globalization and increased competition, leading to a continual need to improve efficiency from productivity and to increase service levels. Thus, vertically integrated services were no longer seen as the best organizational arrangements for gaining competitive advantage. The idea of extending the organization's capabilities, whether core or non-core, to a third party, is confirmed in recent research in the area by Gottfredson et al. (2005). These authors suggest that competitive advantage can be gained by optimizing uniqueness of function versus the proprietary nature of the organizations' capabilities. Outsourcing combined with digitalization has proven to be a potent mix.

The result of digitalization has not really been the development of post-bureaucratic organizations that was widely imagined in the new organizational forms literature. In fact, what has happened has been a decomposition of existing organization forms, especially bureaucracies, and the externalization of bureaucratic routines into either supply chain inputs or sub-contracted and out-sourced service provision, such as call centres (Frenkel et al. 1998; Wickham and Collins 2004).

Recomposing Bureaucracy through New Organization Forms

Concepts of new organizational forms all point the way to some version or other of a post-bureaucratic future (Heckscher 1994), but no one term, other than the generic 'new organizational forms' (Lewin et al. 2002) and 'virtual organization' (Davidow and Malone 1992; Ahuja and Carley 1999; De Sanctis and Monge 1999; Black and Edwards 2000; Davidow and Malone 1992), has captured the imagination in the way that the term *bureaucracy* once did. Thus, new organizational forms are many but united by one thing— they are all conceived in opposition to the classic model of bureaucracy. For this reason they are sometimes termed post-bureaucratic organizations, as Fairtlough (2007) suggests. At their core he suggests are two main features: reduction of hierarchy and of coercive elements in bureaucracy and a move towards less rigid and perhaps apparently less rationalistic ways of organizing.

For Fairtlough (2007), the alternatives to hierarchical bureaucracy are suggested as *heterachy* and *responsible autonomy*, while Dunford et al. (2007) provide a succinct account of the relationships between design and form. The literature on new organizational forms suggests that modern corporations can become similar to high-tech cottage industries, as everyone is wired from anywhere. Working virtually, there may be no need to concentrate in a few blocks of central business district real estate. In its most virtual new form, organization will be composed of networks of interdependent but independent knowledge-based teams working in different continents and time zones. Such work can be organized on a rolling twenty-four-hour basis and often involves multiple global collaborators. The work activities are often associated with digital data-based projects, such as film or copy editing, computer programming, or graphic designing.

Many new forms of organization are emerging these days: the network and cellular form (Miles et al. 1997), the federal organization (Handy 1993), the creative compartment (Fairtlough 1994), the postmodern and flexible firm (Clegg 1990; Volberda 2002), the virtual organization (Goldman et al., Nagel, and Preiss 1995), and the individualized corporation (Ghoshal and Bartlett 1997). Often, in a generic sense, these post-organizations are referred to as 'new organizational forms'. In Table 9.1 we indicate some of the terms and sources of new organizational forms.

In *The Rise of the Network Society*, Castells (2000) regards the network as the fundamental form transforming post-bureaucracies. Networks can be understood as a long-term relationship between organizations that share resources to achieve common goals through negotiated actions. Castells identified Cisco Systems as the world's leading and most typical network enterprise. Cisco follows a 'networked business model' demonstrating that networks are a means of production at the same time as being the end product of the business. Cisco uses the Internet and web-based technology to maintain a global network of customers, employees, and suppliers.

Post-bureaucratic organizations tend to be technologically fetishist; hence, the digital devotion of which I have spoken in religious terms, only half-jokingly. Managers will routinely invest time in keeping up with evolving technologies—reading, meeting with experts, and working with the technology first-hand. They will develop a network of trusted technical experts—disciples—who can offer guidance and will have to 'unlearn' old technologies, just as the religious convert must unlearn old faiths, which act as barriers to the new. Multiple partnerships, collaborations, and networks mean that successful managers in post-bureaucratic organizations will have to learn to balance and devote time to the demands of multiple and diverse stakeholders—members of their own team, colleagues from other units in the company, external partners, customers, and shareholders in a new and complex community of other faithful who are digitally devolved.

Managing at the speed of the Internet, in fast organizations, means that virtually all of the core assumptions about a company's business, and market trends in general, will be up for grabs. Successful managers seek insight from a range of sources: they will read widely—not just business publications but books and articles on social trends, history—even science fiction. They will network extensively, not just with peers but with contacts in dissimilar fields, industries, or business functions. And they will take an experimental approach, learning-by-doing, by surfing the net, looking for opportunities to structure experiments around new business concepts or Web applications, and to capture and spread the learning that results.

For new firms in the e-economy, the dissaggregation of traditional organization designs that are more social than technological. Barbara Adkins and her colleagues (2007: 922) have recently written that in the 'knowledge

Table 9.1. Concepts of organization structure

Concept	Characteristics	Author and year
Adhocracy	This refers to organizations that have simply grown, without much explicit design. They are characterized by a lack of structure and formal rules. Often small, creative agencies are adhocracies, such as a design studio.	Mintzberg (1983)
Technocracy	Organization structure enabled by technological innovations. Organizations that comprise people who work on a common database from remote locations would be a good example, e.g. the Genome project.	Burris (1993)
Internal market	Flexible markets and internal contracts within an organization structure characterize these forms of organization, often adopted by public sector organizations in search of greater flexibility and efficiency.	Malone et al. (1987)
Clans	A clan organization is based on shared culture rather than formal rules, much as the members of an extended anthropological clan might be in a traditional society. The culture is overwhelmingly oral rather than recorded in formal rule-like statements. For instance, hi-tech start ups in places such as Silicon Valley.	Ouchi (1980)
Heterarchy	A form of organization resembling a network or fishnet. Rather than there being a single chain of authority—a hierarchy—there are plural connections between the individual members. Professional firms, such as law partnerships or accounting partnerships often correspond to this model.	Hedlund (1986)
Virtual organization	An organization linked through virtual networks rather than formal rules, often involving several ostensibly separate organizations, often project-organized. *The crucial factor is that the network relations are virtually enabled.* Often data is moved with great rapidity around the virtual network and separate skill-sets work on it either in series or in parallel. This is often the preferred mode of design-oriented firms, such as architects' studios, working on large projects with many other specialist partners, such as engineers, project management firms, designers, etc.	Davidow and Malone (1992)
Network organization	An organization formed by intersecting and crosscutting linkages between several separate organizations, usually connected on a project basis, such as large scale civil engineering alliances between a public sector organization, such as a major utility, and other specialist construction, design, and project management-related firms. *The crucial factor here is that the partners have a more formal and enduring relationship than in the virtual organization, and are not restricted to work on digital data, such as movies, designs, etc.*	Biggart and Hamilton (1992), Powell (1986), Rockart and Short (1991)
Postmodern organization	This is essentially a bureaucratic organization which has undergone a degree of de-differentiation of its structure; that is, it has become more integrated, less specialist, and more team-based. Japanese automobile companies—learning bureaucracies that are seeking to become less bureaucratic—would be a case in point.	Clegg (1990)

economy... [t]he product is no longer tangible, the process is no longer straightforward, and the outcomes—"success" or "failure"—are no longer exclusively defined by the bottom line. The traditional firm that works independently no longer stands up in comparison with the organizational and professional networks that cross-cut and break down traditional organizational and disciplinary boundaries.'

Certain places become magnets for particular fields of activity, like hi-tech in Silicon Valley, movie-making in Hollywood or Mumbai, or creative design in Brisbane's Fortitude Valley. Let us look at the last one in a little more detail, as Brisbane is a place I happen to know well. Fortitude Valley, or the Valley, as locals refer to it, has long been a slightly seedy area of the city, close to the old wharves on the Brisbane River, separated from the city of Brisbane by a ridge and the undeveloped site of a Cathedral, in the past a place associated with prostitution and illegal gambling, as well as Chinatown. But, like many other edgy areas of major cities, the Valley has become cool. Cheap leases, warehouses ripe for conversion, street-level access rather than anonymous high rises, and a traditional café and restaurant scene have seen many new design businesses locate there.

A specific ecology of business has developed in the Valley, where social and business networks overlay each other in a shared sense of identity and community, as well as dense networks of referrals and problem-solving. Much of the work that individual firms do is digitally based but often involves collaborative project-based work with other creative people in the same neighbourhood. So while much of the work is Internet-mediated, it occurs between people involved in projects that are very much socially mediated. It is not so much the technology that creates new possibilities for organization design that is disaggregated and project-based but a network of ties premised on social proximity, in both a spatial and cultural sense. Projects and project teams are the nodes that connect in a series of value-chain relationships that bind members and projects together. Connected by these nodes are team members, clients, suppliers, users, and other key stakeholders, who comprise a socio-professional community. Digital capabilities maintain and make possible the network but they are not its essence: that resides in the deep embeddedness of the creative teams in a specific place and set of related spaces that constitute the Valley as these creative people experience and use it as a resource, creating symbolic capital in its milieu (Bourdieu 1998).

The ultimate contradiction of the Internet revolution is that although firms could be located anywhere in cyberspace, they still seem to cluster together in specific quarters of global cities such as New York, London, and Sydney. The digital world moves fundamentally towards concentration, standardization, and control, as Castells acknowledges in both *The Rise of the Network Society* (2000) and *The Internet Galaxy* (2001). An obvious reason is that on the average in the Organization for Economic and Cooperation and Development

(OECD) economies, about 36–40 per cent of what is spent in the economy is spent by the national state, in terms of defence, health, education, and so on, and these sorts of expenditures tend to be well-grounded in national capabilities and concentrated, indeed, clustered, in national space.

Castells' account of the digital utopia is premised on seeing extensive organizational subcontracting through inter-firm networks, the use of 'multidirectional' networks of technologically dynamic firms, and the development of a plurality of strategic alliances between small and large firms (Castells, 2000: 163–88). More innovative flexible responses demand both inter-organizational networking and the functional decentralization of managerial structures (Heckscher and Donnellon, 1994; Nohria and Ghosal, 1997). 'Network enterprises' are characterized by decentralized loosely coupled, flexible, non-hierarchical, and fluid forms, horizontally networking, finding their clearest expression in high-tech sectors such as IT, biotechnology, and advanced manufacturing (Castells 2000).

The Internet enables space to supersede time because, in a world of trade in symbolic images such as software, currencies, and other forms of representation, time is no longer an issue. If you have trading facilities in the right time zones, for instance, you can trade twenty-four hours a day, moving money, or other 'signs' of commerce, symbolically, across the globe, from London to New York to Tokyo to Sydney to London. There is an increasing separation of the 'real' economy of production and its simulacra in the 'symbol economy' of financial flows and transactions. A new international division of labour compresses and fragments both space and distance in such a way that not only production but also various business service industries become distributed in unlikely places. Global currencies facilitate trade across the world: MBAs become global warriors in the new world order. New divisions restructure geographic space. In principle, anywhere is virtually accessible by information and communication technologies. In practice, most national capitals can be reached within twenty-four hours of air travel.

The most radical expression of network organization is that of Michael Hardt and Antonio Negri (2002), who envisage a new form of global democratic potential in network organizations, which they term the 'multitude'. They conceive a network in terms inspired by Deleuze and Guattari (1984) who conceived of a network as an open system with no underlying structure or hierarchy, which they termed 'the rhizome'. The term is used metaphorically and is drawn from botanical usage, where it means a thick underground horizontal stem that produces roots and has shoots that develop into new plants. The rhizome can be expressed in terms of several principles, suggests Munro (2007: 273).

1. Any point in a rhizome can be connected to any other (like a distributed network), and objects of different kinds are connected within the rhizome. This is the principle of connection and heterogeneity.

2. The rhizome is defined by its lines of flight rather than by points internal to it. As the rhizome makes connections with the outside, it undergoes a metamorphosis; like a piece of music, it transforms itself with each new note. This is the principle of multiplicity.
3. The rhizome can be broken at any spot, and it will either sprout a new line of growth or continue along an old line. Deleuze and Guattari described this kind of network as 'the wisdom of plants', by means of which they move, expand, and develop their territory. The rhizome moves by following a flow, of wind, of rain, of water. This is the principle of a signifying rupture.
4. The rhizome does not have an underlying generative structure; intensive states and thresholds replace the idea of an underlying topology, this is referred to as the principle of cartography.

Virtual spaces in which information can spread in an unregulated, nomadic fashion would be examples of rhizomatic networks, such as on-line communities for file sharing such as YouTube or Linux, which function by making novel connections and expanding and maintaining internal communal relations. In the new digital world, IT reduces the transaction costs of information flows, increasing the efficiencies which allow an expanded field of operations. On the other hand, these technologies are associated with more flexible and decentralized management and organizational structures, since they allow for highly efficient communication between functionally and spatially separate units. IT networks thus allow quasi-autonomous, geographically dispersed production units to be embedded in ever more integrated corporate structures.

The Politics of Post-Bureaucracy

In contemporary post-bureaucracies, the promotion of socio-economic cooperation is achieved through the manipulation of specific trust/control mechanisms, thanks, above all, to the network form suggests Castells (1996). These hybrids evoke some types of technologies of trust, which make politically viable a fuzzy, but nevertheless active, system of concentrated power. The 'organizational hybridization' analysed by Ferlie et al. (1996) in the British health-care sector, demonstrates the political aspect of the dynamics implied. Classical administrative (bureaucratic) power is maintained, because these post-bureaucratic hybrids 'have the technical and ideological capacity to combine and re-combine selected elements of managerialism with pre-existing structures of political, administrative and professional power' (Reed 2001: 220). As Reed has argued (1999) has argued, these hybrids often generate considerable mistrust, if not downright opposition, on the part of some groups of professional experts wedded to professional norms, who sense a decline in the conditions enabling the exercise of autonomous judgement.

Power in bureaucracy was largely determined through career opportunities. An inability to fit in, to comport in the appropriate way, or to simply blend into the *habitus*, was a sufficient reason, on many occasions, for a person's career opportunities to be questioned and perhaps restricted. Even when the person might appear singularly inappropriate as an organization member in many ways, if their there was good fit in terms of *habitus*, their future was usually relatively unquestioned (see Kim Philby's (1968) account of Guy Burgess' everyday life).

The question of power remains at the core of post-bureaucracy, but it is less the dialectic of *habitus* and career that structures it. The post-bureaucratic hybrid is a 'loosened community' (Courpasson and Dany 2003), where relationships and groupings are temporarily maintained, where individuals' destinies are more and more separated, where the institutionalized dialogues and interactions are operated through sometimes uncertain and barely legible networks of control, of influence, and of friendship. Consequentially, there is far less opportunity for the formation of stable views of the person in situ.

Adler (2001) analyses the general evolution of firms towards 'trust and community systems'. He suggests mapping institutions in a three-dimensional representation, making it possible to consider the variety of possible organizational models entailed by the hybridization process (Adler 2001: 219). Hierarchy can be combined with trust mechanisms, producing first-degree bureaucratic hybrids, such as 'dynamic bureaucracy' (Blau 1955) or 'enabling bureaucracy' (Adler and Borys 1996). He points out the 'refinements of hierarchy' existing within business firms: the introduction of more formal procedures (TQM, product, and software development processes), the strengthening of planning techniques (in HRM, in project management), of control instruments to assess the projects and performances. Simultaneously, in a post-bureaucratic manner, he argues that the necessary sharing of knowledge in business firms 'depends equally critically on a sense of shared destiny...a sense of mutual trust' to improve and reinforce employee commitment. Even the form of trust entailed by contemporary organizations is rational, according to Adler: 'leadership seems to have shifted toward a form of trust consonant with the ethos of "fact-based management", independent inquiry' (Adler 2001: 227). He sees this shift as constituting a bureaucratic hybrid removed from the traditional bureaucratic deference to established authority, but which, simultaneously, relies on a rational and formalized apparatus. The rhetoric of trust and dialogue that constitutes the post-bureaucratic argument must not lead us simply to forget the existence of 'façades of trust' (Hardy et al. 1998: 71), where trust is not necessarily undertaken 'with reciprocity in mind and may, on the contrary, be intended to maintain or increase power differentials'.

The person in post-bureaucracy is not the *épitomé* of the trusting and trusted subject that is sometimes suggested. Lack of trust is the very reason why post-bureaucracies' organizational arrangements are somewhat authoritarian. The pressure to perform is intense, and business leaders implement tough supervisory processes. These underlying authoritarian mechanisms are largely constituted by tight time-reporting schedules for milestones and progress in specific projects. As a hybrid system of tensions between opposed goals, post-bureaucracies build bridges between domination and self-determination (Romme 1999), in 'the paradoxes and tensions that arise from enacting oppositional forms' (Ashcraft 2001: 131). Ackoff terms this relationship between domination and self-determination as one of 'democracy', which he defines as a regime based on three major features:

(1) The absence of an ultimate authority, the circularity of power; (2) the ability of each member to participate directly or through representation in all decisions that affect him or her directly; and (3) the ability of members, individually or collectively, to make and implement decisions that affect no one other than the decision-maker or decision-makers. (Ackoff 1994: 117)

Democracy is founded on a circular form of power because 'anyone who has authority over others is subject to the collective authority of these others; hence its circularity' (Ackoff 1994: 118). But Ackoff is also a 'realist' thinker. He reminds us that 'divided labour must be coordinated and multiple coordinators must be coordinated; therefore, where complex tasks are involved, hierarchy cannot be avoided . . . hierarchies, contrary to what many assume, need not be autocratic' (Ackoff 1999: 181).

What is distinctive about contemporary post-bureaucracy is that the major mechanism of the career has undergone a substantial change. The typical bureaucratic career was an enclosed phenomenon, classically contained within one organization. Post-bureaucracy differs significantly on this dimension. The inherent political dynamics of post-bureaucratic organizations are condensed and concentrated on the figure of the project manager, circulating from project to project, alliance to alliance, and network to network, torn between the *habitus* of their professional background and the reporting needs of the situation in which they are currently located.

Project Management as the Core of Politics in Post-Bureaucracy

Careers will be increasingly project-based in post-bureaucratic organizations. Increasingly, they will be liquid careers, flowing now like mercury and then reconsolidating in a new plane of activity. The project—whether it is focused on innovation, R&D, engineering, marketing, or whatever—becomes the major vehicle for organization networks and alliances and developmental tasks within specific organizations—although, increasingly these will involve team members from other organizations. In such hybrid and often unclear situations, conflict and confrontation are inevitable, so managing emotions becomes a crucial skill. Managers need to create a learning environment—coaching, hands-on-teaching, and mentoring—to stimulate and develop their employees—and to manage expectations about evolving roles in projects. Employees will be sensitive to shifting roles and the signals they send about a person's worth. A popular metaphor for the post-bureaucratic manager is that of a coach trying to build a team out of a group of highly paid free agent talents.

Taking together the characteristics of networks, alliances, collaborations, virtual relations, multiple stakeholders, liquid careers, and work in projects, it is not surprising that the figure of the project manager should have emerged as the point at which all the contradictions of post-bureaucracy are concentrated. The virtual organization, apart from its digital accoutrements, seems too hazy to grab a firm hold of and it is by no means clear that some of those things attributed as its effects, are not, in fact, the working out of the near-total dominance of market values (Kallinikos, 2006: 109).

Recent management writers have seen project management as a circuit breaker for bureaucracy, and have contrasted the bureaucratic past with the future of a project-based postmodern world (Clegg 1990). Elements of empowerment, self-reliance, trust, and peer-based teamwork controls (Barker 1993) are supposed to portray project management as an explicit and concrete appeal to postmodern/post-bureaucratic organizations. Looked at from below, from the perspective of the subaltern recruit, these organizations seem shape-shifters, project-based, with teams composing and decomposing, locations shifting as projects are completed, key performance indicators (KPIs) changing with projects, and one's individual organizational future uncertain. From the perspective of the elites, the story is quite different. They know that they are over the threshold where the golden chains are evident. The largest problem that they must deal with is using the project shape-shifting that goes on outside the threshold as the basis for competitions and tournaments that will decide who may cross the threshold. The hybrid political structure of post-bureaucracy needs both elite differentiation to ensure a credible competition among various centres of power (individuals and/or sub-groups), and elite unification to ensure a relative consensus on basic values and on the legitimate rules of the internal political arena.

Project management is one of the technologies used to design hybrid political structures for post-bureaucracies for at least two major reasons.

Project management encompasses principles of selection and education. Selection mechanisms are used to enhance the circulation as well as rivalries among sub-elite members (namely would-be project managers and actual project managers), while facilitating the control by incumbent oligarchs over local orderings (through appointments of new project leaders, circulation of experts among projects, 'go/no go' decisions at certain critical steps of the projects . . .). Education mechanisms are used to create what Mills terms the 'fraternity of the chosen' (1956: 143). In other words, project management can be viewed as a technology of power helping to create and sustain diffuse networks of acquaintanceship between 'professionals', that legitimates 'educational nurseries' in which project managers learn both the basics of the official body of knowledge, as well as a feel for those underlying values whose meaning they have to decipher (such as those values pertaining to 'what is important to succeed in this place').

Project managers in post-bureaucratic organizations cultivate a culture of ambition and a method of circulation. As they cycle through projects they strive for visibility for their achievements in managing the projects not only as innovative, creative, and exciting but also as timely, on budget, and dependable. Like Weber's Protestants, they strive to show the state of leadership grace moves through them sufficiently to join the ranks of the elect, or at least those elites who are currently elect.

Corporate leaders have a direct interest in shaping, grooming, and educating selected project management aspirants, constituting what might be called subjects with an appropriate comportment, etiquette, and equipage to qualify as disciplined. The question is not to know whether being a project manager constitutes a guarantee that one will be tagged as a would-be leader. Such is obviously not the case. Being made a project manager merely hints, in a weak way, that one has been spotted as someone with potential which the elites wish to test out, to see if the project leader can display certain indispensable characteristics. Mostly, these characteristics pertain to an ability to accept and work creatively with an existing order and existing rules; thus, they go far beyond merely technical and professional expertise. They are the new way of re-invigorating *habitus* when organizational borders have become porous, careers liquid, and professional identities contingent.

Project management directly influences elite power structures in contemporary post-bureaucratic organizations for three major reasons. First, it differentiates between those likely to be able to aspire further and those who will not. The latter will end up either specializing in project management or going back to their initial working environment. Project management therefore helps differentiate between pre-selected individuals. Second, different kinds of top management decisions (such as resource allocation, project termination, team leaders' demotion/promotion . . .) can shape the chances of those in the project roles. Third, project management creates more complex elite strata to traverse and enables a route of social mobility within the organization. Project management is premised on a high degree of transparency of project performance. Creating a powerful network of shared values regarding career and ambition also facilitates the activation and embodiment of common reference points that structure the attention and commitment of project members. Such reference points include milestones, key performance indicators, profit margins, annual performance, respect for deadlines, respect for budgets, deference to which is progressively internalized as incontrovertible business *and* moral values, essential for the healthy survival of the entire organization (Courpasson and Dany 2003). These reference points strengthen the regime through weaving the social fabric of allegiance for would-be leaders.

In the context of post-bureaucratic organizations, it is the circulation of people (especially potentially key people), which provides the elites with the resources to recruit, stabilize, and perpetuate their ilk. From the moment the circulation of sub-elites is monitored from the centre of the organization, it becomes a means of producing knowledge through the diversity of individual experiences.

The Death of a Theoretical Object?

Bureaucracy is both being superseded by post-bureaucracy and not being superseded by post-bureaucracy. While this may sound nonsensical, it all depends on whether one focuses on recomposition or decomposition. If one follows the direction of decomposition, it is clear that in the new electronic panopticons of the call centre, (often globally located on the margins of modernity), bureaucracy is alive and well in a particularly centralized, standardized, and routinized form. Here the bureaucratization of the shopfloor has proceeded into the heart of the white collar, pink blouse, and colourful indigenously attired digital factory. If, on the other hand, one follows the recomposition route into the upper echelons of leaner and more entrepreneurially oriented organizations, then one might conclude that there were, indeed, post bureaucracies that had managed to turn the iron cage into golden chains.

In the land between lies the road less travelled. Here, above and outside the routines embedded in the digital factory are the innovation, construction, design, and research projects through which young Turks circulate. However, in the words of Matthew (22:14, King James Version of *The Bible*), 'Many are called, but few are chosen'. The zone in-between, the arenas through which individual recruits cycle and circulate, managing their careers as they manage their projects, becomes a panoptical space for the elites to watch and for the project managers to be aware that they are under surveillance, never knowing whether this is the project that will lift them out of the in-between zone and get them over the threshold into the promised land.

There are some rather large implications to this recomposition and decomposition. What made bureaucracies bureaucratic, in part, was their unitary nature—the incorporation within them of many separate processes under one central control. What we are seeing with the emergence of the digital economy is a dispersal of the elements that once were incorporated. In fact, in some respects we are seeing the end of organizations as theoretical objects.

Organizations, as theoretical objects (Althusser 1969; Bachelard 1984; Althusser 1968), came into focus through the study of bureaucracy. Weber's ideal type was the anchor point for almost all of the initial post-Second World War development of the area, either as organization theory or the sociology of organizations. In the mid-1960s, when the Aston researchers were collecting data on organizations, they did so with an implicit model that equated the theoretical object—the construct—of organizations with the empirical object of actual organizations. The two were assumed to correspond. It was in Birmingham that Aston's views crystallized, not more than a couple of kilometres from a much earlier harbinger of organization that was far more fluid. These were earlier models of Marshallian industrial districts, (see also Ackroyd, in this volume) that emphasized what we might now think of as important post-bureaucratic tendencies, such as Birmingham's Jewellery District, not far from Aston University (Pollard 2004). Here, since at least the late eighteenth century, jewellery and medallions, shields, presentation cups, etc., had been produced in a dense web of networking and putting out, in which it was rare for any one craftsman to produce a whole item. Instead, the whole trade was based on parts manufacture. It was decomposed. The earlier model of the decomposed industrial district is in many ways a more useful guide to the social organization of spaces such as Brisbane's The Valley, than the models of bureaucracy.

Conclusion

It is clear that organizations still exist as empirical objects. However, their status as theoretical objects has been transformed. The theoretical object of organizations, crystallized in the 1950s and 1960s, froze some elements of becoming. It captured in a series of snap shots a moment in the becoming of the empirical object. It was the age of the organization man, of the complete organization.

Continuing analysis of organizations as stand-alone and complete entities increasingly misses that much of what organizations achieve—both in the past, as in the Jewellery Quarter, as well as today—will be done through virtual linkages. Thus, in the post-bureaucratic era, we may be witnessing not only the emergence of post-bureaucracies but also the decline of the ontological basis for what has been a fairly fruitful line of enquiry these past 70 years or so. To excavate the future, we may need not only new tools but also a renewed scepticism, and a different compass, than that which has brought us, analytically, to a position where we need 'to find out what price [we] have to pay to get out of going through all these things twice' (Dylan 1966). Otherwise, post-bureaucracy will simply be a replay of the old ontology, this time through the mirror darkly, in reverse, as the representations of organization theorists increasingly accord with a moment of intellectual reification, frozen in a language game of their own making, whilst, meanwhile, social reality changes in ways that cannot easily be represented within the contingent language game being played out.

Something is happening and it is not at all clear that this something is a 'new economy'. The something is both more than a singular event and is not novel; it is, in fact, a complex set of processes of decomposition and recomposition, which have at their core an indeterminate and unpredictable set of political practices, that are in part foreshadowed in premodern forms such as the Jewellery Quarter. But there is something else happening; that is the marketization of many aspects of organizational practices. Nowhere can this be seen more clearly than in the unanticipated events that are flowing from the continuing unravelling of the sub-prime mortgages problems in the United States—in part generated by an entrepreneurial project-oriented selling mentality. We should recognize that the most significant aspect of our present situation is its unpredictability and undecidability: we do not know where the ramifications of past projects will lead us. The successful performance indicators of success in past projects, such as entrepreneurial selling of mortgages, can be the harbingers of tomorrow's doom. Political indetermination is the frontier of present practices. Something is happening as bureaucracies unravel into post-bureaucracies through the dialectics of decomposition and recomposition and, while it is not possible to say exactly what this something is, or where it might lead, in this chapter I have sought to bring some 'sociological imagination' to bear on the issue.

☐ NOTE

1. Sourced from http://www.businessballs.com/tompetersinsearchofexcellence.htm.

☐ BIBLIOGRAPHY

Ackoff, R.L. (1981) *Creating the Corporate Future*, New York: John Wiley and Sons.

——(1994) *The Democratic Corporation*, New York: Oxford University Press.

——(1999) *Re-creating the Corporation*, New York: Oxford University Press.

Adkins, B., Foth, M., Summerville, J. and Higgs, P.L. (2007) Ecologies of Innovation: Symbolic Aspects of Cross-Organizational Linkages in the Design Sector in an Australian Inner-City Area, *American Behavioral Scientist*, 50: 922–34.

Adler, P. (2001) Market, Hierarchy and Trust: The Knowledge Economy and the Future of Capitalism, *Organization Science*, 12(2): 215–34.

——Borys, B. (1996) Two Types of Bureaucracy: Coercive versus Enabling, *Administrative Science Quarterly*, 41(1): 61–89.

Ahuja, M.K. and Carley, K.M. (1999) Network Structure in Virtual Organization, *Organization Science*, 10(6): 741–57.

Althusser, L. (1969) *For Marx*, Harmondsworth, Allen Lane.

Ashcraft, K.L. (2001) Organized Dissonance: Feminist Bureaucracy as Hybrid Form, *Academy of Management Journal*, 44(6): 1301–22.

Bachelard, G. (1984) *The New Scientific Spirit*, Boston: Beacon.

Ball, K. (2007) Call Centers, in S.R. Clegg and J.R. Bailey (eds), *The Sage International Encyclopedia of Organization Studies*, Thousand Oaks, California: Sage.

Barker, J.R. (1993) Tightening the Iron Cage: Concertive Control in Self-Managing Teams, *Administrative Science Quarterly*, 38: 408–37.

Beauvallet, G. and Balle, M. (2002) *E-Management Work: The Internet and the Office Productivity Revolution*, London: Writers Club Press.

Bendix, R. (1956) *Work and Authority in Industry*, Berkeley, California: University of California Press.

Biggart, N.W. and Hamilton, G.G. (1992) On the Limits of a Firm-Based Theory to Explain Business Networks: The Western Bias of Neoclassical Economics, in N. Nohria and R. Eccles (eds), *Networks and Organizations: Structure, Form and Action*, Boston: Harvard Business School Press, 471–90.

Black, J.A. and Edwards, S. (2000) Emergence of Virtual or Network Organizations: Fad or Feature, *Journal of Organization Change Management*, 13(6): 567–76.

Blau, P.M. (1955) *The Dynamics of Bureaucracy*, Chicago: Chicago University Press.

——and Meyer, M.W. (1971) *Bureaucracy in Modern Society*, 2nd edn, New York: Random House.

Bourdieu, P. (1998) *Practical Reason: On the Theory of Action*, Stanford University Press.

Burns, T. and Stalker, G.M. (1961) *The Management of Innovation*, London: Tavistock.

Burris, B.H. (1993) *Technocracy at Work*, Albany, New York: State University of New York Press.

Castells, M. (1996) *The Rise of the Network Society*, London: Blackwell.

——(2000) *The Information Age: Economy, Society and Culture. Volume 1: The Rise of Network Society*, 2nd edn, London: Blackwell.

——(2001) *The Internet Galaxy: Reflections on the Internet, Business, and Society*, New York: Oxford University Press.

Child, J. and McGrath, R.G. (2001) Organizations Unfettered: Organizational Form in an Information-Intensive Economy, *Academy of Management Journal*, 44(6): 1135–49.

Clegg, S.R. (1990) *Modern Organizations. Organization Studies in the Post Modern World*, London: Sage.

——Courpasson, D., and Phillips, N. (2006) *Power and Organizations*, Thousand Oaks, CA:Sage.

Courpasson, D. and Dany, F. (2003) Indifference or Obedience? Business Firms as Democratic Hybrids, *Organization Studies*, 24(8): 1231–60.

——Reed, M.I (2004) Bureaucracy in the Age of Enterprise, *Organization*, 11(1): 5–13.

Crozier, M. (1964) *The Bureaucratic Phenomenon*, Chicago: Chicago University Press.

Davidow, W.H. and Malone, M.S. (1992) *The Virtual Corporation*, New York: Burlingame/ Harper Business.

Deleuze, G. and Guattari, F. (1984) *A Thousand Plateaus: Capitalism and Schizophrenia*, Vol. 2, London: Athlone.

De Sanctis, G. and Monge, P. (1999) Communication Processes for Virtual Organizations, *Organization Science*, 10(6): 693–703.

Donaldson, L. (1996) The Normal Science of Structural Contingency Theory, in S.R. Clegg, C. Hardy and W.R. Nord (eds), *Handbook of Organization Studies*, London: Sage, 57–76.

Dubin, R. (1949) Decision-Making by Management in Industrial Relations, *American Journal of Sociology*, 54: 292–7.

du Gay, P. (2000) *In Praise of Bureaucracy*, London: Sage.

——(ed.) (2005) *The Values of Bureaucracy*, Oxford: Oxford University Press.

Dunford, R., Palmer, I., Beneviste, J. and Crawford, J. (2007) Coexistence of 'Old' and 'New' Organizational Practices: Transitory Phenomenon or Enduring Feature?, *Asia Pacific Journal of Human Resources*, 45(1): 24–43.

Dylan, B. (1966) *Stuck inside of Mobile (with the Memphis Blues Again)*, *Blonde on Blonde*, New York: Columbia Records.

Fairtlough, G. (1994) *Creative Compartments: A Design for Future Organization*, London: Greenwood.

——(2007) *The Three Ways of Getting Things Done: Hierarchy, Heterarchy and Responsible Autonomy in Organizations* (International edition), Greenways, Dorset: Triarchy.

Ferlie, E., Ashburner, L., Fitzgerald, L. and Pettigrew, A. (1996) *The New Public Management in Action*, Oxford: Oxford University Press.

Fligstein, N. (1990) *The Transformation of Corporate Control*, Cambridge, Massachusetts: Harvard University Press.

——(2001) *The Architecture of Markets*, Princeton, New Jersey: Princeton University Press.

Frenkel, S., Tam, M., Korczynski, M. and Shire, K. (1998) Beyond Bureaucracy? Work Organization in Call Centres, *International Journal of Human Resource Management*, 9(6): 957–79.

Ghoshal, S. and Bartlett, C.A. (1997) *The Individualized Corporation: A Fundamentally New Approach to Management: Great Companies are Defined by Purpose, Process, and People*, New York: HarperBusiness.

Goldman, S.L., Nagel, R.N. and Preiss, K. (1995) *Agile Competitors and Virtual Organizations: Strategies for Enriching the Customer*, New York: Van Nostrand Reinhold.

Gottfredson, M., Puryear, R. and Phillips, S. (2005) Strategic Sourcing: From Periphery to the Core, *Harvard Business Review*, 83(2): 132–43.

Gouldner, A.W. (1954) *Patterns of Industrial Bureaucracy*, New York: Free Press.

——(1955) Metaphysical Pathos and the Theory of Bureaucracy, *American Political Science Review*, 49: 496–507.

——(1960) The Norm of Reciprocity: A Preliminary Statement, *American Sociological Review*, 25: 161–78.

Hall, R.H. (1963) The Concept of Bureaucracy: An Empirical Assessment, *American Journal of Sociology*, 69: 32–40.

Handy, C. (1993) *Understanding Organizations*, London: Penguin.

Hardy, C., Philips, N. and Lawrence, T. (1998) Distinguishing Trust and Power in Inter-Organizational Relations: Forms and Facades of Trust, in C. Lane and R. Bachmann (eds), *Trust Within and Between Organizations*, Oxford: Oxford University Press, 64–87.

Harris, J.G., De Long, D.W. and Donnellon, A. (2001) Do You Have What it Takes to be an E-manager? *Strategy & Leadership*, 29(4): 10–14.

Hartd, M. and Negri, A. (2002) *Empire*, Harvard University Press.

Heckscher, C. (1994) Defining the Post Bureaucratic Type, in C. Heckscher and A. Donellon (eds), *The Post Bureaucratic Organization: New Perspectives on Organizational Change*, Thousand Oaks, California: Sage, 14–62.

——Applegate, L. (1994) Introduction, in C. Heckscher and A. Donnellon (eds), *The Post Bureaucratic Organization. New Perspectives on Organizational Change*, Thousand Oaks, California: Sage, 1–14.

——Donnellon, A. (eds) (1994) *The Post Bureaucratic Organization, New Perspectives on Organizational Change*, Thousand Oaks, California: Sage.

Hedlund, G. (1986) The Hypermodern MNC: A Heterarchy?, *Human Resource Management Journal*, 25(1): 9–35.

Kallinikos, J. (2006) *The Consequences of Information: Institutional Implications of Technological Change*, Northampton: Edward Elgar.

Landau, M. (1972) *Political Science and Political Theory*, New York: MacMillan.

Lazega, E. (2000) *The Collegial Phenomenon*, Oxford: Oxford University Press.

Lewin, A.Y., Long, C.P. and Carroll, T.N. (2002) The Coevolution of New Organizational Forms, in S.R. Clegg (ed.), *Central Currents in Organization Studies II: Contemporary Trends*, Vol. 8, London: Sage, 323–47; originally published in *Organization Science*, 10: 535–50.

Macaulay, S. (1966) *Law and the Balance of Power: The Automobile Manufacturers and their Dealers*, New York: Russell Sage Foundation.

Malone, T.W., Yates, J. and Benjamin, R.I. (1987) Electronic Markets and Electronic Hierarchies, *Communications of the ACM*, 30: 6.

March, J.G. and Simon, H. (1958) *Organizations*, New York: Wiley.

Martindale, D. (1960) *The Nature and Types of Sociological Theory*, London: Routledge and Kegan Paul.

Merton, R.K. (1940) Bureaucratic Structure and Personality, *Social Forces*, 18: 560–8.

Miles, R.E., Snow, C.C., Matthews, J.A. and Coleman, H.J. (1997) Organizing in the Knowledge Area: Anticipating the Cellular Form, *Academy of Management Executive*, 11(4): 7–20.

Mills, C.W. (1956) *The Power Elite*, New York: Oxford University Press.

Mintzberg, H. (1983) *Power In and Around Organizations*, Englewood Cliffs, New Jersey: Prentice-Hall.

Munro, R. (2007) Network Society and Organizations, in S.R. Clegg and J. Bailey (eds), *The Sage International Encyclopedia of Organization Studies*, Thousand Oaks, California: Sage, 971–5.

Nohria, N. and Ghoshal, S. (1997) *The Differentiated Network: Organizing Multinational Corporations for Value Creation*, San Francisco, California: Jossey-Bass.

Nonaka, I. and Takeuchi, H. (1995) *The Knowledge-Creating Company*, New York: Oxford University Press.

Osborne, D. and Gaebler, T. (1992) *Reinventing Government*, Reading, Massechusetts: Addison Wesley.

——Plastrik, P. (1997) *Banishing Bureaucracy: Five Strategies for Reinventing Government*, Reading, Massachusetts: Addison Wesley.

Ouchi, W.G. (1980) Markets, Bureaucracies and Clans, *Administrative Science Quarterly*, 25: 129–41.

Peters, T. (2003) *Re-imagine! Business Excellence in a Disruptive Age*, London: Dorling Kindersley.

Philby, K. (1968) *My Silent War*, London: Macgibbon & Kee.

Pollard, J. (2004) From Industrial District to 'Urban Village'? Manufacturing, Money and Consumption in Birmingham's Jewellery Quarter, *Urban Studies*, 41(1): 173–93, *Social and Behavioral Sciences*, Oxford: Elsevier.

Postrel, V.I. (1997) The Peters Principle–Interview with Tom Peters, *Reason*, October 1997, http://findarticles.com/articles/mi_m1568/is_n5_v29/ai_20521295/, accessed on August 20, 2007.

Powell, W.W. (1986) Hybrid Organizational Arrangements: New Form or transitional development, *California Management Review*, 30(1): 67–87.

Pugh, D.S. (1966) Modern Organization Theory: A Psychological and Sociological Study, *Psychological Bulletin*, 66(4): 235–51.

——Hickson, D.J. (1976) *Organizational Structure in Its Context: The Aston Programme 1*, London: Saxon House.

Reed, M. (1999) From the cage to the gaze? The dynamics of organization control in late modernity, in Morgan, M. and Engwal, L. (eds.), *Regulation and organizations: International Perspectives*, 17–49, London: Routledge.

——(2001) Organization, Trust and Control: A Realist Analysis, *Organization Studies*, 22(2): 201–28.

Rockart, J.F. and Short, J.E. (1991) The Networked Organization and the Management of Interdependence, in M.S. Scott Morton (ed.), *The Corporation of the 1990s: Information Technology and Organizational Transformation*, Oxford: Oxford University Press.

Romme, A.G.L. (1999) Domination, Self-Determination and Circular Organizing, *Organization Studies*, 20(5): 801–31.

Rothschild, J. and Whitt, J.A. (1986) *The Cooperative Workplace: Potentials and Dilemmas of Organizational Democracy and Participation*, Cambridge: Cambridge University Press.

Rothschild-Whitt, J. (1979) The Collectivist Organization: An Alternative to Rational-Bureaucratic Models, *American Sociological Review*, 44: 54–81.

Schütz, A. (1967) *The Phenomenology of the Social World*, Evanston, Illinois: Northwester Press.

Selznick, P. (1949) *TVA and the Grass Roots*, Berkeley, California: University of California Press.

Ten Bos, R. (2000) *Fashion and Utopia in Management Thinking*, Amsterdam: Benjamins.

Volberda, H.W. (1998) *Building the Flexible Firm*, Oxford: Oxford University Press.

——(2002) Toward the Flexible Form: How to Remain Vital in Hypercompetitive Environments, in S.R. Clegg (ed.), *Central Currents in Organization Studies II: Contemporary Studies*, Vol. 8, London: Sage, 298–322; originally published in *Organization Science* (1998) 7: 359–74.

Weber, M. (1978) *Economy and Society, An Outline of Interpretive Sociology*, R. Guenther and C. Wittich (ed.), Berkeley: University of California Press.

Wickham, J. and Collins, G. (2004) Call Centres as Innovation Nurseries, *The Service Industries Journal*, 24(1): 1–18.

Wilensky, H.L. (1964) The Professionalization of Everyone?, *American Journal of Sociology*, LXX (2): 137–58.

Winiecki, D.J. (2006) *Discipline & Governmentality at Work: Making the Subject and Subjectivity in Modern Tertiary Labor*, London: Free Association Press.

10 The Post-Bureaucratic Organization and the Control Revolution

MICHAEL REED

> The account of life at the heart of what the intelligence sources call 'the grand central station' of international Islamic militancy... stresses the militants' bureaucratic mind-set, and even describes filling in forms in triplicate before sitting exams to test suitability for a suicide attack. (*Guardian Newspaper*, 11.9.09)

Contemporary debates on 'the post-bureaucratic organization' (PBO) have major implications for the changing control regimes associated with 'network-based' forms of institutional governance in the advanced capitalist societies (Rhodes 1997; Thompson 2003; Crouch 2005; Ezzamel and Reed 2008). A growing number of influential commentators (Giddens 1994; Heckscher and Donnellon 1994; Lash and Urry 1994; Castells 1996, 2000a; Van Dijk 1999; Child and McGrath 2001; Mattelart 2003; Barney 2004; Stalder 2006) have suggested that the more widespread diffusion of the PBO will, inevitably, lead to the development and implementation of far more complex logics and modes of organizational control that radically depart from the once dominant bureaucratic control regime.

Some commentators (Castells 2000a) have gone so far as to insist that the 'variable geometry' of the network economy/enterprise will generate sufficient socio-technical momentum and cultural force to generate and sustain another 'control revolution' in which the orthodox mode of bureaucratic control will implode under the combined weight of its internal contradictions and tensions. In its place will emerge a multidimensional organizational control logic and mode that supersedes the core control principle—that is, standardization operation combined with hierarchical coordination—inherent in what Weber labelled 'rational bureaucracy'. The former, unlike the latter, is more than adequately equipped to cope with the discontinuities, uncertainties, and contingencies endemic to organizational life under globalized capitalist competition. Thus, the complex combination of technological, social, and organizational innovations that have fundamentally undermined the cultural authority and operational effectiveness of bureaucratic orthodoxy will necessarily destroy, in time, the control logic and mode on which it depended. The relative speed and comparative scale with which this 'control revolution' unfolds will vary considerably in temporal, spatial, and sectoral terms but the 'writing is on the wall' for rational bureaucratic control regimes and the normative and organizational mechanisms through which they were legitimated and sustained.

The purpose of this chapter is to provide an overview and evaluation of the intellectual synergy between theorizations of the PBO and interpretations of the latest 'control revolution' in advanced capitalist societies and political economies. It will open with a relatively brief characterization of the PBO thesis as it has been developed over the last decade or so by a number of prominent social and organizational theorists. This will be followed by a, somewhat more detailed, analytical specification of the deep-seated shifts in control logics and forms putatively following on from the core structural changes associated with the PBO thesis—as they are identified and analysed in the work of Manuel Castells. The third section of the chapter will focus on 'control hybrids'—and, in particular, 'neo-bureaucratic' modes of control and polyarchic governance structures (Clegg et al. 2006)—as these have emerged as a central feature of the ongoing debates concerning changes in the nature of organizational control within twenty–first-century capitalism. A concluding section will review the arguments developed in previous sections of the chapter and their underlying implications for the future development of organizational control regimes.

The Post-Bureaucratic Organization

Over the last decade or so, a number of diagnoses and prognoses concerning the organizational health and longevity of the modern bureaucratic organization have been developed that selectively draw on a wide range of classical and contemporary social and organizational theory to provide an influential interpretation of 'how we live now' and 'how we are likely to live in the future'. These exercises in organizational evaluation and forecasting can be disaggregated into a number of interrelated analytical components and substantive claims: first, an ideal typical specification of the contrasting structural features of 'bureaucratic' and 'post-bureaucratic' organizational forms; second, a theoretical identification of the contextual conditions under which either of these ideal types of contrasting organizational forms are likely to prove more strategically effective and operationally efficient; third, a substantive assessment of the empirical conditions, prevailing now and in the foreseeable future, at different levels of socio-economic and political activity and within different institutional sectors and fields that are likely to push increasing numbers of work organizations towards administrative forms isomorphic with the post-bureaucratic type. Taken as a complete package, this analysis of the PBO provides a culturally powerful and cognitively persuasive 'meta-narrative' or generic discourse of radical change and system-wide transformation that has indelibly shaped ongoing dialogue and debate over the current condition of, and future prospects for, liberal-capitalist democracies over the last decade or so (Miller and Rose 2008).

However much we may complain about our continued dependence on ideal-type-based theorizing and analysis (Courpasson and Clegg 2006), they remain an essential, if overly seductive, conceptual instrument in the analytical tool box of contemporary social scientists as they struggle to get some explanatory purchase on highly complex, multilevel, and multidimensional developments that often seem to push and pull, simultaneously, in opposite directions. As an indispensable analytical aid to theoretical model building and application, ideal types still play a vital heuristic and interpretive role in social scientific research and analysis that is unlikely to disappear in the short or medium term (Lawson 1997; Blaikie 2000; Parker 2008). But they need to be handled with extreme care and they need to be worked up into descriptive types that are more closely tied into as wide a range of empirical socio-historical contexts as is feasible and practical within the constraints under which contemporary social science research and analysis operates.

This degree of methodological care and empirical caution has not always been evident in the different positions taken-up in the PBO debate; indeed, the latter has often been marked by a degree of over-hasty theoretical abstraction and generalization that would make the most ardent supporter of ideal-type analysis blush, if not cringe, with embarrassment. Nevertheless, we have to start somewhere and, whether we like it or not, the debate about the PBO has its intellectual roots in theoretical and empirical critiques of Weber's ideal type of bureaucracy in its most rational form that emerged in the middle decades of the twentieth century (Reed 2009a). These early critiques of the endemic theoretical limitations and empirical weaknesses of Weber's ideal type of bureaucracy and the explanatory ends to which it was directed have gathered much greater intellectual momentum and ideological force over the last decade or so as advanced capitalist societies and political economies have developed in ways that seem to make them even more remote from the early twentieth-century world in which Weber lived and worked. Yet, we cannot avoid engaging with the various ideal–typical representations of the PBO thesis because these establish the analytical benchmarks against which our attempts to understand the dynamics of organizational change and institutional transformation must be interpreted and assessed.

The ideal–typical contrast between rational bureaucratic organization (RBO) and the PBO is summarized in Figure 10.1.

RBO	PBO
specialization	collaboration
standardization	flexibility
formalization	negotiation
centralization	dispersal
depersonalization	personalization
collectivization	individualization

Figure 10.1. Rational bureaucratic organization (RBO)/post-bureaucratic organization (PBO)

RBO is analytically represented by a reasonably well-integrated configuration of structural elements focussed around specialization, standardization, and formalization of all work tasks and the behavioural routines required to carry them out. Overall coordination of these various structural components is seen to be provided through an extended hierarchical control system in which discrete levels of operational and strategic decision-making are identified by means of an elaborate framework of rules that are, in turn, legitimated by a vocational occupational culture in which the needs of individual employees (and clients) are always subordinated to the collective demands of the organization.

PBO, as we might expect under the methodological protocols underpinning ideal type construction, is analytically represented through a configuration of structural elements that are categorically differentiated from those constitutive of RBO. So, the ideal type PBO is based on collaboration (rather than specialization), flexibility (rather than standardization), and negotiation (rather than formalization). A much looser form of overall coordination between these structural elements is achieved through a horizontally dispersed control system in which the distinction, much less division, between discrete decision-making levels and powers becomes much more blurred and open to a process of, almost continuous, bargaining and interpretation in which institutionalized rules are conspicuous by their absence. Finally, the overarching cultural context in which the PBO is likely to emerge and take root is one in which 'vocationalism' and 'collectivism' are much weaker as the 'symbolic glues that hold the organization together' as a well-integrated and ordered social system. Indeed, the PBO is much more likely to extol the virtues of 'careerism' and 'individualism' as value systems much more in tune and step with a wider global cultural context in which consumption, rather than production, becomes the primary source of group and personal identity. As a result, the PBO rests on core cultural norms in which personalization and individualization are regarded as positive values to be embraced rather than as negative values to be avoided—indeed, resisted—at all costs in order to ensure the maintenance of procedural rationality and vocational probity (du Gay 2000, 2005). The claim that a move towards a PBO culture that embraces the personalization of service delivery and the individualization of the employment roles and contracts occupied by employed staff may prove an unacceptable threat, or at least substantial risk, to the preservation of administrative equity and integrity is either marginalized or ignored.

The much 'looser coupling' between the various structural components of the PBO is likely to make for a much higher degree of fragmentation and ambiguity than is the case with the RBO (Clegg 1990; Nohria and Berkley 1994). Having substantially weakened, if not totally removed, the hierarchical backbone of the RBO, the PBO is left with little or no choice but to depend on devolved coordinating mechanisms that lack the consistency or resilience of centralized control through a strategic administrative mechanism and an elite group that takes overall responsibility for 'the organization' as a collective entity. But this may be the very control logic and form that is required in the socio-material and cultural conditions prevailing under late twentieth century/early twenty-first-century capitalism.

The ideal typical contrast between RBO and PBO has been explicated and critiqued across an extremely wide range of social scientific publications over the last decade or so (Clegg 1990; Heckscher and Donnellon 1994; du Gay 2000; Courpasson and Reed 2004; Reed 2005; Palmer et al. 2007; Johnson et al. 2009). The tendency to counterpose the two models has also permeated the business practitioner literature (Kanter 1990; Davidow and Malone 1993; Ghoshal and Bartlett 1997; Clarke and Clegg 1998; Thrift 2005). The ideal typical contrast between RBO and PBO has thus taken on an iconic status that dovetails with much of the more recent literature that extols the necessity and virtue of network-based forms of organizational control in the network enterprise and society.

The writing of Manuel Castells (1989, 1996, 2000a, 2000b, 2001, 2004) offers the most elegant, coherent, wide-ranging, and powerful exposition of the view that the move towards the PBO necessarily entails a dramatic and irreversible shift towards new logics of organizational control that presage the rise of the network society. It is to an in-depth exposition and interpretation his work—set within the broader context of recent theoretical and empirical work on organizational control—that we turn in the next section of this chapter.

PBO and the Control Revolution

The proposition that organizational control regimes pass through various developmental phases or cycles is well established in the study of work organizations (Edwards 1979; Edwards 1986; Perrow 1986, 2002; Thompson

1989; Ramsay 1997; Thompson and McHugh 2005). A distinction is usually drawn between movements at the level of 'general control'—that is, at the level of the capitalist production process/corporate system—and 'detailed control'—that is, at the level of immediate work processes and relations. The relationship between these two levels of control is often highly problematic such that changes at the level of detailed workplace control regimes (focussed on the monitoring and assessment of task performance and the administration of workplace discipline) cannot simply be 'read off' from changes at the level of general control (Thompson 1989).

However, more recent debates about the 'rise of network society' and the growing influence of the PBO thesis have generated a renewed interest in much more theoretically ambitious and empirically wide-ranging analyses of the latest evolutionary stages in what Beniger (1986) called the continuous 'control revolution' that modern capitalist societies and political economies had been experiencing since the latter half of the nineteenth century. Beniger (1986: 7) defines 'control' in, largely, functionalist terms—that is, as 'purposive influence towards a predetermined goal'—and, in this way, denudes it of its ideological and political significance in terms of its necessary institutional embedding in wider power relations and structures. In this respect, he shares a close intellectual affinity with managerial control theorists who see 'control' purely in technical terms and focus on intra-organizational control mechanisms to the virtual exclusion of higher levels of social organization and analysis (Thompson 1967; Tannenbaum 1968; Berry et al. 1995). Nevertheless, Beniger's analysis is highly sensitive to the complex socio-economic processes and mechanisms through which 'depersonalized control relations' were re-established by means of advances in bureaucratic organization and the material technologies on which it depended to secure effective formalized control over work behaviour. He also identifies, through detailed historical research, a complex series of 'control crises or failures' which modern societies and organizations work through from the mid-nineteenth century onwards—such as the American railroad control crisis in the second half of the nineteenth century—until effective centralized control is gradually achieved during the twentieth century and reaches its apogee in the post-industrial/information society (Webster 2002).

Castells' analysis shares much of the sweeping historical vision and scope of Beniger's evolutionary theory of socio-organizational control. But the former is much more attuned to the discontinuities and breaks within, and between, different control logics and regimes as they develop in response to the radically different types of conditions prevailing under globalized 'informational capitalism'. For Castells, the latter—and, in particular, the key financial sectors within globalized 'informational capitalism'—is, literally, 'out of control' insofar as it operates according to a logic that is driven by market irrationality and lacks any effective stabilizing, much less directing, mechanism.

Thus, he argues, there is an inverse relationship, under the conditions imposed by 'informational capitalism', between micro-level (corporate enterprise/work organization) control and macro-level (global economic system/national economic sectors) control; the more control you have at the micro-level, the less control you have at the macro-level. Hence:

Managers control specific corporations and specific segments of the global economy, but they do not control, and do not even know about, the actual, systemic movements of capital in the networks of the financial flows, of knowledge in the information system, of strategies in the multifaceted network enterprises. (Castells 2000a: 504)

Consequently, the PBO, for Castells, is largely 'flying blind'. Its managerial and technocratic elites are able to design and implement intra-organizational control systems—such as self-managing teams afforded a relatively high degree of decision-making autonomy to identify, design, and pursue their own business projects—that may achieve some, not insignificant, degree of internal order. But these internal control regimes are always likely to be at the mercy of the radically destabilizing extra-organizational chaos prevailing at the level of the global capitalist financial system as a whole. Thus, the emphasis given to 'concertive control' regimes by theorists of the PBO—that is, control regimes that move beyond the core logics and mechanisms of bureaucratic control by shifting the locus of control away from managers and towards the workers themselves (Barker 1999: 40–1)—needs to be tempered by a realistic evaluation of the conditions under which it is likely to be viable as an alternative to bureaucratic control and of the new power dynamics and relations that such a control regime will generate. The increasing emphasis given to normatively or culturally based control regimes within the literature on the PBO/network enterprise (Alvesson and Willmott 2002; Child 2005; Alvesson 2006) must be analytically and empirically situated within an appreciation of the wider structural and ideological movements experienced within the network economy/society.

Castells' analysis of these wider structural and ideological movements within the network economy/society requires further elaboration because it has major implications for the way in which we may interpret and evaluate the new control logics and modes associated with the PBO. Castells' analysis of what he calls the 'variable geometry' of the network economy/society shapes his understanding of, and explanation for, the emergence of the network enterprise and the radically different forms of work relations and control mechanisms that the latter relies on when compared to the orthodox, vertically integrated bureaucratic corporation. The concept of 'variable geometry' conveys Castells' sense of the extreme and pervasive instability inherent in globalized informational capitalism—that is, a form of capitalism that has creatively destroyed, in true Schumpeterian fashion, through the cumulative force of intersecting technological, financial, organizational, and cultural innovations, the material foundations and institutional architecture of the 'old economy'.

The analytic focus on this 'variable geometry' also suggests that the conventional categorical distinctions between 'sectors', 'corporations', 'departments', and 'units' are no longer sustainable in a situation where the basic organizational components of the network logic underpinning the new economy are process flows rather than functional tasks and where the coordination of these flows, such as it is, only becomes possible through loosely interconnected circuits of control operating simultaneously at a number of different levels. Insofar as there is any strategic rationale or direction to this system of 'variable geometry', Castells continues, it is to be found in those individuals, groups, and organizations that are the 'switchers' connecting the various control circuits and coordinating networks; they control access to the inter-operating codes and protocols which have emerged as the key power 'pinch points and relationships' in the new economy/society. This 'variable geometry' creates a world in which inherently contradictory principles, concepts, and forms—of self-renewing and managed systems, of decentralized autonomy and concentrated power, of virtualized reality and materialized symbols, of disembodied relationships and embedded connections—simultaneously coexist in a state of permanent tension and ambiguity. But it is this very instability and unpredictability of 'variable geometry', Castells insists, that gives the network economy/society its dynamic fluidity and adaptability—that is, its core organizational capacity to cope with the 'managed chaos' of globalized informational capitalism.

Castells provides us with a highly evocative and substantial body of theoretical and empirical work to support his analysis of the network economy/society and the organizing logic on which it is based. Overall, his work argues for a fundamental and irreversible shift away from a 'fixed geometry' of stabilized containment and standardized coordination through formalized procedures and vertical chains of 'command and control' towards a 'variable geometry' of dynamic interactions and temporary accommodations through negotiated protocols between 'switchers' positioned at the key connecting nodes within and between networks that rely on non-hierarchical modes of control.

As several commentators (Jessop 2002; Barney 2004; Sennett 2006; Stalder 2006) have noted, Castells' analysis of the shift from 'fixed' to 'variable' geometry—as indeed is evident in much of contemporary network theorizing more generally (Thompson 2003)—is primarily about changing power relations and control dynamics under the conditions imposed by globalized informational capitalism. But, as Stalder (2006: 133–40) indicates, there is a singular lack of detailed discussion in Castells' work about the power inequalities and domination structures that frame the institutional context in which 'switchers' and 'protocols' are embedded, and from which they draw their legitimacy and authority. Castells may be right in suggesting that nation states and bureaucratic corporations are no longer 'sovereign actors' with untrammelled structural power and hierarchical control. But he also seems largely uninterested in the agents, both individual and corporate, that determine the 'rules of the game' and shape the 'variable geometry' of the network economy/ society. Consequently, Castells seems to ignore, or at the very least marginalize, the continuing role of established corporate groups and institutions— such as business corporations and national governments, as well as various elite groups located at the strategic apex of these agencies—in dominating and shaping the conditions under which new power configurations and control regimes are likely to emerge and develop under globalized informational capitalism (Clegg et al. 2006; Savage and Williams 2008; Reed 2009c).

Nevertheless, Castells' analysis does provide us with a wider theoretical and empirical context in which the distinctive modes of controlling prevailing under, respectively, RBO and the PBO can be analytically identified. These are specified, again in ideal typical terms, in Figures 10.2 and 10.3.

As we can see from Figure 10.2, the ideal type bureaucratic control regime can be identified in relation to three interrelated analytical components—the objectives or problems on which it is focused, the design logic that emerges to deal with these objectives/problems, and the structural form or mode which that design logic requires for its realization. The major control objectives on which bureaucratic control regimes are focussed relate to the securing of externalized conformity to standardized rules, the transformation of implicit knowledge into explicit knowledge, the internalization of a vocational work identity, the maintenance of long-term operational continuity through process standardization, and the sustainability of behavioural norms and rules relating to appropriate modes of disciplined work activity.

Each of these control objectives is aligned with a particular control logic or process. Externalized conformity prioritizes collective order over individual autonomy. Converting implicit into explicit knowledge requires knowledge conversion mechanisms that prioritize incremental centralization over decentralized diffusion. An internalized vocational work identity prioritizes intra-organizational careers over extra-organizational incentives. Operational continuity prioritizes hierarchical coordination over horizontal mediation, and maintaining the integrity of work-related behavioural norms prioritizes

Foci	Logic	Mode
Externalized conformity	Collective order	Output monitoring
Explicit knowledge	Incremental centralization	Process rationalization
Vocational identity	Internal career systems	Internalized labour markets
Standardized continuity	Hierarchical coordination	Rule specification
Work discipline	Functional specialization	Task fragmentation

Figure 10.2. Bureaucratic control regime

Foci	Logic	Mode
Internalized commitment	Disciplined selves	Normative discipline
Tacit knowledge	Operational decentralization	Process flexibility
Occupational identity	Portfolio careers	Externalized labour markets
Leveraged creativity	Semi-autonomous teams	Concertive coordination
Behavioural adaptability	Project-based coordination	Process integration

Figure 10.3. Post-bureaucratic control regime

functional specialization over organizational participation. In turn, each of these components of the underlying control logic associated with the bureaucratic control regime is aligned with a specific mode of control. Prioritizing collective order generates the need for an output monitoring system that will protect the integrity of the organization's service provision. Centralized knowledge management requires continuous process rationalization. Organization-based work identities and careers demands internalized labour markets. Hierarchical coordination engenders stratified decision rule systems, and functional specialization encourages a high degree of task fragmentation.

The ideal type post-bureaucratic organizational control regime, as we might expect, has diametrically opposed structural characteristics to those identified under the bureaucratic control regime. The primary control objects or targets for the former are internalized commitment (rather than externalized compliance), tacit knowledge (rather than explicit knowledge), organizational identity (rather than vocational identity), leveraged creativity (rather than operational continuity), and work behaviour flexibility (rather than work behaviour routinization). This set of control objects or targets encourages the development of a very different configuration of control logics to those crystallized around the bureaucratic control regime. The emphasis on internalized commitment prioritizes 'disciplined selves' (Kondo 1990) (rather than collective order). The stress on facilitating tacit knowledge prioritizes operational decentralization (rather than incremental centralization). An orientation towards organizational identity highlights the importance of portfolio careers (rather than internal labour markets). Emphasizing the need for leveraged creativity promotes semi-autonomous teams (rather than hierarchical coordination), and the extension of work behaviour flexibility encourages project-based collaboration (rather than functional/task specialization).

Again, each of these components of the control logic under PBO facilitates the development of a distinctive mode or form of control. Work individualization engenders the need for normative discipline (rather than output monitoring). A focus on tacit knowledge encourages process flexibility (rather than process rationalization). An emphasis on portfolio careers stresses the importance of external labour markets (rather than internal labour markets). The need for semi-autonomous teams leads to a stress on concertive coordination (rather than hierarchical coordination), and the commitment to project-based collaboration facilitates process integration (rather than functional/task specialization).

The ideal type bureaucratic control regime has dominated both the historical and theoretical analysis of changing organizational control logics and forms since the 1970s. Thus, much of the work undertaken within the labour process theory tradition has focussed on the ways in which changing workplace-level, enterprise-level, and corporate-level control regimes have to be understood as the highly contingent outcomes of a complex interplay between 'imposition from above' and 'resistance from below' (Braverman 1974; Marglin 1974; Friedman 1977; Edwards 1979; Montgomery 1979; Storey 1983, 1985; Burawoy 1985; Knights et al. 1985; Knights and Willmott 1990; Jacques 1996).

The broad corpus of labour process theory and analysis indicates that the underlying mechanisms of capital accumulation that constitute capitalist political economies impose significant structural limits on corporate-level control strategies and forms. Consequently, the structural imperative to generate profits and accumulate capital, embodied in the 'genetic code' through which capitalism operates, frames the institutional context within which organizational control regimes emerge and develop. But this does not mean that these underlying structural mechanisms predetermine the control logics and forms that will develop at company and workplace levels or that they will be tightly aligned with higher level corporate-level control strategies (Reed 1989, 1990). More than three decades of research and analysis on the relevant organizational control dynamics indicates a rather more complex interplay of 'structural necessity' and 'contextual contingency' (Thompson 2003; Elger and Smith 2005).

More recently, work carried out within a, broadly speaking, neo-institutionalist perspective has also confirmed the underlying organizational resilience and historical longevity of the bureaucratic control regime (Powell and DiMaggio 1991; Siberman 1993; Adler and Borys 1996; Courpasson 2000; du Gay 2000; DiMaggio 2001; Perrow 2002; Courpasson and Reed 2004; Kallinikos 2004; Reed 2005). These analyses indicate that key features of the bureaucratic control regime have become ubiquitous in contemporary organizations and societies which continue to rely on de-contextualized management systems for monitoring, regulating, and governing through standardized behavioural routines and normative frameworks. This is especially the case in relation to contemporary organizational control regimes that have become increasingly dependent on integrated information and communication technologies as a critical means for monitoring and regulating highly complex and mobile flows of financial, human, symbolic, and linguistic resources through spatially and temporally extended networks (Zuboff 1988; Masuda 1990; Boisot 1998; Frenkel et al. 1999; Kallinikos 2004). Within these extended networks, and the integrated information and communication technologies through which they are regulated and governed, some of the core structural elements of the ideal typical bureaucratic control regime are maintained, if in a somewhat attenuated and diluted fashion.

In this way, neo-institutionalist research on underlying continuities between bureaucratic and post-bureaucratic control regimes has, however unintentionally, helped to raise the issue and profile of 'control hybridization' as a key feature of network-based organizations that combine selected components of different, and quite often contradictory, control logics and forms. It has also surfaced and critiqued ideological debates swirling around the supposedly 'enterprising', 'entrepreneurial', and 'empowering' qualities of the PBO and the much more sophisticated and subtle control logics and forms on which the latter is seen to depend.

Control Hybrids

Much of the more recent work on control hybrids in contemporary organizational research and analysis has taken its intellectual inspiration from a diverse, and often disparate, set of theoretical and methodological developments such as actor-network-theory, post-structuralism, discourse theory and analysis, governmentalist theory, and institutional ethnography (Law 1994; Law and Hassard 1999; Westwood and Linstead 2001; Thompson 2003; Grant et al. 2004; Reed 2005; Smith 2005; Clegg et al. 2006; Latour 2007; Miller and Rose 2008). But drawing on theoretical and methodological resources such as these has given a growing number of organizational researchers some very real and penetrating insights into the micro-level processes and relations through which operational modes of organizational control are assembled and re-assembled—out of an inordinately wide range of material, symbolic, discursive, textual, and linguistic resources—to form workable control regimes.

Recent work has also suggested that viable operational control regimes are likely to require a much higher degree of 'requisite variety', and hence structural flexibility and mobility, when they are expected to co-opt and enrol, if not colonize and govern, a much broader range of stakeholder interests and values that are likely to respond to very different, if not antithetical, governance logics and mechanisms. It also dovetails very neatly with the 'capillary' conceptualization of organizational power relations and control developed out of Foucault's work on 'ascending' modes of power (Foucault 2003) and the inspiration it has provided for the work of the 'governmentalists' on the complex mix of intra-organizational control rationalities and technologies through which the conduct of governance under neo-liberalism has been practically achieved (Flyvbjerg 1998; Dean 1999; Clegg et al. 2006; Miller and Rose 2008; Townley 2008).

Organizational research and analysis on control hybrids—that is, work focussed around the development and maintenance of complex combinations of control logics and forms based on contradictory principles and loosely coupled integrating mechanisms—is by no means a new thing in organizational studies. Indeed, one can trace it back at least as far as the contribution of the modern classics on 'the dysfunctions of bureaucracy' (published between the 1940s and 1960s) and the much more dynamic conception of bureaucracy, bureaucratization, and de-bureaucratization that it engendered (Reed 2009*a*). More recently, an increasingly influential body of research and writing on the growing significance of control hybrids in public sector and public service organizations has called attention to the possibility, indeed probability, of modes of contemporary organizational governance that cannot be adequately analysed and interpreted in terms of an 'either-or choice' between bureaucratic and post-bureaucratic control regimes (Ferlie et al. 1996; Pettigrew and Fenton 2000; McLaughlin et al. 2002; Farrell and Morris 2003; Deem et al. 2007). In turn, these studies and others have suggested that there may be a 'third way' organizational control regime emerging—that is, the neo-bureaucratic control regime embedded within polyarchic governance structures that are ideally suited to the political realities of contemporary organizational life. These structures need to be effectively managed by overlapping and competing elite groups through complex combinations of devolved democracy and centralized autocracy (Ashcraft 2001; Newman 2001; Farrell and Morris 2003; Clegg and Courpasson 2004; Courpasson 2006; Courpasson and Clegg 2006; Clegg et al. 2006).

More recent research (Clarke and Newman 1997; Clark 2000, 2003; Courpasson 2000; Pettigrew and Fenton 2000; Farrell and Morris 2003; Clegg and Courpasson 2004; Courpasson and Clegg 2006; Clegg et al. 2006; Deem et al. 2007; McGivern and Ferlie 2008; Rasmussen 2008) within both public and private sector organizations, has suggested that a distinctive form of 'neo-bureaucratic control' may be emerging in which meso-level control strata and mechanisms are being rationalized out of existence, while strategic control is centralized at the macro-level and operational control further decentralized to the micro-level. The 'hollowing out' thesis has become increasingly influential as researchers have become more sensitive to the 'disconnect' (Thompson 2003; Reed 2005; Sewell 2005; see also chapters by Harris and Ackroyd this volume) between the public discourse of collaboration, partnership, high-trust, empowerment, entrepreneurialism, and personalization that has accompanied much contemporary network theorizing and the political reality of more complex, hybridized control regimes in which power elites have been prepared to devolve a, not insignificant, degree of operational autonomy but only as long as they retain, more streamlined and effective, centralized strategic control. Front-line service providers—often, relatively high status, professionals or 'knowledge workers'—end up regulating and disciplining themselves in line with centrally determined performance metrics and targets that are designed and monitored by technical specialists who are relatively detached from the formal authority hierarchy insofar as they are located within specialist units directly responsible to governing elites. Of course, the potential for resistance, incompetence, confusion, and incoherence is very considerable and should never be underestimated in relation to any grounded assessment of how these hybridized control systems actually operate in practice (Flynn 1999, 2002; McNulty and Ferlie 2004; Miller 2005; Clarke et al. 2007). But the potential for hybridized control regimes to combine or, even more subtly, to 'blend' a complex range of control logics and mechanisms in order to realize a viable synthesis of streamlined and remote strategic control (required by governing elites) with devolved operational compliance through a much more sophisticated 'coalface' surveillance and disciplinary technology, developed and implemented by a new cadre of technocratic managers, should also be evaluated. As a number of researchers have suggested (Farrell and Morris 2003; Miller 2005; Newman 2005; Deem et al. 2007; McGivern and Ferlie 2008; O'Reilly and Reed 2008), neo-bureaucratic control regimes work through a deft combination of remote strategic leadership and detailed operational management that governing elites attempt to legitimate through a discourse of 'modernization' and the key role that it assigns to various hybrid 'manager-professionals' in holding together, if not integrating, the much higher degree of complexity and fragmentation that it necessarily entails. By hybridizing selected elements of market-based, hierarchy-based, and network-based control logics and mechanisms, neo-bureaucratic control regimes blend the operational pragmatism and ideological sophistication that seem to be the discursive and institutional hallmarks of postmodern, network-based governance structures and systems.

It is possible to identify the key analytical components of the neo-bureaucratic control regime, again in ideal typical form, in Figure 10.4.

Foci	Logic	Mode
Demonstrated participation	Team performance	Continuous self-surveillance
Embedded knowledge	Organization specific	Knowledge codification
Discursive identity	Committed subjects	Peer-group regulation
Disciplinary incentives	Market competition	Dual labour markets
Delegated autonomy	Collective empowerment	Managed democracy

Figure 10.4. Neo-bureaucratic control regime

The key foci for the neo-bureaucratic control regime are, respectively: 'demonstrated participation'—that is, transparent and public demonstrations that 'you' are fully involved in the behavioural routines through which organizational membership is confirmed and reproduced. 'Embedded knowledge' is concerned with the tacit understandings underpinning the task routines and supporting conventions through which 'organizational work' gets done. A focus on 'discursive identity' highlights the importance of shared cultural frameworks developed through the enactment and inculcation of shared symbolic values and linguistic understandings communicated through key textual materials and forms (Fairclough 2003). 'Disciplinary incentives' refers to the more elaborate mechanisms through which high-level work performance is stimulated and rewarded. Finally, 'delegated autonomy' makes reference to the structures and systems through which a degree of self-management—for the individual and/or the group—can be combined with overall coordination and regulation of collective performance (Hoggett 1996, 2005; Johnson et al. 2009).

Each of these control objects or targets is, in turn, embedded in a particular control logic. 'Demonstrated participation' emphasizes the crucial importance of team performance and the mechanisms through which it is to be identified and assessed. 'Embedded knowledge' prioritizes organization-specific expertise and skill over organization-transferable expertise and skill—what matters is what you can do for the organization, how you can effectively bring your talents and skills to bear on the issues and problems that the organization faces and help it to deal with them effectively. 'Discursive identity' emphasizes the importance that is attached to employees socially constructing themselves as 'committed subjects'—that is, individuals who prioritize their work-related commitments over non-work commitments and are even prepared to sacrifice the latter in the cause of the former. 'Disciplinary incentives' re-asserts the continued relevance of market competition as a core principle of employee recruitment, retention, and motivation. Finally, 'delegated autonomy' only becomes viable under a control logic in which individual and collective empowerment—that is, giving individual employees and the work teams in which they are embedded the freedom, or at least the discretion, to take risks and develop their own learning routines and capabilities—are continuously promoted (Best 1990; Blackler 1995; Robertson and Swan 2003).

Combining each of these control objects and logics provides us with an ideal–typical identification of the core, interrelated mechanisms that constitute the neo-bureaucratic mode of control. Demonstrated participation and team performance come together in the form of continuous self-surveillance and the various material and ideational technologies through which it is realized. Embedded knowledge and the organization-specific issues and problems to which it is directed are combined through the various knowledge codification systems and techniques that contemporary work organizations rely on to an ever increasing degree. The stress on discursive identity and committed subjects is reflected through the range of peer group regulatory mechanisms and practices that contemporary work organizations experiment with in order to ensure that appropriate levels of worker commitment are generated and sustained (Ezzamel and Willmott 1998; Sewell 1998, 2001; Barker 1999; Frenkel, et al. 1999; Sewell and Barker 2006). Disciplinary incentives and market competition are brought together through the mechanism of dual labour markets in which high status, professionalized 'knowledge workers' are incentivized to compete with one another for scarce material and symbolic rewards (Ezzamel and Burns 2005), while lower level, routine operatives have to prove their worth to managers by continuously pitching for, and hopefully securing, work if their employment, as temporary and casual labour, is to be maintained (Bauman 1998; Grimshaw et al. 2005). Finally, delegated autonomy and collective empowerment are dovetailed through a form of 'managed democracy' in which a balanced portfolio of competitive and cooperative mechanisms, operationally designed and implemented by a cadre of technical specialists and strategically monitored by a complex coalition of governing elites, are developed and maintained (Clegg and Courpasson 2004; Clegg et al. 2006; Courpasson and Clegg 2006).

The neo-bureaucratic control regime attempts to blend, even achieve a partial synthesis between, selected elements of 'the cage' (rational bureaucratic control) and 'the gaze' (post-bureaucratic control) in order to deliver a configuration of regulative mechanisms that can effectively facilitate the practice of contemporary 'governance' (Reed 1999, 2005; Thompson 2003; Crouch 2005). This is particularly relevant within an institutional context in which much of the middle-range control infrastructure associated with rational bureaucratic control—such as detailed first-line supervision and extended supervisory hierarchies—has all but been 'rationalized out of existence' by the development and implementation of new information and communication technologies that can do the job much more cost-effectively and efficiently. On the other hand, the more subtle and sophisticated normative control technologies associated with post-bureaucratic control regimes are still seen to be in their relative infancy and to lack the degree of ideological, discursive, and emotional power often ascribed to them by both their advocates and critics. Hence the need to retain, even selectively strengthen, formal control mechanisms—such as inter-organizational market competition, intra-organizational career competition and circulation, and elite remote monitoring and surveillance—under a neo-bureaucratic control regime that constitutes a hybridized form of political dominance and governance which strives to achieve a workable degree of political stability under conditions of escalating complexity and instability (Sewell 2005; Courpasson and Clegg 2006).

The 'brave new world' of 'high performance work systems' (Appelbaum et al. 2000) or 'knowledge-intensive companies (Nonaka and Takeuchi 1995) or 'network-based societies and political economies' (Van Dijk 1999) may still need to rely on strategic steering mechanisms and operational coordinating routines that cannot be effectively provided through the technological and organizational 'miracle cures' of informational capitalism (Jessop 2002). Neo-bureaucratic control may provide a viable control regime through which the complex political coalitions, circuits, and deals required to achieve some degree of institutional resilience and continuity under the extreme volatilities and insecurities endemic to internationalized capitalism, particularly under its network-based form, can be realized (Harvey 2003, 2005; Thrift 2005).

Discussion and Conclusions

The chapter has provided a broad overview and evaluation of the putative changes in organizational control regimes associated with the development and diffusion of the PBO set within the wider context of ongoing debates about the rise of the 'network society' as promulgated by prominent social analysts such as Manuel Castells. As the chapter has progressed, an increasingly complex interpretation of changing organizational forms and control regimes has been developed in which the dynamics of 'hybridization' and its broader implications for the emergence of a neo-bureaucratic control regime have assumed greater empirical relevance and theoretical importance. Along the way, a range of theoretical, methodological, and substantive issues have emerged that require a somewhat more focussed appreciation in the concluding section of the chapter.

As already indicated, much of the chapter has drawn on analyses in which ideal type construction and interpretation have played a central expositional and explanatory role. As Parker (2008) has pertinently reminded us recently, Weberian ideal types are 'thought experiments' about changing organizational forms and supporting ideological justifications that may be vital instruments in the social scientist's theoretical tool kit but which also bring various methodological risks or dangers with them. In particular, they may bring into play, especially when they are treated as descriptive types rather than theoretical models, a form of quasi-functionalist teleology and linearity in which one form of ideal type is thought to necessarily succeed or replace a preceding type due to the determining force of some underlying historical logic or structural imperative. Such a risk has been evident throughout the analytical narrative constructed in this chapter insofar as theoretical analyses of, and substantive justifications for, the PBO and its associated control logic/regime have been methodologically grounded in forms of ideal type construction and interpretation that all too often skate rather easily over historical complexity and empirical diversity.

The chapter has further argued that ideal type analysis is an indispensable theoretical and methodological tool for developing what Thompson (2003) has called a 'contextualist paradigm' for understanding and explaining the complexities of contemporary organizational life in general and changing governance structures in particular. He directly contrasts this 'contextualist paradigm' with the 'variable paradigm' that has tended to dominate social, political, and economic analyses of changing organizational forms and their broader implications for emerging governance structures and control regimes. While the latter focuses on the formulation and testing of hypotheses drawn from general theoretical models through the application of sophisticated quantitative research tools, the former is geared to the construction and evaluation of analytical narratives about complex chains of interaction over time and place that shape and reshape different types and modalities of collective political action (also see Manicas 2006; Reed 2009*b*, 2009*c*). Consequently, ideal type construction and application is an indispensable analytical tool required to model these 'complex chains of interaction' and to identify the underlying mechanisms which generate and sustain the distinctive organizational control regimes that emerge from them in different socio-temporal and spatial contexts.

Considered in these terms, the 'contextualist paradigm' provides the theoretical and methodological prism through which the ongoing debate about the PBO and its significance for changing logics and forms of control reviewed in this chapter should be viewed and assessed. At its theoretical core, the PBO thesis suggests that fundamental changes *to both the nature and mode of organizational control* in 'network society' have occurred and that these structural transformations can only be understood and explained by identifying the very different type of institutional logic that dominates the development of such a society—that is, the logic of 'variable geometry'.

Nevertheless, as has been alluded to several times in this chapter, network-based theories of organizational control seem relatively weak when dealing with the crucial role of power relations in shaping and reshaping organizational forms and control regimes. As Perrow (1986) argued more than two decades ago, and has reaffirmed more recently (Perrow 2002, 2008), network theorizing tends to ignore the intimate and complex interconnections between 'power' and 'control' in favour of an evolutionary model of institutional development in which various impersonal functional mechanisms—such as 'natural selection', 'technological efficiency', and 'network density'—are seen to determine the process and trajectory of change. Unfortunately, Perrow suggests (1986: 213) this removes 'much of the power, conflict, disruption, and social class variables from the analysis of social processes.

It neglects the fact that our world is made in large part by particular men and women with particular interests. Instead, it searches for ecological laws that transcend the hubbub that sociology should attend to'. While earlier formulations of network theorizing display some degree of sensitivity to the 'power issue' (Powell 1991), later interpretations, focussing primarily on issues such as network structure, density, and design seemed to lose sight of this crucial issue of the complex ways in which power processes and relations shape network dynamics and forms (Reed 2008).

Yet, as has also been demonstrated in this chapter, there is little doubt that ongoing analysis of and debate over the PBO and its implications for changing control regimes has identified a wide-ranging research agenda that will be of continuing interest to organizational researchers as they struggle to understand the key power relations and control dynamics that will shape twenty-first-century capitalism. As two recent overviews (Palmer et al. 2007; Johnson et al. 2009) of the PBO/new organizational forms literature have demonstrated, the debate over changing control logics has intensified as established control regimes come under increasing pressure from wider economic, social, and political transformations that seem to push inexorably in the direction of enhanced delegation, autonomy, and empowerment. But this literature also highlights the fact that these 'developmental tendencies' are embedded within an uneven and contested process of multilevel, multidimensional change in which certain 'clusters of control mechanisms' seem to come together to form distinctive patterns of control that do not conform to the orthodox models. Analyses of the latter also emphasize the continued explanatory importance and relevance of 'non-linear' theories of organizational change that 'explore the relationship between sectoral, national and supranational institutions and firm-level practices, in accounting for persistent but evolving diversities: general change mediated by continuity and difference' (Johnson et al. 2009: 55).

In many ways, the network-based analyses of the PBO offered by prominent social theorists such as Castells is a continuation of the 'reflexive modernization' thesis developed in the early and mid-1990s by social theorists such as Giddens (1994). The thesis suggested, amongst other things, that high or postmodernity exhibited a degree of institutional complexity that would require a qualitatively different form of 'institutional reflexivity' to that prevailing under industrial or managed modernity. This could only be provided through *organizational forms that reflexively monitored and controlled themselves* as well as continuously monitoring and controlling the specific activity domains and sectors for which they were nominally responsible and accountable. Higher level or 'double reflexivity', it was further argued, could not be provided by rational bureaucratic forms of organizational monitoring and control because they fundamentally lacked the more advanced 'disembedding' and 'distancing' mechanisms that continuous and remote self-reflexive monitoring and control demanded. It is but a short step from this kind of theorizing to Castells' theorization of the 'network society' and the institutional logic of 'variable geometry' that drives and reshapes it.

Alternative and perhaps more illuminating analytically structured narratives of changing organizational forms and control regimes may be provided by theoretical models and analyses that give more emphasis to the underlying institutional continuities that continue to shape and define twenty-first-century capitalism. Harrison's analysis (1994) of the 'core-ring' network formation emerging in advanced capitalist political economies, in which the power and dominance of 'the core' of large business corporations becomes more concentrated without becoming more politically and administratively centralized in classic bureaucratic fashion (Ackroyd 2002), may tell us more about the emergent dynamics of contemporary capitalism than Castells 'variable geometry'.

Indeed, much of the downside of the 'brave new world' of the 'network society', at least for the upper and middle ranks of the professional, managerial, and technical members of what Galbraith (1967) called the 'techno-structure' of the modern capitalist corporation—and what we today call the core group of 'knowledge workers' on whom the long-term survival and success of the network corporation is supposed to depend—was anticipated over three decades ago in Fletcher's searing polemic on the 'end of management' (1973). Fletcher argued that the rationalization of control processes and relations in the capitalist business corporation of the mid-1970s had reached a juncture at which ever-increasing numbers of middle-level, and also upper-level, managers and professionals were being made—technically, organizationally, and economically—redundant. He saw little or no possibility of this long-term trend being reversed or even diluted. Instead, Fletcher (1973: 156) foresees a future in which:

... the intricate and delicate management structure will disappear and be replaced by a managerial atmosphere in which highly paid experts execute precise control, observation, and distraction tasks for their masters using machines which also control themselves. By attrition, redundancy, unionization, or revolution management will be finished, and managers themselves are facilitating their own end.

Again, this vision of an organizational future—characterized by a structural polarization between a power elite and a supporting core of, relatively privileged but self-exploiting, knowledge workers—does not seem too far away from more recent analyses of the emergence of 'polyarchic' power structures and control regimes in late twentieth-century/early twenty-first-century capitalist corporations (Clegg et al. 2006). The latter are seen to combine highly resilient and durable forms of oligarchic dominance with partially devolved control systems that are reasonably well equipped to handle the escalating political instability and volatility generated by the interrelated set of structural changes that Castells identifies as constitutive of 'informational capitalism'. As a complex intermediary form made up of selectively combined elements of oligarchic and democratic modes of governance, a polyarchic power structure, and the hybrid, neo-bureaucratic control regime that it generates in order to reproduce itself, establishes a type of political system that seems best-fitted to satisfy the contemporary governance needs of political elites and the organizational needs of technical experts.

If we accept that this theoretical model of the hybridized polyarchic power structure and its supporting neo-bureaucratic control regime has explanatory potential, then there are a number of key issues that are likely to shape the research agenda for organizational analysts over the coming years. First, a renewal and revitalization of research on organizational elites, located at various levels within the polyarchic power structure, and on the multifarious ways in which their internal deliberations and external interactions—particularly in relation to how they respond to challenges and threats to their occupancy of controlling positions within the polyarchic power structure—impact on policy and practice outcomes (Scott 2001, 2008; Savage and Williams 2008; Reed 2009c). Second, developing a better understanding of how the 'soft' forms of power that have become central to the fabrication and implementation of 'concertive coordination' mechanisms within neo-bureaucratic control regimes have been generated and recombined in new and innovative ways by strategic elites and their supporting cast of 'knowledge workers' (Nye 2004; Barker 2005; Lukes 2005; McKinlay 2005; Courpasson 2006; Townley 2008; Reed 2009c). Finally, mapping out the new 'contested terrains' and 'frontiers of control' that are emerging in polyarchic power structures and neo-bureaucratic control regimes such as identity politics, gender politics, spatial politics, and sustainability politics (Darier 1999; Halford and Leonard 2001; Webster 2002; Dale and Burrell 2008; du Gay 2008).

Insofar as polyarchy is a hybrid governance system that combines centralized autocracy and devolved democracy—through a complex, and inherently unstable, institutional synthesis of elite domination and expert delegated autonomy—then it will have a vital ideological and organizational role to play in shaping the neo-bureaucratic control regimes emerging in twenty-first-century capitalism. It would appear that these 'dynamics of domination' will retain their theoretical and empirical significance for some time to come, just as they did for Max Weber in his struggle to interpret the momentous 'control revolution' of the early twentieth century.

☐ BIBLIOGRAPHY

Ackroyd, S. (2002) *The Organization of Business: Applying Organizational Theory to Contemporary Change*, Oxford: Oxford University Press.

Adler, P and Borys, B. (1996) Two Types of Bureaucracy: Enabling and Coercive, *Administrative Science Quarterly*, 41: 61–89.

Alvesson, M. (2006) *Knowledge Work and Knowledge-Intensive Firms*, Oxford, Oxford University Press.

——Willmott, H. (2002) Identity Regulation as Organizational Control: Producing the Appropriate Individual, *Journal of Management Studies*, 39(5): 619–44.

Appelbaum, E., Bailey, T., Berg, P. and Kalleberg, A.L. (2000) *Manufacturing Advantage: Why High Performance Work Systems Pay Off*, Ithaca, New York: ILR Press.

Ashcraft, K.L. (2001) Organized Dissonance: Feminist Bureaucracy as a Hybrid Form, *Academy of Management Journal*, 44(6): 1301–22.

Barker, J.R. (1999) *The Discipline of Teamwork: Participation and Concertive Control*, Thousand Oaks, California: Sage.

——(2005) Toward a Philosophical Orientation on Control, *Organization*, 12(5): 787–97.

Barney, D. (2004) *The Network Society*, Cambridge: Polity Press.

Bauman, Z. (1998) *Work, Consumerism and the New Poor*, Cambridge: Polity Press.

Beniger, J.R. (1986) *The Control Revolution: Technological and Economic Origins of the Information Society*, Cambridge, Massachusetts: Harvard University Press.

Berry, J.L., Broaddbent, J. and Otley, D. (1995) *Management Control: Theories, Issues and Practices*, London: Macmillan Press.

Best, M. (1990) *The New Competition: Institutions of Industrial Restructuring*, Cambridge, Massachusetts: Harvard University Press.

Blackler, F. (1995) Knowledge, Knowledge Work and Organizations: An Overview and Interpretation, *Organization Studies*, 16(6): 1021–46.

Blaikie, N. (2000) *Designing Social Research*, Oxford: Polity Press.

Boisot, M.H. (1998) *Knowledge Assets: Securing Competitive Advantage in the Information Economy*, Oxford: Oxford University Press.

Braverman, H. (1974) *Labour and Monopoly Capital: The Degradation of Work in the Twentieth Century*, New York: Monthly Review Press.

Burawoy, M. (1985) *The Politics of Production*, London: Verso.

Castells, M. (1989) *The Informational City: Information Technology, Economic Restructuring and the Urban-Regional Process*, Oxford: Blackwell.

——(1996) *The Rise of Network Society*, 1st edn, Oxford: Blackwell.

——(2000*a*) *The Rise of Network Society*, 2nd edn, Oxford: Blackwell.

——(2000*b*) Information Technology and Global Capitalism, in W. Hutton and A. Giddens (eds), *On the Edge: Living with Global Capitalism*, London: Jonathon Cape.

——(2001) *The Internet Galaxy*, Oxford: Oxford University Press.

——(2004) Informationalism, Networks, and the Network Society, in M. Castells (ed.), *The Network Society: A Cross-Cultural Perspective*, London: Edward Elgar.

Child, J. (2005) *Organization*, Oxford: Blackwell.

——McGrath, R. (2001) Organizations Unfettered: Organizational Form in an Information-Intensive Economy, *Academy of Management Journal*, 44(6): 43–76.

Clark, P. (2000) *Organizations in Action: Competition between Contexts*, London: Routledge.

——(2003) *Organizational Innovations*, London: Sage.

Clarke, T. and Clegg, S. (1998) *Changing Paradigms: The Transformation of Management Knowledge for the 21st Century*, London: Harper Collins.

Clarke, J. and Newman, J. (1997) *The Managerial State*, London: Sage.

————Smith, N., Wilder, E. and Westmarland, L. (2007) *Creating Citizen-Consumers*, London: Sage.

Clegg, S.R. (1990) *Modern Organizations: Organization Studies in the Post-Modern World*, London: Sage.

Clegg, S.R., Courpasson, D. (2004) Political Hybrids: Tocquevillean Views on Project Organizations, *Journal of Management Studies*, 41(4): 525–47.

——————Phillips, N. (2006) *Power and Organizations*, London: Sage.

Courpasson, D. (2000) Managerial Strategies of Domination: Power in Soft Bureaucracies, *Organization Studies*, 21(1): 141–61.

——(2006) *Self-Constraint: Liberal Organizations and Domination*, Copenhagen: Copenhagen Business Press.

——Clegg, S.R. (2006) Dissolving the Iron Cages: Tocqueville, Michels, Bureaucracy and the Perpetuation of Elite Power, *Organization*, 13(3): 319–43.

——Reed, M. (2004) Bureaucracy in the Age of Enterprise, *Organization* 11(1): 5–12.

Crouch, C. (2005) *Capitalist Diversity and Change: Recombinant Governance and Institutional Entrepreneurs*, Oxford: Oxford University Press.

Dale, K. and Burrell, G. (2008) *The Spaces of Organisation and the Organisation of Space*, London: Palgrave Macmillan.

Darier, E. (1999) *Discourses of the Environment*, Oxford: Blackwell.

Davidow, W. and Malone, M. (1993) *The Virtual Corporation: Structuring and Revitalizing the Organizaton for the 21st Century*, New York: Haper Collins.

Dean, M. (1999) *Governmentality: Power and Rule in Modern Society*, London: Sage.

Deem, R., Hillyard, R. and Reed, M. (2007) *Knowledge, Higher Education and the New Managerialism*, Oxford: Oxford University Press.

DiMaggio, P. (2001) *The Twenty-First Century Firm: Changing Economic Organization in International Perspective*, Princeton, New Jersey: Princeton University Press.

du Gay, P. (2000) *In Praise of Bureaucracy*, London: Sage.

——(2005) *The Values of Bureaucracy*, Oxford: Oxford University Press.

——(2008) Keyser Suze Elites: Market Populism and the Politics of Institutional Change, in M. Savage and K. Williams (eds), *Remembering Elites*, Oxford: Blackwell.

Edwards, R. (1979) *Contested Terrain: The Transformation of the Workplace in the Twentieth Century*, London: Heinemann.

Edwards, P. (1986) *Conflict at Work: A Materialist Analysis of Workplace Relations*, Oxford: Blackwell.

Elger, T. and Smith, C. (2005) *Assembling Work: Remaking Factory Regimes in Japanese Multinationals in Britain*, Oxford: Oxford University Press.

Ezzamel, M. and Burns, J. (2005) Professional Competition, Economic Value Added and Managerial Control Strategies, *Organization Studies*, 26(5): 756–77.

——Reed, M. (2008) Governance: A Code of Many Colours, *Human Relations*, 61(5): 597–615.

——Willmott, H. (1998) Accounting for Teamwork: A Critical Study of Group-Based Systems of Organizational Control, *Administrative Science Quarterly*, 43: 333–67.

Fairclough, N. (2003) *Analyzing Discourse: Textual Analysis for Social Research*, London: Routledge.

——(2005) Discourse Analysis in Organization Studies, *Organization Studies*, 26(6): 915–39.

Farrell, C. and Morris, J. (2003) The Neo-Bureaucratic State: Professionals, Managers and Professional Managers in Schools, General Practices and Social Work, *Organization*, 10(1): 129–56.

Ferlie, E., Pettigrew, A., Ashburner, L. and Fitzgerald, L. (1996) *The New Public Management in Action*, Oxford: Oxford University Press.

Fletcher, C. (1973) The End of Management, in J. Child (ed.), *Man and Organization*, London: Allen and Unwin.

Flynn, N. (1999) Managerialism, Professionalism and Quasi-Markets, in M. Exworthy and S. Halford (eds), *Professionals and the New Managerialism in the Public Sector*, Buckingham: Open University Press.

——(2002) Explaining the New Public Management: The Importance of Context, in K. McLaughlin, S. Osborne and E. Ferlie (eds), *New Public Management: Current Trends and Future Prospect*, London: Routledge.

Flyvbjerg, B. (1998) *Rationality and Power: Democracy in Practice*, Chicago, Illinois: University of Chicago Press.

Foucault, M. (2003) *Society Must Be Defended*, London: Allen and Lane.

Frenkel, S., Korczynski, M., Shire, K.A. and Tam, M. (1999) *On the Frontline of Work in the Information Economy*, Ithaca and London: Cornell University Press.

Friedman, A.L. (1977) *Industry and Labour: Class Struggle at Work and Monopoly Capitalism*, London: Macmillan.

Galbraith, J.K. (1967) *The New Industrial State*, Harmondsworth: Penguin.

Ghoshal, S. and Bartlett C.A. (1997) *The Individualized Corporation*, San Francisco, California: Harper Business.

Giddens, A. (1994) Living in a Post-Traditional Society, in U. Beck, S. Lash and A. Giddens (eds), *Reflexive Modernization: Politics, Tradition and Aesthetics in the Modern Social Order*, Cambridge: Polity Press.

Grant, D., Hardy, C., Oswick, C. and Putnam, L. (2004) *The Sage Handbook of Organizational Discourse*, London: Sage.

Grimshaw, D., Willmott, H. and Rubery, J. (2005) Fragmenting Work Across Organizational Boundaries, in M. Marchington, D. Grimshaw, J. Rubery and H. Willmott (eds), *Fragmenting Work: Blurring Organizational Boundaries and Disordering Hierarchies*, Oxford: Oxford University Press.

Guardian Newspaper (2009) Red Tape and No Bullets—Tales from Bin Laden's Volunteers, 11 September, 18–19.

Halford, S. and Loenard, P. (2001) *Gender, Power and Organizations*, London: Palgrave.

Harrison, B. (1994) *Lean and Mean*, London: The Guilford Press.

Harvey, D. (2003) *The New Imperialism*, Oxford: Oxford University Press.

——(2005) *A Brief History of Neo-Liberalism*, Oxford: Oxford University Press.

Heckscher, C. and Donnellon A. (1994) *The Post-Bureaucratic Organization: New Perspectives on Organizational Change*, London: Sage.

Hoggett, P. (1996) New Modes of Control in the Public Service, *Public Administration*, 74: 9–32.

——(2005) A Service to the Public: The Containment of Ethical and Moral Conflicts by Public Bureaucracies, in P. duGay (ed.), *The Values of Bureaucracy*, Oxford: Oxford University Press.

Jacques, R. (1996) *Manufacturing the Employee: Management Knowledge from the 19th to 21st Centuries*, Thousand Oaks, California: Sage.

Jessop, B. (2002) *The Future of the Capitalist State*, Cambridge: Polity Press.

Johnson, P., Wood, G., Brewster, C., and Brookes, M. (2009) The Rise of Post-Bureaucracy: Theorists' Fancy or Organizational Praxis, *International Sociology*, 24(1): 37–61.

Kallinikos, J. (2004) The Social Foundations of the Bureaucratic Order, *Organization*, 11(1): 13–36.

Kanter, R.M. (1990) *When Giants Learn to Dance*, London: Unwin Hyman.

Knights, D. and Willmott, H. (1990) *Labour Process Theory*, London: Macmillan.

———Collinson, D. (1985) *Job Redesign: Critical Perspectives on the Labour Process*, Aldershot: Gower.

Kondo, D.K. (1990) *Crafting Selves: Power, Gender, and Discourses of Identity in a Japanese Workplace*, Chicago, Illinois: University of Chicago Press.

Lash, S. and Urry, J. (1994) *Economies of Signs and Space*, London: Sage.

Latour, B. (2007) *Reassembling the Social: An Introduction to Actor-Network Theory*, Oxford: Oxford University Press.

Law, J. (1994) *Managing Modernity*, Oxford: Blackwell.

——Hassard, J. (1999) *Actor Network Theory and After*, Oxford: Blackwell.

Lawson, T. (1997) *Economics and Reality*, London: Routledge.

Lukes, S. (2005) *Power: A Radical View*, 2nd edn, London: Macmillan.

Manicas, P. (2006) *A Realist Philosophy of Social Science: Explanation and Understanding*, Cambridge: Cambridge University Press.

Marglin, S.A. (1974) What Do Bosses Do?: The Origins and Functions of Hierarchy in Capitalist Production, *Review of Radical Political Economics*, 6: 60–102.

Masuda, Y. (1990) *Managing in the Information Society: Releasing Synergy Japanese Style*, Oxford: Blackwell.

Mattelart, A. (2003) *The Information Society: An Introduction*, London: Sage.

McGivern, G. and Ferlie, E. (2008) Cancer Networks in the Iron Cage, unpublished conference paper, *European Group for Organization Studies Colloquium*, Amsterdam, July 2008.

McKinlay, A. (2005) Knowledge Management, in S. Ackroyd, R. Batt, P. Thompson and P. Tolbert (eds), *The Oxford Handbook of Work and Organization*, Oxford: Oxford University Press.

McLaughlin, K., Osborne S., and Ferlie E. (eds) (2002) *New Public Management: Current Trends and Future Prospects*, London: Routledge.

McNulty, T. and Ferlie, E. (2004) Process Transformation: Limitations to Radical Organizational Change Within Public Service Organizations, *Organization Studies*, 25(8): 1389–412.

Miller, D. (2005) What is Best Value?: Bureaucracy, Virtualism and Local Governance, in P. du Gay (ed.), *The Values of Bureaucracy*, Oxford: Oxford University Press.

Miller, P. and Rose, N. (2008) *Governing the Present: Administering Economic, Social and Personal Life*, Cambridge: Polity Press.

Montgomery, D. (1979) *Workers' Control in America*, Cambridge: Cambridge University Press.

Newman J. (2001) *Modernizing Governance: New Labour, Policy and Society*, London: Sage.

——(2005) Bending Bureaucracy: Leadership and Multi-Level Governance, in P. du Gay (ed.), *The Values of Bureaucracy*, Oxford: Oxford University Press.

Nohria, N. and Berkley, J.D. (1994) The Virtual Organization: Bureaucracy, Technology, and the Implosion of Control, in C. Heckscher and A. Donnellon (eds), *The Post-Bureaucratic Organization: New Perspectives on Organizational Change*, Thousand Oaks, California: Sage.

Nonaka, T. and Takeuchi, H. (1995) *The Knowledge-Creating Company: How Japanese Companies Create the Dynamics of Innovation*, Oxford: Oxford University Press.

Nye, J.S. (2004) *Soft Power: The Means to Success in World Politics*, New York: Public Affairs.

O'Reilly, D. and Reed, M. (2008) Leaderism and UK Public Service Reform, unpublished conference paper, *European Group for Organization Studies Colloquium*, Amsterdam, July 2008.

Palmer, I., Benveniste, J. and Dunford, R. (2007) New Organizational Forms: Towards a Generative Dialogue, *Organization Studies*, 28(12): 1829–47.

Parker M. (2008) The Seventh City Review of The New Spirit of Capitalism by L. Boltanski and E. Chiapello, *Organization*, 15(4): 610–14.

Perrow, C. (1986) *Complex Organizations: A Critical Essay*, 3rd edn, New York: Random House.

——(2002) *Organizing America: Wealth, Power, and the Origins of Corporate Capitalism*, Princeton, New Jersey: Princeton University Press.

——(2008) Conservative Radicalism, *Organization*, 15(6): 915–21.

Pettigrew, A. and Fenton, E.M. (2000) *The Innovating Organization*, London: Sage.

Powell, W.W. (1991) Neither Market or Hierarchy: Network Forms of Organization, in G. Thompson, J. Frances, R. Levacic and J. Mitchell (eds), *Markets, Hierarchies and Networks: The Co-ordination of Social Life*, London: Sage.

——DiMaggio, P. (1991) *The New Institutionalism in Organizational Analysis*, Chicago, Illinois: University of Chicago Press.

Ramsay, H. (1997) Cycles of Control: Worker Participation in Sociological and Historical Perspective, *Sociology*, 11(3): 481–506.

Rasmussen, B. (2008) Mechanisms of Power in Post-Bureaucratic Organizations, unpublished conference paper, *European Group for Organization Studies Colloquium*, Amsterdam, July 2008.

Reed, M. (1989) *The Sociology of Management*, London: Harvester.

——(1990) The Labour Process Perspective on Management Organization: A Critique and Reformulation, in J. Hassard and D. Pym (eds), *The Theory and Philosophy of Organizations: Critical Issues and New Perspectives*, London: Routledge.

——(1999) From the Cage to the Gaze: The Dynamics of Organizational Control in Late Modernity, in G. Morgan and L. Engwall (eds), *Regulation and Organizations: International Perspectives*, London: Routledge.

——(2005) Beyond the Iron Cage: Bureaucracy and Democracy in the Knowledge Economy and Society, in P. du Gay (ed.), *The Values of Bureaucracy*, Oxford: Oxford University Press.

——(2008) Exploring Plato's Cave: Critical Realism in the Study of Organization and Management, in D. Barry and H. Hansen (eds), *The Sage Handbook of New Approaches in Management and Organization*, London: Sage.

——(2009*a*) Bureaucratic Theory and Intellectual Renewal in Contemporary Organization Studies, in P. Adler (ed.), *The Oxford Handbook of Sociology and Organizational Studies: Classical Foundations*, Oxford: Oxford University Press.

——(2009*b*) Critical Realism: Philosophy, Method, or Philosophy in Search of a Method? in A. Bryman and D. Buchanan (eds), *The Sage Handbook of Organizational Research Methods*, London: Sage.

——(2009*c*) Critical Realism in Critical Management Studies, in M. Alvesson, T. Bridgeman and H. Willmott (eds), *Critical Management Studies*, Oxford: Oxford University Press.

Rhodes, R. (1997) *Understanding Governance: Policy Networks, Governance, Reflexivity and Accountability*, Buckingham: Open University Press.

Robertson, J. and Swan, J. (2003) Control—What Control?: Culture and Ambiguity Within a Knowledge Intensive Firm, *Journal of Management Studies*, 40(4): 831–58.

Savage, M. and Williams, K. (2008) *Remembering Elites*, Oxford: Blackwell.

Scott, J. (2001) *Power*, Cambridge: Polity Press.

——(2008) Modes of Power and the Re-Conceptualization of Elites, in M. Savage and K. Williams (eds), *Remembering Elites*, Oxford: Blackwell.

Sennett, R. (2006) *The Culture of the New Capitalism*, New Haven, Conneticut: Yale University Press.

Sewell, G. (1998) The Discipline of Teams: The Control of Team-Based Industrial Work through Electronic and Peer Surveillance, *Administrative Science Quarterly*, 43(2): 397–429.

——(2001) The Prison-House of Language: The Penitential Discourse of Organizational Power, in R. Westwood and S. Linstead (eds), *The Language of Organization*, London: Sage.

——(2005) Nice Work: Re-Thinking Managerial Control in an Era of Knowledge Work, *Organization*, 12(5): 705–10.

——and Barker, J.R. (2006) Coercion Versus Care: Using Irony to Make Sense of Organizational Surveillance, *Academy of Management Review*, 31(4): 934–61.

Siberman, B.S. (1993) *Cages of Reason: the Rise of the Rational State in France, Japan, the United States and Great Britain*, Chicago, Illinois: University of Chicago Press.

Smith, D. (2005) *Institutional Ethnography: A Sociology for People*, New York: Rowan and Littlefield.

Stalder, F. (2006) *Manuel Castells: The Theory of the Network Society*, Cambridge: Polity Press.

Storey, J. (1983) *Managerial Prerogative and the Question of Control*, London: Routledge.

——(1985) The Means of Management Control, *Sociology*, 19(2): 193–211.

Tannenbaum, A.S. (1968) *Control in Organizations*, New York: McGraw-Hill.

Thompson, P. (2003) Disconnected Capitalism: or Why Employers Can't Keep their Side of the Bargain, *Work, Employment and Society*, 17(2): 359–78.

Thompson, J.D. (1967) *Organizations in Action*, New York: McGraw-Hill.

Thompson, P. (1989) *The Nature of Work: An Introduction to Debates on the Labour Process*, London: Macmillan.

Thompson, G. (2003) *Between Hierarchies and Markets: The Logic and Limits of Network Forms of Organization*, Oxford: Oxford University Press.

Thompson, P. and McHugh, D. (2005) *Work Organizations: A Critical Introduction*, 3rd edn, London: Macmillan.

Thrift, N. (2005) *Knowing Capitalism*, London: Sage.

Townley, B. (2008) *Reason's Neglect: Rationality and Organizing*, Oxford: Oxford University Press.

Van Dijk, J. (1999) *The Network Society: Social Aspects of New Media*, London: Sage.

Webster, F. (2002) *Theories of the Information Society*, 2nd edn, London: Routledge.

Westwood, R. and Linstead, S. (2001) *The Language of Organization*, London: Sage.

Zuboff, S. (1988) *In the Age of the Smart Machine: The Future of Work and Power*, Oxford: Heinemann.

11 Back to the Future: What Does Studying Bureaucracy Tell Us?

HUGH WILLMOTT

Introduction

> When, despite arguments advanced by an official, his superior insists on the execution of an instruction . . . the official's honour consists in being able to carry out [his/her superior's] instruction . . . conscientiously and precisely in the same way as if it corresponded to his own convictions. *Without this supremely ethical discipline and self-denial the whole apparatus would disintegrate.* (Weber 1994: 330–1, emphasis added)

Contributors to this volume have interrogated the claim that management in late modern societies relies increasingly upon organizational forms that go 'beyond bureaucracy'.[1] Most commentators on this question subscribe to the view that contemporary work organization 'ain't what it used to be', at least if Scientific Management and Fordism are taken to typify its past. Elements previously dissociated from 'bureaucratic organization'—such as 'enterprise' and 'innovation'—are seen to prefigure a waning, if not an eclipse, of 'bureaucracy' as a dominant organizing principle. But there is also widespread scepticism about claims that bureaucracy is being killed off by 'post-bureaucratic' forms of organizing. As contributions to this volume show, the situation is perplexing, and not least because there is uncertainty and disagreement about what 'bureaucracy' is, what it once was, and what it is becoming.

When reviewing studies and discussions of bureaucracy, one might conclude that they comprise an endless fight over claims made for its *technical* capabilities. Gathered in one corner are the critics of its technical capabilities, who contend that it stifles creativity, is inefficient and wasteful, and demoralizes employees. Such critics are inclined to commend 'post-bureaucratic' innovations, including Corporate Culturalism (Peters and Waterman 1982) and New Public Management (NPM) (Osborne and Gaebler 1992), which favour other media of governance such as core corporate values and/or markets and networks. Congregating in the other corner are those who stress the distinctive capacity of bureaucracy to clarify responsibilities, ease role stress, and thereby enable employees to work effectively. For them, 'post-bureaucracy' blurs responsibilities, increases dysfunctional pressures, and so compromises effectiveness. Finally, there are those standing in the middle of the ring who seek to reconcile the two opposing camps but risk satisfying neither. Their claim is that a high level of formalization can be meshed with more enabling, 'post-bureaucratic' methods of working as a basis for mobilizing employees' innovative capacities, and thereby secure greater effectiveness (Adler and Borys 1996).

For participants in this contest, the aim is of course to enlighten the opponent or, in the third case, to show how the contest is based upon a misconception. Others, myself included, suspect that the clash is about competing ideologies as much as it is about a preparedness to produce or accept compelling 'evidence' (Alvesson and Thompson 2006). When 'evidence' is generated, selected, and interpreted in the light of particular world-views, reconciliation seems no more likely than victory. Debating the 'management of modernity' is nonetheless important if, as the opening quote suggests, a loss of '*ethical* discipline' (Weber 1994: 331) within 'bureaucracy' or 'post-bureaucracy' risks disintegration of the apparatus of modern administration.

The issue of ethical discipline tends to be sidelined when discussion of bureaucracy and/or post-bureaucracy is directed primarily at their *technical* capabilities as organizational *forms* or socio-technical systems (Trist and Bamforth 1951).[2] There is an issue of whether the *ethos* and *principles* of modern bureaucracy are recognized, valued and maintained, or disregarded and neglected by 'post-bureaucratic' innovations. It will be argued that, historically, the meaning of bureaucracy is embedded in a narrative that endows it with *politico-ethical* significance. When discussing the establishment of modern bureaucratic administration in the United Kingdom during the mid-nineteenth century, Osborne (1994) notes how 'the administrator was not to be a faceless official—the "bureaucrat" of modern parlance—but was to enjoy a certain discretionary autonomy. [The] Northcote Trevelyan [Report] stresses that permanent officials needed to possess the ethical characteristics required in those who were to be relatively autonomous' (Ibid.: 294). The capacity to exercise 'autonomous' judgement is, arguably, a condition of possibility of what makes modern bureaucracy 'a distinctive ethical milieu in its own right' (du Gay, in this volume); and it is also what makes trust, in addition to accountability, a central issue in the analysis of governance (see Höpfl, in this volume). Consideration of the politico-ethical significance of bureaucracy is congruent with Weber's insistence that 'the bureau must be assessed...as a particular *moral institution* and that the ethical attributes of the bureaucrat [should] be viewed as the contingent and often fragile achievements of that socially organized sphere of moral existence' (du Gay 2000: 4, emphasis added). These 'ethical attributes', I will suggest, are closely associated with the rise of formal rationality, insofar as it requires a subordination of personal preferences and allegiances to the calculations of procedural decision-making.

Formal rationality underpins the ethos of modern bureaucracy, which includes the principle of procedural fairness. Without this principle, employees, clients, and customers would be subject to the arbitrary exercise of power that could be influenced only through personal connections or the routine use of bribes. In effect, modern bureaucracy limits and inhibits such abuses. As Amy (2008) has argued, albeit in a rather hyperbolic tone:

> We should *want* bureaucrats to not treat people as individuals... Dealing with us impersonally is what guarantees that our treatment is not arbitrary, discriminatory or abusive... Abuses occur because officials are engaging in personal favouritism and not treating people the same according to a set of administrative procedures... we should try to remember that [impersonal treatment] is an important political safeguard of the modern democratic state.

In reflecting upon the ethical as well as the technical significance of formal rationality, I draw inspiration from Weber's abiding concern with illuminating 'the conduct of life' (see also du Gay, this volume), and more specifically his consideration of the conditions for '*the cultivation of individuals with "person-ality"*' (Ibid. ch. 1, emphasis added) in relation to '*the development of mankind*' (Hennis 1983: 135, emphasis added; see also Mommsen 1974). '*Personality*', it is worth stressing, has for Weber a specialist meaning that is very distant from populist associations with individualism and cults of personality. Weberian 'personality' is forged through a continuous struggle to live a life that is framed and informed by reason, yet critically is fully cognizant of a morally charged obligation recurrently to renew and enact a non-rational commitment to particular values. This struggle is, for Weber, a necessary condition of rendering the world meaningful and living with dignity.

Central to Weber's thinking, then, is the *politico-ethical* question of how the rise of modern formal rationality, exemplified in bureaucratic organization, enables or impedes a fulfilment of the understanding that

> life as a whole, if it is not to be permitted to run on as an event in nature but is instead to be consciously guided, is a series of ultimate decisions through which the soul... chooses its own fate, i.e. the meaning of its activity and existence. (Weber 1949: 18)

Weber, I will suggest, deploys 'bureaucracy' as a *concept* for the analytical purpose of examining modernity, its discontents and its possible futures. Engaged for analytical purposes, the value of bureaucracy as a concept is, for Weber, heuristic, not descriptive.[3] Weber also usefully notes that the impersonality of formal rationality is not necessarily accepted as rational from the perspective of individuals or groups who have their own specific, substantive values, including those derived from tradition or stirred by charisma. As he stresses, what counts as 'rational' is contingent upon an assessment of its relevance for the realization of particular values: 'a thing is never irrational in itself, but only from a particular... point of view' (Weber 1992: 35). The person who wants an office-holder in a bureaucracy to give priority to his or her case is likely to encounter resistance, become frustrated by the slowness of response, and to complain about the irrationality of a 'pettyfogging' system bound up in 'red tape'. Such frustrations inform and legitimize calls and crusades to introduce forms of 'post-bureaucracy'. In their quest for greater efficiency, these efforts tend to disregard the ethos and principles of modern bureaucracy.

The remainder of the chapter is organized into three major sections. The first explores aspects of bureaucracy and 'post-bureaucracy' as means of managing modernity. It emphasizes the centrality of formal rationality and the distinctive way in which the issue of delegation is addressed in modern bureaucratic organization. It also considers the 'variable geometry' of 'post-bureaucracy'. In the second section, the central concerns of this chapter are illustrated by reference to the provision of children's services by a UK local authority. Processes of decomposition and recomposition of bureaucracy within this organization highlight some dangers of 'post-bureaucratic' innovation. The third section sketches an alternative perspective on bureaucracy where the focus is upon the significance of formal rationality for bureaucratic governance and, more specifically, for its ethos. A discussion section and a conclusion complete the chapter.

Managing Modernity: Beyond Bureaucracy?

As other contributors to this volume, notably Reed, have suggested, the concept of bureaucracy is relevant for illuminating the distinctiveness of organizational governance. Practices of governance are here understood to articulate relations of power that became institutionalized. Yet, these relations never become fully institutionalized, since competing logics are also engaged— for example, in Weberian terms, the logics of tradition and charisma as well as legal rationality; and the sedimentation of these relations is subject to forces and 'events' that defy its control, including those that Selznick (1949: 253) terms 'the recalcitrance of the human tools of action'.[4] As he notes, the 'use of organizational instrumentalities is always to some degree precarious, for it is virtually impossible to enforce automatic responses to the desires or commands of those who must employ them' (Ibid.: 10). From this perspective, the exercise of power is not something confined to actions that escape or transgress formal procedures, positions, or structures. Rather, the formal rationality (imperfectly) institutionalized in the procedures and routines of modern organization is itself an articulation of power—in the sense that their engagement privileges the enactment and naturalization of particular social realities. The power vested in social practices or institutions is established and maintained hegemonically: it 'tends to become, but never achieves, a closed system' (Ibid.). Modern bureaucratic organization is unavoidably open to forces of dislocation, implosion, and subversion—as challenges posed by 'post-bureaucratic' thinking and interventions illustrate.

FORMAL RATIONALITY AND ITS DISCONTENTS

Given the (Weberian) understanding that formal rationality underpins the development of modern bureaucracy, it is appropriate to consider its distinctive characteristics. Formal rationality refers to *the calculability of means or procedures*, without regard to the substantive value of the ends or results of its application. Formal rationality is, for Weber, purely technical: it is concerned with calculating the most efficient means of attaining a given end according to the best available (scientific) knowledge. For Weber, formal rationality is distilled in scientific and technical knowledge; it is not derived from, nor guided by, the concerns or priorities of particular groups of actors. Indeed, Weber refers to formal rationality as objective rationality.

Applications of formal rationality are evident in disciplined industrial production and in dependable public administration. In principle, formal rationality provides the most systematic and efficient, or the least uncertain and unreliable, means of organizational control. Of critical importance to the reproduction of modern societies is the predictability of formal rationality, as institutionalized in the design and operation of their legal systems and other key elements of the state apparatus. The very operation of markets, which itself exemplifies the impersonality of formal rationality, is contingent upon the discipline and dependability made possible by the coercive authority supplied by the regulatory frameworks of modern states. As Weber (1998: 1,095) observes of 'industrial capitalism', it 'must be able to count on the continuity, trustworthiness and objectivity of the legal order, and on the rational, predictable functioning of legal and administrative agencies'. For investors and entrepreneurs, the state, and more specifically the legal system, ensures and legitimizes control over both the marketplace and the workplace, or what Weber (1992) terms 'the complete appropriation of all material means of production by owners' (Ibid.: 161). A measure of certainty (e.g. that devised by the architects of 'scientific management') and legal security provided by modern bureaucracy is required for entrepreneurs and investors to risk their time and (often borrowed) capital to create the means of expropriating wealth from productive labour.

With regard to the position of office-holders in public and private bureaucratic organizations, their actions are, according to Weber, routinely guided by the development of impersonal '*rational* rules . . . which meet with obedience as *generally binding norms*' (Weber 1978: 954, second emphasis added). Modern workplaces whose division of labour is based upon a reformed version of Scientific Management are underpinned by the calculations of formal rationality. This division of labour is 'essentially dependent upon the calculability of the most important technical factors [and] this means fundamentally that it is dependent on the peculiarities of modern science, especially the natural sciences based on mathematics and exact and rational experiment' (Weber 1992: 24). Principles of organizational design that ostensibly depart from, or even purport to overturn, Scientific Management do so by claiming to be more rational in virtue of being informed by a more sophisticated and comprehensive (social scientific) understanding of human behaviour. With the benefit of this superior knowledge, it is believed that 'all that stuff you have been dismissing for so long as the intractable, irrational, intuitive, informal organization can be managed' (Peters and Waterman 1982: 11).

The importance attached by Weber to '*binding norms*' is stressed here because, when advancing an analysis of modern organization that places the application of formal rationality at its centre, 'bureaucracy' is not reducible to an organization dominated by rules. As Weber puts it, 'rationally regulated association within a structure of domination finds its *typical* expression in *bureaucracy*' (Weber 1978: 954, first emphasis added). 'Typical' is not the same as universal or most potent. Forms of organization that are regarded as approximating Weber's ideal–typical bureaucracy (see above) may have been 'typical', especially at the time Weber was writing, but 'rationally regulated association' is not limited to such organizations. Organizations in which, for example, there is reliance upon a set of core norms, rather than a detailed set of rules and procedures, may be more *intensively* 'bureaucratic'—in the Weberian sense of being dominated by a logic of formal rationality that deploys these norms instrumentally, with a view to streamlining the means of established ends.

From this perspective, 'post-bureaucratic' features and forms of organization are, perhaps, better characterized as 'hyper-bureaucratic', at least with regard to technical considerations of the calculation of efficiency gains. This claim is, of course, counter-intuitive, since 'post-bureaucratic' innovations are championed as softening, if not radically subverting, organizations commonsensically characterized as 'bureaucratic'. 'Post-bureaucratic' organizational forms and mechanisms are typically held to replace specialization and detailed rule-following with increased teamwork and empowerment, greater involvement and what Heckscher (1994) terms 'interactive forms'. Be that as it may, the advocacy and introduction of such 'post-bureaucratic' innovation is supported by calculations based upon 'rational norms' (Weber 1978: 954) that show how improved performance or better value for money can be achieved.

Those who champion 'post-bureaucratic' innovation, such as the enthusiasts for NPM, emphasize its capacity to improve the efficiency of modern organization, and they largely exclude consideration of bureaucracy as a 'positive moral and ethical achievement' (du Gay 2000: 4). In 'post-bureaucratic' crusades, innovations and reforms that are ostensibly 'humanizing' generally aspire to establish a more condensed or rationalized mode of legal–rational domination that is unsupportive of, if not antithetical to, the bureaucratic ethos. Direct and oblique attacks on bureaucracy parallel the way politicians play upon populist sentiment. Critics of Mandarinism as well as enthusiasts for 'post-bureaucracy' tend to ignore or suppress the virtues of procedural fairness, probity, etc.[5] Advocates of 'post-bureaucracy' generally overlook the protection that, in principle, the much maligned 'pettifogging legalism and red tape' affords with regard to personal abuses of 'office' by evangelical executives or obstructive 'jobsworths'.[6] It is when rules are absent or ignored, and/or when the ethos of bureaucracy is weak, that 'personalization' expands to support or promote diverse kinds of 'goal displacement'—in the form of 'soldiering' (restriction of output), empire-building, patronage, etc., in addition to forms of corrupt and fraudulent activity.

The emphasis of this chapter is upon the contribution of formal rationality to substantive improvements in equity and probity, and its institutionalization in the ethos and principles of modern bureaucracy. But formal rationality incorporates an attentiveness to the consequences of its application: it includes a capacity to challenge and reform present as well as past practices. Scientific Management was accomplished through a critical assessment of the rational deficit attributed to reliance upon 'custom and practice'. In turn, Scientific Management was challenged when the application of formal rationality identified the greater efficiency of alternative—Human Relations and, more recently, 'post-bureaucratic'—ways of attaining established ends.

By hiring personnel or by selectively colonizing and adapting values and motivational techniques imported from the private sector, for example, it is anticipated that 'post-bureaucratic' innovations will cut through 'red tape', improve communication, revive flagging morale, etc. Such expectations are indebted to the calculations of formal rationality upon which modern bureaucracy is also founded. Yet, this shared indebtedness to formal rationality is unacknowledged by advocates of 'post-bureaucratic' reforms. When 'post-bureaucratic' innovations are prescribed or introduced, they are routinely presented as an antidote to bureaucracy, not as continuous with its dependence upon formal rationality. Reference to the principles and ethos of bureaucracy is, at best, muted when they are not unequivocally rejected as deserving of being 'banished' (Osborne and Plastrik 1997, cited by Clegg, in this volume). A one-sided preoccupation with efficiency tends to displace a concern for the ethos and principles of bureaucracy that are attentive to matters of probity and equity.

When whatever is associated with bureaucracy must be 'banished', continuity with its indebtedness to formal rationality cannot be openly acknowledged; and so it is consigned to the shadows of organizations. Post-bureaucratic innovations often either retain or require the construction of shadow systems of bureaucracy—for example, to specify and monitor outsourced contacts and/or to recuperate failings or abuses consequent upon the introduction of 'post-bureaucratic' reorganization. At worst, as we shall see in the Doncaster case (discussed in a later section), a 'post-bureaucratic' crusade may involve a removal of established systems without any effective replacement. What, then, is it about modern bureaucratic organization that merits preservation?

DELEGATION: THE MODERN BUREAUCRATIC SOLUTION

To mount a credible defence of the principles and ethos of modern bureaucracy requires an appreciation of the distinctiveness of the modern, bureaucratic 'solution' to the problem of governing collective organization. The productive power of all forms of collective organization relies upon some division of labour entailing a delegation of power to undertake a bounded range of tasks or duties. These activities incorporate degrees of discretion together with devices for shaping and limiting its exercise. Where power is directed to, and secured by, monopolizing control over material and symbolic resources, there is a recurrent issue of how to regulate delegation of access to, and control of, those resources.

One possible response to the problem of delegation is to harness the loyalty vested in personal ties—for example, by mobilizing bonds of kinship—so as to minimize the risks of ineptitude and expropriation. Patronage is another way of inducing allegiance and obedience, thereby diminishing the hazard that 'delegates' will extend their discretion beyond what is productive for, or valued by, their patrons. Bureaucracy offers yet another, more impersonal, means of addressing the problem of delegation and associated exercise of discretion.

Perhaps the most distinctive and significant feature of modern bureaucracy is the strict separation of the conduct of the office from (*a*) the office-holder's personal preferences and allegiances (associated by Weber with an 'ethic of adjustment' or the 'mean', to be discussed later) or (*b*) the office-holder's private moral absolutisms (e.g. beliefs that certain actions are absolutely right or wrong, regardless of their consequences, a stance that Weber associates with an 'ethic of conviction', to be discussed later). Importantly, the separation of the activities of the office from the connections of its occupant extends to superiors within the chain of command who are responsible for the appointment or advancement of the office-holder. In principle, the holder of an office within a modern bureaucracy, whether in the public or the private sector, 'does not establish a relationship to a person, like the vassal's or disciple's faith under feudal or patrimonial authority, but rather is devoted to impersonal and functional purposes' (Weber 1978: 959). It is not only the design of the office, or set of offices, that is determined objectively according to the calculations of formal rationality. It is also the capabilities of the office-holder that are established on the basis of formal qualifications and relevant experience.

Objectivity of design and execution provides a distinctive, modern bureaucratic means of securing control of the productive power of (collective) organization. Forms and features of 'post-bureaucracy' signal an assessment that other organizing principles are being, or should be, incorporated to remedy the failings attributed to bureaucracy—that is, inflexibility, red tape, etc. As Clegg argues, the contemporary institutional complex of global capitalism—comprising 'chains, networks, alliances and collaborations' and facilitated by information and communication technologies (ICTs)—is corrosive of 'organization conceived on the old model of bureaucracy' (Clegg, in this volume). His observations illustrate how bureaucratic organization 'ain't (quite) what it used to be' as modern organization becomes entangled with, and supplanted by, new, 'post-bureaucratic' features and forms. On the basis of this assessment, Clegg suggests that 'the processes of organizing, the chains, links and networks, the politics of key performance indicators (KPIs), milestones, etc.' should become 'the salient theoretical objects' of inquiry (Ibid.: ch. 9).

Such a focus is indeed appropriate if contemporary developments in modern organization are to be adequately researched and critically scrutinized. A possible danger of following this advice, however, is that attentiveness to emergent 'objects' of analysis may detract from consideration of the bigger (historical and politico-ethical) picture. This picture includes the ethos of bureaucracy and its contribution to justice, and not least to the prospects of those whose lives are in the balance (Clegg 2002). Alternatively, Reed suggests that many 'post-bureaucratic' elements and processes 'retain, even selectively strengthen, formal control mechanisms . . . to achieve a workable degree of political stability under conditions of escalating complexity and instability' (Reed, in this volume). If this interpretation is followed, then innovations such as 'networks' and 'project management' are examined as extensions of, rather than as novel departures from, modern, bureaucratic organization(s), at least in respect of their role in sustaining the prevailing structure of domination. In pursuing this course, there is, however, a danger of focusing upon 'new' or 'hybrid' features of organization (to be discussed in the next section) in a way that again displaces or marginalizes an appreciation of the ethico-political significance of bureaucracy. To be clear, neither proposal excludes a focus upon the ethico-political significance of post-bureaucratic reforms, and there is no objection to empirical studies of the features and forms of organization widely characterized as 'post-bureaucratic'. Rather, my concern is to recall and make central the role of the ethos and principles of bureaucracy in minimizing discrimination, corruption, and so on.

FROM FIXED TO VARIABLE GEOMETRY

Regardless of the position taken on the question of 'continuity' or 'change' in organizing practices, evidence and arguments presented in the previous chapters suggest that contemporary work organizations, and especially in larger firms and public sector organizations, are incorporating elements that are not commonsensically 'bureaucratic', and are in *this* sense both novel and perplexing. 'Post-bureaucratic' developments have been conceptualized as a shift from a 'fixed' to a more 'variable geometry' of organization. Fixity is distinguished by 'standardized coordination', 'formalized procedures', and 'vertical chains of "command and control"' (Reed, in this volume). 'Variable geometry', by contrast, is discerned in the less familiar, less uniform organizational configurations that include 'dynamic interactions' and 'temporary accommodations through negotiated protocols between "switchers" positioned at the key connecting nodes within and between networks that rely on non-hierarchical modes of control' (Reed, in this volume). What kind of difference, or 'shift', is this?

When reflecting on changes in central government, Höpfl (in this volume) observes how innovations, such as task forces and special advisors, have been introduced to enhance, shake up, and perhaps circumvent time-honoured relations between politicians and civil servants, but without necessarily making any improvement in the accountability of the latter to the former, and ultimately to the electorate. Nor have they been conspicuously effective in strengthening relations of trust. Reform may have been intended but the main effect is continuity. Buchanan and Fitzgerald (in this volume) interpret experimentation with variable 'accessories' to a 'fixed geometry' as a supplement to, rather than displacement of, established forms of organization. In analyses of public and private sectors, processes of 'hollowing out' are identified where: activities deemed external to their main competences are outsourced (see chapter by Harris, in this volume); executive agencies (e.g. for prisons) are, in many cases, run by non-career civil servants on fixed term contracts who can be dismissed for underperforming (Höpfl, in this volume); and the application of bureaucratic control shifts from close and detailed management of productive activity to forms of output control where the focus is upon monitoring 'the numbers', often by acquiring companies with potential for short-term profitability (Ackroyd, in this volume). In these cases, there are stronger indications of change but, to repeat Reed's assessment, they may be interpreted as efforts to 'retain, even selectively strengthen, formal control mechanisms...to achieve a workable degree of political stability under conditions of escalating complexity and instability' (Reed, in this volume, chapter 10) to which, it might be added, those ostensibly streamlining measures often contribute.

What a focus upon change in *geometry*, or form, tends to displace, however, is whether changes are accompanied by a reaffirmation, or a neglect and devaluation, of the basic ethos and principles of modern organization. Where there is indifference or neglect, I suggest that a more likely outcome of reform is a displacement or decomposition of 'formal control mechanisms', with potentially damaging, and even disastrous, consequences. This assessment tends to be confirmed by examples where reform has resulted in 'complexity and instability' and loss of control that is perhaps better characterized as disorganization, if not chaos. That tendency is now illustrated by an example that became front-page news in the United Kingdom for several days during the preparation of this chapter.

'Tear Down the Barriers': Reorganizing Children's Services in Doncaster

In April 2009, in the village of Edlington near Doncaster, United Kingdom, two boys of 10 and 11 years old were sexually assaulted and tortured by two brothers of the same age. They barely escaped with their lives.[7] The brothers were from a family that had been known for fourteen years to the authorities, including the children's department at Doncaster Council, who had failed to intervene on thirty-one occasions. Since 2004, seven young people in the Doncaster area have died as a consequence of abuse or neglect.

Doncaster is situated in a comparatively deprived area of northern England with a very high level of referrals to its children's department. Services have been stretched and it has been difficult to recruit staff. That said, it will be suggested that these long-standing difficulties were compounded, not eased, by a 'post-bureaucratic' crusade, launched in 2005, to correct problems (of fragmentation and remoteness) attributed to bureaucracy. Core bureaucratic principles were set aside or neglected and the bureaucratic ethos was apparently abandoned or severely eroded. A Serious Case Review into the death of one child, which occurred in 2007, refers to a 'chaotic and dangerous situation' that had developed in Doncaster's provision of children's services (Booth 2009).

The case came to my attention as a consequence of intense media interest in the vicious nature of the attack by the young brothers. The headline 'Pie Man Was Child Safety Chief', caught my eye when it appeared on the front page of the *Sunday Times*. It was reported that:

The official in charge of protecting the children at the local authority . . . was a former food factory manager who has admitted that he had no 'relevant experience' . . . Hodson joined [Doncaster] council as part of a shake-up and presided over the children's department for two years. During this time, the circumstances of neglect and abuse in which the two children were being raised were allowed to fester until they launched their attack. (Foggo and Swinford 2010a: 1–2)

The newspaper report led me to start digging around on the Internet for more information. To my surprise—as little of the following had been unearthed by reporters on the case—a considerable amount of material was accessible, though dispersed and time-consuming to uncover. This public domain material is pieced together to provide a case study of the post-bureaucratic decomposition and subsequent recomposition of the Doncaster Council children's department.

FROM PIES TO CHILDREN'S SERVICES

It was in May 2005 that Doncaster Council announced the appointment of Mr Mark Hodson (the 'Pie Man') as 'Strategic Director for Neighbourhoods, Communities and Children's Services'. With something of a fanfare, it is noted that he 'joins the public sector with significant senior experience in the private sector, leading a portfolio of businesses in the Fast Moving Consumer Goods market dealing with the top five retailers in the country' (Doncaster Council eNews 2005). I then unearthed an interview given by Hodson to a major national newspaper, the *Daily Telegraph*, a year after his appointment in which he says:

'I came from a very values-driven environment, and part of the change agenda at Doncaster MBC is about driving a change to the culture of the organisation to one which puts the needs of its residents, our customers, at the heart of all decision-making'. He continues: 'We are doing this by *moving away from a traditional "silo" structure to one which is decentralised, with locally based area and neighbourhood teams who are delivering the breadth of council services out in their specific areas* . . . We have restructured the borough into five areas and 15 neighbourhoods to facilitate this new model of working.' (Baker 2006, emphasis added)

After two years in post (May 2005–July 2007), Hodson had an offer to return to his previous employment. He is reported to have said that he was under no pressure to leave Doncaster Council, and that he would not have resigned his position (for which he received a salary in excess of £100,000) if he had not received the offer (Foggo and Swinford 2010*b*). The *Sunday Times* article continues:

Hodson added that he had not paid any attention to the Edlington case the official report that has been so damning about the department that he used to run. He said 'I haven't read anything about the case and I probably won't...' Tim Leader, interim chief executive at Doncaster council, said: 'At the time there was no need for a qualified social worker to be a director of children's services' (Ibid.: 2).

The purpose of this example is not to criticize or blame the 'Pie Man' for applying for, and taking, a job for which he had no 'relevant experience', having previously been employed at Unilever, Unigate, and Asda. Nor is the point to highlight what might be regarded as Hodson's callousness in paying no attention to a horrific case of neglect and abuse that, arguably, could have been avoided, or at least mitigated, if actions had been taken during the period of his tenure by the department for which he was the responsible Director. After all, Hodson did not write the job description; he did not recruit consultants to scour the private sector for suitable candidates; he did not make the appointment decision; and he did not determine that he could continue to be employed at Doncaster for two years before returning to the private sector. Nor, finally, was Hodson the architect of the reorganization at Doncaster (to be discussed below).

Rather than to blame or scapegoat the 'Pie Man', the purpose of this example is to illustrate what can happen when key elements of bureaucracy—such as possession of relevant qualifications for undertaking the duties of a post and then ensuring that the appointed candidate is relevantly qualified and competent to ensure the safe operation of the children's department—are 'decomposed'. Phrases such as 'moving away from a silo culture', 'putting customers as the heart of all decision-making', 'decentralizing into neighbourhood teams' are redolent of 'post-bureaucracy'-speak. As argued earlier, they are potentially consistent with the drive of formal rationality to calculate improved means of attaining existing means. But, when the underpinnings of bureaucratic ethos and principles are neglected, a likely outcome is an escalation of the pathologies of bureaucracy—in the form of paralysis and disorganization—without remedial virtues.

EFFECTS OF THE POST-BUREAUCRATIC CRUSADE

One measure of the impact of the 'post-bureaucratic' crusade launched in 2005 was that, by summer of 2007, no less than a third of the children's social services workforce at Doncaster were agency workers (Ahmed 2009). This situation was directly commented upon in the Special Case Review of the attack on the two boys, where it is judged that 'high reliance on interim and temporary staff at all levels also undermined consistent and safe working' (Doncaster Safeguarding Children Board 2010). A lengthy (unpublished) report written by the former specialist change director at Doncaster Council and published in March 2007, just prior to Hodson's departure, supplied further details of the severity of the problems associated with the provision of children's services:

Filing systems are seriously inadequate, with loose papers, unstructured files and files kept on window ledges and in piles on desks. There is no systematic signing in and out of files and there are numerous examples of case files and papers going missing. Files are transferred between teams by any worker who happens to be around 'chucking them in the back of their car'. This situation is clearly unacceptable from a data protection aspect and because the information is essential to enable safe case management and decision making. (Slack 2009, quoting directly from the Report)

The Serious Case Review of the attack by the brothers also notes that 'the reorganization of council services in 2005 caused disruption to the delivery of core services... The lines of accountability were insufficiently clear and robust'. With regard to the 2005 reorganization of services into neighbourhood teams, the report comments that 'the introduction of antisocial behaviour strategies and locating them in neighbourhood teams had not ensured clear enough working arrangements with other parts of the council' (Doncaster Safeguarding Children Board 2010). This failing was, arguably, a consequence of a devaluation of the ethos of bureaucracy associated with the reorganization led by the Chief Executive, Susan Law, who had been appointed in 2004 and who, in her announcement of her plans, declared the intention to 'tear down the barriers between different council departments' (Doncaster Council eNews 2004). In the absence of an ethos strong enough to withstand this onslaught, it would appear that communications broke down between the newly formed neighbourhood teams and other parts of the council. The Doncaster case suggests that greater recognition and nurturing of the virtues of the bureaucratic ethos might have significantly reduced the risks visited upon its children.

In his chapter in this volume, Clegg commends a perspective that accommodates narratives of change and continuity by interpreting contemporary reforms of bureaucracy as involving moments of decomposition and recomposition. With regard to the Doncaster case, the process of decomposition can be traced back to April 2004 when Martin Winter, Doncaster's elected Mayor, recruited Susan Law, who had previously been employed in Adelaide. For reasons that will be come clear (see esp. note 9), it is not irrelevant to note that Ms Law had resigned her position in Adelaide following a conflict with the Mayor (Adelaide Review 2004).[8] Winter, the Mayor of Doncaster, instructed Law to 'shake up the Council' (Prodger 2009).

In December 2004, Law announced a new structure for Doncaster social services. She said that the new 'structure gives much greater clarity of role and ensures collaborative working and customer focus right from strategy meetings to the doorsteps of the people we serve' (Doncaster Council eNews 2004). And she emphasized that 'its main priority is not cost-cutting or middle-management bashing, but putting the kind of leadership in place which empowers council staff to make common sense decisions which benefit residents' (Ibid.). There are strong strains in this announcement of the 'post-bureaucratic' aspiration of NPM to 'shake up' the public sector, making it more efficient by introducing private sector values and techniques. It would seem that the new Chief Executive was very much a devotee of NPM, since she was intent, or perhaps even hell-bent, on decomposing established vertical and horizontal divisions and associated lines of accountability, so as to 'empower' employees and 'benefit residents'. The 'Pie Man' was one of new team of senior managers appointed by Ms Law to implement the reorganization.

After the assault on the two boys in Edlington became front-page news, Ed Balls, the central government Minister responsible for children's services, was interviewed on the BBC. He identified Ms Law's reorganization as the primary source of the problems at Doncaster: 'I think what had happened was, there was a re-organisation in Doncaster of children's services ... that went badly wrong; that led to the problems which were identified in 2008' (Balls 2010). What the Minister omitted to mention is that the 'chaos' attributed to Ms Law's reorganization had been anticipated by the Pie Man's predecessor, Sharon Docherty. Docherty had resigned in 2005 in protest at Law's reorganization plans. When interviewed by a BBC journalist in March 2009, she said that she had told her superiors in 2005 that children would be unsafe and would die as a consequence of the absence of clear lines of responsibility and accountability in the new structure: 'they were so fudged as to be nonexistent, certainly as far as frontline workers were concerned' (Prodger 2009).[9] A year later, Ms Docherty's assessment was vindicated in the summary of the Serious Case Review undertaken into the attack on the two boys (Doncaster Safeguarding Children Board 2010).

Ms Docherty's criticisms of the Council were elaborated in another interview given to the Doncaster Free Press in April 2009. There she is reported as saying that 'the post that included children's services in its responsibility [to which Mark Hodson was appointed] was originally called director of neighbourhoods and communities and only later had "and children's services" tagged on [and that] a legally-required appointment of a manager for the safeguarding of children in education was "downgraded" and "diluted" with other tasks' (Mason 2009). In this interview, Ms Docherty also alleges that with regard to the reorganization of children's services between 2004 and 2006, central government did not check that Doncaster was implementing statutory posts. A month earlier, in March 2009, and following a report by

Ofsted (Office for Standards in Education, Children's Services, and Skills) into the Doncaster children's department which identified serious weaknesses (Ofsted 2008), Ed Balls intervened to recompose the provision of children's services at Doncaster. He imposed a new senior management team, overseen by an external improvement board reporting directly to him. Set out in a fifty-four-page document, the strategic aims of the improvement plan

'are directly linked to statutory and local performance indicators. Clear milestones underpinning the actions will provide short, medium and long term aims. Progress reporting against both actions and the performance indicators will evaluate the delivery of the improvement plan and this will be reported on an exceptions basis. The Director of Children's Services will report progress against the plan at each Improvement Board meeting' (Doncaster Council 2009)

In short, the plan involves a recuperation and recomposition of bureaucratic principles that had been devalued and eroded during the reorganization of children's services. What is less clear is whether this strengthening of formal control mechanisms incorporates any recognition of, or any concern to revitalize, the role played by a vibrant bureaucratic ethos.

DECOMPOSITION AND RECOMPOSITION

With regard to wider and less pathological processes of decomposition than those exhibited in Doncaster, information and communication technologies (ICTs) can be seen to facilitate new forms of social production in which hierarchy and bureaucracy are reduced as network forms come to predominate (Kallinikos, in this volume; Ackroyd, in this volume). Another example of decomposition is where consultants and executives develop and cultivate differing ways of doing business by, for example, favouring distinctive 'personnel concepts' (Alvesson and Karreman, in this volume). In the Doncaster case, Ms Law appointed consultants 'to push through restructuring and reforming the culture of the council' (Waugh 2006; see also note 9) with what turned out to be very serious consequences. The decomposing effects of her reorganization of services at Doncaster were then checked and reversed by the intervention of central government in the form of an imposed senior management team and improvement board.

This brings us to 'recomposition'. Processes of recomposition intentionally or unintentionally extend and strengthen bureaucratic organization, and not necessarily in ways that merit unequivocal disapproval (Buchanan and Fitzgerald, in this volume). ICTs do not necessarily replace forms of 'fixed geometry' when, for example, they are used to monitor and enforce complex administrative procedures such as service level agreements (SLAs) developed between purchasers and providers for controlling outsourced activities. Most market and quasi-market forms of regulation, whether in the management of supply chains or for outsourced services, rely upon systems of monitoring that tend to fall back upon bureaucratic procedures, and may actively spawn them, rather than diminish their use or effects (see Harris, in this volume). Procedures widely identified as bureaucratic—such as the ostensibly patient-centred clinical guidelines applied to the work of health-care professionals—are introduced and elaborated to supplement and/or weaken forms of self-regulation by occupational groups (see Speed, in this volume). Radical reform of government administration, such as the Next Steps programme, is heralded as an enterprising alternative to an established bureaucratic mode of gover-nance, yet 'it relies for its effects on new kinds and levels of bureaucratization' (du Gay 2004: 53). More generally, what has been termed 'bureaucracy-lite' (Hales 2002) retains some bureaucratic principles while it marginalizes others. The resulting forms of 'post-bureaucracy' tend to be broadly, if not fully, consistent with a logic of hierarchical control, albeit that monitoring of perfor-mance replaces compliance with detailed rules. The casualty is the ethos of bureaucracy that tends to be ignored or diluted in the process of change. It is therefore relevant to reflect upon the (historical) making of modern bureaucra-cy, before considering in more depth its significance as a moral achievement and, more specifically, the plausibility of the claim that formal rationality, enacted in bureaucracy, is predicated 'on what we might term a positive, statist, "ethics of responsibility"' (du Gay, in this volume, chapter 1).

Rethinking Bureaucracy: Enter Morality

So far, the focus of this chapter has been predominantly on formal rationality and its articulation in modern society, especially in work organization(s), identified as 'bureaucracies'. Bureaucratic methods of production and admin-istration involve specialization and careful limitation of positions or 'offices'. Functionalist thinking attributes these divisions—vertical as well as horizontal—to the efficiency of their means in achieving ends *per se*. Weber is more sceptical. He attends to such divisions as (imperfect) articulations of formal rationality, and he thereby raises the question of their substantive rationality.

The 'other' of formal rationality is substantive rationality. Substantive rationality refers to what actors perceive or assess to be rational in the light of their own values. For example, resistance by workers and managers to the application of the principles of 'Scientific Management' or to the application of 'rational norms' (Weber 1978: 954), in the guise of a few core values, indicates the presence of substantive rationalities that deviate from the orga-nizational articulation of formal rationality. Substantive rationality moves recalcitrant actors to oppose, subvert, or conditionally accommodate the disciplinary requirements of formal rationality. Consider the application of formal rationality in the principles of Scientific Management. Reluctant managers may begrudge its restrictions on their personal discretion; and their subordinates may resent and resist the regimentation of their work when it deprives them of opportunities for self-determination and conviviality. In different ways, workers and managers may contest the consequences of applications of formal rationality to the workplace when it offends or impedes the realization of the substantive rationality embedded in their own value-commitments.

THE MODERN 'STRUCTURE OF DOMINANCY' AND THE LIMITS OF FORMAL RATIONALITY

Weber conceives of formal rationality as an outcome, as well as a medium, of an emergent, modern 'structure of dominancy'. He argues that 'the structure of dominancy... is decisive in determining the form of social action' (Weber 1978: 941) and that it 'has played the decisive role particularly in the most important social structures of the past and present, viz., the manor on the one hand, and the large scale capitalistic enterprise on the other' (Ibid.). This implies that the improved functionality of organizations resulting from the application of formal rationality is subordinate to, and conditioned by, the value of this principle in reproducing a modern mode of domination.

From this perspective, the key to making sense of modern ('bureaucratic') methods of production and administration is therefore ultimately not to be found in their claimed functionality, but rather in the articulation and reproduction of a distinctive 'structure of dominancy' that such methods promise to maintain and expand. From this (radical) Weberian standpoint, the application of formal rationality is seen to be contingent upon its mobilization in struggles to change or preserve the status quo. Within a modern 'structure of dominancy', there are currents of resistance as well diverse logics of organization so it is to be expected that 'bureaucracy takes a plurality of forms depending on context and purpose' (du Gay 2004: 53). The actual forms of bureaucracy 'occurring in historical reality' rarely, if ever, correspond to any 'ideal-type' specification. Rather, they 'constitute combinations, mixtures, adaptations, or modifications of "pure" types' (Weber 1978: 954).

When analysed from this perspective, the 'social actions' of the occupants of positions within public and private bureaucracies are studied in relation to the structure of dominancy that renders their work meaningful and legitimate. Formal rationality is of foremost significance in the development of modern organizations, but the actions of organizational members are not reducible to its application. As noted earlier, within organizations dominated primarily by 'rational rules', there are generally elements and residues of logics based upon 'personal authority' founded either in 'the sacredness of tradition', or upon a belief in the charisma of the 'person as a saviour, a prophet, or a hero' (Ibid.: 945), in addition to expressions of careerism, cynicism, politicking, etc. The rules embedded and interpreted within the modern 'structure of dominancy' incorporate hybrid elements, not least because of efforts to colonize 'personal' qualities in order to sustain or fortify administrative potency.

As a consequence of the inherent impurity of bureaucratic organization, in addition to inherent ambiguity and uncertainty, the exercise of judgement and discretion is not only functionally necessary but forms an integral part of the duties of the office. Work in modern organizations—for example, processing inquiries (Zimmerman 1971) or evaluating subordinates' performance (Clegg and Courpasson 2004: 529)—is rarely reducible to following a rule. Indeed, as has often been remarked, 'if everyone really followed the rules... the system would grind to a halt. Indeed, the unions have long demonstrated the effectiveness of the tactic of "working to rule"—following the formal structure to a T' (Heckscher 1994: 21). And, as a consequence, 'informal' media and resources are mobilized to remedy this limitation. 'Bureaucracy' is, in this sense, unavoidably 'personalized' (Ibid.) as it incorporates 'intersubjectively shared governmentality' as well as 'externally imposed regulation' (Clegg and Courpasson 2004: 529). Conversely, and with regard to 'post-bureaucratic' innovations, 'detailed regulations, record keeping and provision of information in standardized formats', etc. are 'crucial constitutive feature(s)' (du Gay 2004: 53) of many ostensibly 'post-bureaucratic' practices. If this is accepted, then it becomes difficult to maintain a clear division between 'bureaucracy' and 'post-bureaucracy', in that the latter routinely relies upon the former as well as being an outcome of the more extensive application of formal rationality.

The key point is that 'bureaucracy' already incorporates aspects of organization that tend to be attributed to 'post-bureaucracy'. Where the calculations of formal rationality prevail, 'intersubjectively shared governmentality' (Clegg and Courpasson 2004: 529) tends to be evaluated, legitimized, and disciplined primarily, though not of course exclusively, by reference to the calculations of formal rationality—that is, by rationally assessing its merits by reference to its contribution to improving the means of attaining existing ends. In Zimmerman's words (1971: 238), the 'judgemental work' of office-holders provides for 'the reasonableness of viewing particular actions as essentially satisfying the provisions of the rule', even though this departs from idealized versions of sociologists' ideas of 'the behavioural acts prescribed or proscribed by the rule'. In other words, office-holders' actions are routinely guided and legitimated not by rules *per se* but, rather, by a '*system of rational norms*' (Weber 1978: 954, emphasis added).[10]

FORMAL RATIONALITY IN 'POST-BUREAUCRACY'

It is only when the institutional embeddedness of 'bureaucracy' and 'post-bureaucracy' is disregarded that their uniformity and distinctiveness are assumed or exaggerated. Contingency and diversity is washed out when a universal (e.g. 'ideal–typical') formulation of bureaucracy is taken as a literal or descriptive benchmark for determining its existence or demise. Anything deemed to depart from some 'ideal–typical' specification is then seized upon as 'post-bureaucratic'. Before rushing to this judgement, it is prudent to recall the pervasiveness of a principle of modern bureaucracy—that is, the separation of the tasks comprising an office or work role from the personal allegiances and moral enthusiasms of the office-holder. It is precisely this separation that makes it comparatively easy to redesign and reconfigure roles in response to changing circumstances without requiring a change of personnel. The separation of the duties of office from the personal allegiances of the office-holder is a condition of possibility for undertaking *inter alia* 'diffuse tasks that demand the constant redesigning of jobs' (Kallinikos 2004: 24) associated with so-called 'post-bureaucratic' developments and organizational forms. Even where 'post-bureaucratic' innovations disregard or subvert this key principle of bureaucracy, they also depend upon it.[11]

At the same time, it is important to recognize the existence of work organization(s) that are minimally governed by bureaucratic principles. Even so, in a context where formal rationality is privileged, organizations are susceptible to pressures to introduce these principles, and arguably for better as well as for worse. Consider *Google* which is often celebrated, or at least fantasized,[12] as a new, post-bureaucratic organization. Even with the benefits of the most advanced ICTs, *Google*'s operation is accompanied by a specialized division of labour and many recognizable features of bureaucratic governance (see Google 2010*a*).

The Case of *Google*

Seven years after being established in 1997, the company 'formalized our enterprise unit with the hire of Dave Girouard as general manager' (Google 2010*b*), a move that was (not coincidentally) immediately preceded by its initial public offering (IPO). More recently, the CEO of *Google* is reported to have said that the goal of the company is to 'use "metrics of performance" to "systematize" every aspect of its operations' (Carr 2007: 4). Part of this process has involved 'ordering its innovation teams to focus upon fewer initiatives' (Ibid.), which implies that *Google* engineers could not be trusted with how they devote the 20 per cent of their time reserved for 'pet projects with little corporate oversight' (Ibid.). Such areas of discretion have become subject to (bureaucratic) audit and performance measurement. As Weber would have anticipated, these interventions do not necessarily address or rectify the shortcomings (e.g. lack of innovation) that they are introduced to correct (see Harris, in this volume), but they do send a clear and reassuring signal to stock analysts and fund managers.

Developments at *Google* illustrate how 'post-bureaucratic' features are promoted and accommodated to enhance existing means of attaining given ends, in the form of innovation as an engine of growth and profitability. When this calculation is found wanting in terms of desired outcomes, another calculation is made that results in tighter direction and monitoring of the activity (see Levy 2007). A recurrent issue is one of the organization of delegation and discretion in the face of a (moral) deficit of trust (see Höpfl, in this volume). In the case of *Google*, it is not difficult to imagine its engineers using the company's resources to develop ideas and products that are assessed by managers to be of little immediate relevance to its businesses or, if sufficiently promising, these ideas are then developed independently (Lashinsky 2008). *Google* is now attempting to make this more difficult by requiring engineers to enter all their ideas on a shared database (Groysberg et al. 2009).[13]

As 'post-bureaucratic' features and forms are introduced, it is not entirely 'business as usual' as there is a relentless search for more formally rational means of doing business 'across manufacturing, private and public services... while retaining a capacity for formalization and central control' (Thompson and Alvesson 2005: 104). Increased teamworking and 'self-management', reduced hierarchical layers, greater 'informalization', and the introduction of quasi-internal markets mean that bureaucracies 'ain't what they used to be'. Experimentation with self-managing 'Trust' hospitals, the use of quasi-market mechanisms, the introduction of performance league tables, etc. in the UK National Health Service illustrate what has been described as 'a bureaucratic revolution' (Le Galès and Scott 2010). Yet, formal rationality continues to inspire and infuse such 'post-bureaucratic' practices of organizing.

Elements of 'post-bureaucracy' are commended and celebrated for counteracting the effects of eliminating 'from official business love, hatred, and all purely personal and emotional elements that escape calculation' (Weber 1978: 975). Yet, 'post-bureaucratic' innovation is itself deeply calculative with regard to the 'personal and emotional elements' that are to be accommodated or nurtured, and what forms of 'love' (e.g. of product) or 'hatred' (e.g. of competitors) are to be promoted or at least countenanced. When encouraged and developed within modern work organizations, 'post-bureaucratic' elements take on the form of *simulacra*: their inclusion and expression is tolerated or even rewarded only insofar as they are assessed to provide more attractive and/or effective means of attaining established corporate ends. The transformational zeal displayed in such 'restless' organizations threatens to despatch the sacred cows of tradition and unforced affect with at least as much speed as those that demand strict adherence to rules; and, in the pursuit of such transformation, elements of charismatic authority are routinely harnessed to provide personalized legitimacy for the domination of the formal rationality distilled in 'rational norms', rather than offering an alternative to them. It is from this perspective that much project management, for example, is plausibly characterized as involving 'the refurbishment of bureaucratic procedures rather than their renunciation' (Clegg and Courpasson 2004: 542).

MORALITY AND THE UPSIDE OF FORMAL RATIONALITY

The formal rationality institutionalized in modern, bureaucratic organizations and the substantive rationality expressed in the value-commitments of office-holders may coincide, or they may be engineered to converge. Employees may be inclined, be prepared, or be induced, to embrace and enact the prescriptions of formal rationality when, for example, managers and/or their subordinates become converts of the objective rationality of Scientific Management and its contemporary counterparts (e.g. Business Process Reengineering), or when public administrators come to identify with, and meticulously enact, 'post-bureaucratic' procedures. Reflecting on this prospect, Weber presents a nightmare vision in which the march of formal rationality within all modern(izing) institutions—churches no less than banks—progressively drains social relations of all qualities associated with the formation of Weber's notion of 'personality'. In the absence of a countervailing force, he anticipates that each person will become increasingly like a 'small cog in a ceaselessly moving mechanism which prescribes to him [*sic*] an essentially fixed route to march' (Weber 1978: 988).

Two kinds of loss are seen to accompany the rise of formal rationality in modernity. First, there is a loss of opportunity to develop and express feelings that escape calculation. Second, and more profoundly, opportunities to develop what Weber terms 'personality' are stunted by a 'steady diffusion of a purely instrumental orientation [that] erodes ultimate value commitments and thereby threatens to subvert individual autonomy from within' (Brubaker 1984: 6). This erosion is illustrated by Clegg and Courpasson's project managers (2004: 542) who 'by pragmatically devoting their abilities to the destiny of their own project, effectively renounce any will to govern collective bodies. Their identities are tied up, literally, with their projects'. These are managers who have become completely identified with creating and lubricating cogs in the machine, and have no interest in, concern about, or control over, its overall purpose or effects.

Weber was deeply troubled by the demoralizing consequences of the spread of formal rationality but he also identifies a possible antidote. He was not resigned to 'metaphysical pathos' as he sought to highlight and analyse the tensions between formal and substantive rationalities—tensions that, arguably, are key to making sense of modernity and the on-going struggles to organize activity within it. The positive that Weber draws from the pervasive influence of formal rationality is its clarification of human beings' responsibility for the values with which they (we) endow the world with meaning. Domination based primarily upon tradition or charisma is seen to occlude such clarity. It is, as it were, taken care of by some higher authority. An effect of legal–rational domination, by contrast, is to compel a confrontation with the (existential) responsibility for endowing the world with meaning, including the meaning that guides the 'ultimate decisions through which the soul . . . chooses its own fate, i.e. the meaning of its activity and existence' (Weber 1949: 18).

When it comes to making choices, of deciding between alternative values, formal rationality (e.g. science) is, by its own reckoning, of limited value. It can inform the process that precedes the making of 'ultimate decisions'. But questions of 'how conflicts between several concretely conflicting ends are to be arbitrated', as Weber (1949: 19) puts it, are beyond rational calculation. 'There is no (rational or empirical) scientific procedure of any kind whatsoever which can provide us with a decision here' (Ibid.). Formal rationality *per se* has no answers for modern, disenchanted individuals, who are progressively deprived of the comforting certainties of tradition and the emotionally gratifying reassurances of charisma. Instead, it confronts them (us) with personal responsibility for whatever choices are made between competing value-commitments. In modernity where, as Marx and Engels put it, 'all that is solid melts into air, all that is holy is profaned', the only option is to identify and choose between available 'ethics' (see below), a choice which Weber associates with determining the 'fate' of 'the soul' (Weber 1949: 18). Three possibilities are identified by Weber: the ethics of 'adjustment', 'conviction', and 'responsibility'.

THREE ETHICS: ADJUSTMENT, CONVICTION, AND RESPONSIBILITY

The Ethic of Adjustment

How are these reflections relevant to the formation of bureaucratic principles and their application by 'bureaucrats'? Consider again the example of the project managers whose identities, according to Clegg and Courpasson (2004), 'are tied up, literally, with their projects' so that they 'effectively renounce any will to govern collective bodies' (Ibid.: 542). Their stance would seem to exemplify what Weber, echoing Nietzsche and anticipating Heidegger, terms an 'ethic of adjustment' (or of the 'mean') where ends (e.g. immediate material self-interest) are taken as uninterrogated givens, and the focus is exclusively upon refining the means.

When we subscribe to an 'ethic of adjustment', we take on whatever values are available and congruent with our immediate wants. Values are embraced with minimal reflection on their merits, or upon alternatives to them. If the adoption of particular values is subsequently experienced as incongruent with the satisfaction of our wants, an adjustment is made as other values are prioritized. When subscribing to an 'ethic of adjustment', we are comparatively unhindered by value commitments. Being expedient, such commitments can be readily replaced. Seemingly, the individual who adopts, or is adopted by, an 'ethic of adjustment' is free, unconstrained by any particular or enduring commitments. Yet, from an alternative perspective, s/he is seen to be tossed around by, and enslaved to, immediate preferences and inclinations.

Adopting an 'ethic of adjustment' is, as Weber (1949) puts it, comparable to 'run(ning) on as an event in nature' (Ibid.: 18) and is antithetical to the development of human 'personality' in the Weberian sense of the term. It is illustrated by abuses of their office by self-serving executives, careerists, cynics, and 'jobsworths' who, disregarding the ethos of bureaucracy, satisfy their immediate material self-interests (as entertainingly caricatured in *The Office* persona of David Brent). The 'ethic of adjustment' is incompatible with the discipline of the bureaucratic ethos, which demands that office-holders commit themselves to performing their duties rather than deriving self-centred gratifications from positions that they occupy.

The Ethic of Conviction

An alternative to the 'ethic of adjustment' is the 'ethic of conviction'. When embracing this ethic, the person has the compass of a resolute commitment to some ultimate value—a value that is chosen in relation to alternative ultimate values. For Weber, this choice, or series of affirming choices, is the basis for the development of 'personality'.

When adhering to an 'ethic of conviction', we strive to exemplify our chosen ultimate value(s) in all aspects of their lives and without regard for their effects. The distinctiveness of the 'ethic of conviction' is that we fully and unconditionally embody whatever value(s) we have embraced. Within this ethic, there is no space for the calculations of formal rationality. Once a commitment to a specific ethic is made, its consequences are ethically irrelevant. Since subscription to this ethic requires that the convictions of the office-holder coincide with performing the duties of the office, its enactment is difficult to reconcile with the application of bureaucratic principles.

The Ethic of Responsibility

The other alternative to the 'ethic of adjustment' is the 'ethic of responsibility'. When embracing this ethic, we are no less committed to an ultimate value than is the person whose actions are guided by an 'ethic of conviction'. The difference is that the choice of the means of its realization is tempered by considerations of consistency with the anticipated consequences of alternative courses of action. The 'ethic of responsibility' incorporates the application of formal rationality in the calculations that are made to identify and minimize incongruent outcomes. It is therefore consistent with modern bureaucratic organization. Indeed, du Gay (in this volume) concludes by suggesting that the formal rationality which infuses 'governmental administration', at least, is predicated upon a 'positive, statist "ethics of responsibility"' (Ibid.: ch. 1).

THE ETHIC OF RESPONSIBILITY AND THE MORAL ACHIEVEMENT OF THE DILIGENT OFFICE-HOLDER

The demands of bureaucratic office, such as adhering to procedure rather than relying upon personal convictions or treating the office as a private asset, are ethically significant. It is wholly implausible to regard and represent office-holders, or at least *diligent* office-holders, as '*amoral* technical expert(s)' (du Gay 2000: 28, emphasis added). *Proficient* execution of their duties repeatedly requires office-holders to uphold procedural fairness in the face of pressures, internal as well as external, to deviate from the ethos and principles of impersonality and impartiality. The disciplined subordination of 'one's ego to procedural decision-making', as Hunter (1994: 157, cited in du Gay 2000: 32) puts it, is a deeply painstaking process. Developing 'the disposition and ability to conduct [oneself] according to the ethos of a bureaucratic office' (du Gay 2000: 28) is no mean moral achievement.

Ethical discipline is a requirement for any administration to operate effectively and reliably with minimal subversion by self-centredness, favouritism, greed, cynicism, and so on. Effective bureaucratic organization 'presupposes an ethical formation on the part of the bureaucrat, a bureaucratic vocation, as opposed to a more or less blind obedience to rules and orders' (Osborne 1994: 309). If office-holders do not set aside personal allegiances and convictions that are extraneous to the objective of diligently undertaking the duties of their office, then equity and consistency are compromised. It is this end, or 'ultimate value', in the form of 'commitment to the purposes of the office' (du Gay, in this volume, chapter 1), that the *dedicated* bureaucrat dutifully serves. Working diligently as an office-holder involves a distinctive kind of ethical discipline and commitment to upholding the ethos and principles of bureaucracy. It is for this reason that the vocation of the office, as Weber characterizes it, should not be viewed as a 'subtraction from the "complete" (self-realizing) comportment of the person' (du Gay 2000: 32). It is simplistic and inappropriate to assess the ethics of the bureaucratic office-holder against some other (e.g. humanistic) formulation of 'ultimate value' as a basis for castigating such dedication as 'bad faith'. An obvious question raised by this assessment is: what does the diligent bureaucrat do when a directive is received from a superior that s/he regards as illegitimate or wrong? Weber's answer is unequivocal:

An official who receives a directive which he considers wrong can and is supposed to object to it. If his superior insists on its execution, it is his duty, even his honour to carry it out as if it corresponded to his innermost conviction, and to demonstrate in this fashion that his sense of duty stands above his personal preference... This is the ethos of the office. (Weber 1994, cited in du Gay, in this volume, chapter 1; see also the quotation from Weber that opens this chapter)

Weber clearly rejects any suggestion that the principles of bureaucratic organization are honoured and properly applied when office-holders automatically carry out instructions and refrain from voicing any objection. To do so would be to exemplify an 'ethic of adjustment' or of 'conviction' (so long as the instruction is compatible with personal conviction). Enacting the bureaucratic ethos demands of the diligent office-holder that s/he assess the legitimacy of directives, not simply accept them or follow only those that accord with his or her convictions. The ethos of the office requires the bureaucrat to raise objections when 'receiving a directive that s/he considers wrong' (Ibid.)—not because it offends personal convictions but because it is assessed to deviate from due process and/or to transgress the ethos of the office.

If the objection is then overruled by a superior, the ethos of the office is upheld and preserved by setting aside the challenge and carrying out the instruction 'as if it corresponded to [the office-holder's] innermost conviction' (Ibid.). The justification for this resides in the importance of maintaining the integrity of the bureaucratic process as this would be rapidly corrupted if office-holders took matters into their own hands by refusing to carry out any instruction to which they personally objected, rather than raising the issue with their superior. Needless to say, the discipline required of the office-holder is exceptionally demanding, as there must be no trace of personal doubt or disapproval in how directives are executed. Otherwise, the principle of separating personal preferences from administrative duties is compromised. If the office-holder finds it impossible to establish or maintain this separation, then the only course of action consistent with the development of 'personality' is to blow the whistle or to resign; and then, if so inclined, the ex-office-holder can engage in a political struggle to expose the shortcomings of the bureau as a basis for defending and strengthening his or her commitment to the ethos. Once released from the obligations of the office, s/he is at liberty to seek alternative employment or to pursue another vocation, such as that of politics where personal beliefs are not only incorporated but form an important element in communicating a convincing, heart-felt message.

Discussion

Narratives, lay and scholarly, that refer to bureaucracy, including those to which this book contributes, necessarily mobilize value-laden assumptions and produce more or less intended effects (see also note 3). Scholarly narratives of 'bureaucracy'—whether interpreted as supportive, hostile or irrelevant, and whether focused upon its principles or its features—inform a wider process of (re)making and managing modernity. In doing so, they play an integral part in the collective reproduction or transformation of modern institutions that concepts, such as 'bureaucracy', aspire to render intelligible.

This chapter has recalled and explicated how the underpinning of modern bureaucracy by formal rationality has politico-ethical as well as technical significance. In circumstances where 'advances' in sciences and technologies are accompanied by escalating risks, it is difficult to imagine how the progressive elements of modern society can be sustained without renewing the ethos of bureaucracy. Devaluing this ethos may garner (probably short-lived) popular appeal; and it may please some office-holders by liberating them from the demands of the discipline required to fulfil their duties in an impersonal and reliable manner. But, as Weber warns, relaxation of this discipline foreshadows the disintegration of modern organization, as illustrated by the Doncaster case.

So long as the values of modernity are widely affirmed, albeit often cynically, the management of modernity is likely to require some rehabilitation of the bureaucratic form and the 'political safeguard(s)' (Amy 2008) provided by the ethos and principles of modern bureaucracy. Whilst the guardians of modern institutions often encourage some populist bashing of bureaucracy (Guardian 2009), the Doncaster case illustrates the ways in which those in authority may act to restore and defend bureaucratic principles when 'post-bureaucratic' innovations have disrupted and disordered the reliable delivery of services.

On the other hand, if the creation of a *post-modern* society is the ultimate value—in the sense of a developing a society that is comparatively unindebted to, and unencumbered by, formal rationality—then the elimination of the ethos of bureaucracy, or hastening its largely unrecorded erosion, will be welcomed. This prospect speaks to Weber's identification of the limits of formal rationality, even when it is articulated through an 'ethic of responsibility' rather than an ethic of 'adjustment' or 'conviction'. A regressive effect of the rigorous application of formal rationality is a solidification and legitimation of existing inequalities and an associated endorsement of the neo-liberal mantra that, economically and politically, there are No Alternatives. Reflecting upon the effects of formal legal equality for disadvantaged (e.g. 'propertyless') members of modern societies, Weber observes that

The property-less masses . . . are not served by the formal 'equality before the law' and the 'calculable' adjudication and administration demanded by bourgeois interests. Naturally, in their eyes justice and administration should serve to equalize their economic and social life-opportunities in the face of the properties classes. *Justice and administration can fulfil this function only if they assume a character that is informal because 'ethical' with respect to substantive content.* (Weber 1978: 980, emphasis added)

Analysis of bureaucracy can stimulate debate on the extent to which we wish to retain and strengthen an ethos of impartiality in the governance of organization(s). Such debate might prompt questioning of whether the problems of maintaining the bureaucratic ethos signal the limits of modernity's promise. In turn, a growing awareness of these limits may stimulate increased experimentation with alternative, radically post-modern forms of sociation, such as those based, for example, upon ecocentricism as a deeply held conviction.

In the absence of a radical rethinking of the values of modernity, which include the premium placed upon a relentless, globally divisive, and unsustainable pursuit of economic growth, it is relevant to interrogate the coherence and viability of 'reforms' of bureaucratic organizations, such as the experiment in NPM visited upon Doncaster. Do such organizational innovations frustrate or facilitate the mobilization of formal rationality (calculability of means and procedures) in the service of substantive rationality (the determination of valued ends)?[14] In what circumstances do 'post-bureaucratic' innovations increase or impair awareness of the bureaucratic ethos of fairness, etc.? Do these developments nurture or marginalize the ethos amongst employees faced with changes in labour markets (e.g. high staff turnover, use of agency workers) and impending cut-backs in public services that result from unprecedented public borrowing to save the financial sector from the consequences of recklessness fuelled by high-powered incentives—incentives that, as Williamson (1999: 325) observes, 'are notably absent in the Weberian description of bureaucracy . . . because high-powered incentives place the fidelity of the system at risk'?

Weber's explication of the distinctive organizing principles of bureaucracy rests upon a clear and compelling logic: *if* a robust and reliable, fair and just, form of administration is valued, whether in the public or the private sector, *then* strict adherence to the core principles of bureaucracy is required. *If* minimizing corruption as well as incompetence in administration is valued, *then* the diligent application of bureaucratic principles provides the relevant means. As du Gay (2000: 2, emphases added) observes:

while we may sometimes experience *a sense of personal frustration* in our dealings with state bureaux, we might learn to see such frustration as a largely inevitable by-product of *the achievement of other objectives* that we also value very highly: such as the desire to ensure *fairness, justice and equality* in the treatment of citizens . . . We may be able to get along with fewer forms and thinner files, but forms and files will always be with us, and the sensible, if not always emotionally satisfying thing, it to learn to live with them.

du Gay's emphasis upon the politico-ethical formation and significance of modern bureaucracy is warmly welcomed. As we have seen, however, Weber's reflections on bureaucracy suggest that the relationship between bureaucratic principles and the enactment of different ethics is rather loosely coupled. It is questionable whether 'governmental administration' is *predicated* upon an 'ethics of responsibility' rather than contingently congruent with such ethics. With this in mind, it is relevant to recall how the effective operation of bureaucratic organization makes significant moral demands upon its office-holders. Unfortunately, it cannot be taken for granted that 'fairness, justice, and equality' are universally desired, or that these principles are placed above other priorities, such as value-for-money or personalized service. Nor can it be assumed that what produces 'a sense of personal frustration' is a by-product of 'the *achievement* of other objectives'. Even if it is agreed that the principles of bureaucracy are intended to ensure fairness, etc., it may be doubted that these principles are adequately recognized, incorporated, or effectively implemented in practical bureaucratic administration, whether in the public or the private sectors.[15]

If this assessment is accepted, then establishing or strengthening an ethos of bureaucracy is not simply a matter of reducing the number of forms or files but, rather, creating and processing those forms and files in such a way that is consistent with the bureaucratic principles of fairness, justice, equality, and so on. Relevant questions to ask include: To what extent is the current design of administrative systems conditioned by the personal moral enthusiasms or allegiances of their designers? Do the office-holders value the bureaucratic ethos, and associated principles, attributed by Weber and/or du Gay to bureaucratic organization?

A condition of possibility of the ethos of bureaucracy being enacted in practice is a fuller awareness, embrace, and prizing of its values and principles by office-holders. It is to be regretted that Weber says comparatively little about the fostering and maintenance of such awareness and vigilance. Weber and du Gay both seem to assume that the principles and ethos inhere in the structure of bureaucratic organization, and do not therefore consider how they are practically constructed and continuously renewed. By default, it is assumed that the ethos is well established and/or readily internalized by office-holders. It is instructive that when Weber (1978) refers to the importance of training, he relates it exclusively to the acquisition of specialized knowledge and examination, and not to fostering a commitment to the bureaucratic ethos. When du Gay (2000: 120) touches on this issue, he emphasizes the importance of office-holders having 'a focus of ethical commitment and duty autonomous of . . . extra-official ties to kin, class community or conscience'. This, however, is a negative conception of the ethos of the office. Its positive constituents, as well as the means of its acquisition and preservation, have to be imputed.

It is unclear what 'conditions provide the bureaucrat with a distinctive ethical bearing and status conduct' (Ibid.). How are the qualities attributed to the '"good" bureaucrat' (Ibid.: 4) acquired, nurtured, and safeguarded so that the 'moral achievement' is established and sustained in the face of pressures (e.g. high staff turnover, use of temporary and agency staff) that may tend to erode it? How, to return to the quotation that opens this chapter, does the office-holder acquire the 'discipline and self-denial' required to enact the core principles of the bureaucratic ethos, and thereby ensure that the apparatus does not deteriorate or indeed 'disintegrate'?

Largely absent from studies of bureaucracy—whether the focus is upon its principles or its forms—is the question of how the moral qualities attributed to the actions of office-holders are constructed and instilled. When, where, and how are office-holders enabled to appreciate and reflect upon the ethical, as contrasted to the technical, demands that are placed upon them? How, and to what extent, is the ethos credited to bureaucratic office and the ethical qualities ascribed to the '"good" bureaucrat' (du Gay 2000: 4) retained in relation to 'post-bureaucratic' innovations? Without becoming overly precious about it, how are office-holders enabled to become 'personalities' by appreciating and fully assuming the responsibilities that are being placed upon them?

Concluding Reflections

The question of how modernity is managed, and should be managed, is plagued by controversy, uncertainty, and disagreement. In this chapter, I have sought to explore the nature and value of modern bureaucratic organization through a narrative that has emphasized the centrality of formal rationality in processes of modernization that are inclusive of 'post-bureaucratic' innovations.

Advocates of post-bureaucracy, including supporters of NPM, have tended to disregard or downplay the virtues of formal rationality and have assumed that the vices of bureaucracy can be removed by having *less* bureaucracy and/or by replacing it with other media of governance, such as markets and networks. This equation marginalizes and inhibits an appreciation of the politico-ethical strengths of modern bureaucracy. Where a shallow understanding of the challenges of managing modernity takes hold, as illustrated by the Doncaster case, the progressive, and even emancipatory, power of bureaucratic organization—with regard to equity and probity—tends to be denigrated and depleted by reliance upon organizational forms and mechanisms that lack equivalent priorities and principles. Markets and networks may play a supplementary and supporting role within an overarching framework that is governed by a bureaucratic ethos and principles. But accompanying their inclusion is the risk that they will subvert and ultimately usurp the *ethos* of bureaucracy underpinning the provision of robust and incorrupt administration in the private and public sectors.

Weber cautions that when applications of formal rationality are harnessed to capitalist expansion, they tend to foster an 'ethic of adjustment' which impedes the collective development of responsibility, dignity, and 'personality'. Where the ethos and principles of bureaucracy are weakened by 'post-bureaucratic' innovations, the resulting work organization has been characterized as a kind of 'soft despotism'.[16] Yet, in weakening traditional and charismatic forms of domination, formal rationality also has a potential to reveal and advance the human capacity to endow life with meaning by recognizing, developing, and exercising the ability to make informed choices between values. For Weber, formal rationality is Janus-faced: its demoralizing effects can also engender greater self-consciousness of its impotence in assessing the value of alternative ends.[17] The evaporation of meaning that was once drawn from the reserves of tradition invites a confrontation with responsibility for developing the capacity, individually and collectively, to make informed, although ultimately unwarrantable,[18] rational choices between, and commitments to, the realization of ultimate, particular ends. When conceived in this way, it is inconsistent to restrict the scrutiny of modern means of organizational governance to debates about the contemporary relevance of ideal–typical features attributed to bureaucracy. Instead, calls for the study of 'post-bureaucratic' innovation should focus on the issue of how the reform of bureaucracy might respect and maintain, (or disregard and weaken), its ethos and principles.

Attending to Weber's reflections on modernity recalls how the most pressing and salient issues of modernity for Weber are moral and political, not technical. The principal danger of the rise of formal rationality is its subordination of the ethical to the technical. Studies of 'bureaucracy', including contemporary struggles to introduce 'post-bureaucratic' innovations, can contribute to debate over, and commitment to, the ultimate values to which we make a commitment, individually and collectively. These studies do not need to be preoccupied with, or restricted to, technical questions of efficiency or design. To date, excessive attention and resources have been dedicated to mapping the changing 'geometry' of modern organization instead of examining how the principles and ethos of bureaucracy are fostered, strengthened, or neglected. Office-holders committed to its ethos and principles are not just filling a role, 'doing a job', or being paid by a private firm contracted to provide services or manufacture products. Equity and probity are assured only by office-holders who, being dedicated to the ethos of the office, are committed to providing the very highest standards of administrative service. A challenge for managers and students of modernity is to better appreciate how an awareness of this ethos can be nurtured and given its fullest engagement.

☐ NOTES

1. I would like to thank Stewart Clegg, Martin Harris, and Harro Höpfl for their assistance in preparing this chapter and for their very helpful comments on earlier drafts.

2. Insofar as it is assessed to support or impede technical capability, ethical discipline is of course also relevant for evaluations of the technical capability of 'old' and 'new' organizational forms.

3. Recalling its heuristic status helps us to resist a tendency to reify bureaucracy as an entity or form, even if it does not cleanse the term of its commonsense meaning (Bittner 1965). For analytical purposes, Weber sought to abstract the distinctive principles of bureaucratic organization into the elements of an 'ideal type'. As a concept, bureaucracy characterizes some aspects of a complex, multifaceted reality that defies capture or reflection. 'Bureaucracy' and 'post-bureaucracy' are invoked to make, or dispute, claims about (emergent) features of the social world that contribute to enacting the reality which such claims aspire to represent. The very term 'bureaucracy' was coined by a physiocrat and advocate of laissez-faire economics, Jean Claude Marie Vincent de Gournay (1712–1759) (see Albrow 1970: 16). His motto was 'Laissez faire et laissez passer, le monde va de lui même' (Let do and let pass, the world goes on by itself). From the outset, use of the term 'bureaucracy'—or what Gourney termed the French illness of 'bureaumania' which he regarded as wreaking havoc—has been 'politically charged' in its conception and application.

4. As Dyrberg (1997: 17) puts it, power 'throws the subject into possibilities of signification which it simply cannot master, but, precisely because of these possibilities, none the less sets up new conditions for their emergence, institutionalization, reproduction, or indeed destruction'.

5. Post-bureaucratic developments may nonetheless be welcomed, or at least accommodated, by employees who are 'humanized' by their introduction, even when the price of reform is increased work pressures and/or additional responsibilities. To the extent that employees are caught up in a modern romance with the efficiencies identified by formally rational calculations, and the associated declamation of rigidities, top-heaviness, 'turf' protection, etc. attributed to bureaucracy, it is to be expected that their anticipated removal will gain a positive reception. Taken-for-granted or simply overlooked is the degree of protection—from favouritism, bullying, constructive dismissal, etc.—afforded by bureaucratic procedures that limit the arbitrary, autocratic exercise of power (e.g. by employers, supervisors, and employees).

6. 'A person in authority (esp. a minor official) who insists on adhering to rules and regulations or bureaucratic procedures even at the expense of common sense'; OED, entry 'jobsworth'

7. According to the police report presented at the first court appearance of the brothers, the younger boy was 'found wandering the streets of Edlington in a dazed state on Saturday barefoot, caked in mud and covered in blood from head to foot. He returned home yesterday after receiving plastic surgery for a cut to his arm that reached to the bone. The 11-year-old, who had been airlifted to hospital in a critical condition after being found unconscious at the foot of a ravine, had a cut five inches long and two inches wide on the back of his head. He remains in hospital and is not yet well enough to be interviewed by the police' (*The Times* 2009).

8. The conflict was over a redevelopment project that threatened to restrict access to the local market.

9. It is relevant to note that the Minister did not mention how Ms Law had been at the centre of allegations about payments in the region of £500,000 by Doncaster Council to a recruitment agency, *Rockpools* (see http://www.rockpools.co.uk/), for the appointment of several senior council officers, a charge that she strongly denied by insisting that she had taken no part in the procurement process. Coincidentally, Aidan Rave, the Deputy Mayor of Doncaster, resigned in February 2006 to take up an appointment with Rockpools in March 2006 (see http://uk.linkedin.com/pub/aidan-rave/5/401/a61; accessed 24 February 2010). Ms Law reportedly claimed that this allegation formed part of a witch hunt triggered by her reporting of the elected Mayor, Martin Winter, to the police regarding alleged irregularities of payments to a community project run by the Mayor (Waugh 2006). Neither of these allegations was substantiated but they led to Law's departure which, inclusive of a £120,000 payment to Ms Law, cost the council in the region of £300,000 and prompted the Audit Commission to threaten government intervention (Local Government Chronicle 2010). Shortly after leaving her employment at Doncaster on 31 March 2007, Law was appointed Chief Executive of Wokingham Council in September 2007 (Wokingham Borough Council 2007). In the announcement of her appointment, Wokingham Council states that she had 'a phenomenal track record in local government' and that she 'developed and implemented the neighbourhood service delivery model' at Doncaster, the model that was at the centre of the reorganization.

10. '*Rational* rules', Weber contends, 'meet with obedience as *generally binding norms*' (Weber 1978: 954, second emphasis added).

11. That said, and as noted earlier, there are forms of productive activity and collaborative arrangements (e.g. peer-to-peer production and distribution, such as *Linux* or Farmers Markets as well as those outlined by Kallinikos, in this volume), that are not primarily governed by bureaucratic principles. Fuelled by a rather anti-capitalist spirit of personal interactions and/or sharing, and ignited by a morally charged antagonism towards the operations and impacts of established bureau-capitalist corporations (e.g. Microsoft, Wal-Mart), these networks are largely unfettered by a central, governing body. Many of them are dependent, however, upon an infrastructure provided by predatory, bureau-capitalist corporations. They are therefore vulnerable to acquisition where they are not legally protected (Willmott 2010)—the purchase of *YouTube* by *Google* being a high profile example.

12. A recent post to Social Media News New Zealand (30 November 2009) is typical in signalling the problem but without considering why the probability of a 'company evolving into a bureaucracy' is so high: 'To keep innovating and achieving, *Google* must ensure it does not turn into a bureaucracy. It should essentially spin off into smaller companies to reduce the risk that by being a big company it might evolve into a bureaucracy. As long as *Google* can continue to inspire young innovators to join them and improve the world, and as long as they can avoid the bureaucracy that plagues so many other large tech companies, it is safe to say *Google* will continue to lead and dominate the Internet' (http://socialmedianz.posterous.com/google-and-the-bureaucracy-plague; Accessed 3 January 2010).

13. In due course, ideas nurtured initially within *Google* that are developed outside may be bought (back). *Google* has been comparatively successful with its acquisitions, although their integration into its businesses has been criticized (Cubrilovic 2008).

14. When discussing NPM, Pollitt and Bouckaert (2004) have proposed an alternative based upon a shift that is responsive to the priorities of clients and identifying where there is scope

for change without compromising basic principles. This proposal is described as '*neo-Weberian*' (see also Drechsler 2005). This, I suggest, is misleading. As has been argued in this chapter, innovations of this kind are entirely compatible with Weber's thinking about the application of formal rationality in the development of modern methods of administration. More novel and urgent is the challenge to develop a *post*-Weberian interrogation of the relevance of bureaucracy for managing modernity—that is, an analysis which builds upon Weber's insights to address the issue of how, in practice, bureaucratic principles and the bureaucratic ethos of procedural fairness, etc. can be more greatly appreciated and readily valued, nurtured, and embedded in public and private sector organizations.

15. A similar agenda has been proposed by Lawton and Doig (2006) who also lament how discussions of NPM have focused upon its values and techniques of personal service delivery rather than starting with 'values like justice and equity' as a basis for examining the implications of NPM (Ibid.: 29).

16. Clegg and Courpasson (2004) go so far as to suggest that the mode of governmentality associated with project management, as an exemplary form of 'post-bureaucracy', operates 'through an immense and tutelary power...It is total, precise, regular, caring and gentle, responsible...thus, day after day, it reduces the need for, and the use of, free-will' (Ibid.: 29: 542, quoting de Tocqueville, their translation). This is somewhat ironic, as it goes well beyond the totalizing *aspirations* that I attribute to Corporate Cult(ur)ism (Willmott 1993), and which Clegg and Courpasson (2004) claim to be 'quite different' from de Tocqueville's idea of 'degrading people without worrying them' (Ibid.: 29: 541, citing de Tocqueville, their translation). Invoking Weber, I argue that subscription to a few corporate values can be appealing precisely because it offers some absolution from the demanding and worrying responsibility of determining one's values (Willmott 1993).

17. At best, it invites us to embrace the values of technocracy by becoming dedicated to refining available means as an end it itself. Its disenchanting logic makes clear that the world lacks any discoverable meaning. An example is the advocate of a management fad, such as total quality management, who adopts it as a personal credo which s/he uses to assess the 'fitness for purpose' of all aspects of life, including the way s/he approaches personal relationships. In case this example seems far-fetched, an ex-colleague unjokingly and evangelically declared this to be the value to which he was firmly committed.

18. Value commitments are rationally unwarrantable because, although scientific inquiry can furnish knowledge relevant for making or supporting a particular decision, ultimately the decision is made on the basis of a value-commitment. It is precisely this commitment to values that scientific knowledge is powerless to defend or condemn. While Weber's position can be interpreted as supportive of 'decisionism' and 'irrationalism', this assessment overlooks his insistence upon the presence of ethics, or 'the ethical', at the centre of human action.

⬚ BIBLIOGRAPHY

Adelaide Review (2004) Gehl Plans Left to Gather Dust, Available at: http://www.adelaidereview. com.au/archives/2004_08/issuesandopinion_story4.shtml (accessed 28 January 2010).

Adler, P. and Borys, B. (1996) Two Types of Bureaucracy: Enabling and Coercive, *Adminstrative Science Quarterly*, 41: 61–89.

Ahmed, M. (2009) Interview with Dr Paul Gray, *Community Care*, Available at: http://www.communitycare.co.uk/Articles/2009/01/22/110521/dr-paul-gray-interview-with-community-care.htm (accessed 25 January 2010).

Albrow, M. (1970) *Bureaucracy*, London: Pall Mall.

Alvesson, M. and Thompson, P. (2006) Post-Bureaucracy, in S. Ackroyd, R. Batt, P. Thompson and P.S. Tolbert (eds), *Oxford Handbook of Work and Organization*, Oxford: Oxford University Press.

Amy, D.J. (2008) The Case for Bureaucracy: An Unapologetic Defence of a Vital Institution, Available at: http://www.governmentisgood.com/articles.php?aid=20 (accessed 24 February 2008).

Baker, M. (2006) The Pie-Man Charts Fresh Career Path as Doncaster Rover, *Daily Telegraph* (13 July), Available at: http://www.telegraph.co.uk/finance/2943231/The-pie-man-charts-fresh-career-path-as-Doncaster-rover.html (accessed 23 January 2010).

Balls, E. (2010) Transcripts of Interviews on the Edlington Case—Interview with Edward Stourton on The World at One, Available at: http://www.edballs.co.uk/index.jsp?i=4633&s=1111 (accessed 28 January 2010).

Bittner, E. (1965) The Concept of Organization, *Social Research*, 32(3): 239–55.

Booth, R. (2009) Doncaster Faces Social Work Inquiry after Child Deaths, *The Guardian* (13 January 2009), Available at: http://www.guardian.co.uk/society/2009/jan/13/doncaster-child-protection (accessed 30 January 2010).

Brubaker, R. (1984) *The Limits of Rationality: An Essay on the Social and Moral Thought of Max Weber*, London: Allen and Unwin.

Carr, N.G. (2007) The Google Enigma, *Strategy and Business*, 49, Available at: http://www.strategybusiness.com/media/file/sb49_07404.pdf(accessed 4 January 2010).

Clegg, S. (2002) Lives in the Balance: A Comment on Hinings and Greenwood's "Disconnects and Consequences in Organization Theory?", *Administrative Science Quarterly*, 47: 428–41.

——Courpasson, D. (2004) Political Hybrids: Tocquevillean Views on Project Organizations, *Journal of Management Studies*, 41(4): 525–47.

Cubrilovic, N. (2008) Why Google Slows Down Acquired Companies, *TechCrunch IT* (16 July), Available at: http://www.techcrunchit.com/2008/07/16/google-where-companies-go-to-die/ (accessed 19 January 2010).

Doncaster Council (2009) Doncaster Children and Young People's Improvement Plan (17 June), Available at: http://www.doncaster.gov.uk/Images/Complete%20Plan%20Vers%2034%2017%2006%2009_tcm2-62836.pdf (accessed 1 February 2010).

Doncaster Council eNews (2004) Council Re-organization—Latest Update, Available at: http://www.doncaster.gov.uk/db/enews/article.asp?Archive=Y&CatID=44&Art=1648 (accessed 25 January 2010).

——(2005) Doncaster Council Appoints New Directors (23 May), Available at: http://www.doncaster.gov.uk/db/enews/article.asp?CatID=&Art=1781 (accessed 1 February 2010).

Doncaster Safeguarding Children Board (2010) A Serious Case Review: 'J' Children: The Executive Summary, Available at: http://www.doncaster.gov.uk/Images/Executive%20Summary%20Children%20J%20-%20published%2022nd%20Jan%202010_tcm2-68351.pdf (accessed 1 February 2010).

Drechsler, W. (2005) The Rise and Demise of New Public Management, *Post-Autistic Economics Review*, 33: 17–28.

du Gay, P. (2000) *In Praise of Bureaucracy: Weber Organization Ethics*, London: Sage.

——(2004) Against "Enterprise" (But not Against "Enterprise", for that would Make no Sense), *Organization*, 11(1): 37–57.

du Gay, P. (2006) Re-Instating an Ethic of Office? Office, Ethos and Persona in Public Management, CRESC Working Paper Series, No. 13, Open University.

——(2008) "Without Affection or Enthusiasm": Problems of Involvement and Attachment in "Responsive" Public Management, *Organization*, 15(3): 335–53.

Dyrberg, T. (1997) *The Circular Structure of Power: Politics, Identity, Community*, London: Verso.

Foggo, D. and Swinford, S. (2010*a*) Pie Man was Child Safety Chief, *Sunday Times*, 24 January 2010, 1–2.

————(2010*b*) Pie Boss Mark Hodson in Doncaster Child Scandal, *Times on Line* (24 January), Available at: http://www.timesonline.co.uk/tol/news/politics/article6999961.ece (accessed 28 January 2010).

Google (2010*a*) Corporate Information: Google Management, http://www.google.com/corporate/execs.html (accessed 4 January 2010).

——(2010*b*) Corporate Information: Corporate Milestones, http://www.google.com/corporate/history.html (accessed 4 January 2010).

Groysberg, B., Thomas, D.A. and Wagonfeld, A.B. (2009) Keeping Goggle "Googley", Case Study # 9-409-039 (Revised 24 April 2009), Harvard Business School.

Guardian (2009) Ed Balls Pledges Child Protection Overhaul (12 March), Available at: http://www.guardian.co.uk/society/2009/mar/12/laming-report-child-protection-ed-balls (accessed 1 February 2010).

Hales, C. (2002) "Bureaucracy-lite" and Continuities in Managerial Work, *British Journal of Management*, 13(1): 51–5.

Heckscher, C. (1994) Defining the Post-Bureaucratic Type, in C. Heckscher and A. Donnellon (eds), *The Post-Bureaucratic Organization: New Perspectives on Organizational Change*, London: Sage.

Hennis, W. (1983) Max Weber's Central Question, *Economy and Society*, 12(2): 135–80.

Hunter, I. (1994) *Re-thinking the School*, Sydney: Allen and Unwin.

Kallinikos, J. (2004) The Social Foundations of the Bureaucratic Order, *Organization*, 11(1): 13–36.

Lashinsky, A. (2008) *Where Does Google Go Next?*, *CNN Money* (12 May), Available at: http://money.cnn.com/2008/05/09/technology/where_does_google_go.fortune/ (accessed 1 January 2010).

Lawton, A. and Doig, A. (2006) Researching Ethics for Public Sector Organizations: The View from Europe, *Public Integrity*, 8(1): 11–33.

Le Galès, P. and Scott, A. (2010) *A British Bureaucratic Revolution?* Mimeo, Institut für Soziologie, University of Innsbruck.

Levy, S. (2007) Google Goes Globe-Trotting, *Newsweek* (12 November), Available at: http://www.newsweek.com/id/67919/page/1 (accessed 16 January 2010).

Local Government Chronicle (2010) Timeline: Doncaster, A Troubled History (28 January), Available at: http://www.lgcplus.com/news/timeline-doncaster-a-troubled-history/5010816.article (accessed 28 January 2010).

Mason, K. (2009) Ex Chief Blames the Mayor, Doncaster Free Press (3 April), Available at: http://www.doncasterfreepress.co.uk/child-care/Ex-chief-blames-the-Mayor.5139510.jp (accessed 1 February 2010).

Mommsen, W. (1974) *The Age of Bureaucracy*, Oxford: Blackwell.

Ofsted (2008) Annual Performance Assessment of Doncaster Children's Services, Available at: http://www.ofsted.gov.uk/oxcare_providers/la_download/(id)/4722/(as)/APA/apa_2008_371.pdf (accessed 25 January 2010).

Osborne, T. (1994) Bureaucracy as a Vocation: *Journal of Historical Sociology*, 17, 3: 289–313.

Osborne, D. and Gaebler, T. (1992) *Reinventing Government: How the Entrepreneurial Spirit Is Transforming the Public Sector*, Reading, Massachusetts: Addison-Wesley.

——Plastrik, P. (1997) *Banishing Bureaucracy: Five Strategies for Reinventing Government*, Reading, Massachusetts: Addison-Wesley.

Peters T. and Waterman, R.H. (1982) *In Search of Excellence: Lessons from Americas Best Run Companies*, New York: HarperCollins.

Pollitt, C. and Bouckaert, G. (2004) *Public Management Reform: A Comparative Analysis*, 2nd edn, Oxford: Oxford University Press.

Prodger, M. (2009) Council was Warned "Children Would Die", *BBC Newsnight* (4 March), Available at: http://news.bbc.co.uk/1/hi/programmes/newsnight/7923188.stm (accessed 28 January 2010).

Selznick, P. (1949) *TVA and the Grass Roots*, New York: Harper Torchbooks.

Slack, M. (2009) 'Arrogant Cover-Up' Blamed for Care Disasters, *Yorkshire Post* (1 April), Available at: http://www.yorkshirepost.co.uk/doncaster-child-tragedies/39Arrogant-cov-erup39-blamed-for-care.5129090.jp (accessed 25 January 2010).

The Times (2009) Brothers Appear in Court over Edlington Torture (8 April), Available at: http://www.timesonline.co.uk/tol/news/uk/crime/article6053832.ece (accessed 1 February 2010).

Thompson, P. and Alvesson, M. (2005) Bureaucracy at Work: Mixed Understandings and Mixed Blessings, in P. du Gay (ed.), *The Values of Bureaucracy*, Oxford: Oxford University Press.

Trist, E. and Bamforth, K. (1951) Some Social and Psychological Consequences of the Longwall Method of Coal Getting, *Human Relations*, 4: 3–38.

Waugh, R. (2006) Doncaster in Turmoil—What the Transcripts Reveal (5 December), Available at: http://www.yorkshirepost.co.uk/news/Doncaster-in-turmoil-What-the.1913300.jp (accessed 28 January 2010).

Weber, M. (1949) *The Methodology of the Social Sciences* (trans. and ed., E.A. Shils and H.A. Finch), New York: Free Press.

——(1978) *Economy and Society* (ed. G. Roth and C. Wittich), 2 Vols, Berkeley, California: University of California Press.

——(1992) *The Protestant Ethic and the Spirit of Capitalism* (trans. T. Parsons), London: Routledge.

——(1994) The Profession and Vocation in Politics, in P. Lassman and R. Speirs (eds), *Weber: Political Writings*, Cambridge: Cambridge University Press.

Williamson, O. (1999) Public and Private Bureaucracies: A Transaction Cost Economics Perspective, *Journal of Law, Economics and Organization*, 15(1): 306–43.

Willmott, H.C. (1993) Strength is Ignorance; Slavery is Freedom: Managing Culture in Modern Organizations, *Journal of Management Studies*, 30(4): 515–52.

Willmott, H.C. (2010) Creating 'Value' Beyond the Point of Production: Branding, Financialization and Market Capitalization, mimeo.

Wokingham Borough Council (2007) Wokingham BC Appoints New Chief Executive (September 11), Accessible at: http://www.wokingham-berkshire.org.uk/site-admin/events/2007/09/wokingham-bc-appoints-new-chief.html (accessed 28 January 2010).

Zimmerman, D. (1971) The Practicalities of Rule Use, in J. Douglas (ed.), *Understanding Everyday Life*, London: Routledge and Kegan Paul.

☐ GENERAL INDEX

Straw, J. 51 n. 10
Supiot, A. 11–12
Sweden 161
Suchman, M. 122
Swinford, S. 268

Takeuchi, H. 246
Tannenbaum, A.S. 235
Tapscott, D. 146
TI Group (firm) 179
Tate and Lyle (firm) 181
taxation 37, 49, 57, 58, 77, 96
technology vii, 5, 7, 105–29, 130, 131, 133,
   136, 142, 144, 147, 148, 185–88, 191,
   193, 194, 197, 205, 214, 221, 242,
   243, 283
   digital 211–13
Ten Bos, R. 206
Tesco (supermarket chain) 66
Thatcher, M. 23, 32, 39, 42, 44, 112, 185
Thatcher government (UK) 112, 185
Thatcherism 39, 42, 45, 103
Third Reich 49
Thompson, G. 237, 240–242, 245, 247
Thompson, J.D. 235
Thompson, P. 234, 235, 258, 277
Thrift, N. 234, 246
Tilley, C. 144
Times, The (newspaper) 288 n. 7
Tocqueville, A. de 290 n. 16
Tokyo 217
Tompkins (conglomomrate) 198 n. 4
Tories 33
Townley, B. 242, 250
Toyota 65–6
trade unions 137, 192
transparency 138, 139
Treasury (UK) 51 nn. 15 and 17
Trist, E. 258
trust, concept of 30, 49, 88, 208, 218, 219, 221
   and democratic accountability 30, 49
   in 'post-bureaucratic' organizations
      218–9, 223
Turner, T. 209

Unigate (firm) 269
Unilever (firm) 269
United Kingdom (UK) 5, 7, 22, 24, 25, 27, 35,
   39, 63, 69, 81, 83, 84, 98, 108, 176, 182,
   184, 185, 258, 267
   accountability in 30–55
   child-care services in 8, 260, 264, 267–73
   child protection in 70

government 31, 32, 34, 39, 40, 83, 109, 112,
   182, 183, 198 n. 1; see also government
   manufacturing sector 7, 176–201; see also
      industries (sectors)
United States 39, 83, 161, 170, 177, 184, 185,
   191, 225
universalism 138, 206, 207
Uhr, J. 21
Urry, J. 230

Van Dijk, J. 230, 246
Vehicle and General Insurance case 45
Victoria Climbié case (London Borough of
   Haringey, UK) 70
vocationalism 233
Volkswagen 182, 184
Von Hippel, E. 131

Wal-Mart 289 n. 11
Wales 60, 109
Walton, E.J. 145
Waltzer, M. 138, 141, 144
Wanless, D. 108
Waterman, R.H. 209, 262
Waugh, R. 272, 289 n. 9
Web 2.0; 147
Weber, M. 3, 22, 23, 24, 25, 26, 27, 38, 40, 41,
   49, 141, 142, 222, 250, 257, 258, 259–60,
   276–80, 287, 289 nn. 10 and 14, 290 nn.
   16 and 18
   on bureaucracy 12–20, 40, 41, 47, 58, 139,
      202–5, 211, 224, 230, 232, 258, 261–2,
      264–5, 273, 274, 281–2, 283–5
Weberianism 14
Webster, C. 123
Webster, F. 130, 235, 250
Wegg-Prosser, V. 122
Weinstock, A. 182, 186, 198 n. 4, 200 n. 7
welfare provision 99
welfare states viii, 1, 99, 198 n. 1
   European vii
   Keynesian 124 n. 6
Wenger, E. 131
'Western PCT' (case study) 115
   PAS implementation in 115–20, 121–2, 123
Westland Affair, The 46
Westland Helicopters 198 n. 3
Westminster model 4, 33
Westwood, R. 241
Whitbread (conglomorate) 189, 196
White, G. 187, 198 n. 4
Whitehall 46
Whitman, W. 22

Printed in Great Britain
by Amazon.co.uk, Ltd.,
Marston Gate.